JONATHAN DOWNES

THE OWLMAN
AND
OTHERS

30th ANNIVERSARY EDITION

Edited by Jonathan Downes
Typeset by Jonathan Downes and Corrina James
Cover and Internal Layout by Mark North for CFZ Communications
Using Microsoft Word 2000, Microsoft , Publisher 2000, Adobe Photoshop.

First edition published 1997 by CFZ Publications
Second Edition published 1999 by Domra
Third Edition published 2001, Jonathan Downes
Forth Edition published 2006 CFZ Press

CFZ PRESS
Myrtle Cottage
Woolfardisworthy
Bideford
North Devon
EX39 5QR

© CFZ MMVI

ISBN: 978-1-905723-02-7

For
Darren Naish, and, Julia Andrews
(and like everything else in my life these days)
Corinna James

*"Left by his friend to breakfast alone on the white
Italian shore, his Terrible Demon arose
Over his shoulder; he wept to himself in the night,
A dirty landscape-painter who hated his nose"*.....

'Edward Lear' by W. H. Auden

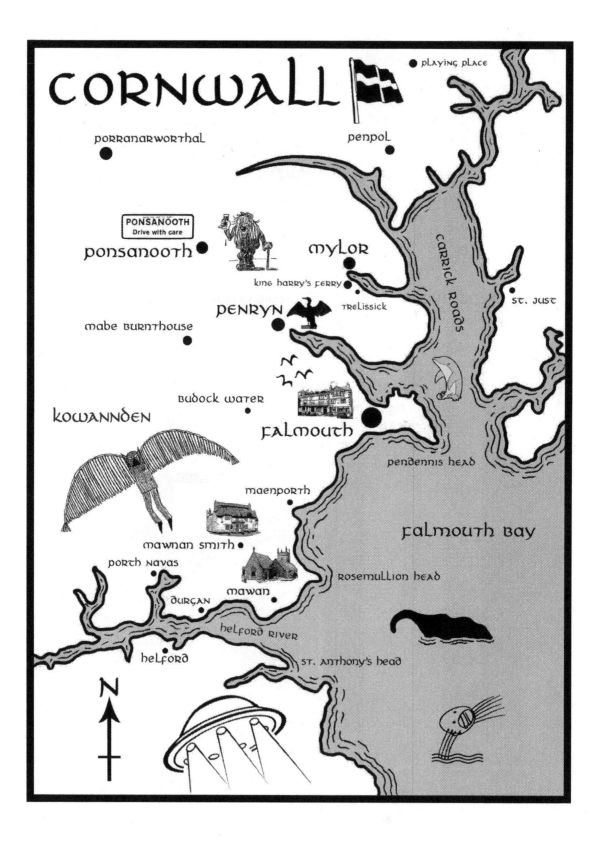

CONTENTS

IN MITIGATION

Nearly every book I have ever read on the subject broadly labelled 'the paranormal' quotes
a Sherlock Holmes story, in which Conan Doyle's fictional detective says that;

*"when you have eliminated the impossible, whatever is left,
no matter how improbable, must be the truth."*

I have always wondered what is wrong with considering the impossible…...

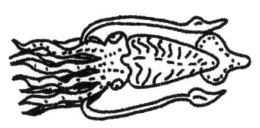

Giant Squid

1976-2006

INTRODUCTION TO THE
30th ANNIVERSARY EDITION:
The Owlman at Thirty!

It must be a mark of me getting older, but it seems that the years are flying past! I first started work on a book about the mysterious events in Mawnan Smith, and the surrounding areas of southern Cornwall back in 1994, and it took three long years to write and research it. It hardly seems like nine years since the book was first published, but it is! The events which make up the body of the book took place mostly thirty years ago, and - again - it is a mark of my increasing age, that not only can I remember the summer of 1976 perfectly well, but it was the last year of my adolescence, and a particularly strange time for me. However, it was an even stranger time for the residents of the Falmouth Bay area, and it is - I believe - interesting, that those events still reverberate to the present day.

The idea for the 30th Anniversary edition of this book can be firmly laid at the door of my friend and collaborator Mark North. He pointed out that although this book has been in print in various editions for a decade now, it had never been brought fully up to date, and that now - with the technology available to us that we simply didn't have ten years ago - we are in a position to make public excerpts from our huge archive of Owlman and "Doc" Shiels related memorabilia - most of which has never been seen before. So under pressure, I agreed to publish.

I never wanted to do this. In some ways this is biting the hand that fed me, because it is unarguable that if it had not been for *The Owlman and Others* I would not be in the position that I find myself today. The Owlman put me and the CFZ firmly on the map, it established me financially, and it established my reputation amongst the first division of fortean investigators…...but it damn near destroyed me as well. In this book I describe how Tony Shiels warned me against the phenomenon of `psychic backlash` which seems to overtake those who spend too much time on the track of a certain breed of monster. This is a series of inexplicable and horrific outbreaks of bad luck that can overtake the hapless seeker

9

after monstrous truth on his way to his goal. I never believed in it until, during the months that I was working on *The Owlman and Others,* two of my pet cats died suddenly, two computers blew up (as did two cars) and my wife left me. It could be argued that my marriage was rocky (to say the least) and that both my cars, computers and cats had seen better days, but it has to be said that over the years, whenever I have found myself on the track of the Owlman and his kin, that this stuff happens again and again.

In the penultimate chapter I tell the story of how I did my best to diffuse the malign effects by use of humour during the early months of 2000, but our bad experiences with psychic backlash continued apace throughout the year. Toby my old dog, and his two feline friends Isabella and Carruthers all died suddenly within a month of each other. Despite a string of media appearances and successful books we were dogged with financial and emotional problems and by the end of the year we had definitely had enough.

On New Year's Day, together with two very powerful witches from Yorkshire, I took part in a nine hour ritual to break the spell once and for all. But one thing is certain: my investigations into His Owliness ended with writing this introduction. The story of the Owlman of Mawnan ain't over yet and I await further developments with interest, but, like Sally G, my involvement *"is firmly in the past"* and I too firmly intend *"to leave it there".*

However, it is undeniable that the saga of the Owlman and his kith and kin, is one of the most important and significant series of fortean episodes to have happened in the United Kingdom during the past hundred years, and is at least as important to those of us who would like to understand the workings of the universe a little more than we do, as the much more widely publicised events at Point Pleasant in the 1960s when the West Virginia Mothman made its appearance. So, here you have it; thirty years of Owlman research, with more supporting memorabilia, testimony, and surrealchemical madness than you could ever wish to shake a stick at.

I would like to thank `Gavin` and Tony Shiels without whom there would be no book, and who remain my close friends to the present day, my darling Corinna (who typed the manuscript), and the ever-lugubrious but eminently loveable Mark North (who was only a few months old when the main events of this book took place), for forcing me to do this edition, and making it into a piece of product far beyond my wildest dreams (and believe me, my dreams can get a little wild)....

Slainte Mhor

Jon Downes
The Centre for Fortean Zoology,
Woolfardisworthy, North Devon
13th March 2006

INTRODUCTION TO THE 2001 EDITION

It still amazes me that five years after I originally wrote this book I still get letters about it. Although my main areas of research have been within more conventional zoology, my investigations into the grotesque Owlman of Mawnan has attracted more interest and more controversy than anything else that I have ever written. My adventures chasing His Owliness were exciting ones, and re-reading this book reminds me of quite how much fun my ex-wife and I had whilst Owlman-hunting.

The events of 1994-6 changed my life beyond measure. Despite the warnings from Doc Shiels *et al*, I was not prepared for the criticism I would get from my peers. In an article posted only a few weeks ago on the Internet, Darren Naish wrote:

"Downes has written numerous articles and a book on these entities: his approach to the subject is arcane, involving the history of surrealist art, the reincarnation of Max Ernst, some mutilated wallabies from Newquay zoo and the claims and counter-claims of Tony Shiels the Irish wizard. I will reserve judgment on all of this, but do read Mark Chorvinsky's article in Strange Magazine 8 (Fall 1991) for a somewhat more prosaic review of the characters involved. Personally I don't think the owlmen and their winged brethren have much to do with cryptozoology in the strict sense - however, they are significant 'indicators' in that how they are interpreted reveals the approach of the investigator.

To Downes and co, these things are so-called zooform phenomena:

phantom-like entities that look like animals but are instead manifestations of an unknown nature. Perhaps these ideas were inspired by similar theories concocted by Janet and Colin Bord, but I'm also reminded of internet devotees who argue that the creature in the Patterson film is an inter-dimensional alien android that can vanish from the camera viewfinder at will. In other words, by making mystery beasts into uncatchable, untestable phantoms one provides an ostensible explanation for the total lack of material evidence. I would more

11

likely side with the folklorists and anthropologists and suggest that group psychology and the power of iconographic tradition are forcing people into believing in animals that really do not exist outside of the human skull."

It may come as a shock to mainstream zoologists like "Our Dazza" but I agree with most of what he has said. It was with great sadness that we received the news a few days ago that Bernard Heuvelmans, the "father" of cryptozoology has died at the venerable age of 86. However, I have a sneaking suspicion that the old chap must be turning in his grave at the thought of what has happened to "his" discipline over the past decade or so. Cryptozoology is the study of UNKNOWN animals - i.e. species that are presently not accepted by mainstream zoologists. It is nothing more and nothing less. There are, however, a number of researchers in the field who, like us, are interested in a variety of related subjects and whilst we are unashamedly cryptozoologists, many of the subjects that we study have little or nothing to do with cryptozoology *per. se.*

British Big Cats, for example are not the purlieu of the cryptozoologist. They are animals of KNOWN species albeit in an alien environment. Similarly the other out of place animals which have been reported in the British Isles over the years and even the so-called "Golden Frogs" of the West Country — a subject which is one of our main study programmes at the moment are not anything to do with pure cryptozoology. Despite the interesting folkloric aspects to these beasties they are nothing more than aberrant colour morphs of a well known and common species. Most spectacularly, there are a whole range of "creatures" that have been reported which are impossible from a zoological standpoint. They cannot possibly exist as three dimensional, flesh and blood creatures. However the owlman, the chupacabra, the Celtic black dogs and various of the stranger lake monsters and man beasts continue to be reported year after year. They have sod-all to do with cryptozoology, but people like us find them interesting.

It is precisely because of these vagaries of definition that the Centre for Fortean Zoology was founded nearly a decade ago. We study a wide range of broadly zoological mysteries some of which are cryptozoological and some most definitely are not! It is mildly irksome to have to repeat this because all this information has been available for years in our magazines, books and on our website. We thought that everyone was aware of the fact, but apparently not.

The Owlman (and others) have nothing at all to do with cryptozoology, but we, at least, never claimed that they had! My research into the Cornish Owlman has convinced me that the sightings of this grotesque entity tell us more about the psycho-social state of the people who encounter it than they do about any of the other living creatures of God's creation. My only caveat is that in my book *"The Rising of the Moon"* (1999) I have presented a hypothesis whereby these creatures of the inner self can achieve a certain transient objective reality.

This, however, is another story.

Slainté Mhôr

Jonathan Downes
Exeter
31 August 2001

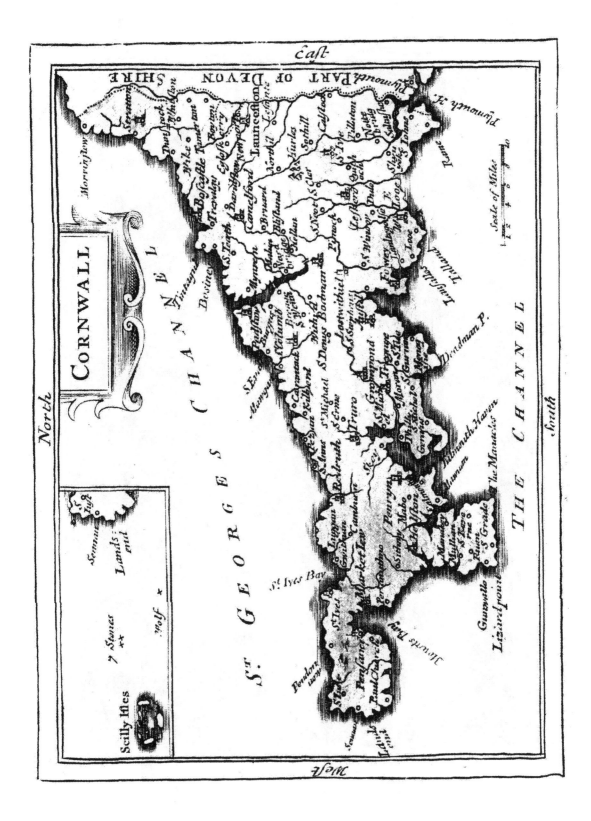

INTRODUCTION
by
Tony 'Doc' Shiels

Melling - Perry - Chapman – Greenwood. Surnames with associations. Melling of the honey, Perry of the pears, Chapman the hawker, and Greenwood of the green woods which surround Mawnan Old Church. Young girls with those surnames encountered Owlman in the Mawnan woods during Cornwall's 'Year of Weirdness, 1976. Do the names signify anything which could, perhaps, trigger manifestations of such an extraordinary apparition as Owlman? I think they do.

Melling and Perry suggest a heady mixture of Cornish mead (the 'honeymoon drink') and pear wine. Sweet intoxicants. Chapman - the peripatetic pedlar - has a sack of surprises. Greenwood, enchanted place of initiation, is the realm of Robin Goodfellow. Consider the symbolism of honey, fruit, and wine; the Tarot-like image of the wandering chapman; those trees overlooking the mouth of the Helford. This is the game of the name. Just one of the tricksy items in a wizard's bag of bamboozlements. Names are magic words with many layers of meaning.

Take 'Loplop' or 'Nnidnid' for example. Word games can reveal some of these meanings.

Twenty years back, I was in the middle of much of the strange stuff happening in Cornwall. Amongst other things, we had Morgawr the sea monster, UFO sightings, witchcraft, mysterious sounds and smells, fairy folk, big cats, and the incredible Owlman. Not only was I involved with these phenomena, but was also often accused of creating them. Such accusations are quite flattering, but all that stuff - apart from Owlman - had occurred in Cornwall over the years, long before I arrived on the scene. Let's just say that, in 1976, I was guilty of a certain amount of surrealchemical conjuration and manipulation. Simply doing my job.

My pal Jon knows something about peddling chapbooks; about honey, pears and wine; about greenwood witchery; about the Owlman. He knows that I am a shameless mountebank and an oxymoronic teller of truthful lies. During the last couple of years, he has bravely attempted to interview me - in London, Exeter, Plymouth, Falmouth, Ponsanooth, Penzance, St Ives and (by telephone) various parts of County Clare, Ireland - on the subject of Owlman, with mixed results. Strong drink was involved with most.. no, ALL of these sessions.

To his credit, Jon did his level best (have you seen him at his 'level best'?) to maintain an appropriately 'open minded' attitude of Fortean scepticism throughout. However, the CASE kept intruding, and Sea Heads surfaced several times to confuse and/or clarify certain areas of investigation. To me, Owlman is a surrealist image and - to quote Rene Passeron - *'the surrealist image is an irrational collision of psychological states'*. It astonishes anyone who experiences it. In this book Jonathan Downes offers a detailed study of the thing.

Armed with facts, gentle reader, if you go down to the woods today…

Doc

Tony 'Doc' Shiels
County Clare, Ireland
November 1996

15

"The Jabberwock, with eyes of flame,
Came whiffling through the tulgey wood."

Through the looking Glass by Lewis Carroll, 1872

CHAPTER ONE: INITIATION

"There must be a lot of people in the world being wondered about by people who don't see them anymore"

Russell Hoban *'Turtle Diary'* (1975)

When you are at the edge of the western world at the end of July at nine in the evening, it is still just about light enough to see a few feet in front of your face. The scent of the wild honeysuckle fills the air, permeating everything with its scent, as heady as any hallucinogen, the horseshoe bats flit through the hedgerows on either side of the ancient, sunken lanes, and in that hour before moon-rise, if you are nearly thirteen years old, and in love for the first time, western Cornwall on a July night is the most beautiful place in the world.

Gavin and Sally were twelve years old and in love for the first time. Sally's family had gone on their annual holiday to Cornwall, and Sally's parents had invited their daughter's boyfriend to accompany them. They were staying just outside Falmouth at one of those tiny caravan sites which spring up like mushrooms on the edges of unproductive farmland every summer.

The farm was on the outskirts of a little village called Mawnan Smith. It boasted a church, a pub, a village shop, and a garage which, as well as petrol, sold a fine collection of picture postcards emblazoned with views of the Falmouth Estuary. It, however, had little in the way of entertainment for young people. The fleshpots of Falmouth (such as they are) were seven or eight miles away and so the young lovers were left pretty much to their own devices during the long, idyllic summer evenings.

Each evening they walked, hand in hand through the gathering dusk and the leafy lanes, doing the things that young lovers do. One evening they were walking along the wooded pathway that leads to Mawnan Old Church and the footpath to Grebe Beach on the banks of the Helford River.

It was gloomy beneath the thick foliage of the tall trees which whispered conspiratorially to each other in the warm breeze which blew in from the sea, only a mile or so to the south. As they wandered further into the woods it got so dark that they needed to use the pocket torches they had brought with them to ensure that they kept roughly to the path.

As they walked along hand in hand, Gavin, a serious young man, kept his torch roughly on the path ahead, whilst Sally waved her flashlight around cheerfully, allowing the beam to play on the leafy branches of the trees above and around them.

Suddenly she stopped dead in her tracks. The beam of her torch revealed a figure on a branch above and in front of them. She opened her mouth to scream, but no sound came out...

CHAPTER TWO: INVOCATION

'Wherever they have shamans they're always the unstable,
the epileptics, the weird ones of the group, people prone to
terrors and depressions like I am"

Russell Hoban *'Turtle Diary'* (1975)

The *Seven Stars* in Falmouth is a pub of the sort that you thought didn't exist any more. Pubs are meticulously marketed businesses aimed at a carefully identified sector of the marketplace, and this usually means either piped music, homogeneous olde worlde mock-oak beams and phony horse brasses, or worse, one of the new brigade of 'theme' pubs and 'fun' pubs, which are springing up like garishly coloured fungi across the decaying corpse of the English countryside.

In a world where even genuine 'olde worlde' oak beams look like they came from B&Q, and where 'traditional' is a synonym for 'corporate', to find a pub that looks *truly* old fashioned is a very peculiar thing indeed. *The Seven Star*s in Falmouth, however, is a very peculiar pub indeed.

As you enter the public bar, the first thing that strikes you is how oddly long and thin it is. The lack of space is accentuated by a large, glass fronted display cabinet selling cigarettes and sweets which stands on top of much of the bar itself. There are very few actual seats and tables. What there is are covered in 1950's patterned formica. Behind the bar is a clergyman pulling the pints. There is no piped music - or if there is, it is inaudible beneath the general hubbub of chatter from the dozen or so regular customers sitting at the formica tables, living out their own exclusive fantasies and drinking pints of bilious yellow lager.

The colours of the pub seem all wrong. The decor is lost in a time-warp of forty years ago: the real 1950's, where post war austerity was ending and the promises of the new Elizabethan age had not yet begun to fade; amidst furnishings and colours seen nowadays only in the less frequented halls of the few remaining provincial psychiatric hospitals, and period dramas on ITV. This is not the 1950's portrayed by films and television, the 1950s of teddy boys, DA haircuts, Elvis Presley clones on every street corner and the cast of *'Grease'* ready to serenade you - given the slightest opportunity - from beneath the bonnets of their highly phallic American cars; but a 1950's where National Service, and even ration books were still in force; where crises like Suez and the Korean War threatened to destroy the

Entering 'The Seven Stars'

fragile veneer of peace, and plunge the world into another war even more terrible than the one that had finished only a few, short years before; a world where although Britain still had an Empire, she knew that within a few short years it would be gone forever.

The Seven Stars, in Falmouth may be a most peculiar pub, by the standards of Cornwall in 1995, but it is still an incongruous place for a young Cryptozoologist and his wife to meet the Wizard of the Western World.

Tony 'Doc' Shiels is unlike anyone else I have ever met. My ex-wife once said that meeting him for the first time was like being struck by a whirlwind. Tony was born in 1938, and over the next fifty-seven years he would be a painter, a conjurer, a gun-slinger, a musician, a playwright and a busker. He is also a self admitted wizard. [1] (He has never claimed magical powers of his own, but then again, he has never claimed *not* to have them either. My own feelings are that Tony is a very similar character to Reg - the time-traveller in *Dirk Gently's Holistic Detective Agency* a science-fiction book by the late Douglas Adams, [3] who discovered the secrets of time travel by accident because he could never be bothered to learn how to programme his video recorder, and who could never figure out alternative ways that he could see episodes of TV shows he would otherwise have missed. I think that Tony developed his very real magickal skills because he could never figure out how to hide the hard boiled egg up his sleeve like a proper conjurer.

Roseland
Cards

PUPPET MASTER TOOK
      SOME JARS,
IN ONE OR MORE OF
      SEVEN BARS,
THEN HE DRANK A GLASS
      OF WINE,
FLAVOURED WITH PURE
      TURPENTINE.
SOON THERE WAS A MERRY
      DANCE,
STEPPING LIVELY IN
      PENZANCE.
THE GAMES AFOOT SO
      JOIN THE CHASE,
AND EARN YOUR STRIPES,
JUST SOLVE THE CASE

REMEMBER
to use the

ADDRESS

'HEN PECKER'

15 HOLNE COURT

EXWICK

EXETER EX4 2NA.

The Seven Stars Public House, The Moor, Falmouth.

MIRANDA

Anthony 'Doc' Shiels, taken in 1996

Inside 'The Seven Stars'

He is shorter than me, (as are most people - but then, I am six and a half feet tall), and has piercing, powerful eyes, which twinkle when he is amused, and cut like a laser beam when he is annoyed. He has short cropped grey hair, and an enormous bushy beard, which bristles magnificently in all directions. He comes over like a cross between a genial Mephistopheles and Captain Birdseye [3] with a cosh in his pocket. He drinks Guinness and smokes small cigars. As we walked into the pub he was standing by the door, deep in conversation with some of his cronies. He bellowed a greeting in an Irish brogue as thick as an upright shillelagh and enveloped us both in an enormous bear hug.

We drank beer, and I brought the subject around to the Owlman of Mawnan:

'Doc' was at a steam fair near Penryn on the afternoon of Easter Saturday 1976. He had recently been involved in a much publicised search for Morgawr, the sea monster of Falmouth Bay; and was known across south western Cornwall as an expert on Monsters. Easter 1976 was an important time for me, and I remember it vividly. [4] It was warm and damp, but the spring sun was shining and picking out the pale yellow of the primroses which were particularly numerous that year. 'Doc' was plying his trade as itinerant busker, performing magic tricks to an appreciative crowd who would, he hoped, reward him with their spare change.

It was also a day out for his large family, most of whom were also members of his theatre group *'Tom Fool's Theatre of Tomfoolery'*. They had just finished one conjuring show, and were relaxing, licking ice cream cones, *"to the strains of a giant fairground organ"* when a *'worried looking man'* approached them.[5] Nineteen years later Tony remembers vividly what happened next:

This fellow Don Melling came up to me. I'd been pointed out to him as being the man involved in the Morgawr business, and he came up to me rather angrily and accused me of having set up some trick that had badly frightened his young daughters. [6]

Don Melling and his wife were on holiday in Cornwall with their two young daughters, June (aged twelve) and Vicky (aged nine). They had arrived at their caravan site near Truro late on the evening of Good Friday, and they spent the following day exploring the countryside in the Falmouth area.

They stopped for a picnic lunch in the woods next to Mawnan Old Church, and, whilst Mr. and Mrs. Melling prepared their alfresco feast, their children played among the decaying gravestones of the ancient churchyard. The peaceful scene was shattered by screams of terror as the two children ran, incoherent with fear, through the lych-gate towards their parent's car, demanding to be taken home as quickly as possible.

Understandably concerned, Don Melling packed his family and uneaten picnic into the car, and drove back to their campsite as quickly as possible. It was only in the comparative safety of familiar surroundings that the two girls would admit what they had seen. [7]

They described hearing a 'funny' noise and seeing a huge, feathered 'bird-man' hovering over the tower of the 13th Century church. [8] Trying to salvage what they could from the traumas that had

Mawnan Old Church

24

The Bell Tower of Mawnan Old Church

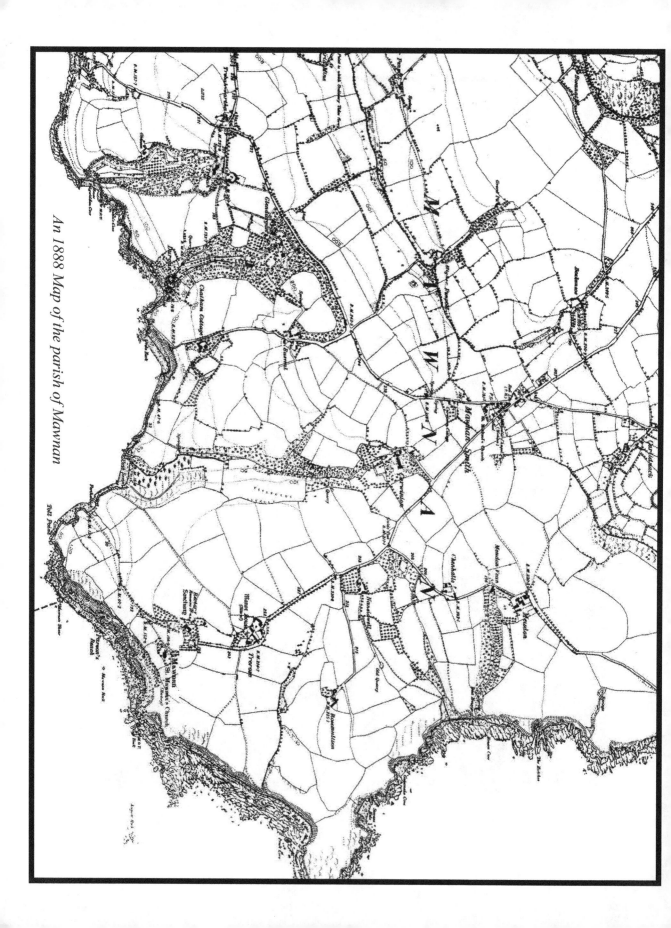

An 1888 Map of the parish of Mawnan

A selection of pictures showing the area surrounding Mawnan Old Church

Above: *The turning off the main road that leads to Mawnan Old Church.*

Below left: *Sign leading to Mawnan Old Church*

Below right: *Old Church Road sign*

Above: *The Red Lion one of the oldest buildings in Mawnan Smith, this thatched cob walled public house, converted from three cottages, is documented to date back as far as the 15th century. The Red Lion is reputed to be haunted by several ghosts*

Below left: *At the back of the former Rectory - known as the Sanctuary - is the Holy Well. The well can be found at the end of a deep, narrow ravine. Though of earlier in origin the well is often thought to be dedicated to the Virgin Mary since the adjoining field bears the name of 'Lady's Field'.*

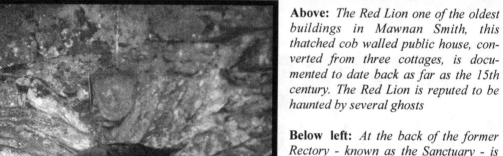

On the exterior above the keystone is an ancient granite corbel-head. The head is of great interest, containing as it does three distinct faces - one full face , the others profile. Mawnan Old Church is an ancient and mysterious place, and the evidence of its antiquity is everywhere that one looks.

blighted the early part of their holiday, the Mellings resolved to behave as normally as possible, which brought them to the Penryn Steam Fair. Tony was pointed out to Don Melling as the man responsible for all the mysterious goings on in that part of Cornwall which explains his belligerent attitude towards the Wizard that holiday lunchtime.

> *"I took a while to reassure him that I hadn't done anything of the kind and how the hell could I have done it anyway? It was broad daylight. I mean it would have been a hell of a trick if you could do it but it would have taken me a long time to work out the method"...* [9]

Tony's eyes twinkled, and he grinned with a slightly absent minded grin as he wondered, for a moment, how it would feel to be a magician capable of such a stupendous feat of prestidigitation.

As he told me this story his sense of humour was tempered with compassion for the little girls who were so badly scared nearly two decades before. He may be the Wizard of the Western World but he is a very kind man and also a father with several daughters of his own, and he is the last person in the world to take any pleasure from terrifying little girls.

> *"What I actually said was that 'If you think that I am that good a magician then I assure you that I will not allow your daughters to be frightened by "IT" again'. I was trying to make the man feel better, but the kids were very scared and just wanted to go home, and get the hell out of Cornwall.. It scared the man. He was frightened by the level of his daughter's fear".* [10].

The Mellings cut short their holiday in Cornwall by three days and returned to Preston the following day. Tony asked Don Melling if he could question the two girls, but their father felt that they had been too emotionally scarred by the experience to go through it again, and although he gave 'Doc' a drawing by June which depicted a strange, flying humanoid creature, be refused to let 'Tony' near either of his girls. [11]

On the 27th April, Tony wrote a letter to *Fortean Times*, the magazine which in 1976 was the only publication in Britain dealing specifically with strange phenomena: [12]

> *"A very weird thing happened over the Easter weekend. A holidaymaker from Preston, Lancs., told me about something his two young daughters bad seen ... a big, feathered bird-man hovering over the church tower at Mawnan (a village near the mouth of the Helford River). The girls (June (12), and Vicky (9), daughters of Mr. Don Melling), were so scared that the family cut their holiday short and went back three days early. This really is a fantastic thing, and I am sure the man wasn't just making it up because he'd been told I was on a monster hunt.*
>
> *I couldn't get the kids to talk about it (in fact their father wouldn't even let me try), but he gave me a sketch of the thing drawn by June."*

The first ever picture of the owlman, which at the time was labelled "Mawnan Bird-Man" was printed below. Incidentally it was an almost exact copy by Bob Rickard, rather than the original which was too large to fit on the page. Tony's letter continued:

> *"There have been no reports. so far as I know, of anybody else seeing the Bird-Man ... even if it turned out to be just a fancy dress hang-glider, you'd think someone else would have spot-*

Mawnan "Bird-Man" based on
sketch by June Melling, witnessed
and drawn 17/4/76.

A sketch of the Owlman
by Tony 'Doc' Shiels, based
on a lost original

*ted him ... but Mawnan is not a place for hang-gliding! I really don't know what to think ...
it's as if a whole load of weirdness has been let loose in the Falmouth area since last autumn!" [13]*

Indeed it had, but we shall return to the wider implications of weirdness in south-west Cornwall between 1975 and 1977 in a later chapter.

Soon after, there was a brief mention of "The Bird-Man of Mawnan" in an 18 page, A6 sized pamphlet
called *Morgawr - the Monster of Falmouth Bay* which was written by A. Mawnan-Peller and published
by Morgawr Productions [14] (see Appendix Five). It has been rumoured, both at the time and since that
the mysterious Mawnan-Peller was none other than Tony, but he has denied it resoundingly, albeit with
a twinkle in his eye as he said so. Not particularly to my surprise, there was no-one with this surname in
the Falmouth, Penryn or Truro area telephone directories at the time of writing in the Autumn of 1995.

It turned out that Mawnan-Peller was not 'Doc', but was another local writer who had written the booklet under a pseudonym. I have been asked to respect his confidence as to his real identity, and although
I *do* know his real name, this I have done. [15]

Another interesting thing about the Mawnan-Peller leaflet is that it contained yet another version of the
first Owlman drawing, again credited as being 'based on' the original. It must be stressed that there is a
mystery surrounding the 'original' (or at least what purports to be the original), image that has been
printed in anything published since 1976. The copy which Janet Bord sent me has a handwritten comment by Tony claiming that this is a copy of the original. [16] As far as I can ascertain, the 'true' original has never been published.

*The Bird-Man of Mawnan as depicted in A. Mawnan-Peller's Booklet Morgawr the
Monster of Falmouth Bay also based on the sketch by June Melling*

The Bird-Man of Mawnan as it appeared in the Fortean Times issues 16 - June 1976, drawn by Bob Rickard, based on the sketch by June Melling

No-one seems to know where the original is. Tony thought that Janet Bord of the Fortean Picture Library had it, [17] and she thought that Tony still had it. [18] Tony claims no knowledge at all on the subject and has suggested that it was probably destroyed along with many of his other notes on the matter when he and his family moved to Ireland in the early 1990's. [19]

Back in 1976, however, the story became more and more interesting.

A month or so later Tony heard a rumour that the 'animal' had been seen near Lamorna on or about the eleventh of May. [20] This story was never substantiated, and although, as we shall see, similar creatures have been seen in South-Western England, this century, the Lamorna sighting - if true - would be the only sighting in Cornwall away from the immediate vicinity of Mawnan Old Church, in recent years.

> *"Yes, I heard about the Lamorna sighting in a Penzance pub",*

he wrote to me in November 1995 [21].

> *"The creature had been seen by a mother and daughter, as I remember. My informant was a*

fellow called Dick Gilbert, a Cornishman who knew the people concerned. Dick used to live at Crowlas near Penzance, but I don't know where he is now".

Dick Gilbert was an artist, but enquiries amongst his old friends in the close knit artistic community of St. Ives were fruitless. No-one has seen him for many years. No-one knows where he is, or even if he is still alive! [22]

On the third of July, the 'creature' was seen again by two fourteen year old girls, Sally Chapman and Barbara Perry. [23] who had been camping in the woods next to the church. According to Tony, writing in a little known article for *Fortean Times* no 17: [24]

"They were camping out for the night among the trees not far from Mawnan Church. These trees cover the banks of the river for a great part of its length, above the rocky beaches. They were brewing up around 10 p.m. when they both heard a peculiar 'hissing' noise close by. Then they saw IT about 20 yards away (no more, they both assured me) standing amongst the trees."

They met Tony on Grebe Beach, below Mawnan Old Church the day after their sighting. Sally, who was from Plymouth, had been staying with her friend Barbara, (who would only admit that she lived 'quite near the river'). Sally approached Tony and said:

"Are you Doc Shiels? We've seen the bird monster" [25]

Sally described what they had seen:

"It was like a big owl with pointed ears, as big as a man. The eyes were red and glowing. At first I thought that it someone dressed-up, playing a joke, trying to scare us. I laughed at it. We both did. Then it went up in the air and we both screamed. When it went up you could see its feet were like pincers!"

Her friend added some details of her own:

"It's true. It was horrible, a nasty owl-face with big ears and big red eyes. It was covered in grey feathers. The claws on its feet were black. It just flew up and disappeared in the trees." [26]

Both girls had read the Mawnan-Peller booklet, [27] but the details given in it were extremely sketchy, and although Tony admitted at the time that it is possible that the two young ladies were trying to hoax him, he is convinced that they were genuine. [28]

He separated the two girls, and had each of them draw a picture of what she had seen. The two pictures are dissimilar enough to rebuff suggestions of collusion, but have enough points in common - both with each other, and with the other accounts of the 'creature' - to be considered as a significant piece of evidence. [29]

Both girls made brief additional notes underneath their pictures. Sally's read:

"I saw this monster bird last night. It stood like a man and then it flew up through the trees. It is as big as a man. Its eyes are red and shine brightly." [30]

And Barbara wrote:

> *"Birdman monster, seen on third of July, quite late at night but not quite dark. Red Eyes. Black Mouth. It was very big with great big wings and black claws.. Feathers grey"* [31]

The two girls agreed on most points with their pictures, although Sally thought Barbara had *"done the wings wrong'.* [32]

During preparation for this book we attempted to contact one or both of the girls, but with nothing more to go on than the fact that Barbara Perry lived 'near the river' and with there being no less than three hundred and something Chapmans living in Plymouth alone, we decided not to bother. [33] Even if the families had not moved in the interim, both girls may well have married and could be living anywhere in the world under any name. My zeal for the truth was blunted somewhat, when I realised quite how many young, Caucasian women called Sally or Barbara, and aged between 32 and 34 at the time of writing, could be living in the world!

However, during the summer of 2000, I received the following email:

> *My Experience of 3/7/1976*
> *Sally G*
> *Pembroke, Wales*
> *July 2000*
>
> *To whom it may concern,*
>
> *Writing this down isn't going to be the easiest thing that I've ever done, so I'll try to get it over with as quickly as possible. I have reluctantly decided to speak on my experience, for reasons that I won't go into here. This is the first time that I have thought about any part of what happened during that summer in years. It took me quite a while to really forget about what I saw and I suppose you could say that it had a definite effect on the way that I lived my life for a number of years following the event. I am a 38-year old career woman who has quite enough going on in her life without dredging up a very upsetting incident that happened 24 years ago. This is certainly the first time that I have written any of this down, and probably the first time that I have willfully remembered it in any detail since I was a teenager. I recently mentioned it in passing to someone whom I am very fond of and he suggested that I contact you, having found you on the net. I am aware of some of the bits and pieces that have been written about my experience in the intervening years, and by-and-large I have no complaint. I remember Mr. Shiels as being quite concerned about my friend Barbara and I at the time. He seemed like a nice man.*
>
> *I have read the essay on your website concerning the incident. There are a couple of discrepancies that you weren't to know about that I should probably clear up. My name wasn't really Chapman at the time it was W***, although I told Mr. Shiels that it was Chapman. Babs gave her real name. You'll probably understand why I did this. I was still VERY upset when Babs and I were walking on the beach the next day. Babs was much more grown-up than me at the time (and probably still is). She was calming me down, trying to make me laugh, because I hadn't slept a wink the night before. She walked up to Tony and told him what had happened. I have no idea how she knew of him, but I gather he was a bit*

Above: *The wooded slopes of Mawnan Glebe, where witnesses have seen the Owlman*
Below: *The nest of the Owlman? No just a weird pile of sticks*

I saw this monster
bird last night. It
stood like a man
then it flew up
through the trees.
It is as big as a man. Its eyes are red and
shine brightly.

Sally Chapman 4/7/76.

Birdman monster. Seen on 3rd July, quite late at night but not quite dark. Red eyes. Black mouth. It was very big with great big wings and black claws. Feathers grey.
B. Perry 4th July 1976.

The pictures given to Tony 'Doc' Shiels by eyewitnesses
Sally Chapman and Barbara Perry's of the bird/man - like creature
they saw at the woods at Mawnan

Looking east towards the wooded slopes of Mawnan Glebe, with the rugged rocks of Parson's Beach just visible below.

This is where one of the most peculiar sightings of the Owlman - and indeed the only one to date when it was seen "in flight" rather than standing, perching or hovering.

The woods here are ancient, magickal, beautiful, and in many places untouched - corroborative evidence for several of the multifarious explanations which have been mooted over the years to explain His Owliness.

of a local character. I didn't really know that part of Cornwall at all.

He had some paper and pencils on him, and had us draw it. He helped me so much that day without even realising it - I remember him making me giggle a bit, and he was so cheery that he really snapped me out of it. I don't think either drawing was particularly good - I'm not really sure that it was as OWLLY as our pictures suggested.

I've just realised that I've been stalling actually describing what happened when we were in the wood that night. This thing STILL has an effect on me all these years later.

It was probably around 9.45pm when we saw it. We had made tea with a little camping stove, and I seem to remember that we were talking about school and boys. There was a boy at home that I was very interested in, and Babs wanted to know all about it. Neither of us had boyfriends before at that point. It was still light. I seem to remember that it hadn't rained for ages, and the woods were very dry and crunchy, if that makes sense. The noise was so abrupt in the quiet of the woods that we both jumped up together. It was a kind of hissing I don't know, I can't really remember. It was loud and sudden. We both looked over into the wood, and there it was.

I had been to see a horror film in Plymouth a few months before, a werewolf film with Peter Cushing. This was the first thing I thought when I saw it, I thought it was the werewolf. The face wasn't really like an owl - thinking back, it was like a frowning sneering black thing. The eyes were burning glaring and reddish. I don't know if it had fur or feathers, but it was grey and grizzled like the werewolf in the film. I remember hearing Barbara start to laugh, but it was a sort of choked, panicked laugh. Tony Shiels did us a great favour by playing down our fear when he talked about what happened to us later on. I think when we saw him that day on the beach that he must have known how upset we really were.

I knew right away it was REAL. It wasn't like a monster in the films that look rubbery and fake. It just looked like a very weird, frightening animal, as real as any animal in a zoo. It looked flesh and blood to me, but there is simply no way it could have been. It couldn't have been something that was born and grew. No way. I have no idea what it was. My head hurts even thinking about it.

It was more frightening than I can really describe. I remember blood rushing to my head, making it pound. It just stood there for what might have been a minute.

I'm not really sure how long. Barbara was laughing, but it was more like a sort of breathless hysterical sound by now. I wanted to run but couldn't. It was so EVIL, intensely so. When it moved, that nearly did it, I nearly started running. Its arms or wings or whatever went out, and it just rose up through the trees. Straight up through the evergreens, it didn't flap, it didn't make a sound. Then, weirdly, I thought 'costume' for the first time, because the legs looked wrong. They looked like a kind of grey trouser material, certainly unnatural. I can't be entirely sure now. And then the feet. Black, hooking things. I have no idea how it had managed to stand up on them. They were like an earwig's tail-piece.

It's difficult trying to remember exactly what happened next. The wood was quiet, but it felt as if it, the thing, could appear again at any second. I think I had nearly fainted at one point. Babs was the same. We were shaking like leaves. I was thinking that someone was

39

going to come out of the woods laughing at their trick, but really I knew that it couldn't possibly have been a trick. On one level, my mind simply wasn't accepting it. It still doesn't in a way. That's how I got over it, I think. By pretending that it hadn't really happened. As I mentioned earlier, in some ways I lost a lot of years to it. Somehow, shaking and crying a bit, we got packed up. That was the worst time, waiting for it to come back. I don't think that I could have coped seeing it again. My mind was POUNDING, ballooning. I don't know how it could have disappeared like it did. The woods weren't that thick. Not thick enough to hide what I can only think of as a monster. I know that sounds silly, but it is perhaps the most apt way to describe it. It seemed to just vanish, like a ghost.

We were originally going to walk back to Babs' home, near Gweek, but it was pretty much dark by now. Obviously as an adult you question why you stayed out, but that's what we did. We moved camp to a place where the woods were thinner, as I recall. I didn't sleep a wink, and neither did Babs I suppose. Yet somehow I knew it was gone for good. The atmosphere was lighter somehow, there were bird noises coming out of the trees, calls and the like. The night crawled by, and eventually it started to get light. We made tea at about six or so, and went for a walk down on the beach around nine. We met Tony Shiels, and told our story.

I really don't know why I decided to write all this down, after so many years. As I have said, someone close to me thought that I should come clean. Actually, doing so has affected me less than I thought it was going to. Reading over it, I feel a little embarrassed. It doesn't seem possible now. I have no idea why or how it happened. I never expect to.

I moved with my family from West Hoe in Plymouth in 1980 to Surrey, and then on to Pembroke to work in a creative role in 1989. I believe that what happened in July '76 shaped my life for years afterwards.

My good friend Barbara emigrated with her husband to Australia in 1987. I haven't spoken to her in many years, but I think that I would hear if anything had happened.

That's about it, really. For what it's worth, I haven't been to Cornwall since I was a teenager. Whatever happened that July is firmly in the past, and I intend to leave it there.

Back in 1976, however, the sightings continued.

At the same time as Sally and Barbara were talking to 'Doc' on Grebe Beach, two other girls, the Greenwood sisters, on holiday from Southport, also saw what Tony refers to as 'his Owliness'. Jane Greenwood described it in a letter to the *Falmouth Packet*. [34]

"Sir. - I am on holiday in Cornwall with my sister and our mother. I, too have seen a big bird-thing like that pictured in 'Morgawr-the Monster of Falmouth Bay'. It was Sunday morning and the place was in the trees near Mawnan Church, above the rocky beach. It was in the trees standing like a full grown man, but the legs bent backwards like a bird's. It saw us and quickly jumped up and rose straight up through the trees. My sister and I saw it very closely before it rose up. It has red slanting eyes and a very large mouth. The feathers are silvery grey and so are his body and legs. The feet are like a big, black crab's claws. We were frightened at the time. It was so strange, like something out of a horror film. After the thing went up, there were crackling sounds in the tree-tops for ages. Our mother thinks

40

THE WIZARD OF PONSANOOTH...

BUILT like a bear with the eyes of a dove, snarling like a pirate, laughing like a schoolgirl, Doc Shiels is a fork - bending, mind - warping, monster - hunting, one hundred p e r c e n t WIZARD.

He also swallows Guinness like air.

Finally, fame has caught up, with the wizard of Ponsanooth Last month he was front - page news when he succeeded — where hundreds had failed — in luring the Loch Ness monster out of her hiding hole.

Now, the powers of wizardry that helped him then have landed him in the limelight of a West End stage.

Ken Campbell, the actor and director who found fame by putting live ferrets in his trousers, has persuaded him to star in a play about his life which will open at the Bush Theatre in Shepherd's Bush, London, in two weeks.

But it isn't written.

Never mind, Doc Shiels is a living theatre.

Stroking his doormat of a beard, Doc considered his theatrical fate 'This play is, I'm afraid, largely about myself.

'I have the honour to be the actor and director of Tom Fool's theatre of Tom Foolery which will present to you a veritable horde of monsters and the like.

'And remember that everything in the play is real, absolutely authentic and very, very true.'

Which takes some believing.

Among the cast of magical monsters which Doc will present are

★ Morgawr, the monster of Falmouth Bay

★ The Owl Man of Mawnan Smith, who was recently seen by some schoolgirls on holiday

★ The Lemonade Man of Ponsanooth, who has appeared in Doc's village twice in the last 100 years

★ Countless Cornish piskies.

Most of what goes on is based on his own experiences with monsters. That is why the play is called The Confessions of a Monster Hunter.

Whether the experiences were really like that doesn't seem to matter. There is a line in the play. 'You don't have to laugh It's only

Can give away stars . . 23 a time

funny if you don't understand it.'

Take, for example, the day that Doc and his friend, John Gordan, became custodians of the entire universe.

'Early one evening, just a few weeks ago, we were walking down to the hostelry. And when we reached the small bridge after which this village of Ponsanooth is named, we heard an unearthly sound.

took photographs of Nessie. And the Owl Man of Mawnan Smith, near Falmouth Bay, has been seen by several young girls.

'They saw an owl-like face and wings and crab - clawed feet. A nice touch that with the crab - clawed feet.'

'And this thing just went up and down without flapping its wings. Which was a rather disturbing thing for it to do, I think.'

When supernatural beings get uppity, Doc turns to his Diddling Doll.

● Doc Shiels . . wizard of Ponsanooth.

'Wow - wow - wow - rip. tip. tip. Suddenly before us appeared an albino extra - terrestial, dressed in a rather neatly tailored suit.'

The strange being, who kept clicking while he spoke, introduced himself as one

Norman Crocadiladine, 'the custodian of the entire universe. But not God, who is someone else'.

Doc recalls that, with much clicking, Norman put forward a strange proposition: 'I have been watching you lads for quite a while and I have decided that you are the ones — being such good lads — to take over my burden. Are you prepared to accept that responsibility?'

'Before those who would do mischief to me start to stick long hat pins in my handsome self, I get my little tie doll out and create a force field.'

Whatever raises a smile is true in Doc's world.

Some of his monster sightings are backed by the word of other eye - witnesses. He

At 39, Doc enjoys playing the proud father; I conceived them and was in at the birth of some of them — which caused drunkenness to occur.'

His eldest son, Gareth, is 18. He sports a glass eyeball on one finger and has already picked up many of his father's magical ways. He is waiting to go to the National Youth Theatre.

Doc's co-stars in the play are his wife Chris, and their five children, as well as Toby, the dog.

ford was more harsh. He made his way as a Punch and Judy man, busker, street actor and mind - reader. Now, he has a grant from the South West Arts Council.

'I don't have a normal, boring day - to - day job. But everything I do is riddled with wizardry.'

Gareth struck a match and casually popped the flame into his mouth.

Doc winked over his Guinness.

Clicking

And that is how they became custodians of the universe with the right to give away stars, 23 at a time.

Images

Doc's youth in Sal-

★ By NICK DAVIES ★

Interview with 'Doc' in the 'Sunday Independent', 24th July 1977

we made it all up just because we read about these things, but that is not true, we really saw the bird-man, though it could have been someone playing a trick in a very good costume and make up. But how could it rise up like that? If we imagined it then we both imagined it at the same time. (35)

'Doc' mentioned the Owlman in a 1977 interview with the *Sunday Independent*. (36)

"They saw *an owl-like face and crab-clawed feet. A nice touch that the crab-clawed feet. And this thing just went up and down without flapping its wings, which was a rather disturbing thing to do I think*".

Tony has never really cared whether people take hum seriously or not, except as a painter. In the same interview for the *Sunday Independent* he claimed that he and his friend John Gordon had been made custodians of the entire Universe:

"Early one evening just a few weeks ago we were walking down to the hostelry. And when we reached the small bridge after which the village of Ponsanooth is named we heard an unearthly sound.

'Wow-wow-wow-rip-tip-tip'. Suddenly, before us appeared an albino extra-terrestrial, dressed in a rather neat tailored suit. The strange being who kept clicking as he spoke, introduced himself as Norman Crocodilidine - 'The Custodian of the entire Universe'. But not God, who is someone else.'

Doc recalls that with much clicking Norman put forward a strange proposition.

'I have been watching you lads for quite a while and I have decided that you are the ones - being such good lads - to take over my burden. Are you prepared to accept that responsibility?'

And that is how they became custodians of the entire universe with the right to give away stars, 23 at a time"...

The same interview mentioned an entity called 'The Lemonade Man of Ponsanooth'. I asked 'Doc' to tell me about the Lemonade Man, and he just cackled maniacally and grabbed the mobile 'phone out of the top pocket of my denim jacket.

He rang a number in London, (I found out later that it was John Gordon, the friend mentioned in the *Sunday Independent* article, whom in fact I had met in London with Tony the previous autumn), and shouted into it:

"You Gobshite! There's a feller here who wants to know if you're still working for Norman Crocodilidine and he wants to know about the Lemonade Man..."

*The lay-by at Ponasanooth alleged to be haunted by
the spectre of the 'Lemonade Man'*

He passed me back my telephone, and John Gordon told me a garbled and mildly incoherent tale about how he and Tony had been walking to the pub in Ponsanooth one night when suddenly someone leapt out of a layby and offered to sell them lemonade. I thanked him politely and switched off the telephone.

A year or so later Miranda, a Cornish Witch who has more to do with this narrative than anyone will ever know, pointed out the layby where the lemonade man lurks, and told us that one has to run past it or drive very much faster to avoid being caught by him. [37]

A conversation with Tony Shiels is full of such tales, and he, together with his enormous circle of eccentric friends, seem to have concocted a complex and diverse mythology about their lives which overspills into the conversation at the slightest opportunity. It is very difficult to differentiate between the myth and the reality (whatever that means), and one would be forgiven for assuming that the Owlman of Mawnan is nothing more than another complex in-joke. Like Morgawr, the Falmouth Bay Sea Monster, however, there is enough corroborating evidence, which is presented throughout this book, to prove that the Owlman has an independent existence outside the fertile Shielsian imagination.

I make no apologies for including the stories of Norman Crocodilidine and the Lemonade Man of Ponsanooth in this narrative, which is, after all, supposed to be a history of the events at Mawnan Old

Church, because, not only are they providing a valuable insight into the Shiels psyche (no lexilink or even pun, intended), but they give the reader some idea of what a conversation with the Wizard of the Western World, with its bizarre lexilinks and tangential storytelling, is actually like.

Two years after the Greenwood Sisters' sighting, the 'thing' was seen again in June 1978. 'Doc' wrote to Bob Rickard, the Editor and founder of *Fortean Times* on the 19th June to tell him about this latest sighting.[38] Before quoting from this letter, and discussing the 1978 sightings in greater depth, we should perhaps take a brief look at Tony's activities that summer.

The *Falmouth Packet* newspaper had announced 'Doc's' intentions at that time to 'summon up' pixies. [39] Whether or not he had any such intention to do anything of the kind, or whether it was part of his ongoing campaign of self-publicity (his play '*The Gallavant Variations*', had, despite initial success been withdrawn prematurely), time does not relate, and I have to admit that I have never actually got around to asking him.

It would seem, however, that Tony was hardly in the position of being short of publicity at that time. *The Sun* ran a full page story on *The Gallavant Variations* and described how:

> *Doc's 16 year old daughter Kate appears topless, and his youngest girl, Lucy, 14, swears throughout the two hour performance. One of his sons, Ewan, 18, wears a pink towelling 'nude' costume sporting three artificial breasts.*

> *Doc - real name Tony - admitted: 'The whole thing is very rude and vulgar'.*

But he added:

> *I don't believe that it is unsuitable for children. It is naïve to think that kids don't have swearing and violence in their ordinary lives.* [40]

In one of the local papers he was reported as saying:

> *Although it was originally a kid's show, it now has something for everyone - surrealism, romance and probably plenty of swearing and nudity..* [41]

As a result of this new spate of publicity, however, he had received several strange telephone calls including one from a man identifying himself as Ken Opie. (Opie is a relatively common name in the Falmouth/Pemyn area, but his precise identity has never been discovered). Opie said that: [42]

> *"He'd read the Packet piece [43] and thought I might be interested in something his daughter had seen a couple of weeks ago. (i.e. about the 4th June). 'A monster, like a devil, flying up through the trees near old Mawnan Church'. I asked the age of his daughter and he said '16', but wouldn't give me her name. I asked him what she was doing near the old church that morning, and he replied that 'she wouldn't have been there on her own'. Then he rang off".*

As Tony insightfully wrote to Bob Richard:

> *"It looks as if our Owlman is back!"*

Stage kids are brought up on sex, violence, nudity and swearing galore

THE WEIRDEST FAMILY IN THE LAND!

SHOWMAN Doc Shiels is shocking audiences with a "rude and vulgar" show featuring his five children.

An average of 15 people a night are walking out of the sex show —which is backed by a £1,000 Arts Council grant.

Doc's 16-year-old daughter Kate appears topless, and his youngest girl, Lucy, 14, swears throughout the two-hour performance.

One of his sons, Ewan, 18, wears a pink towelling "nude"

BY ANN BEVERIDGE

costume sporting three artificial breasts.

Doc—real name Tony—admitted: "The whole thing is very rude and vulgar."

But he added: "I don't believe it is unsuitable for children. It is naive to think that kids don't have swearing and violence in their ordinary lives."

Doc, aged 40, said the play,

called Gallavant, is his own "tongue-in-cheek poke" at sex and violence on TV.

But one playgoer, mother-of-six Mrs Jill Williams, said: "I was horrified. I was even booing. It is a shocking waste of public money."

Bawdy

Mrs Williams, a builder's wife from Redruth, Cornwall, walked out half-way through a performance although she had paid 80p for a ticket.

Falmouth teacher Leonie Hutton agreed that the script was "outrageous."

But she said: "Although it is openly bawdy, there is nothing nasty about it."

At the moment Doc is touring Cornish theatres and village halls with the show, but he plans to take it to London.

He said he got many of his ideas from his own children Gareth, 19, Ewan, twins Kate and Meg, and Lucy.

Investigate

Doc, of Devoran, Cornwall, runs the travelling Tom Fool's Theatre and is well known for his street shows.

But now the South West Arts Council — which awarded his grant — may look into his latest presentation.

Director Ian Watson said: "We could not see Doc's script as it is largely improvised, but we will investigate any complaints."

Freaky family . . . the Shiels on stage in their gear. They are Kate, left, Gareth, Doc, Lucy, Meg and in front Ewan.

The article that appeared in 'The Sun' newspaper 28th April 1978

Thank heavens for tomfoolery

SIR,—So Doc Sheils has the "weirdest family in the land" and the children are being brought up on "sex, violence, nudity and swearing galore," according to the "Sun" newspaper and reported in the "Packet" last week.

I went to see the controversial "Gallavant" production, immensely enjoyed the tomfoolery and wished the advertising posters had not borne the words "not for babes," as I would have liked by eight-year-old to have seen it.

Sex plays no part in the Gallavant, the violence is of the sort favoured by children everywhere; Punch and Judy, the nudity is portrayed by a very funny costume which reveals nought but the facial skin of the wearer. Shocking? Hardly, but very very funny!

I did witness people walking out of the theatre. Two middle aged, blue-rinse ladies waited for the interval to leave and the criticism I overheard as they left was "I can't understand it, there's no story." Over their heads, perhaps?

Doc adds colour to Cornwall and the place would be poorer without him and his talented family. If he and his kind (not that there is anyone quite like Doc) attempted to appease the tight-lipped critics and hypocrites of the public and press, our cultural life would become hatefully dreary.

Long may his tomfoolery prosper and delight its spectators.

P. EFFORD,
Little Oak,
2, Penvale Cross,
Treluswell,
Penryn.

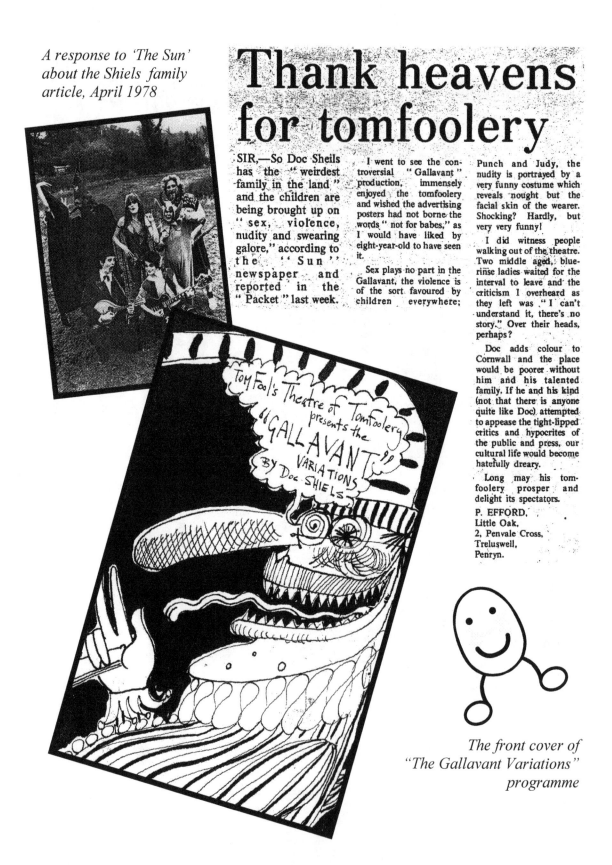

The front cover of "The Gallavant Variations" programme

Nearly twenty years later Tony confirmed:

"Ken Opie exists, or did, and he's a Redruth man, who told his tale to David Clarke of 'Cornish Life' magazine". [44]

On June 26th 1978 he wrote to Janet and Colin Bord:

"The Owlman is certainly back in business, it seems. I poked around his area, around Old Mawnan Church, a couple of days ago, and the atmosphere was positively crackling with 'odd presences', if you know what I mean. As soon as anything really exciting happens, I'll let you know. It would be terrific if I really could get a picture of our feathered friend, but he only seems to pop up for young girls ... and I ain't one!" [45].

The Owlman, as it was now generally known, (it appears that Tony coined the name in late 1976), was seen again on the 2nd August by three young, unnamed French girls. The landlady of the boarding house in which they had been staying told Tony that the three girls had been frightened by something

"very big, like a big, furry bird with a gaping mouth and round eyes"

This was all that the landlady could tell him, so Tony left a message for the girls to contact him, but as always seems to be the case he never heard anything further.

"The French Girls were students (at Camborne Tech - now known as Cornwall College), lodging in Redruth. I think they were on some sort of 'summer school' course. Their land-lady 'phoned me about this sighting. You must remember that at the time I was getting quite a lot of media coverage. People reported weird shit to me.

Two days later Tony wrote to Janet and Colin Bord:

Many thanks for the fiver... I needed it! Yes, things have been going unusually badly for us of late, and it may be a backlash because I've been trying to raise the wee folk and Owlmen, then again it may not. During the last few weeks dozens of things have gone wrong... Kate was thrown by a usually docile horse and broke her arm, Meg has been suffering from all manner of pains and sicknesses, Ewan was almost flattened by a speeding motorbike (he es-caped with just having one of his shoes knocked off - it was very close. The motorcyclist and his bike, by the way were all black; 'very MIB-like' ... he didn't stop), two of our cats sud-denly died of a mystery illness, and I have suffered from strange rashes, sore eyes, and the latest; a painful blow-back when I was doing some fire-spitting as part of our (banned!) street show. You will, I hope, be sad to hear that I lost several inches of hair, beard and skin. I look quite different now! Those are just a few of the hard luck stories.. You will have heard that we've been banned from doing our outdoor shows. Because of this Tom Fool's Theatre is folding. We simply can't afford to carry on, it's so expensive keeping a group of at least half a dozen people on the road. In spite of what some newspapers may have said, we were not banned because of our last stage show... other performers have also been banned. I'll still carry on doing shows, of course, on my own or with just a couple of the kids... but from the end of next month, Tom Fool's Theatre will be no more.

Oh dear, don't I sound miserable. Actually I'm not.

Doc on carpet!

ONE of the Falmouth-Penryn area's zaniest characters has achieved the rare distinction of making headlines in the national Press for a third successive year.

In the spring of 1976, Mr. Tony "Doc" Shiels attracted national and international attention when he announced that he and four nude witches would raise the Falmouth sea monster Morgawr in the Helford River. (They didn't.)

A year later he was on the front pages of the "Daily Mirror" and "Scottish Daily Record" with what he claimed to be the best-ever photograph of the Loch Ness Monster.

But his play not closing

Now, with the help of his five children and under the stage name of Tom Fool's Theatre of Tomfoolery, he has done it again.

VIOLENCE

A banner headline in the "Sun" on Friday described them as "The Weirdest Family in the Land," claiming that the children, aged 14 to 19, are being brought up "on sex, violence, nudity and swearing galore."

Saturday's "Daily Telegraph" also carried a lengthy report on alleged complaints about the family's latest theatre production, "Gallavant," which opened in Falmouth last month.

The "Sun," which also published a photograph of the family, with 16-year-old Kate Shiels topless, said that an average of 15 people a night are walking out of the show.

"That's just plain ludicrous, of course," commented Mr. Shiels, who lives at 3, Vale View, Ponsanooth. "I think one or two people did walk out during our two shows at Falmouth."

Their only performance since Falmouth, in fact, was a street version at Padstow on Monday, although it continues at Davidstowe, near Camelford, tonight and at St. Ives, Penzance and Truro later this month.

Mr. Shiels' three daughters, Kate and Meg (both 16) and Lucy (14) attend Penryn School, but his sons, Gareth (19) and Ewan (18), have left school.

STRONG

"Gallavant" features undeniably strong language to which all his children contribute.

"The point is that they are only acting. Anyone meeting these kids in real life will find they are not the terrifying, disgusting, perverted little darlings that has been implied," said Mr. Shiels.

He added: "I have heard a rumour going round that the show is being stopped or banned. That's absolute nonsense. I would like to see anyone try and stop it!"

Falmouth Packet - February 1977

`Doc's` image was changing. In a bizarre series of events which uncannily predicted the Thatcher government's crackdown on traveller's and those with an alternative lifestyle, during the decade to come, `Doc` was now the target for criticism, and rather than just being seen as a genial eccentric, he was now beginning to be perceived as something somewhat more sinister!

During the next few weeks I'll do what I can to raise the Owlman, aided by the transatlantic vibes of Dr. David Hoy, the American psychic, who's beaming Owlman-invoking thoughts across the ocean. My own daughters may be useful in this experiment; but I don't want to risk them being hurt by any nasty backlash. Recently, as in 1976, there have been a series of UFO sightings around the Falmouth Bay area which, as before, seem to be connected with Owlman's return. I'll keep you posted on all this.

Cheers,

Doc [47]

The *Falmouth Packet*, a newspaper which had always been broadly sympathetic to Tony, covered the 'ban' in some depth:

"A Ponsanooth family have been banned from busking in Falmouth and are meeting with opposition elsewhere in the county. Tom Fool's Theatre of Tomfoolery - alias Mr. Tony 'Doc' Shiels, and his family - had been busking in Falmouth's streets earlier this summer until police began to receive complaints" [48]

Tony was quoted as claiming that:

"I rather got the impression that these complaints were from the same two or three people all the time". [49]

Soon afterwards the family were out busking the streets again, but this time they were in search of signatures for a petition that they hoped to present to the Council in an attempt to get them to change their minds. [50] [51] The papers also noted that another theatre group, *The Footsbarn Theatre,* longtime friends and allies of the Shiels clan, had also been banned from Falmouth, and that there had been generally poor audiences for other theatre shows in the region [52].

Times were changing, and the almost complete collapse of community funded Arts projects that was to take place during the Thatcher era was only just around the corner!

Later that year he wrote to Janet and Colin Bord again:

"Yes, Tom Fool's Theatre is now disbanded and I'll probably give up Showbiz for a while to concentrate on other things... NOT monster-raising, by the by. I've had enough of monsters for a long time. The Owlman-raising experiment was a total failure... though Cornwall was beset, around August and September, with a load of UFO activity. The Owlman has been reported this year by a few people. In June it was seen by 16 year old Miss Opie, from (I think) Camborne. In August (though not during our experiment), he was observed by a trio of French girls. However, as I said, I no longer intend to involve myself in such things...

It seems, as we will see later in this book, as if the experiment might have been more successful than he had thought at the time, though in a new and frightening direction. Despite his decision to quit monster-raising activities, the following year he was to try again.

We should, I think, take note of the discrepancies between the various stories that Tony has told over the years concerning the 'Miss Opie' sighting. Whereas he told Bob Rickard that Opie had telephoned

HE's HERE! IN PERSON!

DOC SHIELS

WIZARD OF THE WEST
PRESENTING
A SERIES OF TRULY AMAZING

IMPOSSIBLE!   **IMPOSSIBLE!**

ENIGMAS OF THE EAST
AND OTHER MAGICAL HAPPENINGS

DOC SHIELS
& company

him, [54] he told me that Opie had given his story to David Clarke. [55] Whilst he told me that Opie came from Redruth, he told Janet and Colin Bord that he was from Camborne, [56] (which he also stated in 'Monstrum'). [58] We should remember that these events took place nearly twenty years before this book was written, (and thirty years before this present revised edition), and the fact that there are discrepancies is something that we should expect. After all, these are the only major discrepancies to date in *any* of his stories, and Redruth is very close to Camborne!

What is more important about the exchange of letters with the Bord's is that this is Tony's first known reference to psychic backlash' a complaint which, he believes befalls monster hunters. [59].

It certainly happened to Tim Dinsdale, [60] and it has happened to me. [60] Tony warned me on a number of occasions about it, and has even, in moments of almost tender concern apologised for any mishaps which may occur to me and my family, as a result of our friendship with him! [61].

Despite his widely reported assertions that the summer of 1978 had seen the end of his monster raising activities, [62] Bealtane [63], 1979 saw another, low key, and practically unknown experiment. [64] On April 24th 1979 he wrote to Janet and Colin Bord:

> *"I'm afraid it looks now, as if I won't be able to let you have anymore witch pictures, involving Kate. Last week she went for a swim in the rather cold waters of Falmouth Bay, hoping to tempt Morgawr to the surface. A couple of days later, she was suffering from a glandular infection. The doctor says she has to take things easy for at least a fortnight. So ....she's out of our final invocation experiment and, as we had both agreed to 'retire' from the game on May Eve (midnight of course), I don't think that she would like to play the part of the witch-girl, after that date, for photographs or for any other reason.*
>
> *This last fling experiment has not been a success, so far. Kate and I have had several rows.... allowing our sense of humour to slip, which is always a great mistake. A lot of the time we've been competing with each other, instead of properly combining our efforts. In fact 'effort' is a dirty word... I think we've, somehow, been trying too hard. The cosmic joker, as usual, seems to be having the last laugh at our expense. The only way to deal with that is to be prepared to laugh at oneself - a trick which I had begun, recently, to forget.*
>
> *The nearest we have come to any kind of result happened about a week ago, near the old church at Mawnan, when... hoping for some sign of Owlman... I heard a loud, nightjar-like 'churring' sound which lasted for several minutes. This happened last year, and it's a sound which I've heard in dreams... a sound which I intend to study from an oneirocritical point of view. I'm convinced that the 'Owlman' is more of a nightjar than an owl (I don't think he ever hoots), that is to say, the collected 'clues', in this case, point more towards the order of Caprimulgiformes than to the Strigiformes (though, it must be admitted, the nightjars are quite close to the owls in the avian evolutionary scale). I know this must sound rather silly, but if when dealing with dragons, (such as Nessie and Morgawr), one considers certain characteristics from a zoological or palaeontological point of view, then surely it is in order to seek clues to the nature and/or meaning of the Owlman in ornithology? He is more like a bird than a man (remember, some birds are man-sized.. and all birds are, like man bipeds). Although I haven't seen the thing (except in dreams... and maybe that's as good as any other way), I have heard the nightjar-style call when attempting to 'call up' the Owlman.*
>
> *The 'nightjar' order... including frogmouths, potoos, oilbirds and whippoor-wills is very*

51

weird. But I'm rambling ... " [65]

As we shall see later in this book, Tony's interest in nightjars continued for some years. A week or so after the last letter, however, he wrote to Janet and Colin Bord again:

> *"The monster-raising experiment conducted a couple of days ago, was something of a flop. Kate decided to re-join for the last few days, and Meg and Gareth turned up for our Beltane celebrations, but, although we all tried hard (too hard, probably), nothing happened except, as before, the nightjar noises, and - on the last night - a great many owl noises. No ... there shouldn't be any 'real' nightjars in this part of the world during April. They usually arrive, from Africa, towards the end of May. Nevertheless, we did hear the 'churring' sound typical of the European nightjar... and nightjars played a part in several significant dreams we (Kate, Gareth and myself), have had lately. Apart from that, however, the experiment failed... Not a single sighting of either the Owlman or Morgawr has been reported (so far as I know), and I don't think any of the Scottish loch monsters have popped up during the period. It seems as if we've lost our touch, so perhaps it is a good thing that we've retired."* [66]

Luck was not with 'Doc' in any of his monster-raising activities that year. In early May he travelled to Ireland, where he unsuccessfully tried to 'raise' at least one Irish Lake Monster or Wurrum. [67] He was to have more success the following year, when coincidentally, both Morgawr and the Owlman were seen again. There are three species of nightjar found in Europe. [68] Two, however are very rare visitors, known only as vagrants. [69] The European Nightjar *(Caprimulgus europaeus),* is as Tony said a summer visitor to Britain migrating from tropical Africa. [70] According to some books the birds arrive in the UK about a month earlier than Tony claimed, [71] and so it is possible that the 'churring' sound, (the distinctive song of both *C. europaeus* and its close relative *C. aegyptius* - The Egyptian Nightjar) [72] could have been caused by 'real' nightjars. Caprimulgiformes are, however, as Tony said to Janet and Colin Bord, [73] very weird birds...

Our personal library does not include a complete run of the Cornwall County Bird Reports, but we have a few copies, and whilst it does seem pointless to go through the records for every year since records began, it seems useful to note the records of nightjars (presumably *C. europaeus)* for the four years, for which, without the exercise of undue effort, we have the data available.

1949. The first record is from 15th May at Mawgan (74)

1958. The earliest record is from Crenver of May 21st. There is a single record from St. Mary's in the Isles of Scilly on the 8th October. [75]

1959. The earliest record is from May 15th at Crenver, and last seen at Par on September 11th. There is a single record from the Scilly Isles on September 24th. [76]

1960. They were recorded at Penanwell Valley, St Just [77] between July 30th and August 4th. The recorder notes that:

AUTHOR'S NOTE: Whilst preparing this 30th anniversary edition, I discovered that there is in fact a *fourth* nightjar on the British List. The Common Nighthawk, *Chordeiles minor* - a North American species, which overwinters in South America and is a rare vagrant in Europe. Adults are dark with brown, grey and white patterning on the upperparts and breast; the long wings are black and show a white bar in flight. The tail is dark with white barring; the underparts are white with black bars. The adult male has a white throat; the female has a light brown throat.

European Nightjar
Caprimulgus europaeus

Red-necked Nightjar
Caprimulgus ruficollis

Egyptian Nightjar
Caprimulgus aegyptius

"They were heard regularly before the war, but this is the first year since 1940 that I have heard them here".

There is also a record for October 7th in the Scilly Isles.

Although some reference books give the arrival date of the species in the UK at the end of April, [80] it seems as if Tony was right when he claimed that the birds do not arrive in Cornwall until later in May.

We shall be returning to nightjars and their relatives later in the book.

As will be seen later in this book, it seems difficult, if not impossible, to separate the phenomenon of Owlman with the other zooform and fortean phenomena in the area. As already mentioned, Morgawr, the sea-monster of Falmouth Bay, was particularly active during the 1970's and early 1980's. What appears to be another sighting of Owlman can be found in an account of a Morgawr sighting on the 13th November 1980.

It is taken from Graham McEwan's book *'The Mystery Animals of Britain and Ireland'*, [81] but he took it almost verbatim from a 'Doc' Shiels article in *Fortean Times*: [82]

> *On Thursday 13 November, 'Doc' was enjoying a lunchtime drink in the Globe Inn on the Falmouth waterfront when a man aged about sixty can over and said that he recognised 'Doc' from a television broadcast, and that he had seen Morgawr the previous afternoon. It was about 4.00 p.m. when he saw the creature off Rosemullion Head and watched as it moved very quickly towards the mouth of the Helford.*

> *Visibility was good and the animal was under observation for two or three minutes. This witness, who called himself 'Martin', said that the animal was gigantic, with a body like a whale and a neck like a python. As if this was not enough, he said that his daughter and grand-daughter had seen an enormous, bird-like creature fly over the Helford River and into the trees near Grebe Beach.*

Back in *The Seven Stars*, fifteen years later, as Tony and I sipped our fourth pints of the evening, he confirmed this sighting:

> *'There was a sighting in 1980, a Mr. Martin's daughter ... but then 1986. That was when I did my bit to upset the Bishop of Truro."* [83]

I'd heard of this legendary 'run in' with the Ecclesiastical authorities. In an article written in 1995 for my magazine 'Animals & Men' Tony wrote:

> *"My Owlman experiments ceased around Hallowe'en 1986, when tricking and treating at Mawnan Old Church upset the ecclesiastical authorities. It was a hoot!"* [84]

In the notorious edition of *Strange Magazine*, [85] which was devoted to a weird cross between attacking and celebrating the Shiels output, Tony wrote:

> *"At the witching hour of midnight, on the 'Feis na Samhain', 1986, 1 invoked the Cornish Owlman at Mawnan Old Church. The event was broadcast over BBC Radio Cornwall and*

54

deeply upset the Bishop of Truro, who considered my conjurations to be blasphemous. They were, in fact, surrealchemical... [86]

(The whole episode of the *Strange Magazine* articles is covered more fully in a later chapter).

In issue number 48 of *Fortean Times*, published in the Spring of 1987, more detailed references were made to the events at Mawnan over Hallowe'en 1986: [87]

> *"While being interviewed by BBC Radio Cornwall - who for some reason considered him as an 'expert' on Hallowe'en, Doc was asked what he planned for that night.*
>
> *Sharp as a whippet, Doe said that he was going to invoke the Owlman. (...) By evening Doc was drunk - 'I had been in a couple of pubs in Penryn bending spoons' - and being followed by radio and newspaper reporters and other sightseers. The crowd found themselves outside Mawnan Smith Old Church. 'It was a last minute decision to go into the church', said Doc. What happened next is obscure...."*

Obscure is the right word. It is quite an entertaining story so far as it goes, but it does not seem to tally with the facts that I managed to unearth during the summer and autumn of 1995. It seems that the story about the BBC radio team is true, but that the 'crowd of reporters and other sightseers' turned out to be one man. His name turned out to be Dave "Shento" Shenton.

> *"What actually happened was, I attempted to invoke the Owlman. Its presence was certainly felt and one or two people were rather scared by the atmosphere. I found my way into Mawnan Church around midnight with a BBC radio crew and a rather nervous person called Dave Shenton. I've never seen Dave Shenton so nervous. He kept repeating, 'you must remember I am a Christian after all...''* [88]

I contacted Dave Shenton, who turned out to be an old friend of Tony's. They'd drunk together and seen each other in various pubs and folk clubs for years. Dave Shenton now lives on a house-boat in another part of southern Cornwall. Tracking him down was a matter of relatively simple detective work which involved leaving messages in a number of riverside pubs until he eventually telephoned our office.

According to Dave, who seems to be known to all and sundry as 'Shento' he was on his way back from work in the early evening of Hallowe'en when he ran into 'Doc' who invited him along for the evening's adventures 'for the crack'. [89]

'Shento' said nothing about Tony bending spoons, but here it should be remembered that for any friend of Tony's this would have been nothing unusual. Tony had been doing this sort of thing around Cornwall for years! [90]

In a 1976 book called *The Shiels Effect* which was credited to Niacail O'Siaghail [91] (it is not entirely a coincidence that Tony's middle name is Nicol and the Gaelic spelling for Shiels is "O'Siaghail"), [92] he describes how he has bent cutlery, nails, keys and even an iron poker at various pubs about the West Country. He also gives explicit instructions as to how this may be achieved by sleight of hand, but this is neither the time nor the place to repeat them.

Tony continued:

"I did a few bits and pieces inside the Church ... There was a lot of misreporting that I was throwing out challenges to God, and saying I'd smack him in the gob. I don't think God has a gob, and I wouldn't do that anyway to the deity. He'd give me a harder smack back wouldn't he?" [93]

According to Dave Shenton:

"We went into the Church. I sat down in one of the pews and said The Lord's Prayer, and Doc muttered something in a foreign language and that was it really. I didn't know anything about the bird-man before this. I actually thought that it was going to be something to do with the sea monster. I think it was all a prank for the radio actually." [94]

According to the report in *Fortean Times*:

"Some say Doc was wandering about the inside of the church, smoking and incomprehensively shouting, ending up on top of the altar threatening God. All of which Doc has denied".. [95]

- and continues to deny. The reports from both 'Doc' and Dave Shenton suggest, although no-one has said as much, that Tony, doing a radio interview to promote the first issue of his surrealist art magazine Nnidnid, [96] hit upon an amusing prank to play upon his hosts at the BBC which would not only guarantee him some more publicity for his new venture, but probably a supply of free beer all evening.

It seems not beyond the bounds of possibility that someone at the BBC, understandably miffed at this harmless jape, (which knowing the amount of Guinness that the man can pack away during the course of an evening - and here we should also remember that by his own admission the 'Owlman raising' exercise did not take place until midnight, which may be a time of occult significance but it is also about the length of time it takes to walk to the Old Church from the pub, after closing time), decided to get his own back mildly by fabricating a story of occult excess.

It seems that the Ecclesiastical authorities took it slightly more seriously.

"The then Bishop of Truro, the Reverend Peter Mumford, thought that they might have to reconsecrate the Old Church." [97]

said Tony, with a wry grin and a sigh, as he took an enormous drag on his hand rolled cigarette.

"but on checking out the situation he found that there was no, um, evidence of my bootprints on the altar cloth or cigar stubs in the holy water or anything like that I telephoned him up and offered to buy him a drink because I'd heard that he was a bit of a whisky drinker..."

Coincidentally, soon afterwards, that Bishop of Truro died, and thus was unavailable to be interviewed for this book. [98]

Back in the pub, as the dog-collared landlord called 'time', I asked Tony whether anyone had actually seen the Owlman as a result of his 1986 adventures:

"Yes, but I think that was pure suggestion wasn't it?"

56

and his eyes twinkled mischievously.

One can gauge a better picture of the events of Hallowe'en 1986 from a selection of newspaper articles in my research notes. The first is from the *Falmouth Packet* of November 1st. [99]

The headline reads:

> *"Wizard Prang!"*

and accompanies one of the stock pictures of Tony taken about six years before wearing his trademark (at the time) tall hat and impish grin. The story is typically eccentric:

> *"One of Cornwall's resident Wizards claims to have been at it again - this time he says he caused a minor earthquake in a pub"..*

There then follows three paragraphs of biographical information which essentially tells much of what you have already read in this chapter, but then the story of the events of Hallowe'en 1986 start with a real bang!

> *"It was unintentional but I was angry at the time", he explained smoking an E.S.P cigar with a Guinness in front of him. I was waving my finger at a picture of the Loch Ness Monster when the plate glass shelves split along the middle, optics fell, and glasses shattered and broke.* [100] *The landlord of the pub confirmed that two shelves had broken but added that he did not blame 'Doc' Shiels. "We don't know why they collapsed but we will find out," he added.*

The rest of the story amusingly corroborates an incident that I had been told by friends of the man himself. It concerned a housewarming party at which 'Doc' had been one of the guests. [101] Tony does not like being asked to perform. Indeed I have always made it a point never to press him on this matter. I have a sneaking suspicion that it would be both undignified and dangerous to treat the Wizard of the Western World as if he were a performing seal.

On one occasion, but history doesn't relate whether it was this specific one, the hostess had been 'hassling' him to bend a spoon, and he was getting angry. According to an eyewitness he waved his hands at a table set with cutlery, and without touching them each item of cutlery on the table bent spontaneously into tortured curved shapes.

As far as the fork bending incident is concerned. I have no compunction in accepting the story at face value. I have stayed with one of his friends where every single piece of her cutlery is bent into bizarre shapes. I have also seen him bend forks, and although I have read his description of how to do so in *The Shiels Effect*, [102] I am convinced that on at least one occasion he performed this feat by totally magickal means.

He asked my wife to hold a spoon with one of her hands on the handle and the other on the bowl. He then, very gently held both her hands and we all saw the spoon bend, with no force behind it, in front of our eyes. We still have the spoon as a *memento mori*, and it has pride of place, together with various other items of arcane decoration in a curio cabinet in our sitting room.

The next newspaper article is from the same newspaper a week later - after the alleged desecration of

Now the Doc claims he caused an earthquake

Wizard prang!

By Clare Morgan

ONE of Cornwall's resident wizards claims to have been at it again — this time he says he caused a minor earthquake in a pub.

Tony "Doc" Shiels is a well-known character in Cornwall, not to mention the rest of England as well as Scotland and Ireland, where he has tried plenty of monster raising.

He has been featured in the Packet in earlier years for trying to raise the Falmouth monster and for bending cutlery like Uri Geller — one of the Packet's reporters had all his forks bent by Doc at his housewarming party.

Doc, aged 49, from Vale View, Ponsanooth, said he realised he had powers when he was three months old.

He rang the Packet last week to say he had just caused an earth tremor in Ponsanooth while drinking his favourite pint, Guinness, in the Stag Hunt Inn.

"It was unintentional, but I was angry at the time," he explained, smoking an E.S.P. cigar with a Guinness in front of him.

"I was waving my finger at a picture of the Loch Ness monster when two plate glass shelves split down the middle, optics shattered and bottles fell and broke."

The landlord of the pub confirmed that two shelves had broken, but said he did not blame Doc Shiels. "We don't know why they collapsed but we will find out," he added.

The Doc has lived in Ponsanooth for about 20 years. He was born in Salford, near Manchester, and travelled to Ireland and Scotland to visit family and raise monsters — including Nessie. He says that his wife, Chris, and three daughters are all witches and his two sons are, naturally, wizards.

His other careers in life included busker, Punch and Judy man, painter, actor, teacher and fire-eater, although he seems to have settled down to wizardry and producing a magazine at the moment.

His most dangerous profession must have been the fire-eating. "It's a mistake to do it if you have a beard and the wind changes," he cautioned.

"I was doing the big blow-out which means you fill your gob with petrol. The wind changed and my head exploded! Guinness saved me then because my wife poured a pint on me."

Guinness is an integral part of his wizardry — perhaps because he has Irish blood. "I use it in my incantation," he explained. He mentions it in the first edition of a magazine he is publishing — Nnidnid — saying he often draws a magic sign in the creamy froth on the pint when raising monsters.

Nnidnidiing is "bombarding a target with nests and potholes" — apparently a very magical thing.

"I had to go to London to have the magazine printed," he said. "No-one in Cornwall would touch it, they considered it subversive."

He said that magic is not evil. "There is no such thing as black and white magic — that smacks of racism! Magic is quite natural, not supernatural."

He declined to give a demonstration of his powers for fear of damaging the tape recorder belonging to a girl from Radio 4, also carrying out an interview.

● The Packet waits for proof, Mr. Shiels!

DOC SHIELS . . . back in action.

Falmouth Packet, 1st November 1986

The Stag Hunt Inn

the church, and is illustrated by a 1986 photograph of 'Doc', his hair by this time, both shorter and a silvery grey, glowering at the camera over a pint of Guinness. There is also a photograph of the lych gate of Mawnan Old Church which purports to have been taken at 1.00 a.m. on the Hallowe'en night.

The tone of the article veers between amused, censorious and frightened, and the headline is:

> *"Black Magic!"..* [103]

The previous week 'Doc' had already said:

> *"There is no such thing as black and white magic. That smacks of racism! Magic is quite natural and not superstitious."* [104]

He has repeated the same thing to me on a number of occasions, and the headline must have been mildly annoying, unless of course it merely referred to his favourite pint.

> *"Publicity seeking 'Doc' Shiels, the man who performed Black Magic in a Cornish church on Hallowe'en night; sat with a pint of Guinness in a pub this week and said: 'If I have upset the Bishop in any way I'm prepared to buy him a pint'.*
>
> *'Doc' (real name Tony), of Ponsanooth had tried to conjure up evil spirits in Mawnan Old Church at midnight accompanied by a Radio Cornwall reporter with a recorder, a freelance photographer and a handful of spectators.*
>
> *In particular, the Cornish eccentric was seeking to invoke the legendary Owl Man, who has 'claws like an eagle, the body of an owl, and the head of a fat man'.*
>
> *Witnesses say Mr. Shiels wandered through the inside of the church smoking a cigarette and mouthing obscenities and ended up on top of the altar 'threatening God'.*
>
> *First reaction of the Bishop of Truro, the Right Reverend Peter Mumford was one of 'horror', and that action night be taken against Mr. Shiels, adding: "It is probable that special prayers may have to be said in the church."*
>
> *And there were reports that Mr. Shiels might be prosecuted for blasphemy.*
>
> *But this week the Bishop issued a considered statement saying that no action would be taken - especially as the church had not been broken into and no damage had been done. There had been no breach of the law.* [105]
>
> *Relaxing in the Stag Hunt pub, Ponsanooth, 'Doc' Shiels, who claims to be a metal bender and monster-raiser, explained the events of Hallowe'en night. "It was a last minute decision to go into the church, although I had already decided to evoke (sic) the Owl Man. I had been in a couple of pubs in Penryn bending spoons and I was drunk.*
>
> *The wrath of the Bishop of Truro was in the church. There was a certain amount of poltergeist activity which could have come from the Bishop himself. However, if I have offended him in any way I am prepared to buy him a pint.*

59

Black magic

But the Doc offers to buy bishop a pint

"DOC" SHIELS . . . "I meant no insult".

PUBLICITY-seeking "Doc" Shiels, the man who performed Black Magic in a Cornish church on Hallowe'en night, sat with a pint of Guinness in a pub this week and said: "If I have upset the Bishop in any way, I am prepared to buy him a pint."

By Jane Reader

"Doc" (real name Tony), of Ponsanooth, had tried to conjure up evil spirits in Mawnan Smith old church at midnight, accompanied by a Radio Cornwall reporter with a recorder, a freelance photographer and a handful of spectators.

In particular, the Cornish eccentric was seeking to evoke the legendary Owl Man, who has "claws like an eagle, the body of an owl and the head of a fat man."

Witnesses say Mr. Shiels wandered through the inside of the church smoking a cigarette and mouthing obscenities and ended up on top of the altar "threatening God."

First reaction of the Bishop of Truro, the Rt.

Rev. Peter Mumford, was one of "horror" and that action might be taken against Mr. Shiels, adding: "It is probable that special prayers may have to be said in the church."

And there were reports that Mr. Shiels might be prosecuted for blasphemy.

But this week, the Bishop issued a considered statement saying that no action would be taken — especially as the church had not been broken into and no damage had been done. There had been no breach of the law.

Relaxing in the Stag Hunt pub, Ponsanooth, "Doc" Shiels, who claims to be a metal bender and monster-raiser, explained the events of Hallowe'en night. "It was a last minute decision to go into the church, although I had already decided to evoke the Owl Man. I had been in a couple of pubs in Penryn bending spoons and I was drunk.

"The wrath of the Bishop of Truro was in the church. There was a certain amount of poltergeist activity which could have come unconsciously from the Bishop himself.

"However, if I have upset him in any way, I am prepared to buy him a pint.

"I did not do anything in terms of sacrilegious vandalism, and I would wish to reassure people that in no way did I intend to insult their faith. I was deadly serious in what I was doing.

"I felt the presence of the Owl Man and I am sure the others did too, but they thought it was the wrath of God."

"I knew he was there. I have an instinct for that type of thing.

"There was a group of witches there already when we arrived, but they were not very pleased with me. They disapprove very strongly of me getting involved with the media.

"I was shouting challenges to God and telling him to face the Owl Man.

"It was probably a foolish thing to do because of the local community. I do most sincerely apologise if they are upset by my actions.

"But I would not ask for divine forgiveness or anything like that."

Churchwarden Mr. Jeremy Simmons, of The Sanctuary, next door to the church, said that he considered Doc Shiels nothing more than a "publicity seeking nut."

Mr. Simmons, who lives in the house that was once the rectory, said that when he went into the church the following day it look "untouched."

"Absolutely nothing was damaged and none of the candles had been used."

"As for the Owl Man of Mawnan Parish Church, all I can say is that I live closer to the church than anyone else and I've never met him!"

1 a.m. scene — as "Doc" seeks the Owl Man inside.

Falmouth Packet, 8th November 1986

The whole affair may have been exaggerated to a ridiculous extent in the popular press, but - luckily for Tony - at least one newspaper did not take the events of All Hallow's Eve 1986 too seriously!

I did not do anything in terms of sacrilegious vandalism, and I would like to assure people that in no way did I intend to insult their faith. I was deadly serious in what I was doing.

I felt the presence of the Owl Man and I am sure that the others did too, but they thought it was the wrath of God. I knew he was there. I have an instinct for that type of thing.

There was a group of witches there already when we arrived but they were not very pleased with me. They disapprove strongly of m y getting involved with the media.

I was shouting challenges to God and telling him to face the Owl Man. It was probably a foolish thing to do because of the local community. I do most sincerely apologise if they are upset by my actions. But I would not ask for divine forgiveness or anything like that." [106]

The article concludes with a quote from a local churchwarden who had lived next to the old church for many years and who had never heard of the Owl Man, and was certain that no such being existed. [107]

In seven days, in the same newspaper, Tony Shiels had gone from being an amiable eccentric who was always good for a story to being a dangerous magician and blasphemer. It is interesting to compare the various accounts that we have read so far. This is the only mention that we have been able to discover of 'witches' at the church. Certainly Dave Shenton, the only person apart from Tony himself who was there that we have been able to talk to, didn't see any.

It is also the only time on record that Tony has contradicted himself in two interviews. In the 1986 interview he is reported as saying that he challenged God, where as in 1995 and 1996 both he and Dave Shenton denied any such thing had ever happened. It is tempting to speculate whether indeed, whoever had written the 'Packet' story had not embellished the account with a few choice quotes of his own.

At least one national newspaper also picked up on the story, which by this time had picked up a number of new embellishments, [108] and also contained, salacious descriptions of the photographic contents of the first issue of *Nnidnid*, [109] his surrealist magazine which was, coincidentally, of course, available at about the same time:

"The Cornish eccentric at the centre of a 'blasphemy' storm has revealed details of his bizarre lifestyle to the Sunday Independent.

Tony 'Doc' Shiels claims to be a surrealist artist and has just published a magazine containing a full frontal nude photograph of his own daughter.

Attractive Katy (21) is a witch, according to Shiels, and had posed for his camera many times..." [110]

This was only the latest in a series of snide attacks on Tony by the national press [111] who were determined, although, to my knowledge, they never printed accusations outright, to accuse him of incest and child molestation. [112] This, as anyone who has ever met the man will know, is the most unfair accusation that could be levelled against him. One has to remember, however that by 1986, when the events recounted here took place, the 'witch-hunts' against the non-existent spectre of satanic child abuse, that were to destroy so many lives over the next few years were only just beginning. [113]

The 1986 story in the *Sunday Independent* recycled most of the main facets of the story, as it was pre-

"Publicity seeking 'Doc' Shiels, the man who performed Black Magic in a Cornish church on Hallowe'en night; sat with a pint of Guinness in a pub this week and said: 'If I have upset the Bishop in any way I'm prepared to buy him a pint'.

'Doc' (real name Tony), of Ponsanooth had tried to conjure up evil spirits in Mawnan Old Church at midnight accompanied by a Radio Cornwall reporter with a recorder, a freelance photographer and a handful of spectators.

Witnesses say Mr. Shiels wandered through the inside of the church smoking a cigarette and mouthing obscenities and ended up on top of the altar 'threatening God'."

First reaction of the Bishop of Truro, the Right Reverend Peter Mumford was one of 'horror', and that action night be taken against Mr. Shiels, adding: "It is probable that special prayers may have to be said in the church."

And there were reports that Mr. Shiels might be prosecuted for blasphemy."

Above left: *The Chancel*

Below left: *The grave of the vicar of Mawnan at the time of the main Owlman incidents.*

Below right: *Despite the rumours there is no evidence whatsoever to support allegations that 'Doc' left cigar butts floating in the font after his Hallow'een sojourn in Mawnan Old Church.*

The one and only issue of *Nnidnid* now fetches astronomical prices on Ebay. An issue sold on the Internet auction site at the end of 2005 went for nearly £500, and the author has been offered similar sums for his copy!

The magazine is most notorious for the naked pictures of Kate Shiels…….

Black magic is in a glass

THE ODD WORLD OF A WIZARD!

Tony Shiels ... basically a showman

THE Cornish eccentric at the centre of a 'blasphemy' storm has revealed details of his bizarre lifestyle to the Sunday Independent.

Tony 'Doc' Shiels claims to be a surrealist artist, and has just now published a magazine containing a full frontal nude photograph of his own daughter.

Attractive Katy (21) is a witch, according to Shiels, and has posed for his camera many times.

He said: 'I have been a practising wizard since I was three months old.'

Of the nude picture of his daughter in the magazine, titled Nnidnid, he said: 'There's nothing wrong with it. It's not obscene.'

Joking

Tony's connections with the world of magic led to his bizarre attempt to raise a mythical figure, the Cornish Owl Man, last week, and to churchmen claiming he had broken the law.

He was being interviewed as an expert on Hallowe'en on BBC Radio Cornwall when the presenter asked him what he planned for that night.

Tony told him he would be invoking the Owl Man.

Since Hallowe'en, the Bishop of Truro, the Right Rev Peter Mumford, has been told of Tony's visit to the church.

At first the Bishop said Tony may have broken the law, but later he relented, and Tony said: 'I'm sorry and I'll buy you a pint.'

But Tony hasn't given up his anti - Christian point of view.

He pointed to his parish church and said: 'I find that stone tower, that huge building, just as offensive as anybody might find my behaviour.'

He claimed he was on the side of good, but would not define his magic as black or white.

'The only black magic I know about is this,' he said, pointing to a pint of draught Guinness.

He lives on the dole, but claims to be a

by Richard Baynes

genuine surrealist.

The home he shares with his wife Christine is a terraced cottage at Ponsanooth.

He speaks with an Irish brogue, and says he is half Irish and half Scottish.

Telepath

And in the past, he says, he has done everything from being an artist to digging roads.

He has also worked as a stage telepath, and admits to being, basically, a showman.

'When this Hallowe'en thing came up I rang a couple of witches to see what they were up to,' he said.

'They told me to get lost. The real occultists probably hate me more than devout Christians.'

The Sunday Independent, 9th November 1986

Weekend Break

By Mike Truscott

In Doc's defence . . .

SEEN any good piskies, UFOs, sea monsters or giant birdmen lately?

Oh come now, don't mock it; we have a reputation for such things down here, after all.

The latest outrageous deeds attributed to "Doc" Shiels — Ponsanooth's "publicity-seeking nut", as he was described last week — only serve to underline this.

When he was shouting and screaming in Mawnan Old Church on Hallowe'en night, he was allegedly trying to evoke the legendary "Owl Man" of that vicinity.

Which prompted me to reach for a fascinating little book I have from a decade ago, published when the hunt for the great Falmouth sea monster Morgawr was at its peak.

This book — "Morgawr, The Monster of Falmouth Bay," by A. Mawnan-Peller — records that during Easter, 1976, the two daughters of a holidaymaker from Lancashire saw "a huge great thing with feathers, like a big man with flapping wings, hovering over the church tower at Mawnan."

The girls were so frightened that the family holiday was cut short by three days.

In the spring of that year, the book adds, a group of "real live Cornish piskies" was photographed by one of the witches who swam nude in the Helford River to try and raise Morgawr.

And flying saucers: "In October, 1975, a group of three UFOs was seen in the sky above Falmouth Docks. Then, in March, 1976, a pair of flying saucers appeared over Perranwell.

"Flying saucers have, of course, been seen by many hundreds of people over the years and Cornwall has had its fair share.

" 'Little people' have been seen, from time to time, coming out of flying saucers. Maybe that is how the piskies first arrived in the area!"

As for this "publicity seeking nut" Doc Shiels, the poor fellow has come in for considerable scorn and scepticism these past two or three weeks.

Queues of radio and newspaper reporters have, for instance, been vainly waiting for him to come up with "proof" of his powers, including his Uri Geller-type cutlery-bending capacity.

So, ever fair-minded, I am pleased to be able to defend him on this count at least.

The Doc, you see, was one of the entertainers I invited to my first and last house-warming party when I moved into my previous abode 10 years ago.

The party was, er, notable in a number of ways.

Not only did one of his witches do a STREAK through the house and out into Budock Terrace, but the Doc — before a dozen witnesses in our kitchen — duly proceeded to bend all our forks and spoons with his mind.

I subsequently did my best to bend them back into shape — but if anyone's interested, I've still got a pile of kinky cutlery!

Falmouth Packet, 15th November 1986

Two contrasting views on the Hallow'een debacle. The Sunday Independent (opposite page) pursued the line that Tony was a strange and somewhat dangerous man, whilst the ever-faithful Falmouth Packet presented a far more reasonable view of him.

sented in the *Falmouth Packet*. but added three very telling quotes from the man himself. The first quote revealed the depth of his particular Celtic spiritual beliefs:

> *He pointed to his parish church and said: 'I find that stone tower, that huge building, as offensive as anyone might find my behaviour!"* [114]

Tony is quite sincere in his beliefs. They are ones that I don't necessarily share, but I respect his right to hold them, and they don't affect my friendship with him. There is, however an undercurrent of irony in this particular quote. During the research for this book Alison and I have spent a considerable time in Cornwall and have spoken to many people about Tony, the Owlman, Morgawr, Celtic shamanism, witchcraft and other related subjects, but the conversation invariably returns to its starting point - Tony Shiels.

I don't think that I have ever met anyone who actually dislikes him. I have heard him referred to, at worst, as 'a loveable rogue', and although there have been individuals who are mildly annoyed about one or more specific incidents, the annoyance is usually only temporary, and very much tempered with a background feeling, that without him, life might not either be so interesting or entertaining.

In our files we have press cuttings, which relate to Tony, dating back at least a quarter of a century, and they all refer to someone who, in his own singular way, enriches the community. There is a photograph of him, smoking a pipe, talking about his club for pipe smokers which met weekly in a pub in Falmouth. [115] There are articles on his activities as a Punch and Judy showman, [116] and there are his regular columns for both *Peninsular West*, [117] and *Cornish Life*, [118] in which Tony held forth with his views on life, and demonstrates simple conjuring tricks. [119]

I have not found anyone, outside, ironically what I call the fundamentalist wing of the cryptozoological community, [120] who is offended by Tony, his beliefs or behaviour. Perhaps, then, we should examine his statement that he finds the tower of the parish church as offensive as anyone finds him, in a new light!

The second important statement in this particular newspaper article concerned his magic:

> *He claimed he was on the side of good; but would not define his magic as black or white.*

> *"The only black magic I know about is this," he said pointing to a pint of draught Guinness.* [121]

The media conception that there are only two types of magic - black and white, good and evil, is both simplistic and dangerous. It represents the school of occultism that has learned everything it knows from watching a few tacky Hollywood horror films, mixed with a few childhood reminiscences of Disney's animated version of 'Sleeping Beauty'. [122] Tony is not, to my knowledge at least, either a necromancer or a nigromancer. [123] To my knowledge as well, no-one has ever claimed that of him. By pointing at his pint and talking glibly of his lack of knowledge about 'black magic' Tony is talking the literal truth. He had no knowledge of 'Black Magic', because, at least in the form envisaged by the reporter who was interviewing him, it doesn't exist. Tony does not dig up graves at midnight, or crucify toads. [124] He does, however, wear a tall hat, [125] on certain occasions at least, and it would be unwise to cross him. Some people have found that out to their cost.

The final statement in this, rather important piece is rather more enigmatic, and is also, like most of

*What happened
to the 'Owl Man'
On Hallowe'en night?
Well, I think he ran
Off somewhere
Scared to death.
Y'see, he hates Guinness...
On a "Wizard's breath,*

Cheers Doc. [130]

VIN'S VIEW

"I think he ran off somewhere . . ."

Above: *Falmouth Packet, 15th November 1986, As if to prove that Tony was once again forgiven by the good people of Falmouth, at least the portion of them that write for 'The Packet', the same issue contained a brief poem, presumably from the man himself:*

what Tony says, probably the truth. Also, however, one has to remember that Tony is a surrealist, and that although what he says is the literal truth, the interpretation of what he says is totally up to the listener, or reader. This third statement reads: [126]

> *"When this Hallowe'en thing came up, I rang a couple of witches to see what they were up to (...) They told me to get lost. The real occultists probably hate me more than devout Christians.*

This is probably true, but as I have said, to date, I haven't found anyone who actually HATES the Wizard of the Western World.

Even the Bishop of Truro was prepared to overlook the events of Hallowe'en 1986; something he would certainly not have done if he had suspected that 'real' blasphemy had taken place that night, and it seems almost certain that he, too, thought of Tony as a loveable rogue.

It is only the newspaper reporters, with their hearts set on the next shocking and self-congratulatory headline, who had anything to gain by suggesting that Tony was a 'real' black magician, and it is probable that even they didn't believe it!

The BBC seemed like the only people who could actually help me ascertain the definitive truth of what happened at Mawnan Old Church on Hallowe'en night 1986. The radio crew had long left, however, and whatever recordings they had made were lost or erased. [126] BBC were helpful in a bureaucratic, and disinterested way, but could, unfortunately, neither prove, nor disprove my assertions.

The backlash against the pseudo-outrage of the moral majority started the following week. Mike Truscott wrote an editorial in the *Falmouth Packet* entitled:

'In Doc's Defence' [(127)]

which read:

> Seen any good UFOs, piskies, sea-monsters or giant birdmen lately? Oh come on, don't mock it; we have a reputation for such things around here.
>
> The latest outrageous deeds attributed to 'Doc' Shiels - Ponsanooth's 'publicity seeking nut', as he was described last week, only serve to underline this. When he was shouting and screaming in Mawnan Old Church on Hallowe'en night, he was allegedly trying to invoke the legendary 'Owl Man' of the vicinity"...

Truscott, who was, and is, and old friend of Tony's, then outlined the history of 'His Owliness', as expounded, in rather more depth in this chapter, quoting large chunks of the Mawnan-Peller booklet, [(128)] before returning to the subject of wizards in general, and Tony Shiels in particular:

> "As for this 'publicity seeking nut', Doc Shiels, the poor fellow, has come in for considerable scorn and scepticism this past two or three weeks.
>
> Queues of radio and newspaper reporters have, for instance, been vainly waiting for him to come up with 'proof 'of his powers, including his Uri Geller-type cutlery bending capacity.
>
> So, ever fair-minded, I am pleased to be able to defend him, on this count at least.
>
> The Doc, you see, was one of the entertainers I invited to my first and last housewarming party when I moved into my previous abode 10 years ago. The party was, er, notable in a number of ways.
>
> Not only did one of his witches do a STREAK through the house, and out into Budock Terrace, but the Doc - before a dozen witnesses in our kitchen - duly proceeded to bend all our forks and spoons with his mind. I subsequently did my best to bend them back into shape - but; if anyone is interested, I've still got a pile of kinky cutlery." [(129)]

By the late 1980's Tony was quite well known outside Cornwall. The Owlman was featured in *'Alien Animals'* [(131)] by Janet and Colin Bord (1980) and in *'Mystery Animals of Britain and Ireland'* by Graham McEwan (1986). [(132)] It was the latter book, and in particular his coverage of the Morgawr incidents of 1976, which first introduced me to the work of Tony 'Doc' Shiels.

It was also ironic that the first issue of *Fortean Times* I read (having got the address from the aforementioned book by Graham McEwan), [(133)] was the issue covering the events of Hallowe'en 1986. [(134)] I have faithfully bought each issue since, and even write for them occasionally!

Nine years later, and I was sitting in the corner of a pub in Falmouth talking to the man. In nine years he had gone from being a weird fellow I read about in a book to being a personal friend. I liked him a lot; I was a great admirer of his paintings; but did I believe him when he told me details of a giant flying Cornish birdman, the evidence for which was mostly attributable to him?

Within the previous few years, Mark Chorvinsky, the well known American fortean writer had dedicated a great portion of an issue of *Strange Magazine*, [(135)] an excellent fortean publication, to 'debunking' Doc's work with both Morgawr and other lake monsters - and by implication his Loch

Lexilinks: 'Doc' points to the word 'Nesse' on the Lych-Gate outside Mawnan Old Church

As it appears today - The Lych-Gate, in which is a granite coffin rest, was built in 1881. The Cornish inscription on the northern face has been translated: "It is good for me to draw nigh unto God"

Ness photographs and the entire canon of evidence in favour of Owlman.

Tony didn't know of any post-1986 sightings, and neither did Mark Chorvinsky, but surprisingly enough, I did.

Luckily for my investigations, and unluckily for the lobby who believed that the whole Owlman affair was nothing more than an elaborate practical joke on the part of an eccentric Celtic performance artist, I had recently uncovered a previously unknown Owlman sighting from 1989, and one which was completely unconnected with Tony, any of his family or his friends. Secure in this knowledge, and with the utter certainty that things were going to get even weirder and more interesting, I finished my drink and, arm in arm, the three of us walked out of the pub and into the rainy Cornish night.

AUTHOR'S NOTE: At the 1998 *Fortean Times* Unconvention, I met Mark Chorvinsky for the first time. I had always been an admirer of his work with *Strange Magazine*, and had looked forward to meeting him. I gave him a copy of my book, and all hell broke loose.

We parted on good terms, and I went off to my hotel room with my then girlfriend for some illicit lechery and to plunder the mini bar. The next morning Mark Chorvinsky was livid. He hated the book and took grave exception to everything I had written about him. He seemed to think that somehow I was casting doubts on his ability and professional reputation as an investigator. "Of course I'm not, dear boy" I said in the calming Old School voice which usually manages to soothe our transatlantic cousins when their feathers have been ruffled. "I'm merely reaching a different conclusion to you" but it was no good.

On his return to the United States he sent vitriolic e-mails to various correspondents, including, I believe, some Internet discussion groups, and from what I can gather told everyone that he could that he regarded me (and presumably still regards me), as some sort of fortean antichrist for daring to claim that he might have been mistaken.

I couldn't be bothered to join in the mudslinging because not only was he not the first person to attack me in print that year, and he certainly wouldn't be the last, but I really didn't care. After all, despite the highly dubious provenance of the Mary F. photographs there was still a reasonably good body of evidence to support the hypothesis that there was indeed some strange creature at large in the waters of Falmouth Bay.

CHAPTER THREE: INTERROGATION

"I had been thinking of it right enough, I often do, I always have the idea of it huddled like a sick ape in the corner of my mind"….

Russell Hoban *'Turtle Diary'* (1975)

After many years of interest in the subject I became a professional Fortean Zoologist, practically by accident, in early 1994.

I had been a member of an organisation called S.C.A.N (The Society for Cryptozoology and the Anomalies of Nature) and, during the eighteen months or so it existed, I became close friends with Mrs. Jan Williams, one of the founders.

When the society folded, just before Christmas in 1993, Jan and I decided that, with her expertise and contacts in the world of Cryptozoology and my knowledge of publishing small press magazines (my wife and I had been running a mildly successful publishing company for some years), we should pool our resources and start a magazine aimed specifically at the Fortean Zoology market.

When we started, it was done on the proverbial shoestring and we were very small fry indeed. However, over the next couple of years the project succeeded far beyond my wildest dreams.

We were not even the only magazine in the UK market which dealt primarily with the subject of mystery animals. There was another magazine, and in the spirit of good-natured rivalry I soon got friendly with its editor.

I am not mentioning either the magazine or its editor by name, purely because, as will become evident in this chapter, I made a solemn promise to respect the utter confidentiality of the main character in this chapter. In order to do so, I have to 'muddy' the trail slightly, because, as I know to my cost, Forteans are great detectives and have a truffle-hound-like tenacity in 'ferreting out' information. In the interests of a readable narrative I shall give him the pseudonym of 'Steve Mabbett', after my old pal Andy Mabbett who for so many years edited the excellent Pink Floyd Magazine, *'The Amazing Pudding'*.

In the early summer of 1994 Alison and I visited Steve Mabbett and his wife at their home in the Mid-

lands, and he gave us many valuable contacts and much useful information. Over the next six months we corresponded in a cheerful but desultory fashion, and it was with some sadness that I discovered, soon after Christmas that he had decided to cease publication.

In April 1995 we again drove up to his house. Again we ate a delicious vegetarian meal, and drank his bountiful supplies of cold beer while listening to his *Doors* CDs.

As Jim Morrison exhorted us all to 'light his fire', I wrote out a cheque for a reasonable sum of money and so became the new owner of his magazine, his archives, what remained of his library (much had already been sold), and four or five large cardboard boxes full of letters.

The next day, nursing a mild hangover, I sat in the back of our Transit Van and, as Alison drove us back down the M5 towards Exeter, I started to sort through the pile of papers.

In amongst the letters were a number from an earnest young student called 'Gavin'. (Again, for reasons that will become apparent this is not his real name). 'Gavin' apparently lived on the south coast and had a deep and enduring fascination with all things cryptozoological. His letters were long drawn out affairs, full of technical detail, and I soon became immersed in reading them. When I read one in particular, however, I let out a yelp of surprise, and nearly caused Alison to drive straight into the back of the vehicle in front!

> *"What the hell did you do that for?"*

she asked angrily..

> *"Listen to this."*

I said, and started to read...

> *Since I last wrote, I've managed to dig out some of the stuff I wrote on Owlman a couple of years back. I've just found my write-up of the sighting I told you about last time (now officially anonymous of course). If you like I can copy it out for you - it'd take too long now. One thing I forgot to say about Owlman last time is that (this is a bit spooky...) practically all (all, actually, as far as I can remember) of the letters I've written mentioning Owlman in the past have vanished! Once, I wrote to say that I was surprised that a letter mentioning Ollie HAD reached its destination; this letter, however, was the one that disappeared! Bleeding typical. So, DON'T be surprised if you don't receive this letter: mysterious forces are obviously afoot (though really I suspect an incompetent postal service and a great deal of coincidence).* [1]

Tantalisingly, the previous letter to which he referred was missing, and although there was another letter from him in the files that corroborated the above paragraph mentioning an ex- girlfriend of his who had seen the creature when she was about twelve years old [2] this, too has vanished into the labyrinthine depths of my filing system, and when I came to write this chapter, it, together with several other documents on the case, were missing. [3]

The episode intrigued me and I resolved to do something about it as soon as I had time.

About a month later I was sitting on the sofa in my sitting room, with my dog Toby and John Jacques, a one-time friend of mine who at the time was my manager and agent. [4] As John smoked incessantly,

and I sipped some red wine, we discussed our latest project.

A few days earlier I had been commissioned to research and present six five minute slots about mystery animals for a West-country TV series called *Mysterious West*. [5] We discussed various options and the subject of 'Doc' Shiels and the Owlman of Mawnan came up. Five minutes later, after a call to 'Directory Enquiries' John was on the 'phone to 'Gavin's' mother. She gave us a telephone number where he could be contacted in the evenings, and eventually, after long and complicated explanations to his girlfriend's mother, (whom it turned out, owned the house where we eventually tracked him down), John spoke to 'Gavin'.

After talking to him for a few minutes John's wrinkled and weatherbeaten face started to beam with pure glee, but after another few minutes he started to look puzzled. He excused himself, pushed the 'mute' button, and passed the receiver to me.

For some reason, no-one seems to trust the efficacy of British Telecom technology, and despite the fact that the 'phone was 'muted', he whispered to me:

> *"Here, you talk to him".*

> *"What's he like?"*

I whispered back, with an equal lack of faith in the technical achievements of the telephone company.

> *"It's bloody weird. He seems genuine enough, but I'm damn sure he's hiding something"....*

I released the 'mute' button, and for the first time I talked to 'Gavin'. We chatted cheerfully about cryptozoology, mostly dinosaurs, for several minutes before, with reasonable skill, I brought the subject around to weirdness in Mawnan woods.

Yes, he confirmed, an ex-girlfriend of his had claimed to have seen the 'creature' in the summer of 1988 or 1989, but he was no longer in touch with her and he was sure that she would be adamant in her refusal to have anything to do with a television programme on the subject Somewhere, he claimed, he had a statement that she had given him - and he would try and find it. He muttered something about a photograph, said that he would write and rang off.

I turned around to John and said:

> *"You're right! He's hiding something. The weird thing is that he doesn't seem at all interested in publicising the Owlman stuff. Whereas the Owlman sighting could be dynamite, the rest of it is interesting if you are a zoologist, but that's about all..."*

John, who never believed in Forteana at all - except as a way of making money, shrugged his shoulders and changed the subject. Five minutes later we were talking to a woman who claimed a 1988 sighting of The Devil's Hunting Pack of Black Dogs on Dartmoor, and was quite willing to share her experience with the millions 'out there in TV land', if the price was right. The subject of Owlman was forgotten, for the time being at least.

The next day, I wrote to 'Gavin', confirming the details of our conversation and assuring him that whatever he told me would be treated with complete confidence:

73

I very much look forward ( ) to your Owlman report. If we do use it for the TV series, or indeed for anything else, we shall respect your confidentiality and that of the young lady concerned. Would you be happy with 'GAVIN' or would you prefer to be something like 'FRED SMITH'? It is completely up to you. You would however have to give us written permission to use your material under a pseudonym but John Jacques the researcher you spoke to last night, can sort that out with no problem. [6]

Three days later, a letter with a south-coast postmark landed on my door-mat. The first paragraph concerned the subscription rates to my magazine *Animals & Men'*, and the second paragraph was about mutated frogs. Except for a couple of lines which I have changed in order to protect his anonymity, I quote the rest of the letter verbatim:

Where, where do I start? This affair is very complicated and I have messed things up by letting my own emotions interfere with what I have told people. My fiancée, with whom I have shared all info, pertaining to this situation finally persuaded me to 'come clean' and tell the whole story, no messing, (don't worry, it's not after all, a hoax).

Well then, as will become evident, I have to say - I HAVE LIED. To both 'Steve Mabbett' and yourself. Why, I'm not exactly sure, but I can think of reasons. You asked if I had seen the creature. Thrown off guard, confused and suddenly alarmed, I had to reply 'No'. Well that was the lie - I DID SEE IT, as did my girlfriend at the time, Sally. ('S' from now on). Referring the whole experience onto her shoulders was a route I took some time ago, and I hope that you will understand why.

Mawnan Owlman is a ridiculous thing that only a bizarre attention-seeker will even pretend to have seen. I am ANGRY that I have seen this creature. The whole thing is so stupid. But because I have seen this - AND I KNOW WHAT I SAW I am prepared to discuss the event intelligently. For the above reasons (the obvious old 'laughing stock' excuse of those who have witnessed paranormal things), I am anxious not to be identified, and the idea that what I say might be on TV scares the living shit out of me! I will return to this issue later, but here are the details of, and the story behind, the sighting!

I have it written down in an old diary and thus don't need to recall the sighting.

I never recorded S's version of events - do bear in mind that we were standing next to one another at the time of the sighting - but my intention was to relay the details as if it were her account. Maybe that way things didn't seem so personal. Though the sighting, particularly the details of the creature, are recorded quite well, things are not so for the exact location, time etc. So that is from memory.

Well, the event occurred late in the 1980s, probably in '88 or '89. It was on a ?camping (sic) to Mawnan, or thereabouts. I cannot remember the site or anything else helpful. I believe the area was near the sea, but can't be sure. 'S' and I went for walks early in the evening, returning not long after it was completely dark. This was probably in June or July, so that would be fairly late. I remember small lanes and paths, a large church and lots of big trees. We had a torch and I was shining its beam across trunks about fifteen feet off the ground. I am fairly sure that the animal was standing in a large conifer tree and the illustration we made after the sighting (but not till we got home actually) does depict the animal in a conifer tree, but I'm not that sure now. Here is the actual sighting as written down in my diary

"Every couple of hours we would walk along the fringe of the wood. This was the third time that evening and it was beginning to get dark. From a distance trees looked black but closer up the branches and trunks could be seen. We saw the animal at about 9.30 p.m. It was standing on a thick branch with its wings sort of held up at the arms. I'd say that it was about five feet tall (but please read on). The legs had high ankles and the feet were large and black with two huge 'toes' on the visible side.

The creature was grey with brown and the eyes definitely glowed. On seeing us its head jerked down and forwards, its wings lifted and it just jumped backwards. As it did its legs folded up. We ran away.

As you can see from the big illustration we had a pretty good idea what it looked like. We didn't know what to do about it, and essentially vowed never to tell anyone. I last saw 'S' about two years ago and talked about it then. She was as unkeen to share the information then as she was earlier, and I promised I wouldn't tell anyone about her involvement but I could 'do what I liked' with my interpretation. I respect this and have never disclosed any information about her.

Seeing this creature has really changed my life. It not only formed a springboard for a personal interest in paranormal creatures, it also opened a different way of looking at the world. 'S' seemed to have forgotten the whole thing, and it certainly didn't make things any different for her. By now I've read all the available literature on this, or similar creatures. Shortly after the event - I emphasise AFTER - I was fortunate enough to chance upon Bord and Bord's 'Alien Animals'. Here was, of course, it all again. I remember reading their chapter 'Giant Birds and Birdmen' at least six times successively. The thing that struck me. and still does, were that all the witnesses were, (as far as I know) teenage girls. At the time of the sighting, 'S' (and I) were between 12 and 13 years of age.

What is Owlman? I think that it's like a ghost; and no way is it a real animal. More to do with the human mind than the world of zoology. Several years ago I began having 'nasty' dreams featuring similar creatures - they were always malevolent but not generally harmful. There's dreams for you. I particularly remember one when I had to hunt and kill a man with a bow and arrow and I was being watched by a BLACK AND WHITE owlman standing at the base of a birch tree. I tried drawing owlman again after this, and, as I was obviously better at drawing animals than previously, was much happier with the result. I enclose a photocopy of this latter interpretation which has caused me to change some of my ideas about the original sighting. Firstly I don't think that it was as big as I (and 'S') originally described: closer to 4 feet than 5. As can be seen from the newer drawing, I found satisfaction in different configurations of the legs and thorax. 'S' and I had agreed early on that the creature had 'bird legs', but we never could agree on the feet. I am sure that they were like black pincers, or what your hands look like if you keep digits two and three pressed together and separate from four and five (which are also pressed together).

'S' though, said that she didn't see separate 'digits' and the feet were like clogs or bulky shoes of some kind. I remember reading in another Bord and Bord book; probably 'Ancient Mysteries of Britain', [7] *that Owlman was probably just an owl after all. Even at the time of the sighting I was extremely familiar with owls, (and other birds) and had even seen several in the wild. This creature was DEFINITELY a great deal bigger than any owl (even the biggest owls in the world - the Eurasian eagle Owls - do not approach four feet in height),* [8]

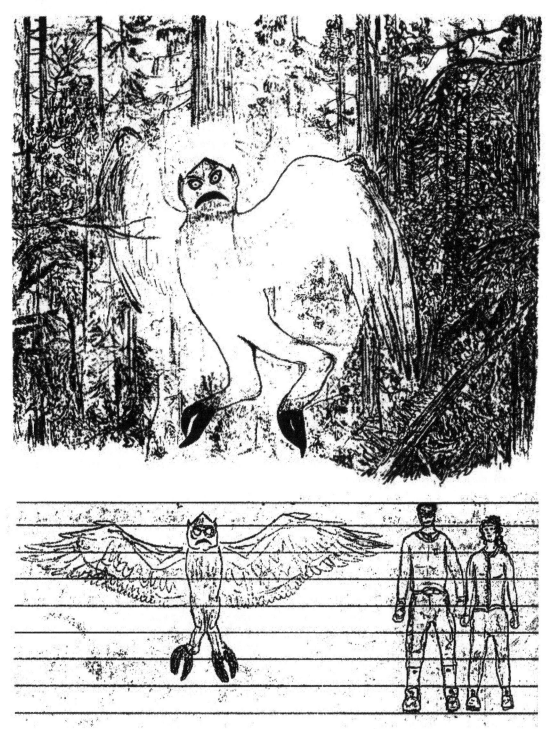

Above: *The Owlman of Mawnan drawn by 'Gavin' several years later*
Below: *Sketch showing height comparisons from 'Gavin's' Diary*

and, as we were sure we knew what the head looked like, it didn't really resemble an owl except superficially.

I do not mind this information being used in any way, just as long as it is not explicitly linked to myself. I hope to eventually become involved in some branch of science, and having a name tarnished by an event such as this really would not be a helpful thing. My family would also be against me, as I have already had enough trouble from my involvement with things cryptozoological/paranormal. Therefore, as I am sure you understand, I would like anonymity and complete confidentiality as regards the personal aspects of this letter. A pseudonym, quite unlike my real name, would therefore be most appropriate. I thank you for your understanding and cooperation, and hereby give you full permission to use the relevant material, obviously with the above conditions. [9]

('Sally' is also a pseudonym, chosen by me at random. The initials of the two 'surrogate' names - G.S did not become significant until later).

On the evening of the day that I received this letter I telephoned 'Gavin'. He was very emotional and I spent most of the duration of our conversation trying to calm him down. Again, we spent most of the time talking about non-contentious topics, again, I mentioned the alleged photograph, again he 'clammed' up, and again he promised to write.

A few days later another letter arrived on my door-mat, and again all the relevant portions have been quoted in full, except where they would provide clues towards 'Gavin's' real identity:

Dear Jon,

Thanks for phoning again, I only wish we could have spoken for longer. It's been more than four hours since I spoke to you and finally I've stopped shaking (that's what the Owlman stuff does to me, not your conversation). I'll start with what I said I'd tell you about the 'other' Owlman stuff but; and I'm not absolutely sure why, I dislike the information here even more, hence my reluctance to share it.

The fact is, we did go back there to see if we could see it again, and we went back with a camera. This time, obviously, we really wanted to see it, and I think that this is why we thought that we did. I am really quite nervous thinking about looking around that place, were I in the same position now as I was then - having only just seen that thing there - I certainly wouldn't do it now!

However, there we were, in pretty much the same place. The thing that I remember is that 'S' said that she could see it and she was looking right at it. I froze and I can remember being really frightened at this point. In fact, imagining this, it seems to be a familiar feeling - looking into the darkness and not really seeing anything, but your mind making shapes out of the shapeless things that are there. 'S' took a photo and I can remember it quite vividly. Of course, it didn't show anything other than trees lit by a camera flash but (this is where the story gets really shameful), we decided to say that it WAS actually a photo of the animal, but as the photo was taken the thing had jumped away/flown upwards, hence its non-appearance in the photo. I don't know if you'd call it a fake photo in that case, but we wanted so much for the thing to be there and for us to capture it on film, if that photo had ever gotten out as it were, then we'd have said that it really showed the Owlman, and that

78

the Owlman was definitely there at the time that the photo was taken. If that had been the case, then we'd have been guilty of some kind of forgery.

This incident, which, I'd like to emphasise is very different from what I know was a genuine sighting previously, I would rather have forgotten about. I don't think it affects the sighting I have previously allayed to you, however, and please don't let it colour your perception. But this isn't all, and the rest of my story is more kind of psychological. You cannot possibly imagine what effect an event such as this can have on your life. Even now, it upsets me very much to recall the details. Well, following our return from Southampton (prepare yourself for a big shock) both 'S' and I kept seeing the Owlman. I saw it in the woods behind my house and 'S' in woods she passed on the way home from school. But though I say 'kept seeing', that might be too graphic a description. A better one, I think; would be 'thought we kept seeing'. I certainly cannot remember my back-garden Owlman as clearly as I can the real one there at Mawnan and now think I must have imagined it because there I was imagining these creatures hiding in trees....

So what about the photo? I was sure that I had the one that 'S' took at the site, of the trees near the church. But what I might have been thinking of is one I have of trees at night behind my garden, which I took at, or shortly after, a time I thought I saw Owlman there (or should I say 'an owlman'), I will gladly show it to you if you want, but now I don't think it shows anything other than that my imagination was running overtime at that point.

I'm really sorry if this has just got too silly for you, or if I've destroyed any believable aspects to this whole tale. I promise you that our original sighting was - no doubt at all - absolutely genuine and anything subsequent such as that I've discussed in this letter, were psychological knock-on effects. You probably think I'm completely mad now...". [10]

There then followed four pages of meticulously observed and recorded natural history, which had absolutely nothing whatsoever to do with giant feathered zooform phenomena, and which suggested that whatever else 'Gavin' is, he is perfectly sane!

Over the next few months I spoke to 'Gavin' a couple of times and we exchanged letters, carefully avoiding the subject of Owlman. During the summer Alison and I met 'Doc' again, and, as recounted in the previous chapter, our investigations into 'His Owliness' began in earnest.

I started to realise that the best card that I held in my hand was 'Gavin', who was, after all, the only person we knew who was an actual first-hand eyewitness. Even Tony had never seen the 'creature' for himself!

In June I filmed my contributions for *Mysterious West*, which included a brief piece on 'Gavin's' experience. [11] I decided, however, that the whole affair was too important to squander on a local TV show, [12] and so I began to make plans as to how I could use the material I had been given to its best advantage.

In early July I wrote to 'Gavin':

I quite understand what you said about Owlman in your second letter.

I look forward to hearing from you. As far as I am concerned the post traumatic shock of

such an experience, especially on what was at the time your adolescent brain, must have been quite severe; and I am not surprised that you imagined seeing the creature again and again.

I would, however suggest that although the whole pattern of your subsequent 'sightings' are important as they show the level of shock that you sustained during the episode, it is only the initial sighting which is a genuine encounter with a zooform phenomenon.

I have written up the episode (with you as 'Gavin') for A&M6, [13] and I recounted your story for Westcountry TV (again without naming you). I will video the show when it is broadcast and I will send you a copy. Why don't you come down for a couple of days over the summer, and you can go through my archives? The house is a bit of a tip but we will make you welcome. Sometime I would like to take you down to Mawnan Smith to see if we can identify the place that you saw the owl thing". [15]

A few weeks later I printed excerpts from 'Gavin's' first letter in issue six of my journal *Animals & Men*, together with a short piece by Tony Shiels, called *'The Case for Owlperson'.* [16] (This wonderful piece of surrealchemical scat rap can be found at Appendix One).

My introduction to the piece read:

THE DOCTOR AND THE OWLMAN

(The references in this piece are not printed in 'superscript' to differentiate them from the references to the main text of this chapter).

The Owlman of Mawnan is possibly the strangest zooform manifestation to have been reported in the British Isles. The sightings of an entity described variously as a feathered 'birdman' and a giant owl took place between 1976 and 1978, and have confounded Fortean researchers ever since. In conversation with Graham McEwan the legendary Fortean Tony 'Doc' Shiels, admitted to being baffled by the whole episode, and even wondered whether the sightings had been all a hoax.(1)

'Doc' Shiels is, himself one of the biggest imponderables in the entire matter. Unfortunately, despite his exalted position as 'Surrealchemist in Residence' to 'Animals & Men', his self admitted claims to being a cheat, a thimble-rigger, a charlatan and a mountebank (2), cast sour doubts on his veracity as a provider of source material.

Mark Chorvinsky, the Editor of the excellent 'Strange' magazine, devoted much of issue eight to part one of an in depth investigation of "Doc's" contribution to the canon of cryptozoological evidence. The articles cast great doubt upon the veracity of the 'Mary F' photographs of the Falmouth Bay Sea Serpent. The inference was that the rest of the series would ask similar questions about the validity of "Doc's" Loch Ness and Irish Lake Monster photographs, but for various reasons the rest of the series was not published.

"Doc" wrote to me in October 1994: (3)

"It most be almost a year since Mark Chorvinsky last slagged me in print. Poor Mark, he gets it wrong, but he means well..."

I think that when Mark Chorvinsky, who I have never met, described "Doc" as a:

'magical wolf amongst fortean sheep' (4)

he was not far from the truth. After all, on a record we have just made, "Doc" admits:

'I don't believe in the Loch Ness Monster even though I've seen the shagger and photographed it...' (5)

In his October letter (6) "Doc" told me to always remember that his attitudes (in connection with almost anything) are strictly surrealchemical, and I sincerely believe that it is this bizarre mixture of art and science, of performance and invocation which provides the key to "Doc" and his work as a whole. "Doc" admits that his evidence is prejudiced, but as he says it is no more prejudiced than any other monster hunter's (7). A great deal of 'Monstrous' concerns "Doc's" relationship with a young Scottish Witch called Psyche. In an earlier book (8), "Doc" suggested how easy it would be to 'invent' a witch called 'Psyche', and to launch her as a media star within the worlds of forteana and stage magic:

"I think that I mentioned that Psyche was a Scots lassie so she would have a certain rapport with Nessie of Loch Ness. There would be great publicity value in Psyche offering to visit the Loch and trying to 'call up' the monster from the deep. She could claim to have done it successfully on a previous occasion...when no spectators were around ... and even to have a photograph as 'proof' of this. A Photograph? Gosh!!!"

Sounds familiar?

Mark Chorvinsky and others (8) suggest that the 'Mary F' photographs, and the 'Patrick Kelly' photograph of the 'Lough Leane Monster' may have been faked by Shiels using a plasticene model affixed to a plane of glass. They may well have been, but equally they may well have not. Luckily, for believers in the Falmouth Bay beastie; there are witnesses if not photographs which cannot, as far as I am aware, be traced back to Shiels. It has been suggested however, that every single 'Owlman' report could be directly linked in some form or other with the man that has been described as 'The Wizard of the Western World'.(9)

That is, until now! We have recently obtained what is, as far as I am aware, the only post-1978 sighting ever to have been published, and also the first sighting by a male witness. Most importantly, however it is the first sighting which cannot be traced back to "Doc" Shiels. This provides unexpected and very valuable corroboration to the Shiels' collected Owlman stories, to Shiels himself and by inference, to his work with other zooform phenomena such as Morgawr and the Scottish and Irish Lake Monsters. In the ongoing battle between the rationalists and the surrealists I strongly suspect that it is the surrealists who will have the last laugh!

I have interviewed the witness and I feel certain that he is genuine. In his witness testimony (…) I have not identified him. I guaranteed him anonymity

because this was the only way in which he would allow us to use his testimony.

We also have two unpublished drawings of the Owlman phenomenon and, coincidentally, my postbag recently contained an article by the good doctor about Owlman which we commissioned from him a year or so ago, and which was accompanied by a photograph, and a note asking us whether a serious magazine dealing with Cryptozoology printed pictures of naked witches. We don't, as a rule, but in this case.. .why not? we thought.

The round up of Owl Man ephemera is completed with a few words from our resident zoologist providing a possible zoological solution for this, perhaps the most bizarre of British Zoomysteries.

REFERENCES:

(1)   McEWAN G. 'Mystery Animals of Britain and Ireland',
      (Robert Hale, London 1986).

(2)   CHORVINSKY M. Ed. 'Of Dragons and Dreams',
      (Strange Magazine No. 8 pp 16).

(3)   SHIELS Tony 'Doc'. personal correspondence with Editor 7.10.94

(4)   CHORVINSKY M. Ed Op. Cit. pp.5

(5)   AMPHIBIANS FROM OUTER SPACE LP TRACK:
      'Invocation of my daemon brother' (1995)

(6)   SHIELS Tony 'Doc', 'Monstrum; a wizard's tale'.
      (FORTEAN TOMES; London 1990). pp.103.

(7)   O'SIAGHAIL N. 'THE SHIELS EFFECT'; A manual for
      the psychic superstar' (LYNN/RAVEN; New Jersey 1976).

(8)   CHORVINSKY M. Ed. Op. Cit pp 10.

(9)   SHIELS Tony 'Doc', 'Monstrum' Op Cit.

NOTE: For some reason, probably due to editorial incompetence the article promised in the final paragraph of my introduction never materialised).

For much of August 1995 I was in a recording studio just below the ancient Dartmoor mountain of Haytor, [17] itself a giant granite phallus with sinister geomantic connections. I was putting the finishing touches to an album called *The Case*, [18] another name which was soon to assume great importance. [19]

The day we finished the final mixes, I resumed the hunt for the Owlperson and wrote to 'Gavin', and finally took the bull by the horns and invited him to visit me for the weekend. [20]

Much to my surprise, because he had been showing less and less enthusiasm for a project which, by his own admission, was beginning to 'freak him out' mightily, he accepted. [21]

I made careful arrangements for his visit. I wanted to obtain a definitive, 'first hand' account from him, preferably on video; but I wanted to ensure that I put him through as little stress as possible. I also wanted, and this was perhaps the most important thing of all, to do my best to assure myself that my initial reactions to his testimony were, in fact, correct, and that 'Gavin' was not engaged in some monumentally complex student prank or hoax.

John Jacques and I discussed the matter at length and read all the available literature, some of which I have quoted in the previous chapter, to ensure that we knew as much as possible about the weird goings on in Mawnan Woods, and that if 'Gavin' was 'trying to pull a fast one', we would be in a position to catch him out.

For ten years between 1981 and 1991, I had been a qualified nurse, working with the mentally handicapped, and during my student years I had undergone a certain amount of psychiatric counselling training. John is a trained Counsellor, and as he says himself, is not interested in psychic phenomena, but is interested in people and their reactions. Together we were fairly confident that we could build up some semblance of a truthful profile of 'Gavin', by which we could evaluate his testimony.

At this stage. 'Gavin' was only a voice down the telephone and a name on a piece of paper, and neither of us had any more than the slightest insight into what sort of a person he actually was. His writings on subjects less contentious than that of winged humanoids were concise and scholarly, far beyond his years, and he did not seem, on the surface at least, to be the sort of person who would pull such an elaborate hoax, especially on our 'home ground'.

The summer of 1995 was disgustingly hot, and in many ways was reminiscent of that other long, hot summer nineteen years earlier, which had seen the original bizarre goings on in the lands surrounding the Fal Estuary. [22] By the autumn, the oppressive heat had mostly gone for good, and the weather was glorious. Saturday the 24th of September was a beautiful late summer day of the sort usually only portrayed in edenic [23] children's books set in an idyllic England that never really existed in the years between the wars. [24]

At eleven o'clock in the morning I was quite happy to sit on a bench on platform four of St. David's station in Exeter, waiting for 'Gavin's' train to arrive.

As I sat, I stared into the empty blue sky and wondered almost nervously what he would be like and whether, meeting him face to face would be fruitful or not. I speculated, almost nervously, on what questions I would ask him that evening, and as to whether or not this whole episode would prove to have been a pointless waste of time.

As the train pulled in, I got to my feet, and waved in greeting as a good looking young man of about twenty walked briskly along the station platform to meet me. I was immediately impressed. He looked younger than I had imagined, but was neat and tidy, and obviously 'sane'. I must confess that I had originally had some misgivings, after all it is not every day that even the man described by *Fortean Times,* as 'one of the country's few professional Cryptozoologists', has a house guest who claims to have had a first hand encounter with a winged humanoid creature from the outer edge.

I liked him immediately, but was sure that he must have had the same misgivings about his first meeting with us as we had about him; and I resolved that, whatever transpired, I would try to ensure that the weekend would be a pleasant one for him.

We exchanged pleasantries as we walked slowly across the footbridge which spans the main platforms of the old Victorian station, and we walked together through the faceless, modern ticket hall, through the double automatic sliding doors which provide a nastily jarring modern note to an otherwise glorious piece of classic architecture, and out into the September sunshine where Alison, parked illegally in a taxi rank, and John Jacques were there to meet us.

83

I introduced 'Gavin' to my wife and my manager, who, after more pleasantries went off to do his own inimitable thing as Alison drove 'Gavin' and me out of Exeter and towards the motorway.

I had already decided that it would be a good idea for 'Gavin' and I to get to know each other on 'neutral' ground, as it were; and, as Alison had business in Taunton, thirty five miles away, I decided to treat 'Gavin' to a day out, firstly to the Somerset County Museum, where I wanted to photograph a case of stuffed Great Bustards (an impressive bird similar to a turkey, which had, sadly been hunted to extinction in Britain in the early part of the 20th Century), [25] [26] and then to the adjacent public house, where I planned a liquid lunch.

By the time Alison came to collect us at three o'clock, 'Gavin' and I had formed a bond based on mutual interests such as Cryptozoology, beer and smutty stories. By the time we finally arrived home, I was convinced that 'Gavin' was a highly intelligent and completely genuine young man, who had been badly frightened by an incident in his youth, and that, far from 'leading us up the garden path', he was intent on exorcising his own personal demons by talking to us about his experience, even though in doing so, he was re-living an ordeal he would far rather have forgotten about.

A few years ago a BBC film crew came to my house to interview me about my work. They were shocked at what they found. "We thought you had a zoology centre", they said, looking around at a tiny, rather badly built mid-terraced house crammed to bursting point with thousands of books, what seemed like dozens of cats, guitars, filing cabinets and bits of computer equipment. (See Footnote).

They were not alone. My house is a little daunting to those uninitiated into its mysteries. 'Gavin' took it all in his stride, and within minutes he had made himself at home and was becoming firm friends with Carruthers, the elderly British Blue tom cat, who has, over the years, appointed himself a one-cat welcoming committee to our myriad of visitors, who have ranged from politicians to pop-stars and from zoologists to computer programmers.

That evening John Jacques arrived at our house, and after a couple of hours of social chit chat, a light meal and some rather good Chardonnay, we broached the subject of the video.

'Gavin' was quite willing to be interviewed but, he asked that the video should not actually show his face because, he was adamant that nothing exist that could personally 'incriminate' him.

We set up the video according to his wishes, and started to film the interview. After a couple of false starts, caused either by the technological gremlins which plague fortean researchers worldwide, [27] or more likely by our antiquated video camera refusing to work properly, we finally got what we wanted.

The transcript that follows is verbatim other than a few 'ums' and 'ers' which have been removed for the sake of readability.

The most striking thing about the interview was that socially, 'Gavin' was a very fluent, accomplished and suave young man; even slightly over-confident, with the over-confidence that comes from someone

---

FOOTNOTE: All this has now changed. In February 2006 my father died and I inherited the old family home in rural North Devon. At the time of writing (March 2006) we are planning to open a proper Visitor's Centre complete with museum, laboratory and library, here in Woolfardisworthy, and hopefully by the time that you read this it will have become a going concern.

who is secure in the knowledge that he is extremely well informed on his own particular subject.

As soon as he started to recount his experiences, his articulacy level plummeted, his hands began to sweat and he was obviously going through some fairly severe psychological stress. Several times he stopped for a glass of water, and on at least one occasion he seemed on the edge of tears.

John and I both felt a great empathy with him, and were as gentle as we could be with our questions. In the interests of good research, possibly we should have been more probing in our choice of questions, but in the interests of common humanity we could not bring ourselves to do so. He was so obviously hating every minute of his ordeal that we resolved to be as quick and as merciful as possible.

The interview started at about eleven o'clock in the evening and lasted, with a few breaks for glasses of water, for about sixty minutes.

John Jacques: We're talking about the summer you were twelve. You were on holiday with your girl-friend in the vicinity of Mawnan Smith.

'Gavin': We went out in the evenings just as it was getting dark. It was summertime so it got dark quite late. We allowed ourselves enough time to go around the area and get back before it got too late; ten o'clock or so. Mostly this is like little lanes or woods. I think I remember the church but I wouldn't swear to it. I had a torch and maybe both of us did. I was just playing with the beam as we walked past the woods in the dark. I shone the beam up a tree for no particular reason, and there about fifteen foot off the ground was this creature that is the Mawnan Owlman. I shone the beam on it, and when the beam was shone onto a surface it projected like a halo of light, and this was projected onto the whole animal.

The animal was in the beam. It reacted to being in the beam. For all the time that we saw it it was looking in our direction. Maybe, specifically looking at us..I can't tell. I still remember the way it looked. It was similar to a man in shape, and about four or four and a half feet high. It was grey, and with a texture like that on a bird with soft feathers. and the torch made it brighter than I think it was. The torch caught the eyes so they were reflected in the light and were bright yellowy, I think.

It had a torso like a man, but had legs which were in proportion to its body, again similar to a man. It was actually standing on this branch which would have been quite a thick branch and virtually all of its feet were wrapped around the branch. The feet were black and looked like pincers. They were really black and they looked like your hand if you press the first and second finger and the third and the fourth finger together.

The Author: Like the *Star Trek* 'Live Long and Prosper' salute?

'Gavin': Yeah. About half way up the legs was an ankle with the legs bending back, with no visible knee like in a person's knee. The torso would have been spindle shaped; broad at the top and at the bottom, so that it tapers down towards the legs and went straight down.

The head was really odd shaped. A really flat face, without any real outstanding features like an animal with a snout or anything. It had a black mouth curling down quite sharply at the corners, like an inverted 'V', and with no other features on the face apart from the eyes, really.

John Jacques: When you talk about a mouth, are you talking about something resembling your mouth,

or something resembling a beak?

'Gavin': More as if there were an opening that was overhung by a ... more like a human mouth, that was wider than a human mouth and dark. The top of the head was pointed and it had flaps at the side of the head about the same level as the eyes, that I think were pointed. It had quite large arms, or wings, with long feathers, the same colour as the rest of the body - a light grey - which weren't folded; they were held at the side so that the very tips of the feathers were like hanging around, nearly touching the branch that the animal was standing on. Having said about the mouth, I now think that whatever it was that is the mouth is something that was black and not open; because, if it was, the torch beam wouldn't have seen the black.

John Jacques: So what did this thing do then?

'Gavin': I captured the whole thing in the beam of the torch, so it was illuminated and it was looking at it. The thing did a quick jerk of its head, and the head like ... when I first looked at it the head was in a relaxed position above the chest, but it sunk into erm ... I wouldn't say that it had shoulders but it sunk into the body. The difference between the thorax and the head .... you wouldn't see the difference. This all happened in a couple of seconds....

John Jacques: Sure.

'Gavin': The head went down and the wings were brought up to the sides and swept around in front of the animal. As the wings were swept round, in the same motion, the animal jumped backwards off the branch it was standing on and it jumped down into the space behind the tree. For a second we stood there and we weren't making a noise, I'm pretty sure 'Sally' had her torch on it at the same time. We ran back .... we ran away.

John Jacques: Did it frighten you?

'Gavin': I was very very scared!

John Jacques: So, you were walking along, you shone a torch, you saw a strange creature that disappeared behind a tree. You didn't see it again?

'Gavin': That's right.

The Author: When you saw this thing, were you on a road or a path?

'Gavin': I think it was on the road.

The Author: A tarmac road?

'Gavin': Yeah, but with a small gravel verge, before the trees start. But the trees are pretty close to the road.

The Author: Do you remember whether you were walking towards the church or away from the church?

'Gavin': Towards the church. The way I picture this in my head is with the Church in front of me. I

wouldn't swear to this, but I am thinking of the church to the front of me and to my left, with the animal to my right and me turning to look at it on my right.

The Author: Did you enjoy the rest of your holiday?

'Gavin': Well, all the time I was thinking about this 'thing' and not wanting to. We didn't talk about it, 'Sally' and I. I think I can say the same for both of us. I wanted to see it again in that it might give us a chance to show somehow that I'd seen it. Maybe to take a photograph of it and maybe to get a second glimpse and find out more about it. But, the amount the animal scared me I wouldn't want to see it again.

John Jacques: Did you both speak about it? Did you say 'My God, what was that?' or that sort of thing?

'Gavin': Not much, but when we'd seen it we didn't talk at all until we'd gotten back to the caravan. We decided that if we could get some evidence, or get a photo then we'd feel better about it, but, like I said, although I'd like to find out more about it, I wouldn't like to see it.

John Jacques: So 'Sally' saw it as well?

'Gavin': Definitely.

The Author: Was this near the beginning of your holiday or near the end?

'Gavin': Neither. We'd done stuff before and we did stuff afterwards.

The Author: Was the rest of the holiday, before you saw the 'thing', a happy holiday?

'Gavin': Yeah, it was fine. It wasn't particularly exciting. I've done a lot of holidays to the Westcountry that were pretty similar. Nothing much happened.

John Jacques: What we are getting at: there was nothing particularly important happening in your life at the time. It was just another run of the mill holiday?

The Author: Was that the first holiday that you'd been on with 'Sally'?

'Gavin': Yeah.

The Author: So it was nice that you'd gone on holiday with your girlfriend for the first time, but, it wasn't a situation with your girlfriend's father chasing you around the camp-site with a pick-axe for getting their daughter back too late or something?

'Gavin': They'd invited me to go, because we were especially close at that time and spent a lot of time together, especially during that summer; and they were kind enough to offer me a place, and invite me along.

John Jacques: Yeah, I've done that sort of thing.

The Author: Girls didn't talk to me much until I was about eighteen you lucky so and so.

(Everyone laughs)

(Author's Note: The stress level in the room had, by this time, reached a considerable level. 'Gavin' was very upset and his level of fear was communicating itself to the other people in the room. Although the transcript quoted here does not show it the atmosphere was becoming very strange indeed. My pathetic attempt at humour was an attempt to defuse the situation. Surprisingly, because such attempts do not usually work, it was a success. 'Gavin's' laughter was infectious and the stress of the situation was immediately diffused).

The Author: You were saying in your letters that you went through quite a lot of emotional upheaval afterwards.

'Gavin': Still now, even today, if I look at trees. I look for the shape of an Owlman in the trees. For quite a long time afterwards, at least the next year or so, I was very very nervous of going near trees in the dark   Well, me and 'Sally', when we went back to school in September. We'd meet to go to school. We went to different schools but we'd meet to go to school. We wouldn't talk about it really, but occasionally, when we were alone we would say that we were worried about it, because at the time we both seemed to feel the same way about it .... that we both had experienced something that made us worried.

I would make... If I was looking into the darkness, which I couldn't help, because we lived near some very dense woods, I would look into the branches and would be able to make an Owlman shape out. We both said that we had seen the same thing in our own area. I saw it, like, really close to my own house, but as I said to you, I am sure that it was my imagination.

John Jacques: Have you ever seen an owl. A living owl?

'Gavin': I've seen wild owls in flight and standing in trees. What I saw didn't look anything like an owl, although what I've noticed is that if you take the shape of an owl, forget about its legs and take it totally out of focus it does LOOK like an Owlman. I'm convinced that the Mawnan 'creature' is not an owl. It cannot be an owl, they don't look like that., they don't stand like that, and I've got a pretty good idea about how big it was.

The Author: Do you ever dream about your experience?

'Gavin': Yeah, I do. I have quite a few nasty dreams, that you would call nightmares, where I would wake up really scared, and often they were quite freaky. I still have them. Recently I had them when I first started thinking about coming on this trip.

The Author: I'm sorry about that.

'Gavin': It's OK.

The Author: Have you ever done psychedelic drugs?

'Gavin': Not at the age of twelve.

The Author: Or since?

'Gavin': No.

(AUTHOR'S NOTE: John Jacques and I were never seriously suggesting that even in this day and age 'Gavin' had indulged in recreational hallucinogens at the age of twelve, but we were hoping that if he had partaken of the psychedelic experience in later life, he might have relived his childhood trauma.

The use of psychedelic drugs for recreational purposes is widespread enough (especially since the introduction of MDMA or Ecstasy to the commercial sub-culture), to make this a very real possibility.

It has to be remembered that Hoffman first synthesized Lysergic Acid Diethylamide 25 as a tool for psycho-analysis, [28] *and it was used as such for many years. Everyone from Huxley* [29] *and Osmond,* [30] *onwards have referred to its powers in reliving traumatic experiences, both real and imagined. I refer the curious reader to 'The Doors of Perception' by Aldous Huxley).* [31]

The Author: Is there anything else you would like to say?

'Gavin': (pause) Yeah. About the freaky dreams. I think of Owlman now as a malevolent entity, which is a thing that isn't just there, but is bad. I'm not going to say 'evil' because 'things' can't be evil. I'm not saying Owlman is an animal. An animal can't be evil, right?

I think that Owlman is maybe like other psychic phenomena. It has a kind of projection towards people that it involves.

This is only from my own personal experience, but in the dreams that I had about Owlman, I had to kill people. It sounds stupid, but..

John Jacques: Had you ever heard or read about the Owlman before your experience?

'Gavin': I was not aware that such things existed!

The Author: How did you feel when you first read about it in .... *Alien Animals* [32] wasn't it?

'Gavin': I picked up the book by chance in a local library shortly afterwards - well, a couple of years afterwards - and I was elated. I was really happy, but at the same time it brought it all back.

The book *Alien Animals* was where I first realised that perhaps other people had seen the same thing. The book *Alien Animals,* means a lot to me. It's like, um ... this one book, and I've seen the same things in lots of publications since; showed that other people had seen the thing which was definitely the same as what I saw.

Although from the pictures that people have done of the thing, they haven't captured the animal as I have described it; they haven't been totally accurate about it ... I understand that, but there is no doubt that the thing that they saw and drew is a perfect match for the thing that I saw at Mawnan.

Here the interview ended. 'Gavin' was clearly distraught, and whilst there were other questions that we wanted to ask him, for compassionate reasons we decided that enough was enough. John went home, and 'Gavin' and I proceeded to demolish a number of bottles of wine, and swap off-colour stories.
The next stage of our investigation would have to wait.

'Gavin' went home a couple of days later. John and I discussed the interview in some depth and, whilst we agreed on some of our conclusions, we were totally at odds on others. Our relationship was only to last a few more months as we had a number of unresolved (and probably irresolvable), personal and business differences. He is therefore unavailable for comment as I write this book, ten months after we interviewed the young man I 'christened' 'Gavin'.

At the time, however, John and I were totally in agreement that 'Gavin' was sincere in what he told us. Neither of us had any doubt, nor indeed had Alison or anyone else who has seen the video, that 'Gavin' believed that what he was telling us was the truth. This is where John and I differed. John believed, and presumably still believes, that what 'Gavin' saw was merely an owl. I believe that, for a number of reasons, which are discussed in some depth at the end of this book, that this cannot be so; and that what 'Gavin' saw was something far less tangible.

There were a few other things, that, with the benefit of hindsight, I wished that I had asked 'Gavin'. I hadn't asked him at the time, mostly out of personal embarrassment. After all, I did not know him very well and it was a peculiar situation. Ten months later I have no such reservations. 'Gavin' and I are now firm friends and so, as almost the last piece of research conducted for this book, I ascertained a few final facts. [33]

It seems that 'Sally' was physically mature at the time. She had started menstruating, although 'Gavin' has no idea if she was doing so at the time that they saw the Owlman. This is, I believe important; because, as I shall describe in more depth in the final chapter, there does seem to be a link between the Owlman and young women at the onset of puberty. It should also be noted that several authors [34] have made connections between 'Bigfoot' type phenomena and menstruating women. This may be purely because the added sex hormones being released act as an attractant to a hominoid species who is very closely related to our own, or it could be something far more subtle in nature. I have written elsewhere, [35] about my belief that, whereas some North American BHM sightings are undoubtedly those of bona fide cryptids, [36] [37] [38] some are zooform phenomena more akin in nature to entities such as the Owlman of Mawnan.

The other piece of information that I obtained from a mildly embarrassed 'Gavin' [39] was that he and Sally did not become sexually active until about a year after the events described in this chapter. I believe that this is significant. Most people are not sexually active at the age of twelve. The much maligned Kinsey Report, [40] [41] states that only 12.5% of boys of 'Gavin's' age at the time, who grow up to go to University, have had any kind of heterosexual contact and only 3.5 % have had sexual intercourse.

What is without doubt, however, is that there were large amounts of sex hormones, and, perhaps even more important, adolescent angst, floating around Mawnan Woods that night in 1989, and as we will see, this is probably very important.

Looking back towards the wooded confines that surround Mawnan Old Church

Prisk Cove, Mawnan

CHAPTER FOUR: IMITATION

"Just let go of everything - like a falling star. The far
away ones, when you see their light it's already happened
millions of years ago. This too, my brief light, maybe it
had flashed across the darkness long long ago..."

Russell Hoban *'Turtle Diary'* (1975)

Ever since the human species gained the evolutionary plateau of consciousness which allowed these shambling ape-like creatures to achieve, for the first time, the twin gifts of self-determination and self-awareness which set us apart from the rest of the animal kingdom, we have populated the nether regions of our imaginations with diverse strange and wonderful beings.

We have always been an extremely egocentric species, hardly surprising when you think about it ... we were, after all the first species to develop an ego, and it is entirely logical that our Gods and demi-gods, our Angels and Daemons, our Trolls, Pixies and faerie folk, should be created in our own image. It is not by coincidence that the nether regions of the imaginations of people from every culture on earth should be populated by beings based loosely upon the form of an omnivorous, evolved primate, whose own shape was near enough to his simian ancestors for him to justifiably fear what he might evolve into.

Bernard Heuvelmans, the 'father' of Cryptozoology wrote in 1958 that *terror is more dreadful when it wears a human face*. [1] C.S.Lewis, the acclaimed Christian academic and author of children's books wrote:

> But in general, take my advice, when you meet anything that's going to be human, and isn't yet or used to be human once, and isn't now, or ought to be human and isn't, you keep your eyes on it and feel for your hatchet.. [2]

As man expanded his iconogography, it invented sub-human, moronic beings who still shamble across the wild places, providing not only a cultural reminder of our humble genetic origins, but also 'creatures' that we can simultaneously fear, scorn, pity and despise. He also created superhuman demi-gods and daemons, who could do things that mere men could only dream about. Beings with superhuman strength, beings who could swim beneath the sea, and beings who could fly effortlessly

through the air.

We have populated every sea on earth with Merfolk. We have populated every cave beneath the earth with Trolls, Goblins and Tommy-knockers, we have filled every woodland with Dryads and Elves, and we have filled the skies of every country with mysterious flying 'people', with the potential power of both good and evil.

The humanoid culture-icons of all races, from the Hindu Garuda, [3] to the Judaeo-Christian Angels and Devils, from Mercury the Messenger of the Gods to the winged snake God Quetzacoatl [4] of the ancient peoples of South America, were all super-human beings. The basic 'model' of the human form with all the optional extras that an earthbound being could only dream of.

Man also created subhuman flying entities, creatures whose zeitgeist was normally, (but not exclusively) evil or malicious. Harpies, which as Bob Rickard points out are *"suggested byJungians as a symbol of the negative anima "*,[5] Cherubs and Imps, could fly but lacked the divinity of the Gods and Devils who were usually, if not always, their masters.

These beings were as real as any of the creatures that roamed the Green Hills of Earth. [6] The socio-cultural process which created them, breathed life into them, and in the days when the earth was young, these figures were familiar sights in the skies above the planet *'I think therefore I am'*, said Rene Descartes. [7] *'I think therefore It Is'*, said early man, as he gave three dimensions and a semblance of solidity to his etheric, pan-dimensional thought forms.

I do not see that it is my position as a fortean researcher and commentator to pass judgement upon other people's deeply held beliefs, but it has always seemed to me, at least that the Theosophical Society [8] is fundamentally unsound. Their beliefs have always appeared to be a bastardised mish-mash of semi-occult beliefs from a range of often conflicting Eastern religions. Many of their sacred writings, especially those of the legendary Madame Helena Blavatsky [9] are completely absurd, and in common with many researchers within my field I treat their claims with a certain degree of scepticism.

Geoffrey Hodson was an early Theosophist, and although I find his code of beliefs fundamentally unsound, this passage from his book *'Fairies at Work and at Play'* (1925), [10] [11] describes the deva (or guardian spirit) of a pine wood that he 'saw' in the Lake District:

> *My first impression was of a huge, brilliant crimson, bat-like thing, which fixed a pair of burning eyes upon me. The form was not concentrated into the true human shape, but was somehow spread out into the shape of a bat with a human face and eyes, and with wings outstretched over the mountainside. As soon as it felt itself to be observed it flashed into its proper shape, as if to confront us, fixed its piercing eyes upon as, and then sank into the hillside and disappeared.*

Hodson's description is included, because it provides a rare glimpse of an apparition which appears to be mid-way between a conventional religious vision, and an Owlman type of 'creature'.

Later on in his book Hodson describes tree-devas who move about in the upper branches of their trees, occasionally flying into the sky but, never descending to the ground.

Hodson's devas, and similar beings described by other mystics and occultists, appear to be benign creatures, far removed in essence, if not in form from the Owlman and his kin. It should, perhaps, as Bob

Illustration of the demon 'Andras'
from Collin de Plancy's *Dictionnaire Infernal*, 1863

"He is a Great Marquis, appearing in the Form of an Angel with a Head like a Black Night Raven, riding upon a strong Black Wolf, and having a Sharp and Bright Sword flourished aloft in his hand. His Office is to sow Discords. If the Exorcist have not a care, he will slay both him and his fellows. He governeth 30 Legions of Spirits."

Some explanation may be useful in clarifying this description. The term night raven, was another name for an owl. Black Wolves were once fairly common in Europe, however it could also refer to demonic Black Dogs . Both wolf/ dogs and owl were considered in the past to be animals of evil.

The magician performing the evocation is called the "exorcist" in the English translation of the Goetia preserved in manuscript in the British Library (Sloane ms. 2731). We would not apply the term exorcist to the magician today since the magician is calling the spirit forth to visible appearance, rather than driving it away. However, the term exorcist was once used more generally to describe someone who commanded spirits. Magicians traditionally had at least one assistant, usually more than one, to help them in their rituals. They stood inside a magic circle for protec- tion. If the evoked demon could tempt or deceive the magician or his assistants to step out from the circle, the de- mon could then injure the careless human beings.

Rickard pointed out, [12] be noted, that both Hodson's deva and the Owlman of Mawnan have appeared in conjunction with coniferous trees.

It says something very disturbing about the human psyche that whereas, very few people report sightings of the super-human winged entities any more, what few contemporary eye-witness reports of 'angels' I have, seem to be inextricably linked with either fundamentalist religious, or 'New-Age' philosophies, [13] there have been a steady stream of sightings of the lesser beings, the winged sub-humans, from antiquity to the present day.

As the human race evolves, there seems to be a parallel process of de-evolution amongst its spiritual creations. This isn't a new concept. A century ago Rudyard Kipling wrote:

Puck

The fact is they began as Gods. The Phoenicians brought some over when they came to buy tin; and the Gauls and the Jutes, and the Danes, and the Friesians, and the Angles brought more when they landed. They were always landing in those days, or being driven back to their ships, and they always brought their Gods with them. England is a bad country for Gods. Now I began as I meant to go on. A bowl of porridge, a dish of milk; and a little quiet fun with the country folk in the lanes was enough for me then, as it is now. I belong here, you see, and I have been mixed up with people all my days. But most of the others insisted on being Gods and having temples, and altars and priests, and sacrifices of their own (...). If it wasn't men, it was horses, or cattle, or pigs, or metheglin – that's a sticky, sweet sort of beer. I never liked it. They were a stiff-necked extravagant set of idols, the Old Things. But what was the result? Men don't like being sacrificed at the best of times; they don't even like sacrificing their farm horses. After a while man simply left the Old Things alone, and the roof of their temples fell in, and the Old Things had to scuttle out arid pick up a living as they could. Some of them took to hanging about trees, and hiding in graves and groaning o'nights. If they groaned loud enough and long enough they might frighten a poor countryman into sacrificing a hen, or leaving a pound of butter for them.. [14]

Those words were spoken by Puck the Hedge-Goblin, one of the last of the 'good people' of Old England. He summed up this 'de-evolution process', the 'de-deification' of the Old Gods, even more succinctly:

First they were Gods. Then they were the People of the Hills, and then they flitted to other places because they couldn't get on with the English for one reason or another! [15]

Tony Shiels also wrote about Puck: [16]

"'Fairy' is a relatively recent word derived from 'Fay-erie', meaning the enchantment of Fays or Fates. Morgan le Fay played the role of bad fairy, or witch, in Arthurian legend, and is linked with the shape-shifting Irish Morrigan. Fays are human size, but the term fairy is used to describe all classes of diminutive humanoid entities: Elves, Goblins, Boggarts,

Leprechauns, Trolls, Dwarves and so on. In a Celtic context, it is perhaps significant that etymologists have linked Piskies with both Picts and Pygmies. In the Scottish Lowlands the wee folk are often referred to as peichts. It is no great jump from Pesky to Pooka, and from Pooka to Puck. These elemental earth or nature spirits, aboriginal midgets, and shape-shifting personeens are known, now, collectively, as fairies. I have seen them..."

Tony is not alone. In the far western counties of the British (or as T.H White pointed out [17] the 'PICTISH') isles, the past (as Alfred Aloysius 'Trader' Horn, remarked about Africa in his memoirs belatedly published in 1927), [18] has hardly stopped breathing. People still see the 'little people' on a regular basis, and belief in them still flourishes, if a little less overtly than when the following report was published in the *Transactions of the Devonshire Association* by the great Devonian Folklorist the Reverend Sabine Baring-Gould:

> *In 1879, a farmer on the west side of Dartmoor, whose name I know, and also the name of his farm, having had sickness amongst his cattle, sacrificed a sheep and burned it on the moor above his farm, as an offering to the pygsies. The cattle at once began to recover, and did well after, nor were there any fresh cases of sickness among them. He spoke of the matter as being by no means anything to be ashamed of, or that was likely to cause surprise. I do not, however wish to give his name. [19]*

A typical sighting of a Dartmoor Pixy was reported to the Devonshire Association by Mrs. Gwen Herbert: [20]

> *Though I am a grown woman with three sons, I still firmly believe in pixies and in fairies. When a child of seven I saw a pixie, and in recent years I have been 'pisky-lead' on Dartmoor.*
>
> *I saw the pixie under an overhanging boulder close to Shaugh Bridge (on the southern edge of Dartmoor), in the afternoon. I cannot say more definitely as to the time, but I remember running in to my mother after an afternoon walk and saying I had seen a pixie - and being laughed at. This was in 1897. It was like a little wizened man about (as far as I can remember) eighteen inches or possibly two feet high, but I incline to the lesser height. It had a little pointed hat, slightly curved to the front, a doublet and little, short, knicker things.*
>
> *My impression is of some contrasting colours, but I cannot now remember what colours, though I think they were blue and red. Its face was brown and winkled and wizened. I saw it for a moment and it vanished. It was under the boulder when I looked, and then vanished.*
>
> *It was about three years ago when I was 'pisky-led'. I did not see the pixie, but, although it was a bright, fine day and I was riding on a part of the moor I know well, I was suddenly - to use a Dartmoor expression - 'mazed'. [21] I knew the places and yet was utterly befogged.*
>
> *I felt I was pixie-led, and started to turn my pockets inside out. While I was doing so, I suddenly knew where I was exactly. I may add that I am psychic, but do not know whether this has anything to do with any pixie experiences.*

This account is included in full, because there are several parallels to the Owlman sightings recounted in the earlier chapters of this book. The Owlman sightings seem to be made exclusively by young girls (as was this sighting), and on the one occasion when a boy saw the creature, he was in the company of,

and emotionally involved with, a young girl. Most pixie sightings are made by young girls and unmarried women, and like the Owlman phenomena they do seem to be associated with a particular geographical location. As the late Miss Theo Brown, the legendary Devonshire folklorist wrote: [22] [23]

> *The general idea about pixies is that nobody sees them NOW and this has been the verdict from Chaucer's time onwards. The fact is that a very few people do see them, but the majority do not. It is a gift which is unaffected by education, though it is modified by tradition and the surrounding scenery. I know three people who see pixies in our generation, but they tell me that pixies seem to prefer the fringes of the moor rather than the centre. This may be due to the forestry schemes, for pixies like open clitter into which they sink at dawn - or little wooded dells with minute waterfalls. They seem to have left the conifer plantations; when these have grown up shall we develop a new kind of woodland spirit?*

As we have seen, the devas of the Theosophists, and the Owlman of Mawnan are associated with pinewoods. Perhaps these are the 'new woodland spirits' foreseen by Miss Brown.

The Pixies, however are still seen. Although the habitat of the pixies has changed along with the changing face of the landscape of the areas in which they 'live', their behaviour and habits seem to have survived relatively unchanged. [26]

Theo Brown again:

> *The old stories of pixies show that they helped the farmer with his threshing, and they haunted the hearth and did the housework if rewarded with a dish of cream on the doorstep. Or in naughty mood they rode the farmer's horses and tangled and knotted their manes - a cousin tells me she has found her horses in 'pixy-ridden' condition in the stable. But a changing folk-life changes the spirits. what can pixies make of combine-harvesters, and calor-gas, or the 'little people' of Land Rovers? [27]*

and she concludes:

> *There is no tradition of Dartmoor Pixies being associated with prehistoric remains, as in other parts of Europe; and none of the Miners 1 have talked to has admitted hearing the 'knockers' at any time. [28]*

It is interesting to note that as recently as the 1950's folklorist Ruth Tongue wrote that on at least one farm in the heart of Dartmoor, dishes of milk were still being left out for the 'little people'. In 1965 she wrote:

> *Until about seven years ago I would have considered the Dartmoor Pixy as dead as Puck and Queen Mab in other parts of the country. Then, however, at the end of a lecture a man in the audience told me of a moorland farm in which he averred a bowl of milk was left out in the cow shed each night for the pixies. [29] [30]*

In a 1994 paper for *'Promises and Disappointments',* [31] I described a number of accounts of people being 'pisky led', a phenomenon in which the afflicted person experiences a feeling of utter alienation, becomes 'lost' in surroundings which are often perfectly familiar to her or him, and sometimes experiences 'time slips', and pointed out the parallels between some of these experiences and the more modern accounts of alien abductions. I have many more accounts on my files, but this is neither the time,

nor the place to list them.

It is tempting, however, and in a way, almost re-assuring to speculate that although the years roll on, and the names have been changed, and although the cultural subtexts to the experiences are years apart, the phenomena themselves remain relatively unchanged.

Maybe it is something to do with the geographical area. Many people, including Tony Shiels, claim that the South-West, and particularly Cornwall has little to do with the rest of the country. [33] This part of England certainly appears to have a much thinner veneer, of what we laughably like to call 'modern civilisation', upon it than has much of the rest of the country. [34]

Here, on the outer edge of the Celtic fringe, the old ways, and the old 'things' have not entirely vanished. Pixies still live on the moorlands, the ancient black dogs of the Devil's hunting pack still pace inexorably up and down the more deserted roads and almost within living memory, bizarre daemons were still encountered in the sunken lanes of Devon and Cornwall.

We have already discussed pixies at some length. They are usually described as 'tiny people', with human features and morphology. One account on my files describes them somewhat differently and leads on, rather conveniently to sightings of Owlman type entities elsewhere in the West-country.

> *Mrs F of Widecombe, told me that her grandfather and father used to see pixies in the dimpsey, in the mires at Buckland. Her grandfather, a very religious man, used to say that they came up from Hell, and were sent as a warning to drunkards, gamblers, and such like, and that Hellfire would be the punishment for the wicked. He described the pixies as having long legs and red heads like a ball of fire, and he regarded them as 'the vapours of hell'.* [38]

The true explanation was probably that the old men witnessed a spectacular manifestation of incandescent methane or marsh gas. Before dismissing the above story as the supernatural ramblings of a superstitious old man, one is tempted to remember another quote from C.S.Lewis:

> *"'In our world', said Eustace, 'a star is a huge ball of flaming gas'. 'Even in your world, my son, that is not what a star is, but only what it is made of...'"* [38]

There is also evidence to support the hypothesis of 'de-deification', that I have extrapolated from Kipling's *"Puck of Pook's Hill"*. [39] It may have been merely a work of fiction but Mr Kipling did write extraordinarily good books! [40]

The Romans never established more than a figurative foot-hold in the far South-West, but there were Roman Settlements in Exeter, Barnstaple and along the Devon-Dorset border. [41] Recent experiences of what appear to be genuine parapsychological events suggest that the Romans left their influence on the psychic infrastructure of the area.

A "Man with a Calf's Head" is said to be 'sometimes seen on a crossroads one mile from Shirwell and three miles from Barnstaple'. [42] The folklorist who submitted this record to the folklore section of the Devonshire Association suggested, without any supportive evidence, that it could have been the ghost of a man who had been knocked down and killed by his cattle. [43] I would suggest, that this phantasm is far more ancient and has certain Mithraic [44] overtones, and may be a tulpa-like thought form, somehow associated with Mithraic rites in the Roman settlements nearby.

There are many water spirits from the region. The waters of the river at Lydford Gorge scream for their next victim, [45] and the mer-folk sing on the shores at Lynton. [46] These are also the 'People of the Hills', described by Kipling. The folklorist Rodney Legg, however described one particularly interesting water spirit which again perfectly illustrates the 'de-deification' theory extrapolated from Kipling.

The late Mary Collier told him of her experience at a place she dubbed 'Whispering Corner', by Lytchett Matravers, near Poole in Dorset:

> ...from the sound of voices ahead I must be intruding on somebody, most likely love's young dream making the most of its lunch-hour. But nobody was there.

> The whispering continued. All around rather than from one single place, part of the woods and the hillside itself. Voice or voices, male or female, it was impossible to distinguish. Continuous, its volume sometimes rising and falling a little, sometimes a little breathless; definitely the sound of a human voice. Hardly the traditional hour of ghosts, yet I seemed to be hearing one, or more than one, loud and clear into the bargain. The most perplexing aspect was, that, try as I might, I could distinguish no words. If words were, indeed being formed, they were in a language unknown to me! [47]

Both Legge, and Mary Collier tried to analyse these voices and to discover a historical event which could, at least attempt to explain them, but to no avail. They finally summised that these were ghosts from the original medieval village of Lytchett Matravers which had been wiped out by the plague.

Mary Collier continues:

> Moving into Devon some years later with Whispering Corner far from my thoughts, a friend living near Branscombe remarked one day "we've got a stream near here with a water spirit! Spirits seem to follow water you know, it seems to attract them in some way. I don't know why. Yes, I suppose you'd call me psychic or somewhat so - I'm a dowser anyway. I've always felt a 'something' about that stream, and there's a field too, we call Pan's Field. One day a friend and I heard a voice whispering by the stream - quite a distinct whisper - and then we felt sure that the 'something' is a water spirit

> Whispering Corner sprang to my mind. 'I think I've heard a water-spirit too! Whispering and whispering quite loudly'.

> 'Could you distinguish any words? We couldn't'

> 'Not one', I replied 'but I'm thinking - wouldn't it have been some very long past language? Wasn't Sylvanus the god of the springs?'

> Had Whispering Corner found its answer? Sylvanus, the God the occupying Romans had prayed to along with Mithras; the God who kept the streams running to water their lands. 'Sylvanus was good enough for my father and grandfather before him. . He's good enough for me!' declared the more cautious when confronted with Christianity. 'Somebody or something got him into a huff the other summer and you remember what happened then. Better to play safe than dry up! [48]

Mary Collier continued:

> *Still part of Roman life when the legions left Britain, Sylvanus was but one of his names, for he had always been part of the rising springs, old as sweet waters themselves, his spirit their spirit, his speech the tongue of earth and sky, of light and darkness, of the things of the earth and its waters.*

The account above was submitted by Mary Collier to Rodney Legg for inclusion in a book they wrote together with Tom Perrot (of the Ghost Club) in 1974. [49]

I contacted Tom to try and gather more information on Mary Collier and her experience [50] but unfortunately, it appears that she died several years ago. I was equally unsuccessful at contacting Rodney Legg, who is, now, apparently, the warden of a nature reserve on the tiny, and practically inaccessible island of Steep Holme in the Bristol Channel. Attempts to contact him failed, and therefore, because I particularly wanted to include the above story in this book, I am forced to go against my usual practice and include it unverified and without having the benefit of a supporting interview.

There are similar stories from throughout the region. Kevin and Sue Wright; from St. Neot in Cornwall told me of a series of psychic phenomena that have been experienced by them, their family and friends in the vicinity of their home. [51] They, too, have a water spirit, and they can also hear the sound of what appears to be a distant playground full of small children, by a spring on their property. There is a magickal oak tree by the stream which appears to have grown at an extraordinary rate over the last few years. They have also experienced other phenomena more directly related to the material in the main body of this book, and we shall return to them later in this chapter.

Centuries after they were last worshipped as deities, the images of Sylvanus and Mithras are still embossed upon the ether. The Ancient Gods became the Old Faith Spirits, who slowly metamorphasised into mere folk memories and entries in tourist guide-books. Occasionally, however, they still venture forth and people, unaware of their true nature, and antecedents, occasionally see them.

The events at Mawnan Old Church also have several precedents in the Westcountry.

An incident in North Devon is particularly interesting. [52] The entire documentary evidence comes from two letters published in the *Western Morning News* of the 16th and 19th February 1932 respectively:-

WILL O'THE WISP?

Sir,

> *A few nights ago another man and I were, one dark November night at about eleven o'clock, on a hillside near the river Torridge far from any road, footpath or house.*

> *We were long netting rabbits. Between us and the river lays a stretch of marshy ground, perhaps one hundred yards wide. On the other side of the river the ground rose abruptly covered in timber.*

> *Suddenly we saw quite near us apparently about fifty feet above the marsh, an oblong object floating in the air.*

Ignis Fatuus or Will O' Wisp

I cannot describe it better than saying that it looked like a conglomeration of very dim stars. It appeared to be about three feet by two feet in size and was clearly outlined against the dark background of the opposite hillside. It sailed about with a sort of circular motion, something like a swallow hawking over a pond.

For five minutes or so we watched it as it swept around in ever-widening circles; finally it sailed off up the river and we saw it no more.

I have sent this letter, before forwarding it to you, to the man who was with me at the time, and he corroborates all that I have said.

F.W.H.
North Devon February 15ᵗʰ. [53]

The Headline refers to the country name for 'marsh gas' which, as I wrote above, is an incandescent form of methane that rises from rotting vegetation. [54] As already noted, it seems very likely that the episode of the 'flaming pixies', recounted earlier [55] was probably based on a sighting of this bizarre

natural phenomenon but it seems almost impossible that this episode, could be equally explained. Marsh Gas is also known as 'Jack O'Lantern', hence the opening words of the next letter which appeared four days later, and which again I quote verbatim:

ONLY A WHITE OWL?

Sir,

'Jack' does not dance fifty feet above the ground. You will not see him on a dark November night; neither does he move with a circular motion.

As a youth I was lucky to see a superb display over some bogland on our common. This land has since been reclaimed and cultivated.

What 'F.W.H' and his companion saw was a white owl.

E.E.Rudd
Torrington February 17th. [56]

Although I agree with Mr Rudd that what F.W.H saw could not have been marsh gas, it could not have been a white owl either. I have yet to meet any species of bird that is rectangular, two feet by three feet, and consists of a 'conglomeration of dim stars'. The precise physics behind what the two men saw over sixty years ago remain obscure, but what seems certain is that the Owlman of Mawnan has some antecedents that have remained obscure even within the canon of fortean literature as a whole.

One slight anomaly which should, perhaps, be noted is the inconsistency of the dates. The letters were written, and published in February 1932 and refer to events happening 'a few nights' before. The same paragraph refers to them happening on a 'dark November night'. [57] Obviously both statements cannot be true. There is enough corroborative evidence, however, to persuade us not to reject this report out of hand because even this, apparently singular occurrence as far from unique. I have already made brief mention of the Wright family from St Neot. [58] Amongst the other psychic and parapsychological anomalies which they have experienced are a series of anomalous occurrences, which appear very similar to those which happened in the Torridge estuary during 1932.

On several occasions during recent years various members of their family circle have reported seeing swirling clouds of 'pinpricks' of pale light amongst the uppermost branches of trees on their property. These have happened at various times of the year and seem inconsistent either with the physics which govern the incandescent properties of methane or, indeed the behaviour of glow-worms or fire-flies. [59]

On one occasion, one of their sons reported to me that he had been surrounded by a swirling mass of incandescent ectoplasmic light, and other witnesses have told me that the myriad points of light appeared to be moving in concordance with each other! [60]

There are other, similar reports from the region.

The wife of a former Vicar of Ilsington saw a very large, white 'owl-like' figure 'flitting about' between gravestones in the churchyard of her husband's parish at some time during the 1950's. This record is included because the lady concerned was adamant that what she had seen was bird like in form.

There are, unfortunately, no other details. [61]

Hurley's 1973 book *The Legends of Exmoor* [62] recounts a number of stories surrounding the legend of a witch called Mother Leakey, who lived in the north Somerset port of Minehead. Her activities caused so much concern locally that eventually the Bishop of Bath and Wells headed an enquiry into the matter.

The Commission's report, which was endorsed on February 4th 1637 read:

> *"We are of the opinion and do believe that there was never any such apparition at all, but that it was an imposture devised and framed for some ends, but what they are we know not."* [63] This statement was powerless to quash the legend, and it is said that: *"It became one with wings that took the old bird up to the mainmasts of ships, where she perched to whistle up the winds and provoke great storms that destroyed vessels and cargoes".* [64]

It appears, however, that nearly three hundred years later, in the early years of the 20th Century, this particular winged demon was being blamed for inclement weather in the seas off Minehead. Rodney Legg described some mysterious air-borne 'creatures' in Dorset during the first half of the 19th Century:

> *Till about 1840 there was an ancient burial mound beside the Ashmore to Fontmell Magna cart track by Folly Hanging Gate at Washers pit (Ordinance Survey map reference ST 898 168). This solitary place was notorious for the weird sounds of creatures in the air, called Gabbygammies, or otherwise Gappergennies. Though the strange sounds could be imitated by human lips, Mr Stephen Hall, of Manor Farm had another explanation and said badgers were the cause. Villagers at Ashmore, however, were sure the place was haunted.* [65]

Badgers, incidentally were also suggested as the cause of one of the greatest and most insoluble Westcountry mysteries of all time. The 19th Century mystery of the Devil's footprints, also known as the 'Great Devon Mystery'. It has also been suggested that these mysterious prints which appeared in the snow one winter's night, across much of South Devon, could have been made by a giant, winged creature, [66] but there is little evidence to suggest such an explanation. The most lengthy and erudite over-

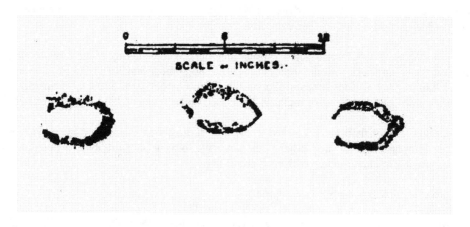

SCALE ~ INCHES.

The Devil's Hoofprints that
appeared in south Devon in February 1855

view of the phenomenon can be found in Mike Dash's paper in Steve Moore's *'Fortean Studies Volume One'.* [67]

Apart from the Owlman of Mawnan itself, possibly the best known incident of an anomalous feathered being in the region was first reported in the *Cornish Echo* on the fourth of June 1926. [68] The account has been printed in several books, including the Mawnan-Peller leaflet [69] (the first as far as I know), *'Alien Animals'* by Janet and Colin Bord, [70] and Bob Rickard's piece for *Fortean Times* in 1976 which has already been source material for much of this chapter. [71]

Two boys were attacked by a peculiar, very large and aggressive 'feathered thing' between Mount Hawke and Porthtowan. It was hunted and eventually killed (some accounts claim that the two boys themselves killed it), and the body, apparently defied identification. In Bob Rickard's account of the incident, he also points out that:

> *According to Frank Hamel's "Human Animals" (1915 and 1973), when English witches flew to their Sabbat, they frequently took the form of an Owl, more so than any other bird.* [72]

One of the most bizarre aspects to the above account is the lexi-link, between a large feathered creature being found at Mount Hawke. The coincidence goes further than this, however.

In my paper on Eagles in Devon which was published in the *Centre for Fortean Zoology 1996 Year-book*, [73] I listed the Cornish and Devon records of one of our rarest avian visitors: The Spotted Eagle *(Aquila clanga)*. The first British record was of a bird shot in the mid 19th Century at ... Mount Hawke!

The mixture of an amusing lexi-link and a bizarre piece of synchronicity is, I think, notable.

It does appear, however that the link between the creature from Mount Hawke and the Owlman of Mawnan is not as straightforward as it might seem. When one examines the original source material from the *Cornish Echo* in 1926, one finds that the story, whilst interesting has less relevance than some researchers have supposed. The headline reads:

"Boys attacked by strange bird"

with a sub heading reading:

"Unpleasant experience near Porthowan"

The story itself is unusual, and more than a little bizarre:

> *While proceeding along a road on Sunday evening midway between Mount Hawke and Porthowan, two lads had their attention drawn to something fluttering on top of a mine burrow. The younger boy ascended the burrow to ascertain what it was, and on finding a large bird, apparently dead, proceeded to examine it. The boy was instantly attacked and ran back to his brother; who just managed to throw his coat over the bird to prevent any injuries being done.*
>
> *The bird, however, escaped from the coat and attacked the older boy, who defended himself*

BOYS ATTACKED BY STRANGE BIRD.

UNPLEASANT EXPERIENCE NEAR PORTHTOWAN.

While proceeding along a road on Sunday evening, midway between Mount Hawke and Porthtowan, two lads had their attention drawn to something fluttering on top of a mine burrow. The younger boy ascended the burrow to ascertain what it was, and on finding a large bird, apparently dead, proceeded to examine it. The boy was instantly attacked, and ran back to his brother, who just managed to throw his coat over the bird to prevent any injuries being done.

The bird, however, escaped from the coat and attacked the older boy, who defended himself with a stick, and eventually killed the bird, but not before he had received a severe bite on the hand.

The bird measured 6ft. 3in. from tip of the one wing to the other, and was 3ft. in length. It had a powerful pointed beak six inches in length, short legs, full webbed feet striped with green and yellow, and a duck-shaped body. The plumage was of cream colour, tinged with brown on the beak, and also on the upper wing-coverts, the tips of the wings being black. The bird had a severe wound under the right wing, which, no doubt, had caused it much pain, and must have infuriated it. The creature was in a very poor condition, and, owing to rapid decay, was soon buried. Many villagers saw the bird, but none were able to name it.

This article from the Cornish Echo, 4th June 1926- here printed in a public forum for the first time in eight decades - should be reproduced in every book on contemporary fortean zoology as an object lesson in how NOT to jump to conclusions.

As Sigmund Freud was wont to say—"sometimes a cigar is only a cigar".

with a stick, and eventually killed the bird, but not before he had received a severe bite on the hand.

The bird measured six foot three inches from the tip of one wing to the other, and was three feet in length. It had a powerful pointed beak six inches in length, full webbed feet striped with green and yellow, and a duck shaped body. The plumage was of cream colour, tinged with brown on the beak; and also on the upper wing coverts, the tips of the wings being black. There was a severe wound under the right wing, which, no doubt had caused it much pain and must have infuriated it. The creature was in a very poor condition, and owing to rapid decay was soon buried. Many villagers saw the bird, but none were able to name it. [74]

Two items of interest come immediately to mind. One is the rapid rate of decay, which in itself is not unusual, but is somewhat reminiscent of the extremely rapid rate of decay reported in conjunction with the corpses of Dartmoor Ponies found in mysterious circumstances. [75] The other is that this is no Owlman. This is not even an owl, and appears to be some type of waterfowl. I must admit, however that like the Cornish villagers in the 1920's, I am unable to identify the unfortunate bird.

It may be apposite to mention the luminous owls which were reported in Norfolk in the late 19th and early 20th Centuries. This appears to be a similar but entirely unconnected phenomenon, which is mentioned here, only for the sake of completeness. The excellent account in Steve Moore's *'Fortean Studies Vol. 1'*, leads one to suppose that here we are dealing with ordinary specimens of *Tyto alba* afflicted with bioluminescence, probably from a fungal or algal infection. [76]

Owls have, however been treated as birds of ill-omen in the South West. As recently as July 15th 1957, W.J.Wallis wrote in the *Western Morning News*:

Once again I have come across a stuffed owl complete with glass case, pushed into a dustbin outside a picturesque thatched cottage. The poor old bird looked sad enough, head downwards behind smashed glass.

I had a word with the tenant who told me that she had experienced a run of bad luck and a neighbour assured her she would continue to do so if she didn't get rid of the owl.

This was the explanation I expected. She admitted her luck had been quite good until recently, so I said the unfortunate owl could not have been so bad after all.

I think that it is a blessing in disguise that this superstition exists. We can ill afford to lose any owls! [77]

A 'creature' superficially similar to Owlman was reported from Kent in 1963. A group of young people were walking down a country road near Hythe when they saw a light in the sky. Then they realised that it seemed to be slowly descending towards them. Afterwards they reported that they felt 'cold all over', and ran away but the light seemed to be keeping pace with them eighty yards away and ten feet above the ground.

The light then, apparently, disappeared behind some trees, but the witnesses reported a feeling that they were 'being watched'. The next thing that they knew was that a dark figure with bat's wings and webbed feet, but apparently without a head, was shambling towards them across a field. The young people decided that discretion was the better part of valour and ran away.

Over the next few days there were several reports of strange lights in the sky, flattened crops and huge footprints. [78]

In the Lochs of Argyllshire in Scotland a creature known as the Boobie or Boobrie is said to exist. The descriptions are of a giant grebe-like creature with leathery wings and clawed, webbed feet. Similar creatures have been reported from The Isle of Skye, and (naturally) from the regions surrounding Loch Ness. [79]

If you refer back to the November 1980 sighting of the Owlman by "Mr Martin's Daughter", you will note the similarities between the Mawnan 'creature' and these Harpies of the Highlands. Perhaps we should also note another piece of quasi-lexilinking – the 1980 sighting took place at Grebe Beach. [80] [81] [82] Grebes are amongst the most primitive flying birds, and they are very reptilian in their appearance. There have been many reports from several parts of the world of flying creatures which appear to be reptilian in form and/or structure. Although the rest of this chapter deals with flying mystery 'beings' from around the world, I have deliberately excluded both the phantom pterodactyl sightings from Africa, the United States, Central and South America and elsewhere [83] and the even more notorious big bird sightings from across the United States. [84] These appear to be either 'genuine' unknown animals, and therefore outside the scope of this book, which is predominantly about winged humanoid type creatures, or are paranormal phenomena of an entirely different type.

I hesitated in excluding the 'big birds' sightings from this book, because as will be seen in the next chapter, I am theorising that there is some kind of weird link between all the odd happenings in Cornwall and Devon during 1976 and 1977. There may also be connections with fortean events worldwide. The cattle mutilation episodes in Cornwall and the U.S.A certainly happened simultaneously, and the best known spate of 'big bird' sightings in the southern U.S. also occurred concurrently, but as author I had to make the decision to stop somewhere.

Before moving on to the next section of this chapter, however, we should, perhaps, point out that there is one connection between the Mt. Hawke creature and the last few entities described above. Unlike most accounts of the Mawnan Owlman they all have webbed feet. Whether this is significant or not remains to be seen.

Similar phenomena have been reported from all over the world; there is not room to relate every winged humanoid sighting on my files, but some are of such especial interest that they must be mentioned.

A particularly interesting event took place during the Vietnam war, at Da Nang in July or August 1969. One night at between one and one-thirty a.m. pfc Earl Morrison was on guard duty, chatting with two colleagues, when suddenly all three looked into the sky and saw a glowing figure coming towards them. They described it as moving:

> *"...real slowly. All of a sudden we saw what looked like wings, like a bat's only it was gigantic compared to what a regular bat would be...it looked like a woman. A naked woman. She was black. Her skin was black ... her wings were black, everything was black. But it glowed. It glowed in the night, a kind of greenish cast to it ... she glowed and cast off a radiance".* [85]

The creature was silent, and even its great flapping wings made no noise at all. The three soldiers stared at 'her' in amazement and could see that the wings appeared to be supported by normal human arms.

108

The soldiers said that each arm had:

> "...a hand and fingers and everything, but they had skin from the wings going over them ... it looked like (THEY) didn't have any bones in them, because they were limber just like a bat". [86]

The soldiers stood watching this peculiar apparition for three or four minutes. When the 'creature' was was about ten feet away from the soldiers they:

> "started hearing her wings flap. And it sounded ... like regular wings flapping". [87]

This particular account of the winged woman of Da-Nang was paraphrased from Bob Rickard's article, 'Birdmen of the Apocalypse', in issue 17 of *Fortean Times* from the summer of 1976. Two particular sets of cultural references come to mind, however, when one considers the above sighting. Firstly, the recurrent rumours, which most recently re-surfaced in the closing episodes of the first series of the excellent quasi-fortean T.V. series, *The X-Files* that on at least one occasion during the Vietnam war a U. F.O was shot down and its extra terrestrial occupant captured and/or destroyed. [88] Secondly, and somewhat churlishly, one has to remember that the recreational use of psychotropic and hallucinogenic drugs by U.S servicemen in 'Nam was legendary, and that many authors, most notably Shelton and Mavrides in *The Fabulous Furry Freak Brothers - Idiots Abroad*, [89] have noted, albeit in a jocular fashion the bizarre hallucinations often reported by G.I's in the jungle!

The Jersey Devil is probably the ultimate shape-shifting zooform phenomenon. It is also, together with the Loch Ness creatures, the 'Beasts of Exmoor and Bodmin' and to a certain extent with the Yeti and Bigfoot, one of the only Zooform Phenomena or Cryptids who have actually entered the popular consciousness on a truly trans-cultural level.

There is even a 'bootleg' LP by New Jersey's other great cultural icon, the massively overrated Bruce Springsteen called *The Jersey Devil*, [90] it has been the subject of an episode of at least one popular television programme, and I have no doubt that it has served as the basis of a thriving tourist industry.

Variously described as kangaroo-like, as a flying creature, as an undefined mystery carnivore and even as a Bigfoot' type creature, [91] there is little doubt that something out of the ordinary has happened on occasions in the vast pine forests of New Jersey.

Loren Coleman described it as having been the state's 'official demon' since the 1930's. [92] Long before that, however, stories had been circulating about strange happenings in the area.

The Jersey Devil

It is one of the basic tenets of cryptozoology that the presence of a cryptid can often be suspected from its presence in the local folklore. [93] The native Americans, or Red Indians, were the first people to notice the presence of a strange animal in

New Jersey Pine Barrens and the world's rarest Bruce Springsteen record

the area. According to Indian folklore, the animals first appeared in what is now Bucks County, where many alleged sightings of the Jersey Devil have been made in recent years. The Indians were so in awe of the place that they named the creek near what is now the boundary line with Philadelphia, 'Popuessing', which means 'the place of the dragon'. It is also perhaps significant that Swedish explorers who reached the same place in 1677 noted strange footprints and renamed the site 'Drake Kill' which also refers to the dragon. [94]

In almost complete contradiction of the proceeding evidence, the most commonly told story to explain for the anomalous phenomena in the New Jersey Pine Barrens reads as follows:

> *"In 1735 a Mrs Leeds of Estellville NJ., upon finding that she was pregnant for the thirteenth time and less than exhilarated about it, snorted that if she was going to have another child it might just as well be a devil - and it was.*
>
> *It was born with an animal's head, a bird's body, and cloven hoofs instead of feet. Cursing its mother (it could speak at birth), it promptly flew up the chimney and took up residence in the swamps and pine barrens of southern New Jersey where it has lived ever since.* [95]

Folklore across America, and indeed across the world as a whole, is full of stories like this whereby a person, usually a woman's, rash words rebound upon them, but it is seldom that the results of those rash words are seen flapping and screeching their way through deserted woodlands for the next two hundred

and fifty years. I feel that it is certain that the above story, entertaining though it undoubtedly is, is simply a piece of conveniently invented folk history designed to provide a 'neat' explanation for a puzzling zooform phenomenon that had been seen in the area since times immemorial. [96]

One of the most well known phenomena of this type was the mothman of West Virginia, which was investigated by veteran ufologist John Keel during 1967. This phenomenon which appeared mostly at

Oh, That 'Bird!' It Was Seen Again

Mason County"s famous "Bird" is apparently still with us and has made its appearance in the daytime for the first time..

Tom Ury, a Clarksburg resident, told the Sheriff's office he had an experience with the "bird" this morning at 7:15 a.m. as he traveled north on State Route 62.

Ury, an assistant manager of the Kinney Store in Clarksburg, was enroute back to the northern city after spending Thanksgiving here with relatives when he encountered the "bird".

"I know people think you're crazy when you tell of seeing something like this", Ury said" but I've never had such an experience. I was scared

In giving an account to the Register, the frightened young man said as he went up the road he spotted a flying object that seemed to come from the woods on his right.

After his description of the area it was determined it came from the area back of the Homer Smith residence..

"It came up like a helicopter and then veered over my car. It began going around in circles about two or three telephone poles high and kept staying over my car" he added.

While his first thought was that of fear, Ury noted "I tried to get away and was going 70 miles an hour, but it kept up with me easily."

He stated that it kept soaring over his vehicle until he got to the Kirkland Memorial Gardens and then it made its way to the left and over toward the river.

Appearing still shook up" Ury said "I have a convertible and at first felt it was going to come through the top,, but after it stayed in the air at about the same height. I didn't feel it would attack."

"I've seen big birds, but I've never seen anything like this" he commented.

In giving a description he said it was grayish-brown color, was some six feet in length and had at least an eight to ten foot wing spread.

Ury said he saw a bill, but not unusually big. He did not see red eyes that have previously been given as a characteristic. Some theorized the daylight could have accounted for this.

Mr. Ury is the son of Mrs. Frank Ury and the son-in-law of Mrs. Dorothy Rhodes both of Point Pleasant.

That Mothman: Would You Believe A Sandhill Crane?

By RALPH TURNER

The case of the Mason County monster may have been solved Friday by a West Virginia University professor.

Dr. Robert L. Smith, associate professor of wildlife biology in WVU's division of forestry, told Mason Sheriff George Johnson at Point Pleasant he believes the "thing" which has been frightening people in the Point Pleasant area since Tuesday is a large bird which stopped off while migrating south.

"From all the descriptions I have read about this 'thing' it perfectly matches the sandhill crane," said the professor. "I definitely believe that's what these people are seeing."

Since Tuesday more than 10 people have spotted what they described as a "birdman" or "mothman" in the area of the McClintick Wildlife Station.

They described it as a huge gray-winged creature with large red eyes.

Dr. Smith said the sandhill crane stands an average of five feet and has gray plumage. A feature of its appearance is a bright red flesh area around each eye. It has an average wing spread of about seven feet.

"Somebody who has never seen anything like it before could easily get the impression it is a flying man," he said. "Car lights would cause the bare skin to reflect as big red circles around the eyes."

While such birds are rare to this area, Dr. Smith said this is migration time and it would not be too difficult for one or more of the birds to stop off at the wildlife refuge. There are no official sightings of such birds in West Virginia, although there have been unconfirmed reports in the past, he added.

The birds are rarely seen east of the Mississippi now except in Florida. Distribution mainly is in Canada and the population is increasing in the Midwest. They winter in Southern California, in Mexico and along the Gulf Coast.

According to one book, the sandhill crane is a "fit successor" to the great whooping crane which is almost extinct. The book states that the height of the male when it stands erect is nearly that of a man of average stature, while the bird's great wings carry its compact and muscular body with perfect ease at a high speed.

Dr. Smith said that while the birds are powerful fliers they cannot match the 100 mph speed one couple reported the "thing" attained when pursuing their car.

Dr. Smith warned that while the sandhill crane is harmless if left alone, that if cornered it may become a formidable antagonist. Its dagger-like bill is a dangerous weapon which the crane does not hesitate to use when at bay and fighting for its life. Many a hunter's dog has been badly injured, he said.

Some of those who reported seeing the "monster" remembered best the eerie sound it made. The description of the sandhill crane also fits there.

"The cry of the sandhill crane is a veritable voice of nature, untamed and unterrified," says one book on birds. "Its uncanny quality is like that of the loon, but is more pronounced because of the much greater volume of the crane's voice. Its resonance is remarkable and its carrying power is increased by a distinct tremolo effect. Often for several minutes after the birds have vanished the unearthly sound drifts back to the listener, like a taunting trumpet from the underworld."

Meanwhile, for the fourth night in a row, an area of the wildlife station again was clogged Friday night with the curious searching for the "thing."

The latest reported sighting came Friday morning from two Point Pleasant volunteer firemen, Captain Paul Yoder and Benjamin Enochs.

"As we were going into the picnic area in the TNT area, Paul and I saw this white shadow go across the car," Mr. Enochs reported.

"This was about 1:30 a.m. Paul stopped the car and I went into the field, but couldn't see anything. I'd say this definitely was a large bird of some kind."

Meanwhile, authorities issued a warning to "monster hunters."

If the "thing" is a migratory crane they had better not shoot it. Migratory birds of all kinds are protected by federal and state wildlife laws.

Sheriff Johnson said he would arrest anybody caught with a loaded gun in the area after dark.

There were earlier reports of armed people in the area.

Sheriff Johnson also warned that the scores of persons searching the abandoned powerhouse in the TNT area after dark risk possible serious injury.

The Herald Dispatch, 19th November 1966

Mason Bird-Monster Presumed Gone Now

By RALPH TURNER

POINT PLEASANT — Authorities here have concluded that the so-called Mason County monster was a large bird of some kind and either has been or soon will be frightened out of the McClintic Wildlife Station area by hunters.

It was a week ago today that the first sighting was reported of a large red-eyed winged creature in the McClintic area. Since then there have been about 10 or more similar reports.

The latest report was by four teen-aged youths who said they saw a large bird with red eyes fly away from their car at a very high rate of speed. This was 3 a.m. Sunday.

Monday was the first day of open deer hunting season in the McClintic reserve and Chief Deputy Millard Halstead of the Mason County sheriff's office said the influx of hunters undoubtedly would bring any large bird out in the daylight. All "monster" sightings have been at night.

Duane Pursley, wildlife biologist and manager at McClintic, believes small game hunters, which have numbered about 200 a day over McClintic's 2,450 acres, would have flushed any such bird out earlier.

He said he didn't think a large bird, if it did exist, would stay in the area more than a day with all the commotion and hundreds of people searching at night for it.

A West Virginia University wildlife biologist suggested last week that the "thing" is a rare Sandhill Crane.

Mr. Pursley suggested that maybe the "thing", crane, or whatever the people reported seeing, wasn't as large as they thought it was during their excitement.

"We have a lot of Canadian geese stop over here during migration periods, but nothing the size of what these people report," said Mr. Pursley.

He said the hundreds of "thing hunters" had caused a littering and vandalism problem for the wildlife station. He said the area has been littered with cups, cans, bottles and paper and some signs have been damaged.

"There was so much pressure — some people came in here with guns after dark — that we were ready to close off the station area tonight (Monday), but it's eased up and that doesn't appear to be necessary."

Just what was seen in the dark of the night may never be firmly established. The Mason County monster may become a legend. Maybe a new tourist attraction has been born.

The Herald Dispatch, 22nd November 1966

Dorset Evening ECHO

Telephone WEYMOUTH 4804   PRICE 4d.

SATURDAY, DECEMBER 16, 1967.   No. 14,476

Many die as 75 vehicles plunge into river

BRIDGE COLLAPSE HORROR

From Reuter reporter: Point Pleasant, West Virginia, Saturday.

SCORES of homegoing travellers and Christmas shoppers plunged to death in the ice-cold Ohio River in ten seconds of horror as the Silver Bridge at Point Pleasant caved in under peak-hour traffic last night.

Only a handful of survivors were rescued from the swirling 70ft. deep waters after the suspension bridge crumpled an hour before darkness fell.

Divers and rescue boats working under searchlights recovered 12 bodies and 22 injured survivors from the twisted steel and concrete wreckage of the bridge, and the estimated 75 cars and lorries which had been jammed on it.

Eye witnesses said it was only seconds from the first sharp crack of the bridge snapping until, as Ohio State highway patrolman David Proth put it: "The whole thing went to the river bank, below.

There just wasn't any more bridge at all," Patrolman Proth added. Only the two concrete toppers, piers and the road apron remain.

GROPING

Another eyewitness, Mrs. Amy Lander, said, "It sounded like a paper bag. It was the most horrible thing I ever saw. There was a trailer truck at the point where it broke."

Today a giant floating crane groped in the tangled debris on the muddy bottom of the river for more bodies, but the authorities said it would be days before the exact toll was known.

Many of the cars were reported to be carrying four or five home-going office workers.

The 46-year-old, 1,500ft. long bridge linked Kanauga, Ohio, with Point Pleasant. It had two...

A new bridge across the Ohio, six miles to the north, due to be opened on Monday, would have eased the heavy traffic normally carried by the Silver Bridge, which weighs...

(Continued in Back Page)

Wreckage of the Silver Bridge, linking Point Pleasant, West Virginia, and Kanauga, Ohio, which collapsed last night. In the foreground, a tangle of cars and trucks. In the background, one of the bridge supports. —Associated Press wire photo.

40 die as buses crash

FORTY people were killed and 42 injured in a collision between two buses, according to reports reaching Stockholm, Finland, today.

The accident was said to have occurred near Rovrania, 60 miles east of Stockholm. —Associated Press.

Five houses on fire: Only one injured

AN early morning blaze in Queenstreet, Failsworth, near Manchester, today, destroyed one house, severely damaged two more homes and caused slight damage by fog others in the row of property affected by the fire.

But only nine persons—a mum herabove at the bridge where the fire started—was injured and he managed with slight burns.

Bridge horror
(Continued from Front Page)

...have been put into semi-retirement.

Local citizens said the Silver Bridge was condemned three years ago. But a West Virginia Highway Authority spokesman said it underwent routine inspection in 1965.

CLINGING

Hours after the bridge collapsed, the West Virginia and Ohio Governors, Mr. Hulett Smith and Mr. James Rhodes, flew to the stricken area and then opened the new bridge, which links Williamsburg, West Virginia, and Marietta, Ohio.

The river, one of America's main inland arteries, was closed by the Coast Guard. It normally carries a heavy volume of barge traffic, mostly moving Pennsylvania coal and chemicals and oil from Ohio plants to the south.

The White House was kept closely informed of developments and President Johnson promised all help to the State authorities.

Some of the injured survivors were found clinging to parts of debris. Dazed, they were still above water, but many witnesses could only stand by and listen helplessly to the screams of victims as they were swept away and drowned.

One of those who escaped was schoolteacher John Mays. He said he would have been on bridge if he had not stopped for petrol. He was just turning on to it when it collapsed.

"The whole bridge went down," he said. "I saw one trailer-truck floating in the river but the bridge buried everything under it."

MISSING

A Highway Patrol spokesman said the current was very swift.

"It might be days before we know for sure how many cars fell in," he added. "It might be weeks before we get in all the missing reports."

Lieutenant Jay Powers, of West Virginia police, said: "There was bumper-to-bumper traffic in both directions when the bridge caved in.

"There is no accurate estimate of how many vehicles were on the bridge at the time, but it is known there were three tractor-trailers among them."

One eye-witness said he saw a log passing under the bridge when it went down, but he did not know what happened to the vessel.

Front Page News: *The Dorset Evening Echo 16th December 1976, covers the awful tragedy that befell Point Pleasant later that year. The Silver Bridge, which connected Point Pleasant to neighbouring Kanauga, Ohio, suddenly collapsed into the Ohio River, killing 46 people trapped in rush-hour traffic. Some claimed that the catastrophe was triggered by a sonic boom from Mothman's wings. Others believed that Mothman had been sent to warn the people of Point Pleasant, although his message was obviously lost in translation. Whatever the connection may have been, Mothman disappeared after the bridge fell down.*

Above: *Part of the Head of Sinbad panel in the San Rafael Swell (Utah), This two thousand year old cave painting depicts two humoid figures, one with the head of an owl and the other a moth?*

Below Left: *In 2002, Point Pleasant held its first Mothman Festival. In 2003, Gunn Park was renamed Mothman Park, and a 12-foot-tall stainless steel sculpture created by sculpturor and artist Bob Roach of the Mothman was unveiled to commemorate the strange events that happened at Point Pleasant in 1966.*

night was very closely linked to UFO phenomena as well as other strange happenings at the time. Keel's account of the happenings at that time is one of the most important ever written in this field, and I urge all readers of this book to obtain a copy of Keel's writings on the subject and read it in conjunction with this present volume. [97] At the time of writing, the most recent occurrence took place in Washington State in the Pacific Northwest of the USA in April 1994. [98] The Pacific North-West is one of the more prolific window areas for fortean zoological phenomena, and is famed for its Bigfoot sightings and for mysterious falls of poisonous jelly. [99] This latest outbreak started when 18 year old Brian Canfield was driving home to the isolated settlement of Camp One from the nearby town of Buckley at 9.30 in the evening. The engine of his pickup truck died and the dashboard lights fell dark and the vehicle stopped suddenly. His headlights were still functioning and they lit up the shape of a nine foot figure descending from the sky to the road in front of him. It had blue tinted fur, yellowish eyes, the feet of a bird, tufted ears and sharp straight teeth. Its wings were folded and attached to its back and broad shoulders.

> "It was standing there staring at me like it was resting, like it didn't know what to think", said Brian. "I was scared, it raised the hair on me. I didn't feel threatened. I just felt out of place". [100]

The newspaper report goes on to describe Brian in terms which make him seem almost saintly by comparison to the usual media representation of young people from that part of America, [101] and stressed that not only had he never had any paranormal experiences before, but he didn't take drugs, drink, play 'Dungeons and Dragons' or listen to heavy metal music. Although it doesn't sound like he would be much fun at a party his description of the apparition was clear and succinct:

> "its eyes were yellow and shaped like a piece of pie with pupils like a half moon. The mouth was pretty big. White teeth. No fangs. The teeth were like a wolf'. [102]

The general consensus of opinion both amongst his family and his friends and of the reporter from the *Tacoma News Tribune* who carried the story on the 24th April 1994, is that young Brian saw something but no-one is prepared to say quite what. They have given the creature the stomach churningly twee name of 'Batsquatch', but no-one, as far as I can make out, has equated this latest apparition with the well attested 'winged things' of previous years. The last word, I think should go to Brian himself:

> "I'm really not into this stuff. It boggles my mind really hard core. I really can't explain it. It's weird, definitely weird. I don't like it. Usually this stuff happens to someone else". [103]

We at the Centre for Fortean Zoology await further developments in the skies above Washington and Oregon with great interest.

I have already extracted the Hampshire and Vietnam bird-person sightings from Bob Rickard's 1976 article, but before we leave worldwide sightings of winged humanoids, and return to Cornwall, I would like to extrapolate one, final, and rather chilling after-thought:

> "The sixteenth of April 1976 was the first day of the year 1338 in the Burmese Calendar - and according to a note in the Bangkok Post (17.4.76), astrologers have pointed out that this is the appointed time in which the king of celestial beings will come down to earth with a sickle in one band and a scimitar in the other to fight the 'galon', a gigantic bird with supernatural powers. As if on cue, the 'Owlman' of Mawnan was first seen on the seventeenth of April". [104]

Gyllyngvase Beach, Falmouth

CHAPTER FIVE: IMPLICATION

*"I don't think I've ever seen anyone pick up a box of matches without shaking it.
Curious. It takes more time to shake the box than it would to open it straight away
but it's less effort. It's pleasant to her a lot of matches rattling in the box, one has
a feeling of plenty. No-one wants to open a matchbox and find it empty…"*

Russell Hoban *'Turtle Diary' (1975)*

The year of 1976 was a particularly weird in southern Cornwall. Tony Shiels wrote to me in March 1996: *"About 1976 there was a lot of UFO activity. Lights in the sky, weird noises, smells, explosions, etc."* [1]

He had described the high strangeness of the year before, both at the time, in *Fortean Times*, [2] And later in other publications. [3] It wasn't, however, until we managed to access the newspapers in the archives at Truro and Redruth libraries that we discovered quite how weird a year it had actually been. [4]

Tony had always described the lights in the sky, [5] the sulphurous smells, [6] the weird 'crackling' sounds like static electricity in the trees, [7] but he hadn't managed to encapsulate more than a fraction of the zeitgeist of what was, both by all the accounts that we have managed to unearth, and from my own memories, a very strange year indeed.

There is something particularly 'odd' about reading a year's worth of newspapers, especially when they are preserved on microfilm and you are winding them along on a continuous strip of celluloid. One becomes immersed in the year one is studying, and one soon starts to discern patterns in human behaviour and the sociology of the time which have little or nothing to do with what you are actually researching. I became engrossed in stories about unruly youth clubs, car crashes and petty crimes, and I often became sidetracked. [8] Slowly, however, a pattern began to emerge.

As my conception of the year became stranger and stranger I decided that, in the interests of scientific accuracy, I should check the papers both before and after the year that I was studying. I found, not altogether to my surprise, that the weirdness had apparently started in the closing months of 1975, and continued on to about February or March of 1977. Before and after those dates, Falmouth. Penryn, and the surrounding villages were apparently sleepy, quiet places in which nothing much happened. I am sure that this is far from true, but it is undeniable that something 'not quite right' was in the air during

117

the fifteen months under review, and being the committed fortean that I am, I am loth to believe that all these occurrences are not in some way all connected.

"There's no such bloody thing as a coincidence,' Doc told me once, and I am sure that he is right. In this chapter I have attempted to give some sort of a picture of the strange events of the year, as gleaned from newspaper reports, interviews, and conversations with some of the main people involved.

Unfortunately, what I, before starting this book, had considered to be a potential goldmine of information, the Shiels archive itself, was no longer available - to me or to anyone else. Tony wrote to me in early 1996:

> *Before moving here - to Ireland in 1993, I ditched and/or burnt a vast amount of paper junk including lots of old notebooks, letters, press clippings and suchlike, much of the stuff related to monstrous happenings in the seventies. A pity perhaps, from a researcher's point of view but what's done is done - and what the hell! I'm far more interested in my painting/ sculpture activities than in all that seventies sorcery, and my side of the story was told in 'Monstrum' anyway...*[9]

Unfortunately for many Shiels watchers, who are not either in the right place at the right time, or who have not got my ferret-like ability to get hold of whatever I want (whether I am supposed to or not), most of 'Doc's' books are not available to the casual buyer. They are works on stage magic, [10] which because of the secretive nature of the trade, are not widely available outside the profession. One notable exception is *Monstrum* [11] a wonderful book which describes, in Tony's own words, the high strangeness of those particular summers.

In 'Monstrum', Tony describes the Falmouth area of Cornwall during the spring and summer of 1976:

"There was witchcraft in the air." [12]

In the Morgawr leaflet, Anthony Mawnan-Peller wrote:

> *"In October 1975, a group of three UFOs was seen in the sky above Falmouth Docks. Then, in March 1976, a pair of flying saucers appeared over Perranwell.*
>
> *In the spring of 1976, a group of 'real live Cornish piskies' was photographed by one of the monster-raising witches."* [13]

He continued:

> *"Flying saucers have, of course, been seen by many hundreds of people over the years: and Cornwall has had its fair share.*
>
> *There would be nothing particularly unusual (by normal saucer-spotting standards) about the Falmouth sightings if they had not coincided with the other odd sightings.*
>
> *'Little People' have been seen from time to time, coming out of flying saucers. Maybe that is how the piskies first arrived in the area!"* [14]

118

Three unidentified 'fireballs' were seen in the sky over St Mawes and Flushing, by a Falmouth house-wife on the first of July. The lady, who asked to remain anonymous, said:

> *"I had come downstairs for a cigarette and looked out of the window when I saw three fire-ball-like objects. One was bigger than the other two, and they were going eastward, reflecting in the water. I was high up and saw them when they passed over St. Mawes.*
>
> *They were definitely real - a fantastic sight. One of the three lost its fire-ball outline but remained in sight with the others.*
>
> *I feel this experience must be personal to me, if no-one else saw them. Keeping my mind completely open, it may be some intelligence contacting me as an individual."* [15]

There was another UFO sighting, this time of a single object over Redruth a week or so later. The *West Briton,* on the 15th July reported:

> *"For about four minutes on Friday, three adults and about ninety children at Treleigh CP School, Redruth, watched a spherical object cross high in the mid-day sky ... and what exactly it was is a mystery to them.*
>
> *Most of them - they watched from the school yard - agreed that it resembled two dinner plates face to face.*
>
> *'It was white and spinning', said Miss Deborah Foster, a teacher. 'It appeared to be very high up and came from the Truro direction. We lost sight of it over Carn Brea. It was saucer shaped and seemed to have an aura or halo'.*
>
> *Another teacher, Mr Sam Hawkins, said that he clearly saw silver and yellow flashes at 90 degrees to the object's direction.*
>
> *He said, 'It was travelling very slowly. It went through high cloud, yet we could still see it,' he added.*
>
> *Mrs. Sylvia Harris, the school secretary, agreed it was round and whitish. She also saw flashes from it. They were like lightning and were spasmodic', she said. 'I have never seen anything like it before'.*
>
> *Miss Foster added, 'It was a little frightening. I do not like anything I cannot explain'.*
>
> *Pupils said that there was no sound and that the sphere changed to a green hue when it went behind high clouds.*
>
> *They agreed that it was spinning and they saw flashes from it. They were certain there were no markings."* [16]

The Headmaster, who was actually interested in such things, was unfortunate enough to miss the incident altogether, but in an interview with the same newspaper added that unidentified flying objects had been seen in the vicinity of the school a few years before. [17]

UFO sighting sets school a mystery...

FOR about five minutes on Friday, three adults and at least 90 children at Treleigh CP School, Redruth, watched a spherical object cross high in the midday sky... and what exactly it was is a complete mystery to them.

Most of them—they watched from the school yard—agreed that it resembled two dinner plates face to face.

"It was white and spinning," said Miss Deborah Foster, a teacher. "It appeared to be very high up, and came from the Truro direction. We lost sight of it over Carn Brea. It was saucer-shaped and seemed to have an aura or halo."

Another teacher, Mr. Sam Hawkins, said he clearly saw silver and yellow flashes at 90 degrees to the object's direction. He said it was travelling very slowly. "It went through high cloud, yet we could still see it," he added.

Mrs. Sylvia Harris, school secretary, agreed it was round and whitish. She also saw flashes from it. "They were like lightning and were spasmodic," she said. "I have never seen anything like it before."

Miss Foster added: "It was a little frightening. I do not like anything I cannot explain."

Pupils said there was no sound, and the sphere changed to a green hue when it went behind high clouds.

They agreed it was spinning and say they saw flashes from it. They were certain it bore no markings.

Mr. Sidney Thorne, headmaster—who is interested in unidentified flying objects—missed the sighting. He said it could not have been a weather balloon, as the object's journey included a distinct manoeuvre.

He added that unexplained objects had been sighted at the school and by parents at North country, Redruth, in March and November 1973.

Falmouth Packet 15th July 1976

As 1976 progressed it just got weirder for the residents of Falmouth Bay....

Close encounters with 'red mushroom'

A CLEAR sighting of a UFO which looked "like a giant red mushroom" was reported this week by Mr. Bill Wroath, a lecturer at Falmouth School of Art.

A woman at Truro gave the same description to an object she saw hanging in the night sky above the city. Both these sightings were on Sunday.

Other red objects in the sky were reported on Monday night by people at Camborne and Carnon Downs.

Mr. Wroath saw his UFO at St. Ewe. He said: "I would estimate that it was about 100 feet across and it stood about the same distance above the ground.

The stem of the mushroom was like a pillar of light, or a vast metal column, suspended from the base of the cap and surrounded by flames such as might have been produced by burning gas.

"Around the dome wisps of cloud formed continuously and disappeared almost immediately in a continuing cycle," he said.

"Where the shaft of light reached the ground it was concealed by a white mist like a smoke ring. The whole area beneath it was bathed in an eerie white glow."

Mr. Wroath said the only sound was of a quiet high pitched "ringing".

The UFO stood about half a mile from him. It was stationary for about 30 seconds and then sped off towards St. Austell Bay at "an astounding rate".

Mrs. Lynn Francis, of Bassett street, Camborne, described an object she saw at 10 pm on Monday as "saucer-shaped and moving across the sky quite slowly."

A spokesman at RAF St. Mawgan said they had calls on Sunday night from people who reported seeing orange lights in the sky above St. Austell and Falmouth.

Aircraft were taking off and landing that night, in the search for the missing German barge carrier Munchen, the spokesman added.

Falmouth Packet 1976

Below: *However, as this 1900's postcard of a circus elephant in Falmouth Bay during the 1900s shows, Morgawr and the Owlman were far from being the first strange beasties to be spotted there.*

I know very little about UFO's. It is not a subject that interests me, except when, as in this case they seem to have a direct bearing on other events which are of greater importance in my eyes. This sighting, however, would seem to be an important one, if only because of the sheer number of witnesses available. At this distance in time it is impossible to find out whether the witnesses cited were in collusion with each other, but the sightings they describe are all remarkably similar.

There was very nearly another UFO report at that time, but the perpetrator, our old friend 'Doc', didn't actually complete his hoax in time. [18]

He had planned to produce a faked photograph of UFO's flying in the sky behind a pattern of five telegraph poles with connecting cables, so that when one looked close enough, they were seen to be musical notation, depicting the four note phrase familiar to anyone who has ever seen Spielberg's *Close Encounters of the Third Kind*. [19] Like so many good ideas, and potentially hilarious jokes, however, nothing came of it!

There were other phenomena that year that were certainly not hoaxes, although it is arguable whether they had anything to do with the aforementioned UFO reports.

A series of mysterious bangs were heard in the sky. They became a regular occurrence across southern Cornwall over the final few months of 1976 and although it was claimed that they were sonic booms from the regular flights by Concorde, nothing was ever proved to anyone's satisfaction.

The earliest record we managed to find of this singular phenomenon was in the *West Briton* of October 21st 1976, which reported that:

> *"Mullion Parish Councillors agreed on Tuesday to join other Parish Councils on The Lizard peninsula in trying to find the source of mysterious sonic booms which have shaken several villages."* [20]

The councillors decided to write to the Department of the Environment and to the local M.P. for St. Ives. The Chairman, Roy Hendy, spoke out in the best traditions of both paranoid conspiracy theorising and small town journalism and insisted that:

> *"The time has come for everyone to be told what is causing the booms, whether or not it is a Government project."* [21]

Paranoia was rife. There had already been suggestions that the noises had been caused 'by Concorde, but this had been denied." [23]

Twenty years later, it is unclear who had made the initial denial.

About three weeks later the story broke nationally. People all along the south coast began reporting noises which some people in Somerset and Devonshire described as 'small underground explosions'. [24]

Cornwall seemed to bear the brunt of them, however, and on Thursday November 18th, *The West Briton* reported:

> *"The story boomeranged back into Cornwall with first hand reports from half a dozen 'West Briton' readers who had heard the baffling boom - not at The Lizard, but in such*

places as Troon, Frogpool, Marazion, Three Mile Stone, Truro and Fraddon.

Although some point the finger increasingly at the French Concorde, Air France were still not shouldering all the blame, admitting at most the possibility that some of the bangs could have been theirs.

In London. a Department of Trade official said that it certainly seemed that some of the booms coincided with the movement of Air France planes. But several callers to The West Briton complained of a boom on Sunday evening – and the Washington-Paris flight runs only on Monday, Thursday and Saturday."

Air France denied the allegations, claiming not only did their pilots decelerate when approaching mainland Britain, and were therefore travelling at speeds beneath the sound barrier, but also that they had attempted to correlate the reported booms with their flight activity and found that at least 60% of them could not have been made by their aircraft. [26]

Several private individuals started investigations of their own. One man who lived at Frogpool near Truro carried out an experiment one Sunday evening:

"When everything was switched off and quiet in the house, and there was no traffic noise, he went upstairs into a bedroom - and at exactly 9.5 (sic), came a rumble which shook the windows.

He neither saw nor heard any aircraft before, or shortly after the sound - and he could not believe that it was caused by an aircraft." [27]

The accounts of mysterious booms continued. Police investigated quarries and military installations, to see if they could uncover any evidence of unauthorised explosions. More claims were made about Concorde, and a source on the Scilly Isles claimed that some, at least of the unaccounted - for sounds were down to unauthorised flight patterns by Concorde aircraft belonging to Air France. [28]

On the 9th December, President-elect Carter, of the United States, became involved in the saga, when The *West Bri*ton claimed, under the headline:

"ALL QUIET ON BOOMS BECAUSE OF CARTER". [29]

that a local MP had said that:

"The government are playing things deliberately 'softly softly' over the mystery nine o'clock booms (...) because of the implications if Concorde is proved to be the culprit." [30]

He also claimed that Jimmy Carter was "rather anti Concorde". [31]

Several other MPs made similar claims and gained valuable column inches and career exposure by giving the newspapers their own particular slant on the mystery. [32] Air France denied the claims, [33] and the British Government said nothing at all until the week before Christmas when the aerospace minister admitted that some of the booms did indeed coincide with flights by Concorde. He also claimed that the flight procedures which had caused these booms had been changed, and that there should not be any further trouble. [34] There wasn't.

122

What was never explained, however, were the well-reported booms which took place on nights when Concorde was NOT overhead. It would perhaps be both over-paranoid and simplistic to attempt to correlate them with some of the other phenomena reported in this chapter - the UFO's for example, and to wonder whether the Government of the time was telling the whole truth?

Sonic booms have been associated with UFO reports in the past and, no doubt, will be associated with them in the future. Another phenomenon often associated with UFO reports are mysterious disappearances of domestic livestock.

Sometimes, such disappearances prove. on investigation, to have a prosaic explanation. Sometimes, they are never explained satisfactorily.

The *West Briton* for the 26th November 1976 carried the following story:

> *"The disappearance of a bullock from a field in the Nance Valley near Lelant, brings the number of cattle which have disappeared from the area over the last twelve months to five."* [35]

The Penryn farmer who had lost another animal earlier in the year complained that the police had been unable to do anything. The police, however claimed that the animals had both been registered as 'lost' rather than as 'stolen'. The same newspaper item reported that over the summer, cattle from herds belonging to several different farmers had become mysteriously 'mixed up', and had somehow been transported from their own fields to other locations in the area. After their owners had eventually sorted out whose cattle were whose, they found that two were in fact missing.

No-one, it seems, had seen the animals being driven from their own fields to the ones in which they were found. If it had been done by a human agency, it was seemingly done without a motive. If not, then it is truly deserving of inclusion within the pages of this book.

A similar story was reported by *'The Falmouth Packet'* in July when an 18 month old Fresian heifer was found in a slurry pit. The pit had been covered with railway sleepers to prevent such an accident happening, and when the animal was found the timber was still in place. The seventy five year old farmer was convinced that it had been pushed in by a malicious attacker or attackers, and the local police tended to agree with him. The attacker was never caught, and like the events recounted in the previous paragraphs the incident seems both motiveless, and an ultimately fruitless exercise. [36]

Cats were also disappearing from Redruth, Falmouth and Penryn over the summer. According to a representative from the Cat's Protection League, abnormally large numbers of cats were missing from their homes. The spokesman for the charity claimed that they were being sold to vivisectionists. but that is a common story used to explain such spates of missing creatures, and is, I feel, unlikely to be true. [37]

Cats are amongst the easiest creatures in the world to breed. There is never any shortage of kittens free to a good home, and were vivisectionists, (or cat furriers), to want a supply of such animals it would be extremely easy to arrange a constant supply without the need of breaking the law. It is also unlikely that the market forces would demand a particularly large number of such animals, and it is almost certain that any hospital, research laboratory, or chemical firm worth its salt would buy their experimental animals from reputable suppliers rather than from the sort of shady character who would attempt to make a living from selling stolen pears.

Spates of missing cats almost certainly have a different explanation. but they are of great interest to the fortean. It is a well known fact that the number of missing cats reported rises according to the number of sightings of alien big cats in the vicinity. Zoologists who believe in such things will claim that this is because Pumas. the animals most likely to be responsible for the vast majority of 'genuine' (whatever that means) ABC sightings, are partial to the taste of the flesh of their smaller, domesticated cousins. [38] Joan Amos, a friend of mine and a UFO expert from Tavistock, has a richer and far more intriguing theory to account for these disappearances, but that is. as they say, another story.

When Falmouth cats were not being abducted by person or persons unknown during the summer of 1976, they were, apparently terrorising a middle-aged lady who lived at Swanpool.

Under the headline *"Woman claims cats 'imprison me in my own home'"*, The *Falmouth Packet* related an extraordinary story of how her home was invaded by wild cats who destroyed her belongings and wrecked her furniture:

> *"She doesn't' t dare leave windows or doors open, has to continually clear up refuse they drag out of her dustbin, and says she is worried by the possible threat of disease."* [40]

Her property was broken, her life was being made a misery, and she was appealing for help. A local animal charity agreed that it was a very real problem.

Birds also behaved in a manifestly peculiar manner that year.

In the summer of 1976, *Fortean Times* printed an excerpt from a letter from Tony Shiels to editor Bob Rickard:

> *"Birds have been acting strangely in a Hitchcockian manner down here, recently. Is it a coincidence that both Daphne du Maurier (who wrote 'The Birds') and Frank Baker (who wrote 'Our Feathered Friends, a nice horror story on which 'The Birds' was based), live in Cornwall...? A fellow called Paul Francis, a fisherman, was telling me how oddly the gulls were behaving these days, attacking fishing boats, stealing bait from mackerel lines. It all fits in of course!* [41] [42]

The same issue reported that:

> *"The Daily Telegraph and Daily Mail of the 14th June 1976 announced that the dream home of Mrs Margot Swatton, of Paul Hill, Newlyn was under attack from a kamikaze rook division. For a week the birds had been dive-bombing the house from trees and nearby power-lines, hurling themselves against the windows, and then dazed and bleeding flying back to their posts to begin again."* [43]

Cornish newspaper reports claimed that Mrs Swatton and her daughters had never been personally attacked by the birds, even when they had beaten them off with sticks. They had tried putting up large cardboard cut-outs, painted black, to frighten the birds away, but to no avail. The attacks only stopped when a friend of Mrs Swatton's shot a bird, and hung the corpse up 'pour encourager les autres'.

Mrs Swatton gave further details to The *West Briton*, which made the events seem even more nightmarish!

Woman claims cats 'imprison me in my own home'

A HORDE of rampaging cats have virtually imprisoned a Swanpool woman in her own home, she claimed this week.

She daren't leave windows or doors open, has to continually clear up refuse they drag out of her dustbin and says she is worried by the possible threat of disease.

Fifty-five-year-old Elizabeth Proctor has lived by herself at 19, Tremorvah, Swanpool, for the past 12 months and complains she's had to put up with the problem ever since she moved in.

Now she wants action to control the animals—before they do any real damage.

"I don't dislike cats as a rule but these animals are nothing more than wild," she says. "They invade dustbins, climb in through any open window and recently one even broke a valuable piece of china of mine.

"The mess they leave is appalling. People are continually aware of the dangers of rabies but what about these animals, what kind of harm could they do? I would honestly rather have rats.

"What kind of life is it when you have to make sure all doors and windows are continually locked for fear they might get in the house?

"Somebody has got to do something about it. The RSPCA must take some kind of action to bully the Post Office into enforcing licences for these animals. They really must be controlled."

'FRIGHTENED'

But Mrs. Kay Beesley, secretary of the West Cornwall branch of the Cats Protection League, warns: "The neighbours must be visited first to establish if they are pets. Only if they are genuinely wild can any action be taken to get rid of them.

"In 25 years with the Cats Protection League I've always known about this problem. It happens all over the country and never seems to improve. And now with the rabies scare on people are really beginning to get frightened."

Falmouth Packet 27th August 1976

Suicide birds: Why did they attack?

A WOMAN complained this week over the lack of advice and help she received when her house was under attack from birds.

Mrs. Margo Swatton, whose house at Newlyn was besieged day and night by birds "as big as chickens", said she contacted everyone she could think of, but no-one could tell her how to stop the attacks.

"Now that it's all over," she said, "people are coming up with suggestions. I would have liked some at the time."

During the attacks, reminiscent of the Hitchcock film, "The Birds," windows on the north side of the house, Panorama, Paul Hill, were battered by a "suicide squad" of birds.

It ended after nearly a week when one of the birds was shot by a friend and hung over a balcony.

They kept coming

German-born Mrs. Swatton was alone with her two young daughters—her husband was in Libya.

"The birds would dive straight into the glass, knocking themselves out and falling on to the balcony," she said. "Even though the blood was running out of them, they would keep coming. There was blood all over the windows."

Mrs Swatton said the birds did not attack her or her daughters, even when she tried to beat them off with a stick.

"People have suggested they were attacking their reflections in the glass, but could the birds have seen anything at night?"

"It also has been suggested the cause is in the birds' flight-line. But the house was here last year as well and they never came then."

All black

The birds, she added, were "all black and as big as chickens: definitely not jackdaws, but rooks or crows, I think".

The shot bird was identified as a crow.

"It was a most harrowing experience," Mrs. Swatton went on. "We hardly slept all week and there were times when we thought the birds would get into the house.

"I am still having nightmares about the cries they made—the screaming all night. It was horrible."

Ornithologist Mr. Bernard King, who lives at Newlyn, commented: "I have never heard of anything like this. I feel the answer could have been reflection. Birds do attack their own reflection, especially during the breeding season, because they think it's opposition."

MASSED BIRDS WIN THE BATTLE OF BEACH-ROAD

NEWQUAY, which has suffered from seagulls for years, has a new bird problem. Thousands of starlings have massed in trees in the Beach-road area and efforts to move them have failed.

Now people living in the road have sent a protest petition to Restormel. The council's environmental health committee were told on Monday that there was no explanation why the starlings had massed in that area.

The chief environmental health officer, Mr. Cliff Quantrell, said they had tried everything they could think of to move them on. The only solution would be to cut down the trees—and the residents would not like that.

Members suggested shooting (not allowed in a town) and poisoning, but in the end agreed to take no action except to ensure that the area was cleaned regularly.

It was the same story with seagulls.

Mr. Quantrell said slaughter was not the answer, but owners or occupiers of land on which gulls were nesting could destroy nests or take the eggs, thereby discouraging the gulls.

Umbrella guard

Mr. M J Roberts said the problem at Mevagissey was becoming acute. He knew of a woman who carried an umbrella when she did her gardening because gulls attacked her. They were becoming a real hazard. He could not hear his television when the window was open in the summer.

Mr. Peter Cocks said there were an awful lot of seagulls and if they were pulled the space left would soon be filled by gulls from outside the town. The real answer was to deprive them of food. They had to persuade people not to feed them.

Mr. Ralph Burnett said a woman at Fowey bought 12 loaves every day and sent her maid to feed the gulls.

But no-one was prepared to second Mr. Roberts's proposal that the environmental health officer should look at the problem again.

Left: *Falmouth Packet, 17th June 1976*

Right: *Falmouth Packet, 23rd September 1976*

Below: *A sign on Falmouth quay warning the general public about aggressive seagulls*

Seagulls expecting to be fed by hand can become aggressive and possibly dangerous to young children

IN THE INTEREST OF SAFETY,
PLEASE DO NOT FEED THE SEAGULLS
& they will return to their natural food supply

Carrick

"The birds would dive straight into the glass, knocking themselves out and falling on to the balcony. Even though the blood was running out of them they would keep coming. There was blood all over the windows." [44]

The bird which was shot was identified as a crow, but Mrs Swatton claimed that some of the birds which had attacked her house were "as big as chickens". [45]

A local ornithologist who was called upon to comment on the incidents was baffled, and the affair was never satisfactorily explained. The last word should however go to Mrs Swatton who said:

"I am still having nightmares about the cries they made - the screaming all night. It was horrible." [46]

Crows are diurnal creatures and we have not been able to discover any other reports of their nocturnal 'screaming'.

In the first year of the Owlman, Mrs Swatton was not the only victim of unusual avian behaviour. In September The *West Briton* reported that:

"Newquay. which has suffered from seagulls in recent years has a new bird problem Thousands of starlings have massed in trees on the Beach Road and efforts to move them have failed." [47]

The starlings were causing a serious health problem because of their droppings and the noise that they made. The seagulls of Newquay had also taken to attacking people, and were causing a worse problem than they ever had before. One woman apparently had to carry an umbrella with her whenever she went into her garden because she was repeatedly under attack from marauding seabirds! [48]

Not only cats and birds, but dogs were also behaving in a peculiar manner.

Villagers at Ponsanooth, a small village on the road between Redruth and Falmouth, and incidentally, once the home of the Wizard of the Western World, was terrorised by a ferocious dog in July. Three hundred people complained to the local parish council that they were afraid to use a footpath through Kennal Woods, providing not only another example of aberrant behaviour amongst the local livestock, but another gem for the lexilinkers. [49]

The local Women's Institute also complained about the animal, [50] and no records appear to exist to suggest that the dog was ever caught, or that it ever had an owner. One suspects that it probably did because, despite the enormous numbers of feral cats across the country, UK records of true feral dogs are very rare.

Even domestic dogs were causing problems that summer, as only a few weeks later, the Union of Post Office Workers issued an ultimatum that if the animals in the Falmouth area were not kept under control, industrial action would be taken. There had been a number of serious incidents where postmen had been menaced and even bitten by domestic pets who had 'got out of hand.' [51]

There were a number of attacks on sheep during the year. Most of them were blamed on dogs, but in a number of cases the culprits were never identified. One particularly interesting episode happened near Mawnan Smith itself in October. Fourteen were killed, or so badly mutilated that they had to be de-

stroyed, during a period of two weeks. The police discovered large paw marks but no animal was ever caught or identified. [52]

Early the following year there was another series of attacks in the same vicinity, and this time it was claimed that two dogs, a black Labrador and a black and white terrier were seen carrying off the corpse of one of the lambs. No conclusive evidence was ever presented to prove that it was, in fact these two dogs which carried out the particularly distressing series of attacks. [53]

In the summer of 1977, another series of attacks, this time almost certainly by dogs, took place at a farm near Gweek. [54] There is no evidence to suggest that these previous attacks at Mawnan Smith were not, as claimed, the work of marauding dogs, but in view of the other reports of rogue dogs, and even more importantly, in view of the other sinister events at Mawnan, reported elsewhere in this book, we felt it important that these incidents were included in our survey of anomalous and unpleasant happenings in the Falmouth area during this particularly peculiar period.

To move onto an area where the fortean aspects of the story are even less in doubt.

The *Falmouth Packet* of August 13th reported a bizarre ghost story from a pub in Penryn. A couple on holiday were settling down to their first night at the *King's Arms* when:

> *"A door began to open where no door should have been, and a drawer full of clothes dislodged itself from a chest of drawers and ended up on the floor, with all the clothes still neatly folded."* [55]

53 year old Ernest Williamson told the reporter from *The Falmouth Packet*:

> *"My wife and I had driven down from Hertfordshire and after checking into the Kings Arms had gone to bed around 12 midnight.*
>
> *I'm a light sleeper by nature, and after I'd been asleep about an hour I woke with the strangest feeling that someone or something was prowling around the room.*

Then it happened.

> *A door in the room began to open. I could see the light around the door quite clearly - and my first thought was that we had a burglar. I sprang out of bed and went towards the door, and then tripped over a drawer full of clothes that neither I nor my wife Winnie had left there.*
>
> *Then Winnie woke up, and she, too saw the light around the open door. I was practically at the door and was about to push it open when Winnie turned the bedroom light on - and to my astonishment where the door should have been there was just blank wall. I don't think either of us was really scared but when we got up the next morning the drawer full of clothes was still lying there on the floor. That's what convinced us both that we hadn't been dreaming.*
>
> *I know that it all sounds very strange, but I'm not making it up and I'm certainly not round the bend. I never did believe in ghosts and I'm not sure even now if I do. But I hope it comes back - I'd certainly like to meet it."* [56]

Right: *Falmouth Packet, 16th July 1976. This story has always fascinated and intrigued me. Even when I first read it on a wonky microfiche in the Cornish Studies Library in Redruth, I experienced a frisson of excitement at the thought of a mysterious animal, fiercely guarding the lonely footpath through the woods. Whilst I have no doubt that it was nothing but an ordinary dog which had gone feral for a time, there are so many parallels here between the animal and ancient legends of spirit guardians and gatekeepers, that it is impossible for me not to wonder whether it could - possibly - be something far stranger than just a stray pet.*

The fact that it took place in Ponsanooth, then the home of the Sheils Clan and the legendary `Lemonade Man` just makes the story even better.

Below: *The Village of Ponsanooth*

Villagers 'afraid of footpath'

A "FEROCIOUS" dog made people afraid to use a footpath in Kennal Woods, Ponsanooth, it was claimed at a meeting of Stithians parish council last week. Further, the path was obstructed.

Eight Ponsanooth villagers attended the meeting in support of a petition signed by 300 residents, asking for action to ensure that a right of way was maintained.

Supporting letters were received from Ponsanooth WI and Mr. R. W. Beard.

The clerk to the council, Mr. D. Thomas, confirmed that, although the path was not shown on the definitive map, it could be used by the public. It had been proved by evidence that it had been used for very many years.

Mr. Beard warned that if the obstruction were not removed, other action would be taken. It was decided to write to Kerrier Council, and the County Council, demanding the removal of the obstruction.

DISAPPROVAL

Members of the council expressed strong disapproval of statements made at Kerrier development committee, that the Council were out of touch with parishioners concerning a proposed housing development at Crellow Fields.

The suggested plans had been before the council some years ago, and a parish meeting was called to put residents in the picture. No objections had been made.

The parish had been fully consulted at all times, and it was felt that some of the comments were very unfair.

It was decided to write to the district planning officer to tell him that the parish council had always acted with the full knowledge of parishioners.

Falmouth Packet, 13th August 1976

A friendly ghost calls at the Kings Arms

IT was enough to make the coolest customer turn white with fear....

There were the happy holiday couple settling down to their first night in room one at the Kings Arms Hotel, Penryn, when stranger than strange things started happening.

A door began to open where no door should have been and a drawer full of clothes dislodged itself from a chest of drawers and ended up on the floor, with all the clothes still neatly folded.

But let 53-year-old Ernest Williamson tell the story. After all, he was there.

"My wife and I had driven down from Hertfordshire and after checking into the Kings Arms had gone to bed about 12 midnight.

"I'm a light sleeper by nature, and after I'd been asleep about an hour I woke with the strangest feeling that someone or something was prowling around the room. Then it happened.

"A door in the room began to open—I could see the light round the frame quite clearly—and my first thought was that we had a burglar. I sprang out of bed and went towards the door, and then tripped over a drawer full of clothes that neither I nor my wife Winnie had left there.

"Then Winnie woke up and she, too, saw the light round the open door. I was practically at the door and was about to push it open when Winnie turned the bedroom light on—and to my astonishment where the door should have been there was just a blank wall.

"I don't think either of us was really scared, but when we got up the next morning the drawer full of clothes was still lying there on the floor. That's what convinced us both that we hadn't been dreaming.

"I know it all sounds very strange but I'm not making it up and I'm certainly not round the bend. I never did believe in ghosts and I'm not sure even now if I do. But I hope it comes back—I would certainly like to meet it."

Strange happenings, it seems, are not that uncommon at the King's Arms. The 300-year-old hotel has seen its fair share of ghosts over the years.

Even landlord Bill Dowsett, who has been there just 14 months, has experienced his moments.

"I remember being tapped on the shoulder one night in the bar," he recalls. "But when I turned round there was no one there. And other landlords, too, have reported seeing ghosts in the past.

"But the important thing is that whatever it is seems to be friendly—even a bit of a comedian. I don't think anyone here is really afraid of it."

Mr. and Mrs. E. Williamson and landlord Bill Dowsett, looking at the blank wall where a door disappeared.

According to the accompanying report, the 300 year old pub has a reputation for being haunted, and even the landlord at the time had seen it. It does seem unlikely, however, that the two holidaymakers would have been influenced by local stories on what was, after all, only their first night in the county!

It is, however, one of the manifest disadvantages of researching a book, twenty years after the fact, that you simply don't have the time or, indeed, the resources to research every aspect of the narrative to the extent that one would wish for, in an ideal world. One is forced, as in the case of the ghost in the *King's Arms* at Penryn to rely on the testimony of twenty year old newspaper articles, rather than checking one's sources as thoroughly as one would wish. We have, for example, no real way to locate the couple in question, who would now (if they are still alive) be in their mid-70's. We know only that they drove to Cornwall from Hertfordshire, and although, I suppose, in theory at least, we could contact the *King's Arms,* and go back through the hotel registers for the past twenty years in search of Mr and Mrs Williamson's address, or at least the address where they were living twenty years ago, the quest would not only be fiendishly difficult, but ultimately pointless.

The important thing is that the story appeared in the local press, not necessarily whether or not it is true. By appearing in the local paper, it added just another strand of weirdness to what was already an exceedingly weird summer.

There were a number of aberrant bird sightings, apart from those of giant strigiforms [57] during the period under review. One particularly notable episode occurred when a Naumann's Thrush *(Turdus naumanni)* [58] [59] from Siberia was seen in Falmouth, in February 1977, but unfortunately, what would certainly have been the most aberrant piece of ornithology, outside the Owlman himself, turned out, when investigated, to be nothing more than an unfortunate misidentification.

In October 1976, Mrs. Boase of Falmouth reported seeing a tiny light brown creature with a yellow tail hovering in front of a flower in her garden. Having seen similar creatures in Canada she unerringly identified it as a Humming Bird. This would, as the expert from a local Bird Gardens said, have been totally unlikely, although, in theory just about possible, because although the chances of a naturally occurring vagrant are so slim as to be statistically impossible, they are occasionally kept in captivity and one could possibly have escaped. The expert finished her interview with the *Falmouth Packet* by claiming that it was:

"More likely to be a Goldcrest or a Spotted Flycatcher." [60] [61] [62] [63]

In fact it was neither.

Mrs Boase was so tired of being disbelieved that she kept a watch out to see if the 'humming bird' returned. When it did, she caught it in a hair-net. It turned out, as any keen entomologists reading this would no doubt have suspected, to be a Hummingbird Hawk Moth *(Macroglossum stellatarum).* A pity, but true. [64] [65]

Other peculiar stories from the region do not fit into any established pattern.

- In April, a long standing Falmouth resident, Laura, a 28 year old parrot died. She had the honour of being the only parrot, as far as we know, ever to have been invited to speak at a charity dinner in London. [66]

- Several children and at least one adult were taken to Treliske hospital in Truro during July after they had been poisoned by eating Laburnum seeds they had found in a local quarry. [67]

- There was an increased level of violence, lawlessness and even some particularly brutal murders in the region that summer. Some, as far as we have been able to establish, have never been solved. [68]

- There were a number of unexplained fires. [69] Some were probably accidental, some were undoubtedly caused by the extreme weather conditions which we shall discuss shortly, and others were almost certainly arson - another by-product of the increased level of civil disobedience that was rife during the long, hot summer. Some, however, like the fire at a chicken farm at Crowan in August which left 11,000 chickens dead remain unexplained. [70]

As already noted, the 'year' of weirdness in the Falmouth area actually lasted something in the region of fifteen months, and a story which appeared in the local newspapers in early January 1977 was as bizarre as any of the others that we have listed in this chapter.

- A severed human arm was found in a builder's skip full of rubble. The police were obviously notified, but the arm turned out to be an anatomical specimen, which, because the preservative used was of an archaic type, probably dated from at least the 1940's and maybe before. The house that was being demolished had once belonged to a doctor, and it was theorised that it had been lying, forgotten in an attic. [71]

- Two months later a human jaw was washed up on the beach at Porthcurnick. When examined by the County Pathologist it proved to be a century or more old, and had probably come from a shipwreck. The police decided in view of this that they would take no further action. [72]

These last two stories symbolise the end of the period of high strangeness in Southern Cornwall. Whereas the stories in the newspapers during 1976 had been genuinely strange, and often with a menacing and somewhat sinister undercurrent, the stories that unfolded the following year became, merely odd, and more and more of them ended up with rational explanations.

The most striking thing about 1976 was the peculiar weather. I was a teenager at the time and was working at my first summer holiday job, and I still remember the scorching hot weather, which was unprecedented at the time. There were water shortages, heath fires and the same undercurrent of social unrest that was so noticeable in the equally hot, and equally disturbing summer of nineteen years later.

It was a strange and momentous year for me. It was the first year that, whilst not exactly an adult I was no longer a schoolboy. I fell in love for the first time, had my first job, got drunk for the first time, and began to put aside childish things. This however is another story. I mention it only because as the memory of 1976 is so vivid to me, the implications for my own life and work have over spilled, certainly on a subconscious level, and probably conscious, into my narrative of the fortean events of twenty summers ago. Such is life, and life both mirrors art, and confuses it.

Everyone who was alive at the time remembers the scorching hot weather, but what has not become engraved into the collective consciousness of the British public is the torrential rain, and the excessive cold weather which followed the end of the drought.

The one time it rained during the summer, the rain was reportedly *"a dirty brown colour"*, [73] but when the drought stopped in October it did so with a vengeance.

The headline in the *Falmouth Packet* on Friday 1st October read:

"Day that the rain came down...and down...and down." [74]

and the story reported that after the hottest summer on record Falmouth had experienced the most severe floods that had been recorded for many years. The rain continued intermittently for the rest of the year causing many hundreds of pounds worth of damage.

A farmer at Maenporth was actually stranded in his house by the rising floodwater, and the local council, the water board, and the fire brigade were all stretched to their maximum capacity. [75]

As the floods at Maenporth spread, the emergency pumps were unable to cope, and by the beginning of December the rising torrent of floodwater was washing raw sewage out onto the beach. [77] A councillor for Mawnan was reported as describing the situation there as 'terrible'. The floodwaters rose, and by the end of this extraordinary year gale force winds were battering the ships in Falmouth Bay. [78]

The bay at Maenporth

The year ended with what was one of the coldest spells on record. Boats were actually frozen in as the water of the Penryn River froze solid. The official recorder claimed that it was the coldest weather that he had ever recorded. [79]

Lost archaeological treasures were rediscovered across the region. A beautiful fourteenth century silver crucifix and a stretch of wall thought to be connected with Glasney Abbey were found under mildly mysterious circumstances during July, [80] [81] and portentously enough a fifteenth century map of the region which depicted sea monsters off the coast was found in the September. [82]

For it is sea creatures, and most importantly sea serpents, that were the most notable events of that peculiar summer.

Before we examine the most famous cryptic inhabitant of Falmouth Bay, we should take a brief look at some of the other, less well-known visitors to the bay, and to the rest of Cornwall. Morgawr was not the only aberrant marine visitor to the shores of Cornwall during 1976. Something peculiar was definitely afoot. Quite apart from the mysterious carcass found on the banks of the Helford [83] which may or may not have been that of an unidentified sea animal, there were larger than usual numbers of whale strandings. A fifteen-foot whale was washed up at Perranporth in November, and was carried on a lorry to Hayle where it was taken to a knackers yard, cut up and turned into fishmeal. [84] The same newspaper reported a number of other incidents of whales and seals being found dead on Cornish beaches.

There was a shark scare at Treyarnon Bay near Padstow in July, [85] and another at Portreath in August. [86] On both occasions terrified bathers were called ashore after a huge dorsal fin was spotted. On neither occasion were sharks definitely confirmed from the area, but at Portreath an equally unpleasant visitor, a Portuguese Man O'War jellyfish *(Physalia physalis),* was found. [87] [88]

A 49lb 6oz Sunfish *(Mola mola)* was caught at Fisherman's Cove in July, [89] [90] and the same month two rare Triggerfish [91] (species unrecorded) were caught in lobster pots in Falmouth Bay. Both species are vagrants from much warmer climes, and some reporters suggested that the dorsal fin which sparked off the shark scare at Treyarnon Bay might have been that of a Sunfish rather than any more sinister visitor. [92]

Another unwelcome visitor was a plague of tiny shrimps *(Asellus aquaticus)* which invaded the water mains of Newquay in November. Their numbers reached epidemic proportions before the pipes were flushed out with a chemical agent to destroy them. [93]

A letter published in the *Falmouth Packet* on the 27th August complained that the size of sea bass caught during the summer of 1976 was much less than that of fish caught in previous years. [94] The mackerel catches were also tiny [95] and it was obvious that something strange was happening in the seas off Cornwall.

Playing 'Yin' to the 'Yang' provided by Morgawr was 'Beaky' the Dolphin. He was generally regarded as somewhat of a pet by local people. A local witch called Miranda, who has been invaluable in my researches into everything connected with this (and the) case, told me that he could often be seen in the enclosed harbour beneath *The Chain Locker* pub on the waterfront where he would perform in the water and live royally on scraps of food thrown to him by locals and tourists alike. [96]

By the time we got to Falmouth 20 years later, 'Beaky' was long gone and the only animal inhabitant of the tiny harbour was a large and rather moth eaten looking seal, with one eye, who was obviously fill-

Falmouth Fish Quay -The Chain Locker can be seen in the background

Falmouth Fish Quay - looking east across the harbout

ing the same ecological niche that 'Beaky' had filled twenty years before, by lolling on the surface and begging for scraps of cheese sandwiches from the occupants of a small pleasure cruiser tied up to the harbour wall.

The papers of the time, however, were full of 'Beaky' and his exploits, some of which were quite fortean.

The earliest reports that we found were from *The West Briton* [97] and portrayed 'Beaky' as a genial cetacean, full of fun and always ready to oblige waiting tourists with an unforgettable photo opportunity.

On July 8th, however, he fell from grace, when the headline in *The West Briton* read:

"Swimmer goes to hospital after meeting Beaky". [98]

The story read:

> *"Beaky the boisterous dolphin put up a black mark last week when a 25 year old St Ives swimmer was taken to hospital suffering from shock and exhaustion.*
>
> *Mr Glyn Vaughn, of Bellair Terrace dived off Smeaton's Pier, intending to swim to a raft off Porthminster Beach and was joined by Beaky.*
>
> *The dolphin swam round him continuously, getting in his way so much that he scrambled ashore only after a tough struggle.*
>
> *'It was fun at first' said Mr Vaughn, but then it became boring and then alarming. When I got to the beach I couldn't stand."*

It is difficult to blame the dolphin, who by the photographs was probably a Bottle-nose Dolphin *Tursiops truncatus*), for the incident. He was probably only trying to be inquisitive and friendly. A local RSPCA inspector pointed out that, despite his reputation for playfulness, people forgot that he was not only a wild animal but weighed 650 pounds. [99]

A week or so later, 'Beaky' bit a swimmer off the same beach. The swimmer managed, after a struggle to get his arm out of the dolphin's eponymous beak, and was taken to hospital with bleeding teeth-marks on his left fore-arm. [100]

The front page of *The West Briton* a week later reported a strong rumour that fishermen from St. Ives were planning to shoot the dolphin, because of his reported predations on the local fish stocks. This, predictably caused a storm of protest which prompted a plan by a number of local businessmen and diving experts to capture the dolphin and then release him in his original haunts of Mount's Bay, away from fishing areas and unwary tourists. [101]

Ironically, in early September, 'Beaky' returned to Mount's Bay, after some ten weeks in the St Ives area, apparently of his own volition. [102] This could well prompt speculation in some areas that he somehow had figured out that he was in danger, and had decided to move, but it seems more likely that his return to his original haunt was prompted by some more prosaic, cetacean-orientated piece of reasoning.

136

Beaky makes a splash

BEAKY the dolphin had a ball with holidaymakers in Falmouth harbour at the weekend.

Beaky was first spotted by the Norwegian boys on Saturday morning, as he swam round their boat. So Bjorn Gunnar Nervik and his brothers Leif Tore and Eivind hopped over the side and joined him in a two-hour frolic.

"He let us ride on his back and stroke him and even let me put my arm in his mouth at one stage," said 20-year-old Bjorn. "He was full of fun, and didn't frighten us in the least."

The boys, their father and mother, are in Falmouth on board the 50ft. Norwegian fishing boat Boeken and are waiting for better weather before setting sail for Spain.

'PLAYFUL'

Another seaman to capture Beaky's attention was Joe Bowden, of Gyllyngvase Terrace, Falmouth, who was sculling in the harbour between Prince of Wales Pier and Flushing when he received a surprise visitor.

"I was rowing out to my yacht when he came alongside," said Mr. Bowden. "He kept nudging the boat. I suppose he was being playful, but obviously didn't know that I don't swim too well and could easily have flipped the boat over."

Passengers on the "Look at Falmouth from the Water" cruise had a special bonus when the dolphin swam alongside for a while.

"We first saw him about 100 yards west of Trefusis Point. He rose out of the water on the starboard bow and everyone shouted 'Beaky'," said Mr. Derek Toyne, of Falmouth Civic Society.

"Then he followed us and everyone forgot about the buildings to concentrate on him. We couldn't compete with that. Perhaps we ought to enrol him as an honorary member."

Falmouth Packet, 24th September 1976

Beaky comes alongside the Nerviks' yacht in Falmouth Harbour, and (below) happily takes 20-year-old Bjorn for a spin, pick-a-back style.

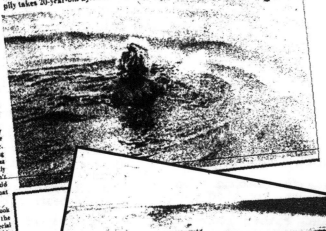

Hello, Beaky!

IT'S Beaky! Cornwall's playful dolphin was up to his tricks this week in Falmouth harbour.

He is pictured taking a close look at a working boat during racing on Saturday.

He later undertook some racing of his own. Turn to page 9.

Falmouth Packet, 24th September 1976

Swimmer goes to hospital after meeting Beaky

BEAKY, the boisterous dolphin, put up a black mark last week when a 25-year-old St. Ives swimmer was taken to hospital suffering from shock and exhaustion.

Right: *West Briton, 8th July 1976*

Beaky grabs swimmer

BEAKY, the playful dolphin, who has been a familiar sight off the beaches of Cornwall during the summer, became rather attached to one holidaymaker who had been playing with him.

When the holidaymaker decided to swim back to Porthminster beach at St. Ives Beaky grabbed his arm. The holidaymaker. Mr. Malcolm Johnston of Glasgow, jerked his arm out of Beaky's mouth and after being taken ashore was treated for bleeding teeth marks on his left forearm.

Above: *Falmouth Packet, 16th July 1976 - The saga of `Beaky` - "The Anti-Flipper" grabbed headlines in Cornwall throughout the summer of 1976. This remarkable cetacean was variously credited with attacking swimmers, and saving them from drowning., and as such was variously hailed as an animal-hero and a dangerous hazard who should be destroyed. In the end no-one seems to know what happened to him.*

Mr. Glyn Vaughan, of Bellair-terrace, dived off Smeaton's Pier intending to swim to a craft off Porthminster Beach— and was joined by Beaky.

The dolphin swam round him continuously, getting in his way so much that he scrambled ashore only after a tough struggle.

"It was fun at first," said Mr. Vaughan, "but then it became boring and afterwards alarming. When I got to the beach I couldn't stand."

SURROUNDED

West Cornwall RSPCA inspector Mr. Brian Sanders said too many people were getting into the water with Beaky. He had watched as the dolphin was surrounded by rubber dinghies off St. Ives.

Beaky appeared to get excited and jump around after a while when a lot of people were around— "and people don't realise he weighs 650lb."

Mr. Sanders said he did not think Beaky could be blamed for his behaviour, because of the games people were playing with him.

At Mount's Bay it was suggested that Beaky left his old haunts off Penzance because he was being pestered by divers and swimmers.

Falmouth Packet
22nd July 1976

'Shoot Beaky' rumours prompt move plan

RUMOURS that some fishermen in St. Ives might be planning to shoot Beaky, the town's playful dolphin, have led to plans to move the creature around the coast to Mount's Bay, its original Cornish home.

The plans have in turn angered local traders—who see the dolphin as a major tourist attraction and fear business could suffer if it goes.

Mr. Bob Carswell, organiser of a diving centre in Penzance, said the measures would be considered only if Beaky was in danger. He had heard that fishermen were thinking of shooting the 650lb. dolphin, because it had unknowingly placed bathers in danger and had "stolen mackerel".

Mr. Brian Sanders, West Cornwall's RSPCA inspector, said he had also heard the rumours.

"I hope it never happens," he said. "People should treat Beaky with the respect he deserves."

Mr. Carswell said he had suggested to the St. Ives harbourmaster that Beaky should be moved only if fishermen and locals did not want it in the bay and harbour. "We would only take Beaky away as a last resort."

'Female' lure

Mr. Carswell added that an idea to lure Beaky away by using a rubber dinghy as an "imitation female" could not be guaranteed—and Beaky might not stay away.

If its life was in danger, however, Mr. Carswell thought it might be necessary to frighten the dolphin away for good by using small amounts of explosive—Beaky left the Isle of Man because of rock blasting.

Mr. Carswell thought that some people in Mount's Bay did not like Beaky either.

Mr Oakley Eddy, former Mayor of St. Ives and a businessman in the town, said Beaky would be a tourist attraction wherever he went.

"Like a lot of people," said Mr. Eddy, "Beaky prefers to live in St. Ives rather than Penzance. I'm sure that if Beaky is lured away he'll come back again if he prefers it here." He described the whole affair as "a lot of nonsense".

Mr. Sanders said that if the threat rumours became more substantial, he hoped Mr. Eddy might use his influence to protect Beaky.

"Mr. Sanders said the dolphin was a free agent. If it preferred to stay in St. Ives, that was fine by him.

[Picture—Page 11]

Falmouth Packet
16th September 1976

Beaky ends his 10-week 'holiday'

BEAKY, the friendly 650lb. dolphin, has ended his ten-week holiday at St. Ives and swum around Land's End, back to Mount's Bay.

Since the first week of July he has delighted thousands of holidaymakers on the beaches at St. Ives—and his departure was as unexpected as his arrival.

"Beaky just appeared at the bottom of the slipway again," said Penlee lifeboat mechanic Mr. Geoff. Bold. "He has been swimming in Newlyn harbour and around the ship just as he was before."

'FOLLOWED US'

Penzance Sub-aqua Club also welcomed Beaky back. "He followed us back from beyond Mousehole," said diver Mr. Tony Hall.

"He was excited and glad to see us. We hope he will stay here for the winter. The rough weather at St. Ives has probably brought him here for shelter and company."

Stories of dolphin/human interaction predate the TV Series 'Flipper' by thousands of years. One of the most famous is found in the writings of Pliny the Elder, and such accounts carry on to the present day. Several children's books have been written on the subject, including a particularly moving book by Monica Edwards.

However, there is a dark side: In recent years there has been at least one person successfully prosecuted for bestiality with a dolphin

West Briton
22nd September 1976

Beaky explores —or does he have a friend?

BEAKY, the friendly dolphin, is certainly getting around and about. Or could it be that other dolphins are taking an interest in our shores?

As we reported last week, Beaky returned to his "winter quarters" off Newlyn after providing an entertainment spectacle for thousands of holidaymakers at St. Ives during the summer.

Now three more dolphin sightings have been reported—at Mullion, on the other side of Mount's Bay, in the Percuil River, near St. Mawes, and in Falmouth harbour.

The Mullion dolphin, which could well have been Beaky, was spotted by Royal Navy divers who were testing new equipment. Lt Glyn Jones, diving officer at RNAS Culdrose, said the dolphin several times popped down to investigate the divers. It even let them scratch its stomach and at one stage put his nose within nine inches of Lt Jones's face-mask.

Later he accompanied the divers' dinghy into harbour.

If it was Beaky who greeted two Ajax class yachts when they sailed out of Percuil River to take part in a race he was certainly a considerable way from his base.

After swimming around the boats for about ten minutes the dolphin began pushing the craft along and rearing up to look over the foredecks.

At Falmouth, a dolphin took a particular fancy to the Customs launch Guardwell going right alongside several times, and was also seen close to Custom House Quay and Flushing Quay.

His antics have included jumping over small boats.

Mr Peter Davey, a Customs and Excise officer at Falmouth, said the dolphin was first seen early on Saturday and had been seen at regular intervals until Monday evening.

"He was a very friendly dolphin," said Mr Davey. "He was about 12 feet long and must have been near Beaky's weight—about 650lb."

By the end of September he was back in Falmouth harbour where he was photographed swimming with two boys from a Norwegian fishing boat. He was once again the pet of the town, with everyone from *The Falmouth Packet*, (the headline on the front page read 'Hello Beaky'), to the secretary of the Civic Society welcoming him home. [103]

Later in September *The Falmouth Packet* speculated that there might be more than one 'friendly' dolphin in local waters, with a rundown of several sightings of what appear from the descriptions to be two or more different animals. They also provided what was probably the most sensible reasoning behind the return of 'Beaky' to Falmouth waters - it was probably, they said, a seasonal migration. [104]

By the end of the year, the animal had been ingrained so deeply within the consciousness of the people of Falmouth that the *'Packet'* even printed a rather revoltingly twee poem by a local schoolgirl, which was 'very nice if you like that sort of thing. [105] [106]

'Beaky' was in St. Mawes harbour in mid February 1977, [107] and only a few weeks later he was back in the news again. *The Falmouth Packet* on the 18th March wrote:

"A seaman on the Cypriot vessel Cloud, counts himself lucky to be alive this week. When his ship left Falmouth on Monday after minor engine repairs, he fell overboard by the harbour - and claims to have been rescued by Beaky the dolphin. Beaky was seen to come from beneath the waves, pushing the man to the surface.

The seaman feels embarrassed about the incident, for no-one believes him except for his colleagues.

The vessel has since returned to Falmouth for more repairs, and he is trying to substantiate his story".
[108]

The best-known Cornish mystery of that peculiar year was that of Morgawr, the semi-mythical Cornish sea serpent that, during 1975 and 1976, became almost a common sight along the coastline of southern Cornwall. It would be impossible to write a book about the fortean phenomena associated with the Mawnan Owlman without mentioning Morgawr, but because a separate book is planned on the subject, we shall only include the Morgawr reports from 1976 in this chapter. Because we intend to publish a companion volume to this book which we intend to be the definitive work on the subject, this chapter does not cover Morgawr in perhaps as much depth as it deserves.

Some of the material presented in the following section has not, we believe, been presented to a fortean readership before. The first item is a case in point. According to all other commentators on the subject the year began excitingly with what Anthony Mawnan-Peller described as a:

'Strange (and, so far unidentified) carcass (...) discovered on Durgan Beach, Helford River, by Mrs. Payne of Falmouth." [109]

A few weeks later, however *The Falmouth Packet* reported that a young naturalist living locally believed that he had found the answer to the mystery:

"The mystery of the bones of Durgan beach may have been solved this week by 13 year old Toby Benham. a keen student of skeletons. Toby believes the bones found at Durgan by Mrs. Kaye Payne of Falmouth, come not from a 20-foot sea monster as suggested, but from a whale. He came to this conclusion because he thinks that the bones form part of a skeleton

140

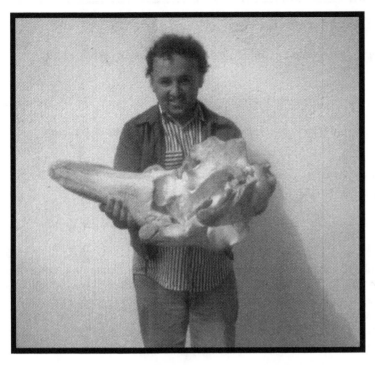

*John Fuller of the Centre for Fortean Zoology,
holding the Durgan Beach Whale Skull*

*Durgan Beach, where the skull and bones
of the whale was discovered*

Falmouth Packet - 5th May 1976

Not a sea monster, says Toby

THE mystery of the bones of Durgan Beach may have been solved this week by 13-year-old Toby Benham, a keen student of skeletons.

Toby believes the bones, found at Durgan by Mrs. Kaye Payne of Falmouth, come not from a 20 foot sea monster as has been suggested, but from a whale.

He came to this conclusion because he thinks the bones form part of a skeleton, he discovered on nearby Prisk Beach just after Christmas.

Toby of 17, Castle View Park, Mawnan Smith, studied the "Packet's" photograph of Mrs. Payne holding a bone from the beach, and he is convinced it is one of those he saw.

"I am sure it is from a whale," the young naturalist said emphatically.

STORM TIDES

His explanation for their appearance at Durgan is equally emphatic. Storm tides swept them around from Prisk, he says.

The original skeleton was about ten feet long and the skull which is now one of the prizes in Toby's collection of bones, looks like that of a whale.

He said the skull had what appeared to be blow-holes and it seemed very similar to pictures he has of whales' heads.

he discovered on nearby Prisk Beach just after Christmas.

Toby (....) studied the 'Packet's' photograph of Mrs Payne holding a bone from the beach, and he is convinced that it is one of those he saw.

'I am sure it is from a whale' said the young naturalist emphatically.

His explanation for their appearance at Durgan is equally emphatic. 'Storm tides swept them around from Prisk,' he says.

The original skeleton was about ten feet long, and the skull, which is now one of the prizes in Toby's collection of bones, looks like that of a whale.

He said the skull had what appeared to be blow boles and it seemed very similar to pictures he has of whales' heads. "[110]

Unfortunately, although several books report Mawnan-Peller's description of the finding of a 'carcass' on the beach, none, that I have been able to find have reported the fact that the 'carcass' was actually a headless skeleton, and that there is every likelihood that the skeleton itself was actually that of a whale. Only one book actually acknowledged the whale theory, and that was *Monstrum* by Tony 'Doc' Shiels, and for reasons known only to themselves, the fundamentalists amongst the world of forteana have decided to take it upon themselves to ignore everything that 'Doc' ever says!

Also in January, Duncan Viner, a dental technician from Truro saw Morgawr while he was:

"*...swimming 'a few hundred yards off Rosemullion Head'. At first, he thought it was a whale, as only a dark hump was visible, but as he watched it started to rise in the water and a long neck appeared*". [111]

According to Mawnan-Peller, he estimated the total length of the animal as being between thirty and forty feet.

The front page of the same issue of *The Falmouth Packet* that printed Toby Benham's theory earned the banner headline:

AUTHOR'S NOTE: We embarked on a quest to see if we could get hold of Toby Benham and the elusive whale skull. By dint of some major detective work we managed to track down Toby`s mother who said that, unfortunately, Toby was no longer living at home. As, by this time he would have been nearly as old as me this did not come as any great surprise, but we asked diffidently, whether there was any chance that his mother knew what had happened to the elusive skull. Of course she did, she told us. When Toby had grown up and fled the nest he left the skull behind, and for many years it had been lying open to the weather in his mother`s garden where it doubled as a door stop and a somewhat macabre garden ornament. After some years she had got tired of it and donated it to a local educational institution.

Three weeks later in a dusty cupboard of a locked classroom in a local college this is where we found it. The proprietors of the college were happy to let the CFZ have it as a specimen for our nascent collection of cryptozoological memorabilia, And so we carried it gingerly out to our van and took it home which is where it resides to this day. We had it identified by an expert at Plymouth Aquarium and by Dr Karl Shuker who both correctly stated that it was the somewhat damaged skull of a baby pilot whale thus vindicating what Tony Shiels had stated all those years before.

The Helford River, Durgan Beach is to the right

Duncan Viner's Morgawr seen off Rosemullion Head in 1976

143

"Sir: kindly find enclosed one sea-serpent" [112]

and featured three photographs, one admittedly faked by the staff photographer of the newspaper, and two purporting to be by someone identifying herself only as 'Mary F'. Mawnan-Peller wrote:

> *"The 'Falmouth Packet' newspaper published two photographs of Morgawr, taken in February by a lady who called herself 'MaryF'.*
>
> *They showed a long-necked, hump-backed creature, at least eighteen feet long, swimming in the water off Trefusis Point, near Flushing. 'Mary F's' monster was described as 'black or very dark brown', with a snake-like head and 'humps on the back which moved in a funny way'.* [113]
>
> *After publishing those historic photographs, the 'Packet' received a flood of letters from people who claimed to have seen Morgawr. Estimates of the creature's length varied from twelve to forty five feet".* [113]

The *'Packet'* also printed a letter from the lady which had accompanied the photographs. It read:

> *"Dear Sir,*
>
> *The enclosed photos were taken by me about three weeks ago from Trefusis. They show one of the large sea -creatures mentioned in your paper recently. I'm glad to know that other people have seen the great humped sea serpent.*
>
> *The pictures aren't very clear because of the sun shining right into the camera and a haze on the water. Also, I took them very quickly indeed. The animal was only up for a few seconds. I would say that it was about fifteen to eighteen feet long. I mean the part showing above the water. It looked like an Elephant waving its trunk, but the trunk was a long neck with a small bead on the end like a snake's head. It had humps on the back which moved in a funny way. The colour was black or very dark brown and the colour seemed to be like a sealion's.*
>
> *My brother developed the films. I didn't want to take it to the chemist. Perhaps you can make them clearer. As a matter of fact the animal frightened me. I would not like to see it any closer. I do not like the way it moved when it was swimming.*
>
> *You can put these pictures in the paper if you like. I don't want payment, and I don't want my name in the paper about that. I just think you should tell people about the animal.*
>
> *What is it?*
>
> *Yours sincerely,*
>
> *Mary F.*
> *Falmouth"*
> [114]

This letter has been quoted many times in books on Forteana, folklore and mystery animals. *The Falmouth Packet* however, reproduced the original handwritten sheets, and sitting here with the photocopy of the front page of a twenty year old newspaper in front of me, I can clearly see something that I believe has been missed by other commentators on the case.

The woman who wrote the letter, whoever she was, seems to have been under a great deal of stress. The handwriting is shaky, but not in the way that an old person's handwriting is shaky. The obvious inference to draw from seeing the original letter is that Mary F was very frightened when she wrote the letter. There are other clues. The letter is constructed in very short sentences but is also grammatically correct. This also gives the appearance of terror.

Unfortunately, no-one has ever managed to identify Mary F with any certainty. Twenty years later Doc told me that he honestly has no idea who she was or is. In *Monstrum* he wrote:

> *"Various sympathetic and serious investigators attempted to contact Mary F, and odd rumours about her possible identity began to circulate amongst the cryptozoological community. She was said to be a titled lady, a famous spiritualist; or a nun from the local convent"..* [115]

The 'titled lady' that was rumoured to be the true identity of Mary F. was, by all accounts, Lady Falmouth, [116] but as far as I can ascertain, this is completely untrue. Tony continues:

> *"I also, eventually, received a letter from the mysterious lady imploring me to drop my enquiries concerning her identity. It seems that, quite unconsciously, I came too close for comfort. She told me that I could publicise her photographs but not her name. She was, perhaps, being a wee bit over cautious. I still don't know the full name of 'Mary F', but can tell you that she no longer lives in Cornwall".* [117]

A fortnight later the *'Packet'* announced that a local author, Tony Shaw, from Feock, was planning a book on Morgawr, and appealed for any witnesses who were interested in helping him to come forward. [118] [119]

Also in March the first of Tony's friends arrived on the scene. Mawnan-Peller wrote:

> *"Towards the end of March 1976, a 'professor of metaphysics, from Albuquerque, New-Mexico, USA arrived in Falmouth with a plan to capture the monster. Professor Michael McCormick a fire-eater and travelling showman, intended to trap Morgawr and to exhibit the beast in his 'Matchbox Circus'. But by the beginning of May, the 'professor' had left Cornwall ... without his sea -serpent".* [120] [121]

The story is, of course, more complicated than that. Tony Shiels had sent McCormick a copy of *The Falmouth Packet* containing the Mary F photographs, [122] and McCormick decided to come to Cornwall by sea, leaving New York on St Patrick's Day. [123] *The Falmouth Packet* wrote on the 26th March:

> *"A self-styled dragon hunter from Alberquerque. New Mexico is on his way to Falmouth, having received cuttings from the 'Packet' reporting sightings of a sea monster.*
>
> *Prof. Michael McCormick has been monster hunting in various parts of the world and is bringing with him 'strange and exciting' specimens..."* [124]

145

Sir: kindly find enclosed one sea serpent

Comment by an anonymous "Packet" reader.

Above: *First appearance of the Morgawr photographs - Falmouth Packet, 5th March 1976*
Below: *Falmouth Packet, 19th March 1976*

Beware, Nessie! Tony is on your tail

SIGHTINGS of a "sea monster" off Falmouth—another of which is reported in today's Letters to the Editor column—have attracted the attention of Mr. Tony Shaw, author of a book on Cornish folk lore.

Mr. Shaw is anxious to talk to anyone who has seen the creature, and would like them to contact him at Pillar Cottage, Penelewey, Feock.

He told the "Packet" he had heard similar reports about five years ago, and said that there had been recent sightings of monsters off the Irish coast.

Mr. Shaw himself doubts the existence of such creatures, but feels compelled to investigate.

He is a member of the Folk Lore Society, which he says was formed in the early 1800s and is based at Kings College, London.

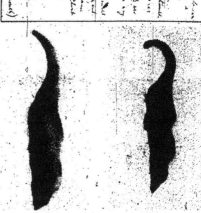

Mr. Tony Shaw

There is little doubt that the Mary F photographs are fakes. The only serious doubt is over the matter of who took them. Forteana is a very strange business by its very nature, and Tony Shiels told me on a number of occasions that there really isn't any such thing as a coincidence. Therefore, I was saddened, though not particularly surprised when, as I was putting the finishing touches to this chapter in late January 2001, I received a letter from Tony telling me that the person that I had always suspected has been the real hoaxer of the Mary F photographs had recently died. His name was John Gordon, and during my long and tortuous researches into the truth about what happened during the long, hot summer of 1976 at least three people hinted strongly that John had been the real perpetrator of the Mary F hoax.

'The Chain Locker', Fish Quay, Falmouth

The 'specimens' were a 'stuffed basilisk' and the skeleton of an imp, [125] but neither the people of Falmouth, nor the *'Packet'* itself, were particularly impressed by his claims that he would shrink the animal to a tiny size by magickal powers, and imprison it in a bottle. [126]

Tony Shiels was quoted as saying:

> *"he was personally too lazy to keep watch for the monster but was awaiting a 'telepathic hunch in the head', whereupon he would go out and call it"...* [127]

Shiels and McCormick called a press conference at the end of March and *The Falmouth Packet* wrote:

> *"The great Falmouth monster hunt got underway this week with the arrival in the town from America of a 36 year old Professor of Metaphysics, Michael McCormick who plans to devote the summer to his search.*
>
> *The professor called a press conference in the 'Chain Locker'* [128] *on Falmouth's waterfront on Monday, when he was accompanied by his 'psychic advisor', 'Doc' Shiels of Ponsanooth. He had with him a number of strange relics from previous monster hunts, including the*

It's cost me a wad, says the professor

THE great Falmouth sea-monster hunt got underway this week, with the arrival in the town from America of a 36-year-old Professor of Michael Mc-Memphtsology, Cormick, who plans to devote the summer to his search.

The professor called a Press conference in the Chain Locker on Falmouth's waterfront on Monday, when he was accompanied by his psychic adviser, "Doc" Shiels, of Ponsmouth.

The professor, who is also a fire-eater and juggler, is causing some problems for his partner.

Said Mr. Shiels: "The whole place is throbbing from the things Mike has brought over. I shall have to do something to stop the headache."

He had with him a number of strange relics from previous monster hunts, including the skeleton of an imp.

WITH HORNS

This was about 18 inches long, with a miniature human-shaped skull out of which horns protruded. It also had chewed feet and wings, and did not, smell too wholesome.

He also produced a small, clawed foot, wrapped in a red cloth, which promptly caused oscillations on the sound-recording equipment brought along by television engineers.

Prof. McCormick said he had recently been lecturing at the University of New Mexico on the basic need for monsters from a long-ram point of view.

He said he had come all the way from Albuquerque, New Mexico, as a result of reports in the "Packet" about sightings of the Falmouth monster.

VARY SIZE

"It has cost a wad of money," he said, "I shall spend the next few months in a dedicated focusing effort, using 'Doc's' remarkable mental powers to produce the beast."

He said he thought the monster was probably migratory, and thought it could vary in size at will.

Prof. McCormick—and his skeleton of 'an imp'.

Fire-eating professor joins the Falmouth Dragon hunt

A SELF-STYLED dragon hunter from Albuquerque, New Mexico, is on his way to Falmouth, having received cuttings from the "Packet" reporting sightings of a sea monster.

Prof. Michael McCormick has been monster-hunting in various parts of the world, and is bringing with him "strange and exotic" specimens.

The "Packet" cuttings were sent to the professor by Mr. Tony Shiels, of Vale View, Ponsmouth, who is well known for his mystical interest in dragons and the like.

Mr. Shiels told the "Packet" that Prof. McCormick was planning to sail from New York on a Polish ship on St. Patrick's Day, and was due to arrive in Falmouth tomorrow.

PUBLIC DISPLAY

"I assume he got away, although it is difficult for an Irish-American to make much progress on St. Patrick's Day," he said.

The professor, who is in eating fire—has said he wants to capture the Falmouth monster alive and put it on public display.

Mr. Shiels said he was personally too lazy to keep watch for the monster but was awaiting "a telepathic hunch in the head," whereupon he would go out and call it.

He has also had news from America of a plan being hatched there for a witch to swim naked in Falmouth Bay to attract the monster. As yet, further details appear to be hazy.

I'll try to capture one: Letters to the Editor, page 8.

Prof. Michael McCormick—fire-eater.

Above: *Falmouth Packet, 2nd April 1976*

Below: *Falmouth Packet, 26th April 1976*

skeleton of an imp.

This was about eighteen inches long, with a miniature human shaped skull out of which horns protruded. It also had clawed feet and wings, and did not smell too wholesome.

He also produced a small, clawed foot, wrapped in a red cloth, which promptly caused oscillations on the sound recording equipment brought along by television engineers.

Prof. McCormick said he had recently been lecturing at the University of New Mexico on the basic need for monsters from a Jungian point of view.

He said he had come all the way from Alberquerque, New Mexico, as a result of reports in the 'Packet', about sightings of the Falmouth monster.
'It has cost a wad of money', he said 'I shall spend the next two months in a determined focussing effort using "Doc's" remarkable mental processes to produce the beast'.

He said that he thought the monster was probably migratory and thought it could vary its size at will.

The professor, who is also a fire-eater and juggler, is causing some problems for his partner.

Said Mr. Shiels, 'The whole place is throbbing from the things Mike has brought over. I shall have to do something to stop the headaches'." [129]

This slightly bizarre approach to monster hunting probably provoked the next instalment of the ongoing saga. On Friday April 2nd, *The Falmouth Packet* printed two photographs of an unlikely looking monster, which appeared to have been constructed from oil drums, floating in the Penryn River. Ironically the larger of the two pictures is very reminiscent of one of the more contentious Nessie photographs taken at about the same time by Mr. Frank Searle. [130] [131]

The headline read:

"Yna omma ow-tos an Morgawr" [132]

and there was an asterisk next to the final word which obviously referred to a smaller subtitle in English reading:

"Here comes the Sea Giant".

The story which accompanied the pictures read:

"What must have been a close relative of the Falmouth Sea Monster reared its ugly head in the Penryn River at 9.30 a.m. yesterday to see what all the fuss was about.

Cries of here Morgawr, which is Cornish for sea giant, greeted its appearance. But it seemed strangely disinterested and set off, all four green humps aloft on a slow run down river.

150

Yna omma ow-tos an Morgawr *

WHAT must have been a close relative of the Falmouth sea-monster reared its ugly head in the Penryn River at 9.30 a.m. yesterday to see what all the fuss was about.

Cries of "Here, Morgawr"—which is Cornish for sea-giant—greeted its appearance. But it appeared strangely disinterested and set off, four green humps aloft, on a slow run down river.

Possibly due to neuralgia, brought on by the Cornish damp, its 20-foot red-and-green neck developed an ominous crick, and it proceeded with its mouth skimming the water.

Monster-hunters. "Doc" Shiels, of Ponsanooth, and Prof. Michael McCormick, of New Mexico, watched with interest from the end of Prince of Wales Pier as the beast slipped slowly by.

COASTGUARDS

Morgawr, obviously, found something attractive about the trawler "No No," which it followed relentlessly. Its presence was sternly ignored by the Falmouth Coastguards, who decided that disbelief was the better part of valour.

The Falmouth Pilot cutter went alongside for a close inspection—and a tanker en route for Coast Lines Wharf hooted a neighbourly greeting.

Captain David Banks, Falmouth's deputy Harbourmaster, was among those to sight Morgawr.

"It was heading seaward when I saw it," he said. "It had about four humps, and appeared to have been caught by a trawler."

The monster was last seen shortly before noon on what was, after all, April 1....

* Here comes the Sea-giant

Falmouth Packet – 2nd April 2006

Penryn Quay

Morgawr comes to Shag Town

Falmouth Harbour

Possibly due to neuralgia brought on by the Cornish damp. its 20 foot red and green neck developed an ominous crick and it proceeded with its mouth skimming the water.

Monster hunters, 'Doc' Shiels, of Ponsanooth, and Prof. Michael McCormick of New Mexico, watched with interest from the end of the Prince of Wales pier as the beast slipped slowly by.

Morgawr obviously found something attractive about the trawler 'No No' which it followed relentlessly. Its presence was sternly ignored Falmouth Coastguards, who decided that disbelief was the better part of valour.

The Falmouth pilot cutter went alongside for a close inspection - and a tanker en route for Coast Lines Wharf hooted a neighbourly greeting.

Captain David Banks, Falmouth's deputy harbourmaster, was amongst those to sight Morgawr.

"It was heading seaward when I saw it", he said. "It had about four humps, and appeared to have been caught by a trawler".

The monster was last seen shortly before noon, on what was, of course, April 1st". (133)

It was a hoax by students from the local Art College. According to Tony:

> *"After this merry jape, Professor McCormick, feeling somewhat deflated himself, quickly altered his plans, and waved goodbye to Cornwall ... and Morgawr!".* [134] [135]

This whole incident was important from one point of view. Previous to the art students' hoax. the animal had been known as 'The Durgan Dragon', [136] but this name had never really captured the imagination of either the press or the public. After the first of April 1976, there was only one name it could possibly be known as ... Morgawr! [137]

There was only one further mention of Prof. McCormick in *The Falmouth Packet*. This was in a jokey news item from April 23rd which claimed that he was suffering from a heavy cold. 'Doc' is reported as saying that it was: *"...the result of spending too much time knee-deep in Falmouth Bay"*.

The same news item reported the advent of the next important group of players in the drama of Morgawr and Falmouth Bay. The naked witches! The paper reported:

> *"The hunt for Morgawr, the Falmouth Sea Serpent took a new turn this week when three witches took up the chase.*
>
> *Two of the ladies have already taken experimental dips into the Helford River in an attempt to attract the monster. Last week, a witch known as Psyche arrived from Inverness, and on Saturday a second witch, known as Vivienne, from London, surprised Easter holidaymakers on Grebe Beach by swimming in the nude.*
>
> *Unhappily Morgawr the monster did not appear, although both witches claimed the beast was 'near'.*
>
> *Now both Pysche and Vivienne intend to repeat their experiments on April 30th when they will be joined by Amanda, a Cornish witch from Liskeard '* [139]

During the summer, several bands of witches, many, but not all in conjunction with the Wizard himself, attempted to invoke Morgawr by a number of methods, including swimming 'sky-clad' in the waters of Falmouth Bay. Mawnan-Peller wrote:

> *Another magical personality, involved in the hunt, is Psyche, a beautiful young witch from Inverness, who, in the company of several members of her coven, swam naked in the waters of Falmouth Bay in order to attract the monster to the surface. Since Psyche's initial dip, several nude witches have attempted to raise the sea-dragon...".* [140]

'Psyche' was Pat Scott-Innes, the daughter of an old friend of Tony's, who had come from Inverness in search of the monster. [141] Unfortunately for the sake of a simple and uncluttered narrative, 'Psyche' was also the stage name used by Tony's daughter Kate, 16 at the time, and a witch in her own right, who was involved, as much as Tony, the Inverness 'Psyche', or anyone else in the events of that summer. [142] [143] There was, however, a third 'Psyche', a mythical young lady 'invented' by Tony for inclusion in his 1975 book *'The Shiels Effect - manual for the psychic superstar'*. [144]

153

Witches (one in the nude) join hunt for Morgawr

THE hunt for Morgawr, the Falmouth sea-serpent, took a new turn this week when three witches took up the chase.

Two of the ladies have already taken experimental dips into the Helford River in an effort to attract the monster.

Last week, a witch known as Psyche arrived from In-verness, and on Saturday a second witch, known as Vivienne, from London, surprised Easter holidaymakers on Grebe Beach by swimming in the nude.

Unhappily, Morgawr the monster did not appear, although both witches claimed the beast was "near."

Now both Psyche and Vivienne intend to repeat their experiments on April 30 when they will be joined by Amanda, a Cornish witch from Liskeard.

HEAVY COLD

Meanwhile in the hunt for the elusive beast, Prof. Michael McCormick from New Mexico is suffering from a heavy cold.

"The result of spending too much time knee-deep in Falmouth Bay," said Doc Shiels who is partnering Prof. McCormick in the search for the monster.

Falmouth Packet , 23rd April 1976

Parsons Beach - Witches invoking Morgawr - The Cornish Sea Serpent

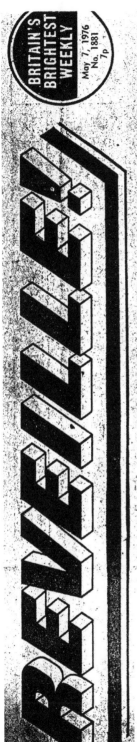

BRITAIN'S BRIGHTEST WEEKLY

May 7, 1976
No. 1881
7p

REVEILLE!

LOCH NESS MONSTER GOES WEST!

By FRANK DURHAM

TWO attractive young women who s they are witches swam naked in t sea off the Cornish coast in an uns cessful bid to lure a sea monster to the su face.

The witches, dark-haired Psyche, from verness, near the home of that other monst Nessie, and blonde Vivienne, of London, a said incantations.

But the monster people claim to have seen nicknamed Fessie— failed to make an appea ance, although there have been at least sev reported sightings.

People who have seen the creature—includi one woman who took pictures—say it h

Continued on Page

Front Page of Reveille, 7th May 1976

NEVER LET THE TRUTH GET IN THE WAY OF A GOOD STORY:
Although the local papers had been full of the weird goings on in Falmouth Bay, this was the first time that any of the national publications started to take an interest, and within months, devotees of the weird and wonderful from across the globe started turning up in the area. It was a great boon to tourism, and a boost to Tony Shiels' ever more eccentric career, but once the boys from Fleet Street became involved, the lines between what was real, and what wasn't soon became very blurred.

Young witches go swimming to lure a monster from the sea

Continued from Page 1

a humped back, long neck and a head like a snake.

Fessie started her hide-and-seek game with people who live near Falmouth just after Christmas.

One Fessie-spotter, 29-year-old Duncan Viner, of St. Georges Road, Truro, said: "I was out walking along the coast path watching sea birds.

"My first impression was that it was a whale as only a dark hump was visible. But, as I watched, it started to rise in the water and a long neck appeared.

"It looked about and then sank back under the surface. It was several hundred yards off the beach."

IT MOVED FAST

Mr. Viner, a dental technician, went on: "I think it must have been 30 or 40 feet long."

Gerry Bennett, aged 36, of Seworgan, near Falmouth, was out with his wife Jean and their four children, when he saw the monster.

He said: "I had left the rest of the family on the beach when I saw this thing going towards the Helford estuary. It was about 50 yards out.

"When I first spotted it, I thought it was a dead whale, but it started to move away and I could see it was not like any other creature I've seen.

"The part of it I could see above the water was about 12 feet in length, with an elongated neck. It moved quite fast."

LETTERS

The man at the nerve centre of the monster sightings is Roy Standring, editor of the Falmouth Packet newspaper.

He explained how a spate of letters describing sightings came in after he had published pictures, said to have been of the monster, sent in by a woman reader.

Mr. Standring said: "I was sceptical at first, but the letters made me think that the writers must have seen something.

"A naturalist has suggested that the creature is some sort of long-necked seal."

Now 38-year-old "Doc" Shiels of Ponsanooth, near Falmouth, who says he is a wizard, plans to capture the beast with the help of an American showman.

NAKED

Shiels told of the first bid to trap Fessie when the two witches swam "sky-clad"—the witches' term for naked.

He said: "They are both beautiful. Psyche is about 18 and Vivienne is in her early twenties.

"I received a letter

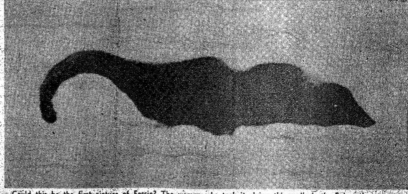

Could this be the first picture of Fessie? The woman who took it claims this really is the Falmouth monster.

Gerry Bennett saw the monster for five minutes

Duncan Viner: "It must have been 40ft. long"

from Psyche, telling me she was coming to try to raise the monster.

"She made her swim very early in the morning. I watched both her and Vivienne two days later. Both girls said an incantation. Psyche's was in Gaelic."

PRESENCE

Vivienne later wrote of her experience to the Falmouth Packet.

She said: "I swam sky-clad, in the Helford River in the name of Cernunnos. I called up the creature and I could feel its presence."

But despite the naked swimming and ritual chanting, Fessie failed to turn up.

Now wizard Shiels plans to have a go at enticing the sea monster from its lair. "We are

going to set up a series of cameras on tripods in the form of a magic circle. Then we shall use ancient invocatory techniques to lure the beast up.

"That should get over its camera shyness.

"If this doesn't work we shall consider a netting operation. It would be fairly easy to drop a net from a line of mackerel boats.

HELP

"There are some good shark fishermen round here, too. With their help, we should be able to grab hold of the beast."

And if all that fails, another witch will join Psyche and Vivienne in a three-woman nude swim to try to communicate with the monster.

"Doc" Shiels banging a drum to raise Fessie

Continued on page 21 of Reveille, 7th May 1976

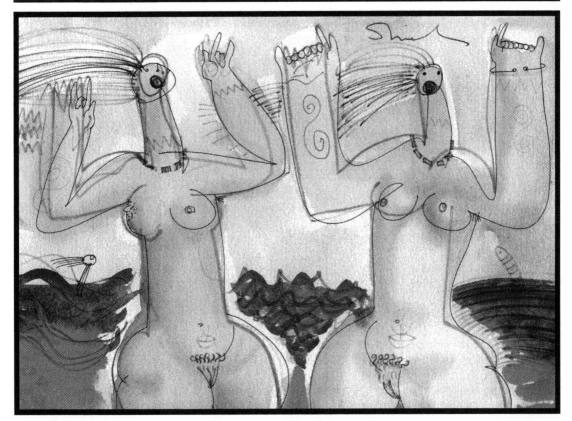

Painting by Anthony 'Doc' Shiels entitled 'Two Green Witches by the Ocean'

He described his concept of her:

> "Let's invent a young witch. We'll call her 'Psyche '.... A young girl, a good looking girl in her late teens, with, say, long black hair, and dark brown eyes. She must be intelligent, a good actress, a quick learner and keen to succeed. Let's give her a slightly Scottish accent (I've always thought the Celts were made for this kind of work). She should be willing to be photographed in the nude. Oh, sure, a lot of people will regard this as quite dreadful, but Psyche is an artist untroubled by prudish inhibitions and her sense of humour is well developed.
>
> Naturally she must be protected from the heavy sexploitation boys... " [145]

Shiels went on to explain how he would train and promote 'Psyche' as a media witch, in his terms, a 'Psychic Superstar'. He also suggests that 'Psyche' should be promoted as attempting to invoke 'The Loch Ness Monster'.

There are so many cross-references in the previous paragraphs that it is hard to know exactly where to begin. Shiels suggested that 'Psyche' should be Scottish. Pat Scott-Innes was from Inverness. [146]

Shiels suggested that 'Psyche' should invoke the Loch Ness Monster - Shiels did exactly that two years

later, and the book which contains Shiels' writings on 'how to be a psychic superstar' is lavishly illustrated by many nude, but neither particularly erotic or explicit photographs of the 'other' Psyche' - his daughter Kate.

Tony Shiels has received a great deal of criticism over the past twenty years for his 'naked witch' photographs, most of which were of his daughters, some of whom were under the age of consent at the time.

He is shocked and hurt at the criticism.

"The problem wasn't getting them to take their knickers off". [147]

he laughed when I questioned him about the witch pictures one spring morning in 1996.

"The problem was getting them to keep them on!"

He is very hurt by veiled accusations that he conducted any sort of incestuous relationship with his daughters. [148] He is emphatic that:

"I wouldn't do that.. it would be wrong. Completely wrong!"

Although the *Sun* Newspaper described the Shiels Clan as *'The Weirdest Family in the Land'* in 1978, [149] they are a very loving and close family, and not the slightest bit maladaptive or dysfunctional.

Indeed, twenty or more years after the first photographs, featuring her as a naked witch, Kate seems perfectly happy about the whole affair. Writing in 1989 she said:

> *"Some serious feminists, deeply involved in the women's movement have been rather critical about allowing myself to be photographed nude in those days. They see it as a kind of exploitation, cheap cheesecake. or something of the sort. I disagree. As well as being a witch, I was in showbusiness. I always retained full control during the photo sessions, and most of the photographers and reporters were a wee bit scared, afraid and in awe of the Shiels clan. Nothing was ever published without my permission. If anyone was being exploited, you could say that the witches - some of us anyway - exploited the press. Yes, I know some people are shocked by nudity when it is associated with witchcraft. They see it as utterly wicked and depraved. I feel sorry for those small-minded puritans.*

> *They must live horribly frustrated lives. I feel free to do whatever I wish to do, so long as it harms no one. I see nothing harmful in those photographs. For one thing they help to dispel the popular notion of a witch as an evil, ugly old hag. That is just one aspect of witch nature, as perceived by man".* [150]

I have only met one of the 'naked witches'. Miranda only became involved in Tony's invocational activities relatively late in about 1980, but in a quiet Cornish voice she explained to me that Witchcraft was women's magic and women's power. [151] I am sure that she is right. In my own limited experience, women are more powerful figures than men [152] and if the artistic and invocational activities of Tony and others can help dispel the image of the wizened old crone, or the 'wicked witch of the west', [153] then, if they achieved nothing else, they had done something very worthwhile.

158

Witchcraft in Mawnan Woods

Invoking the Owlman

However, it seemed that they succeeded in most of their aims because soon after the first invocations by the naked witches the Morgawr sightings came in thick and fast.

The national papers began to pick up on the story. *Reveille* tried to nickname the Falmouth Bay beast Fessie (short for "Falmouth's Nessie"), but the name 'Morgawr' had taken firm hold in the public consciousness. The *Reveille* story provided a neat overview of the events to date, together with interviews with some of the main protagonists. Part of the story described the early invocational experiments by the skyclad witches:

> "Shiels told of the first bid to trap 'Fessie' when the two witches swam ' sky clad' - the witches' term for naked.
>
> 'He said: 'They are both beautiful. Psyche is about 18 and Vivienne is in her early 20's. I received a letter from Psyche telling me she was coming to try and raise the monster.
> She made her swim very early in the morning. I watched both her and Vivienne two days later. Both girls said an incantation. Psyche's was in Gaelic'.

Vivienne later wrote of her experience to The Falmouth Packet:

> She said: 'I swam sky clad, in the Helford River, in the name of Cernunnos. I called up the creature and could feel its presence'.
>
> But despite the naked swimming and ritual chanting, Fessie failed to turn up.
>
> Now wizard Shiels plans to have a go at enticing the sea monster from its lair. 'We are going to set up a series of cameras on tripods in the form of a magic circle.
>
> Then we shall use ancient invocatory techniques to lure the beast up. That should get over its camera shyness.
>
> If this doesn't work we shall consider a netting operation. It would be fairly easy to drop a net from a line of mackerel boats. There are some good shark fishermen around here too. With their help, we should be able to grab hold of the beast.
>
> And if all that fails, another witch will join Psyche and Vivienne in a three-woman nude swim to try to communicate with the monster'. " [154]

The invocations must have worked, because in early May Morgawr was seen again. Mawnan-Peller wrote:

> "At the beginning of May, two London bankers, on a fishing holiday, saw a pair of monsters in the mouth of the Helford River". [155]

The Falmouth Packet printed the story of the two men, Tony Rogers and John Chambers, Merchant Bankers from London, in much greater depth:

> "The men are both keen shore fishermen. They said that on Tuesday of last week at 10.15 a. m. they were on the rocks at Parson's Beach near the mouth of the Helford River. Mr Rogers said: 'Suddenly something rose out of the water about 150-200 yards away. It was

160

The Packet has earned a niche in the annals of zoology

SIR.—Despite the efforts of dead whales and your photographic department to pass off imitations, it seems to me that the reports and photographs of Falmouth's Sea Serpent are the real thing.

As the author of a recent book on lake monsters and sea serpents, I am familiar with reports from Loch Ness and elsewhere. There is no doubt in my mind that these animals exist.

Those described by Mary F and Miss Amelia Johnston are in no way unusual. Indeed, down to their minor details and the way both witnesses reacted, they recall many other reports.

Though there are many photographs of the Loch Ness monsters (including the very strange and unconvincing set published just before Christmas), these photographs are actually the first ones of a sea serpent which have ever been published.

FRONT PAGE

I wonder if your paper realised what it was doing when it put them on the front page? You have ensured the "Falmouth Packet" a small niche in the annals of zoology or at least in my books.

Mary F's original report was very revealing (as was that from Miss Johnston), but I would be very grateful if she would contact me.

It would be a pity if her anonymity were to cast doubt on her important contribution to unravelling the mystery of the Great Sea Serpent

PETER COSTELLO,
28, Eaton Square,
Monkstown,
County Dublin.

Left: *Falmouth Packet, 9th April 1976*

Below: *Falmouth Packet, 23rd April 1976, could the black seal have been mistaken for Morgawr?*

Black seal

A BLACK seal was spotted by Sussex holiday-maker Dr. A. Shaw, in the river, near King Harry Ferry during the Easter weekend.

King Harry Ferry

Merchant bankers spot Morgawr—and a second monster

TWO merchant bank employees from the London area, on holiday in Falmouth, claimed this week to have sighted the Falmouth monster, Morgawr, near the mouth of the Helford River.

Both insisted they had no prior knowledge of its alleged existence, and one said he had in fact seen TWO monsters.

The men are Mr. Tony Rogers, 30, of Epsom Road, Croydon and Mr. John Chambers, 26, of Oakes Avenue, Crystal Palace. Mr. Rogers is branch collection controller of a bank in Croydon and Mr. Chambers is its litigation manager.

The men are both keen shore fishermen. They said that on Tuesday of last week, at 10.15 a.m., they were on the rocks at Parson's Beach, near the mouth of the Helford River.

Mr. Rogers said: "Suddenly, something rose out of the water about 150 to 200 yards away. It was greeny-grey in colour and appeared to have humps. Another, smaller one, also appeared. They were visible for about ten seconds and looked straight towards us."

Mr Chambers said: "If I had been on my own, I would have thought I'd gone round the twist. I didn't see the second one."

Mr. Rogers said: "Not having been confronted by anything like this before, I wondered what to do. We went back up the cliffside and met a man walking his dog and told him what we had seen."

The man told them it sounded like the Falmouth monster, and that there had been reports in the "Packet" about it."

The holidaymakers went to Falmouth library to look through back numbers and as a result of what they read, contacted Mr. Tony Shaw, of Pillar Cottage, Pencleuy, Feock, who is compiling a book on Morgawr.

Mr. Shaw in turn put the "Packet" in touch with the visitors. Out of the numerous claims, Mr. Shaw is taking seriously five sightings of the monster.

Mr. Rogers said he thought it quite reasonable to believe there was an unknown species living in the sea, and thought research with sonar equipment might be worthwhile from a natural history point of view.

Falmouth Packet, 14th May 1976

Although there have been sea monster reports from the coastal areas of southern Cornwall for centuries, the subject of Morgawr (and the jury is still out on the subject of whether this name is indeed the ancient Cornish for `Sea Dragon` or whether someone just made it up because it sounded better than `Fessie` - short for `Falmouth's Nessie` , which is what the tabloids christened it) came to the fore during 1975 and 1976.

And although the Mary F photographs are probably fakes (and it is hard, three decades later, to see why anyone ever took them seriously), there is a significant body of evidence to suggest that there is indeed an unknown marine animal which occasionally strays from its ocean haunts into the waters of southern Cornwall.

The mouth of the Helford River, looking towards St. Anthony's Head

The mouth to Carrick Roads, Falmouth Bay

Loch Ness man to investigate the Morgawr reports

A MAN who has made a 50-minute TV documentary for the BBC—due to be screened on Tuesday night—on the subject of the Loch Ness monster has arrived in Falmouth to conduct research into the sightings of Morgawr, the Cornish sea-giant.

He is Mr. Tim Dinsdale, of Reading, who is a member of the Royal Photographic Society and the author of four books about monsters.

Mr. Dinsdale, who says he numbers Sir Peter Scott among his friends, is taking a serious interest in Morgawr and believes the monster could well be related to the breeding colony of monsters which he is convinced inhabits Loch Ness.

His interest was aroused when he received cuttings from the "Packet" reporting the series of sightings of the local monster, generally at the mouth of the Helford River.

'MARY F'

Mr. Dinsdale would be pleased to hear from anyone with authentic information or pictures at his home, 17, Blewbury Drive, Tilehurst, Reading.

Early this week, he was working in conjunction with Mr. Tony Shaw, of Pillar Cottage, Penelewey, Feock, who told the "Packet" he was particularly anxious to contact "Mary F" who started the Morgawr saga some months ago.

Mr. Shaw is also the author of books about monsters and is busy delving into the comings and goings of Morgawr.

The THINGS THAT GO BUMP IN THE NIGHT page

★

IT has been a funny week, one way and another, for the unexpected.

Hard on the heels of the publication of a booklet, "Morgawr—the Monster of Falmouth Bay" (A Mawnan-Peller, 15p), the "Packet" has received two independent sightings of the beast.

Further bizarre reports followed—of a red-eyed birdman of Rosemullion, and of three unidentified flying objects over Flushing.

The "Packet" presents the facts, with no comment other than to confirm the bona fides of the correspondents.

Falmouth Packet, 9th July 1976

Grumpy Spaniel

SIR,—You may like to know that, in the company of my husband and four of our children, I saw Morgawr the sea-monster last Sunday morning.

They saw it, too, but my husband is unwilling to write to you himself, saying you wouldn't believe him and that he's not sure if he believes it. So I thought I'd better give you the news.

At about 9.30 a.m. we were on the Mawnan side of Grebe Beach, in the rocky part. After a swim, we sat in the sun.

"Doc" had brought a pair of binoculars (saying, "you never know") and was the first to see "something." He raised the glasses, and the thing immediately disappeared. This, he said, happened three times before he mentioned it to the rest of us.

He says he saw a dark shape of a head and long neck, first of all, about 500 yards away, towards the mouth of the river. Then it suddenly vanished.

A few minutes' later, two dark humps appeared moving through the water. Again, the thing vanished as soon as he tried to focus on it. Then, a head on the end of a long neck

---

My husband is convinced you won't believe this, but . . .

rose up and he shouted to us, then swore as it faded away.

We missed it that time, but within a few short minutes the kids started pointing and yelling, "there it is ... the monster!" Finally, I saw it (or them) myself.

It was at the edge of my vision, and when I tried to focus on the image it simply and suddenly wasn't there.

IT WORKED

After two or three frustrating attempts to get a clear picture of the thing by staring straight at it, failing each time, I decided to allow it to be coy, to stay in the "corner of my eye" so to speak. This worked.

For several seconds, I saw a large, dark, long-necked, hump-backed beast moving slowly through the water, then sinking beneath the surface.

Now, my husband, of all people, suggests that we were all hallucinating because of the unusual heat and strong sunlight.

In short, he seemed rather thrown by his own family and himself actually seeing Morgawr! He says he will have to think about it; meanwhile, I thought you would be interested in our experience.

CHRISTINE SHIELS, Ponsanooth.

Three fireballs in the sky

THREE unidentified flying objects have been reported over St. Mawes and Flushing by a Falmouth housewife.

The housewife—who prefers to remain anonymous—lives near the Beacon, Falmouth, and sighted three "fireball" type objects at about 12.30 a.m. on July 1, reflecting their images in the water.

They gradually lost height over the hills beyond St. Mawes, though, from the Beacon the objects remained visible for a further ten minutes before finally disappearing in a glow.

"I had come downstairs for a cigarette and looked out of the window when I saw these three fire-ball type objects," she said.

"One was bigger than the other two, and they were going eastward, reflecting in the water. I was high up, and saw them when they passed over St. Mawes.

"They were definitely real—a fantastic sight. One of the three lost its fire-ball outline but remained in sight with the others.

"I feel this experience must be personal to me, if no one else saw them. Keeping my mind completely open, it may be some intelligence contacting me as an individual."

I wish I'd had harpoon

THREE min-Morgawrs have been seen by a 17-year-old skin diver off Grebe Beach, in the Helford River. They were about five feet long, and disappeared into weeds.

Mr. Roy Peters, a hotel worker from Helston, told the "Packet" that the three "serpent-like things" were swimming quite happily just beneath the surface.

"I frightened them, and they swam for shelter. They had skin like seals, but because of their ugly heads and necks were definitely not seals," he said.

"I wished I'd had a harpoon gun with me. It would have made a good capture."

Slanting eyes, feathers of silver grey

SIR,—I am on holiday in Cornwall with my sister and our mother. I, too, have seen a big bird-thing like that pictured in "Morgawr the Monster of Falmouth Bay."

It was Sunday morning and the place was in the trees near Mawnan Church, above the rocky beach. It was in the trees standing like a full-grown man, but the legs bent backwards like a bird's. It saw us and quickly jumped up and rose straight up through the trees.

My sister and I saw it very clearly before it rose up. It has red slanting eyes and a very large mouth. The feathers are silvery grey and so are his body and legs. The feet are like big, black crab's claws.

We were frightened at the time. It was so strange, like something in a horror film. After the thing went up there was crackling sounds in the tree tops for ages.

LIKE A LIZARD

Later that day we spoke to some people at the camp-site, who said they had seen the Morgawr Monster on Saturday, when they were swimming with face masks and snorkels in the river, below where we saw the bird man. They saw it underwater, and said it was enormous and shaped like a lizard.

Our mother thinks we made it all up just because we read about these things, but that is not true. We really saw the bird man, though it could have been somebody playing a trick in very good costume and make-up.

But how could it rise up like that? If we imagined it, then we both imagined the same thing at the same time.

JANE GREENWOOD, Southport.

Falmouth Bay

Pendennis Point, Falmouth Bay

West Briton,
2nd September 1976

Resort 'sea monster' is back again

THE first sighting of the Falmouth "sea monster" for nearly two months was reported this week.

Mr. Bramwell Holmes, a director of the Penryn furniture firm Bramwell David Ltd., said he, his wife, Pauline and son Andrew (17), saw two humps rise above the surface in Carrick Roads, off Restronguet Point.

"The humps were a dark greyish colour and mottled. They were each about two feet high and five feet across the water," said Mr. Holmes. "The water seemed to boil before they broke surface."

He added: "It was very interesting but also a little frightening. Whatever it was submerged but came up again briefly after we had turned our boat round to get a better look at it."

The sighting occurred on Friday evening as the Holmes were returning to their home at Crest Cottage, Feock, in their 17ft. motor-boat, after a trip to St. Mawes.

Falmouth Packet,
30th July 1976

Fishermen 'sight' Morgawr

Fishing 25 miles south of the Lizard recently, Mr. George Vinnicombe, of Glasney Road, Falmouth, and Mr. John Cock, of East End, Redruth, say they saw Morgawr.

They described him as being 20ft. long with a back like corrugated iron. The sea was calm and at first they thought it was a huge tyre in the water.

Then a head "like an enormous seal" came out of the water. Morgawr glowered at them for a moment and then slowly submerged.

"We're not nuts. There is definitely something out there." Mr. Vinnicombe said.

Falmouth Packet,
30th September 1976

Morgawr back in business

MORGAWR, Falmouth's very own sea monster, has raised its ugly humps again.

The latest sighting was in Carrick Roads on Friday, when Mr. Bramwell Holmes was returning by boat from St. Mawes to his home at Crest Cottage, Feock.

He said: "The sun was just setting, and there was hardly a ripple. We saw it three times within ten minutes. The water boiled before it appeared."

One, and then two humps were visible just off Restronguet Point, and Mr. Holmes, a director - of - the Penryn furniture manufacturers, Bramwell David Ltd., also spotted a "snake-shaped head."

"It was not like anything I have ever seen before," he said.

More of Morgawr

A FALMOUTH man who confesses he viewed with scepticism reported sightings of Morgawr, the monster of Falmouth Bay, is not laughing any more.

Mr. Donald Ferris, of 4, Penarth Road, Falmouth, saw Nessie's Cornish cousin for himself early on Wednesday morning, while taking his dog for a walk on Gyllyngvase beach.

"It was ten past seven, and the thing that first caught my eye was that the diving raft was at a funny angle.

The creature looked to be coming from the direction of Swanpool, and I saw it for fully three minutes.

"It was between the raft and the beach. It was a massive thing, 50 to 60ft. long. There was a fair bit of mist out to sea, but I could see quite clearly so close to the shore," he said.

"We have laughed so many times at the reports of sightings by visitors. I believe it now."

Falmouth Packet,
10th September 1976

'Monster' seen again off resort

THE Falmouth "sea monster" reportedly came within 40 yards of the shore at the resort's main beach last week.

Mr Donald Ferris (63), of 4, Penarth-road, Falmouth, was exercising his dog on Gyllyngvase Beach at about 7.10 a.m.

He said: "I saw what looked like a small boat coming towards Gyllyngvase from Swanpool. When it got closer, I realised it was a creature like a giant eel, at least 60ft long and dark grey."

As it submerged, its back reared out of the water in a hump formation.

Mr Ferris, a toilet attendant employed by Carrick Council, added "Until now I was convinced this monster thing was a big joke. But I've never seen anything like this in my life. It shook me."

Morgawr off the Scillies

IS Morgawr, the monster of Falmouth Bay, a family man?

The question has been posed by art historian and sailing enthusiast Mr. Patrick Dolan, of Cardiff, following a sighting 30 miles NNW of the Scillies.

Mr. Dolan was sailing his 28ft. sloop, Daisy from the Scillies to Kinsale in Ireland when he saw Morgawr—or a close relative—on the high seas, well away from his normal habitat in the Falmouth Bay/Helford River area.

'DISTURBANCE'

He was sailing single-handed on August 11 when, at about sunset he "suddenly saw a peculiar disturbance in the water."

"I could see quite distinctly a kind of worm-like shape in the water and the neck was about 8ft. out of the water.

"I was extremely nervous. I have plenty experience of single-handed sailing and though I have seen fishes, porpoises and whales, I have never seen anything like this. It was about 40ft. long and propelled itself with an undulating movement.

"It was moving at 10-12 knots and it overtook me. I must have had it in my vision for about 20 minutes," he said.

Mr. Dolan has just returned from two months at sea. He left Falmouth on July 9 and though his boat is now at Kinsale he has kept it for the past four years at Flushing.

Left: *West Briton, 16th September 1976*

Right: *Falmouth Packet, 24th September 1976*

Shy Nessie sends her relatives

AN INTERNATIONAL team of psychics claimed success yesterday after their bid to raise the Loch Ness Monster.

Nessie did not actually appear . . . . but the psychics say several of her relatives around the world did.

The team, led by Mr David Hoy, an American writer and lecturer on extra-sensory perception, concentrated all their thoughts on Nessie for three days.

They hoped to draw her up from the depths by 'psychic energy.'

Nessie apparently stayed put. But there were two reported sightings of a legendary monster called Morgawr in the sea off Falmouth, Cornwall.

Telepathist Mr Tony Shiels was busy thinking about Nessie at the time, at his home near Redruth.

'Something unusual' was seen in Loch Morar, Invernesshire, while Major Leslie May was concentrating from his home in Edinburgh.

And the Indian member of the team, Jadoo Chandrao from Calcutta, claimed he was responsible for a 50ft. monster reported in a Russian lake.

'He was just a bit off target,' said Mr Shiels.

'We don't know why all these things happened, but we do think it is highly significant that they did.'

American Mr Hoy now plans to establish psychic contact with a dolphin—and bring it to Loch Ness, to contact the monster.

Daily Mail, 4th February 1977

Morgawr spotted again

A FAMILIAR head broke the surface of Falmouth Bay last Wednesday. Morgawr was back in business.

He was spotted by Mr. David Clarke, editor of the Cornish Life magazine, who had been photographing local entertainer Doc Shiels "invoking the monster" on the shoreline beneath Mawnan old church.

"It was a cold morning and I was all for leaving when he started shouting that there was something in mid-river," said Mr. Clarke.

"I saw a small dot moving towards us, which I presumed to be a seal. It came across the river to within 60-70 feet.

"It started to zig-zag backwards and forwards, and I could see movement in the water well behind the head

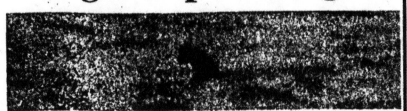

which suggested it was a great deal longer than a seal."

He found through the telephoto lens of his camera that the object was much thicker set than any seal. Then his dog barked at the apparition, and it sank from view.

But Mr. Clarke is reluctant to confirm the existence of such a beastie.

"I am suspicious. I know Doc as an entertainer and illusionist. I have seen him saw a lady in half, and I know that to be a trick. I have seen him bend spoons in front of my eyes by ESP and suspect that to be a trick, although he denies it emphatically."

But if it was an illusion, how was it done? Mr. Clarke confesses he has no idea.

His camera jammed at the crucial moment of the monster's appearance, and he had no admissible prints. The picture we have published was taken by Doc Shiels—though Mr. Clarke says it shows what he saw in the water.

Falmouth Packet, 13th December 1976

COCK COQUE BERBERECHO
GURNARD SOAP AQUS GRILLED
                SARDINES
PANCHOWDERINGS SURROUNDING
SEA HEADS AND MORE
            SEA HEADS
GIGANTIC SPERM AND SALT
            COD PIECE—

WHALE OF A TIME
        TASH TEGO
    HARPOONEER

MISTER BIG

15 HOLNE COURT

EXWICK

EXETER
DEVON EX4 2NA

CORNWALL

Photo: Dave Bastilow, **2DC 1887**
Published by John Hinde Ltd., Redruth, Cornwall. Printed in Ireland. ©

greeney-grey in colour and appeared to have humps. Another, smaller one also appeared. They were visible for about ten seconds and looked straight towards us.

Mr Chambers said: 'If I had been on my own I would have thought that I had gone round the twist. I didn't see the second one'.

Mr Rogers said: 'Not having been confronted by anything like this before, I wondered what to do. We went back up the hillside, met a man who was walking his dog, and told him what we had seen'.

The man told him it sounded like the Falmouth monster and that there had been reports in 'The Packet' about it"... [156]

In early June, veteran monster hunter, the late Tim Dinsdale, from Loch Ness visited Falmouth to carry out some research into the monster. Apart from the fact that he became "good friends" with 'Doc', it is unclear at this distance of time how much, if anything he achieved. [157]

About six weeks earlier, Peter Costello from Dublin, another well-known figure in the annals of Cryptozoology, became involved in the search, tangentially at least, when he wrote a letter to *The Falmouth Packet* which pointed out that although there had been several photographs taken of Lake Monsters across the world, the Mary F photographs were actually the very first pictures ever published of a sea-serpent. [158]

Another letter in the same issue made an extraordinary claim about the creature:

"Sir - I would like to clear up the mystery of the 'Falmouth Monster'.

In 1936 I was strolling along Castle Beach when to my utter amazement I saw thousands of limpets detach themselves from the rocks and attach themselves to a huge piece of seaweed.

I was astounded to see that on the other end of the seaweed were thousands of winkles. There then ensued a 'tug of war', ending in the whole disappearing about two miles off-shore. I did photograph the things but had no film in my camera.

On returning to my squadron. I discussed this with the Station Education Officer. He came up with the solution that such a happening occurred every forty years and that as each contest is inconclusive, the intervening years are spent in special training by each side.

Perhaps this year one side will obtain a result and become holders of the 'Sea weed Cup'".
[159]

The letter was signed by John J. Bickenson from Hornsea, and I can only think that it must have been a joke. I have never heard of any other reports of such a preposterous nature.

In July there was another letter to *'The Packet'*, this time from Mrs Christine Shiels, wife of the Wizard:

Sir - You may like to know, that in the conpany of my husband and four of my children, I saw Morgawr the sea monster last Sunday morning. They saw it too, but my husband is un-

'Mrs S'

willing to write to you himself, saying you wouldn't believe him, and that he's not sure if he believes it. So I thought I'd better give you the news.

At about 9.30 a.m. we were on the Mawnan side of Grebe Beach, in the rocky part. After a swim we sat in the sun.

'Doc' had brought a pair of binoculars (saying 'you never know'), and was the first to see 'something'. He raised the glasses and the thing immediately disappeared. This, he said, happened three times before he mentioned it to the rest of us.

He says he saw a dark shape of a head and a long neck, first of all, about 500 yards away, towards the mouth of the river. Then it suddenly vanished.

A few minutes later, two dark humps appeared moving through the water. Again, the thing vanished as soon as we tried to focus on it. Then, a head on the end of a long neck rose up and he shouted to us, then swore as it faded away.

We missed it that time, but within a few short minutes, the kids started pointing and yelling, 'there it is ... the monster!' Finally, I saw it (or them) for myself.

It was at the edge of my vision, and when I tried to focus on the image it simply, and suddenly wasn't there. After two or three frustrating attempts to get a clear picture of the thing by staring straight at it, failing each time, I decided to allow it to be coy, to stay in the 'corner of my eye', so to speak. This worked.

For several seconds I saw a large, dark, long-necked, hump-backed beast moving slowly through the water, then sinking beneath the surface.

Now, my husband of all people, suggests that we are all hallucinating, because of the unusual heat and strong sunlight.

In short, he seems rather thrown by his own family and himself, actually seeing Morgawr! He says he will have to think about it; meanwhile I thought you would be interested in our experience". [160]

The same letters page included the report of the St Mawes fireballs, recounted earlier in this chapter. The letter from Jane Greenwood, quoted in full in chapter two, and yet another Morgawr sighting; this time one that also presented some peculiar aspects:

"Three mini-Morgawrs have been seen by a 17 year old skin-diver off Grebe Beach, in the Helford River. They were about five feet long and disappeared into weeds.

Mr Roy Peters, a hotel worker from Helston, told the 'Packet' that the three 'serpent-like things' were swimming quite happily just below the surface.

'I frightened them and they ran for shelter. They had skins like seals, but because of their ugly heads and necks were definitely not seals', he said.

'I wished I'd had a harpoon gun with me. It would have made a good capture'." [161]

Later in July, Mr. George Vinnecombe, a staple attraction on many TV shows about Morgawr over the next twenty years, [162] was in his boat twenty-five miles south of the Lizard. With him was John Cock. They were fishing when they saw Morgawr:

"They described him as being 20 feet long with a back like corrugated iron. The sea was calm, and at first they thought it was a huge tyre in the water.

Then a head, 'like an enormous seal', came out of the water. Morgawr glowered at them for a moment and then submerged". [163]

Mawnan-Peller recounted other encounters with Morgawr during 1976:

"Miss Amelia Johnson, on holiday from London, was taking a walk in the Rosemullion area when she saw a 'strange form suddenly emerge from the water in Falmouth Bay'. She describes 'a sort of prehistoric dinosaur thing with a neck the length of a lamp-post'.

Gerald Bennett of Seworgan, saw a creature swimming in the Helford, one afternoon. The part of it above the water was 'about twelve feet in length, with an elongated neck'.

Amelia Johnson's Monster, 1976

On Good Friday, 1976, a fifteen-year-old schoolboy from Helston spotted a 'weird animal with two humps and a long neck like a snake', moving up the river between Toll Point and the Gew. The monster was 'slimy, black and about twenty five feet long'. He took a photograph of the animal which was later shown on BBC television in the Spotlight programme". [164]

This last sighting was somewhat peculiar, and is often considered to be nothing more than an elaborate hoax. The circumstances surrounding the report are described more fully by Tony Shiels in his book *Monstrum – a Wizard's Tale*:

"'Hello', said a voice, and there stood a schoolboy in a schoolboy's blazer. He looked about thirteen or fourteen. 'You're Doc Shiels', he told me, and I nodded philosophically having been told the same thing a thousand times before. 'Hello', he said again, 'I'm Andrew'. I nodded again believing him. Andrew carried an impressive looking 35mm SLR camera with a telephoto lens..." [165]

It turned out that 'Andrew' came from Helston, and claimed to have taken, what 'Doc' described as a 'fuzzy looking' print of the monster. He gave this to the bemused Wizard, but refused to tell him his full name or address. 'Doc', was very suspicious and believed, both then and now, that he was being set up as part of a schoolboy prank.

It would, we believe, be unwise to consider this peculiar episode too seriously as supporting evidence for the existence of Morgawr, although it is undoubtedly, corroboration of the general feeling of strangeness that imbued the whole of that singular year.

There were no sightings of Morgawr in Falmouth Bay or the Helford River during August, perhaps because the animal was further west. On 11th August, a sailing enthusiast from Cardiff was alone on his 28ft sloop, when his sighting occurred:

174

"I could see quite distinctly a kind of worm-like shape in the water and the neck was about eight feet out of the water. I was extremely nervous. I have plenty of experience of single-handed sailing and though I have seen fishes, porpoises and whales, I have never seen anything like this. It was about 40ft long and propelled itself with an undulating movement.

It was moving at 10-12 knots and it overtook me. I must have had it in my vision for about twenty minutes". [166]

In September, Mr Bramwell Holmes was travelling from St. Mawes to Feock by boat when he saw the creature:

"The sun was just setting, and there was hardly a ripple. We saw it three times within ten minutes. The water boiled before it appeared'.

One, and then two humps were visible just off Restronguet Point, and Mr Holmes (...) also spotted a 'snake shaped head'.

'It was not like anything I have ever seen before', he said". [167]

Mr Holmes was with his family at the time and they described the humps as being a dark greyish colour and mottled. They were about five feet high and two feet across the water.

A week or so later there was another report of an animal between 50 and 60 feet in length just off Gyllyngvase beach. One does feel that the witness, a Falmouth man called Donald Ferris, may have unknowingly exaggerated the size of the creature as his estimate was double the size of most of the Morgawr reports, he described the creature as being like a 'giant eel', which is also somewhat different from most of the sightings of Morgawr reported from the south Cornwall coastline. [168]

The last sighting of 1976 was perhaps the most exciting. Tony Shiels was on the shoreline below Mawnan Old Church with David Clarke from *Cornish Life* magazine who was doing a photo shoot on him. He wanted photographs of Tony invoking Morgawr to illustrate a feature he was planning. Tony duly obliged, and David Clarke was taking photographs when:

"I saw a small dot moving towards us, which I presumed to be a seal. It came across the river to within 60-70 feet. It started to zig-zag backwards and forwards, and I could see movement in the water well behind the head which suggested that it was a great deal longer than a seal". [169]

His dog started to bark at the animal and it sank from view. He was immediately suspicious of Tony and accused him of setting up the illusion by some kind of trick. This is something that Tony has always strenuously denied.

The interesting thing is that while Tony's pictures, which were taken on an inferior camera without a telephoto lens, came out properly, although the image was indistinct and not really conclusive, the 'jinx' which has bedevilled fortean researchers for many years, and in many continents, struck again, and David Clarke's camera malfunctioned causing pictures which were seriously double-exposed. They were however probably the most convincing pictures yet obtained of the mysterious creature of Falmouth Bay.

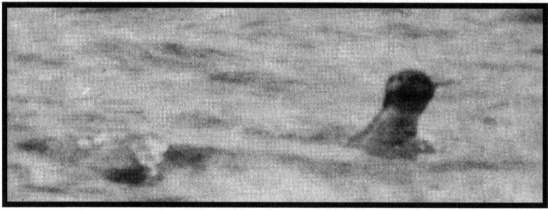

Above: *Triple exposure of 'Doc' Shiels and Morgawr taken by David Clarke, 17th November 1976.*
Below: *A enlargement of Morgawr's head and neck*

Above Left: *A highly enlarged section of negative showing the creature's head swimming towards the camera.*
Above Right: *An enlargement of the negative showing the profile of the Morgawr's head and neck.*

Morgawr approaches the shore of Parson's beach,
photographs taken by Gerry Bennett early in the morning of 31st January 1977

Telegraph, February 1977

Western Morning News, 1977

The wizard disappears to see shots of monster

A SIGHTING of Morgawr, the Cornish sea monster, has been reported to psychic and wizard Tony "Doc" Shields.

For three days, up to midnight on Wednesday, Doc was using his psychic powers in the Falmouth area to try to raise Morgawr from the deep.

Yesterday he received a report that Mr. Gerry Bennett had spotted the long-necked monster near Mawnan Smith and taken colour slides of the beast. Last night, Doc Shields was heading from his home in Ponsanooth to assess the quality and authenticity of the pictures.

On Monday he had received an unconfirmed sighting from a schoolboy near Durgan.

In a transatlantic phone link with Kentucky at midnight on Wednesday Doc discussed his results with Mr. Tony Hoyle, one of six psychics taking part in the chain of concentrated thought to raise monsters from the deep.

WILD THINGS

"We have had some wild things in Paducah," said Mr. Hoyle. "It started with a flock of 40 or 50 pigeons landing on my lawn."

Mr. Hoyle said he had had a "fantastic response" in America. The conversation was being transmitted over several radio stations in the United States, and Doc said he was "delighted with the results in Cornwall so far."

Mr. Hoyle was all set to leave for Marine Land, Florida, with the hope that a dolphin would respond to his psychic messages.

"I'm getting it trained and I will bring it over to Britain and let it loose in Loch Ness and Loch Shiel to ferret the monsters out," he said.

Doc told him about Beaky, the friendly Cornish dolphin, and Mr. Hoyle replied that he would come over to this country and transmit his thoughts to Beaky, who could act as "a messenger to raise Morgawr from the depths."

Is it a monster hoax or not?

The WMN Diary

IT is enough to give any self-respecting monster the hump. Since 1933, there have been 10,000 reported sightings and numerous photographs taken of the Loch Ness monster and yet there are still those who refuse to believe in its existence.

Today author Stuart Campbell publishes his own work, The Loch Ness Monster, and after sifting through all the evidence claims that every sighting can be dismissed or explained away as a wave formations or otters or deer swimming across the loch.

To settle the question for once and for all, I set off in search of Doc Shiels, the genial Irishman who took some of the clearest published photographs of the monster in May 1977.

This column has an unswerving faith in the good Doc since on St. George's Day this year we asked him if he could arrange for the little-seen Cornish sea monster the Morgawr to rise to the surface by way of a celebration of the George and the Dragon legend.

I had contacted the Doc then by way of a sort of joke. But within days of our report of his invocation of the Morgawr I began getting unsolicited letters from readers saying they had seen the beast rise from the deep.

I found Doc Shiels in his home from home, the Stag Hunt Inn, at Ponsanooth, downing a pint of draught Guinness from which he claims he draws his mystical powers.

"Of course Nessie exists," he says quaffing his stout. "I've seen her and so have thousands of others. I've even taken photographs as have others — not that I would necessarily want to argue that a photograph constitutes positive proof of existence."

The Doc published his own theory two years ago that Nessie is an elephantine squid, which he claims is the only explanation that fits in with the descriptions in all the sightings and with the ancient engravings of the Picts.

"I think it must be a type of giant squid," he says. "Biologists now admit that such creatures exist though they are rare.

The Doc, though, is not a figure taken too seriously in the zoological and biological worlds.

His doctorate, for example, was bought for just a few dollars from an American "university" and during his invocations of monsters from the deep he likes to be accompanied by naked witches.

"That's the old beauty and the beast idea," he explains, "and anyway it has its compensations even if the beast doesn't turn up.

"But it does work against me. The establishment refuse to believe that someone like me should see Nessie when they with all their diplomas, scientific research and expensive equipment cannot."

The Doc's own involvement with the monster began back in 1975 when reports of Cornwall's own Morgawr began to circulate.

"The fishermen began coming back into Falmouth saying that there was something out there eating all the mackerel in 1975.

"By 1976 people were taking pictures of it and they were beginning to appear in the papers

"So, as I was working as a stage magician at the time, I thought it might be good for business if I claimed to have brought the thing out of the water myself.

"My claims got a fair amount of publicity and eventually came the day when someone wanted me to put my powers to the test.

"I went out with the editor of the Cornish Times and started waving my arms about like someone out of a medicine show and lo and behold the thing came out of the sea.

"The editor of the Cornish Times was supposed to be taking pictures but his camera jammed, but anyway loads of other pictures were taken of the Morgawr and I have to admit I was more than a little baffled myself with these new found powers.

"So I thought I would test them out on Nessie. Up I went in 1977 did the same thing and she appeared, too, and this time I took the pictures.

So what does he think of Stuart Campbell's claims that the Loch Ness monster does not even exist?

"Well," he says, supping once more from a fresh pint of Guinness, "I know she's there, my photographs were authenticated by the Royal Photographic Society.

"So I think Mr. Campbell's book must be a hoax. In fact, I've seen no evidence at all so far to show that he even exists.

"Until I see proof to the contrary I shall refuse to believe that there is such a beast as Stuart Campbell."

Fraser Massey

Six months later, 'Pendennis' a columnist in *The Falmouth Packet*, who took his name from one of the most prominent features of the Falmouth area topography, included the following piece in his weekly column:

"It's 20 feet long with three humps and a long neck! Yours aye, The Doc". [170]

read the enigmatic headline. The story beneath was no less extraordinary, especially at the time, although, the events it recounted were soon to become a major part of fortean and cryptozoological history.

> *"My mail in the past fortnight has included several excited communications sent from the shores of Loch Ness in Bonny Scotland, each signed 'yours aye – The Doc'.*
>
> *Mr Tony 'Doc' Shiels from Ponsanooth is once more trying to astound the world by raising 'Nessie', and hopefully several other legendary beasties including Falmouth's own Morgawr.*
>
> *As previously explained, it's the thought that counts.*
>
> *Mr Shiels, whose many and varied titles include 'Wizard' and 'Professional Psychic' is trying to raise Nessie by means of telepathy. The Doc tells me that within minutes of his arrival in Fort William a sighting of the Loch Shiel monster was reported (20 feet long, three humps and a long neck).*
> *'I am naturally counting this as a sign of success', said the Doc.*
>
> *The Doc says in a later letter that he has since spotted Nessie twice in Urquhart Bay.*
>
> *And yes, he did take photographs, but it will be some time before we can see them, he explains, because the negatives have to be sent off, undeveloped, to the Natural History Museum for authentication.*
>
> *Watch this space".* [171]

As we all know, despite a bizarrely surreal series of misadventures he did manage to take what are almost certainly the finest photographs ever taken of the Loch Ness Monster. But this, like the post 1976 sightings of Morgawr is, like they say, another story!

*The **CASE** for the <u>G</u>reat <u>S</u>erpent*

It's Nessie -in colour close-up

Now she's putting on two shows a day ... says Wizard of the West Tony Shiels, but it's all due to his psychic power

by FRANK DURHAM

HERE she is, that world-famous tourist attraction, the Loch Ness monster, as you have probably never seen her before ... in close-up and full, amazing colour. She popped her head out of the water 100yd from holidaymaker Tony Shiels and posed just long enough for him to take a couple of pictures.

Tony, who is 38 and comes from Cornwall, explained: "It was about 4pm and I was in the tower of Urquhart Castle, which overlooks the loch. I was taking pictures and turned round for another view ... and there she was.

"She was strong and rigid, greenish-brown with a muscular neck. The head and neck were standing perhaps about 4ft out of the water.

"I took the picture as the monster was looking towards me, then she faced away and went down tail first as smooth as silk. What I remember most was the fleshy, frog-like mouth.

"The monster was hideous ... and looked really grotesque."

It was the second time that day that Tony, a professional Punch and Judy man, had seen Nessie. He said: "I was staying at Inchnacardoch Lodge. At 8am I was in the lodge car park with five other people. Suddenly, my wife Chris pointed out three humps gliding through the water.

"We couldn't have been mistaken because the water was mirror-smooth. I watched the humps for about 10 seconds. I measured them by eye against some sheep that were grazing on the bank of the loch.

"Each hump, which was a dark colour, was twice the size of a sheep. Unfortunately, my camera and binoculars were upstairs."

Tony says he wasn't surprised Nessie so obligingly appeared for his camera. At home in Ponsanooth, near Truro, he is known as the Wizard of the West.

● ● ●

At the time Nessie popped up, Tony and six other psychics round the world were taking part in an operation they called Monstermind '77. They planned to bring the monsters to the surface "by psychic means".

Tony said modestly: "I am sure Nessie appeared as a result of my psychic powers. I knew the weather would be perfect that day.

"Conditions were absolutely right for a special happening . . . and there was one. I personally think the loch is full of these monsters. They have been breeding there for the last 70 million years at least."

Tony claims that the two photographs he managed to snatch in the few seconds Nessie was on the surface have already caused a monster-sized stir.

He said: "The pictures have been described by Tim Dinsdale, whose books include *The Leviathans* and *The Loch Ness Monster*, as 'earth shattering'.

"They are to be used in lectures by Sir Peter Scott and will be submitted for computer analysis in the United States."

Technical note on those Nessie snaps: Tony Shiels used high-speed Ektachrome film in his 35mm SLR, Zenith EM fitted with a 150mm telephoto lens. The speed was 1/500sec at between f11 and f16.

With a fleshy, frog-like mouth, the monster Tony Shiels snapped (top) looks very much like the classic photograph (above), taken in 1934. Left, a distant cousin? This decomposed corpse, netted in April off the New Zealand coast, has led to speculation that there may be other prehistoric beasts still roaming in the depths

Titbits, 15-21 September 1977

Tony Shiels's Loch Ness monster photographs are still causing controversy, three decades after he first presented them to the fortean omniverse.

Many people believe that they do - indeed - show the mysterious lake monster of the Great Glen, but others claim that they are merely photographs of a cleverly executed oil painting. `Doc` is certainly a skilled enough artist to have produced such a painting, but still claims that they are exactly what he has always claimed them to be - photographs of the world's most famous unknown animal!

CHAPTER SIX: INVITATION

*"Something very slowly, very dimly, has been working in my
mind and now is clear to me: there are no incidences there
are only coincidences"*

Russell Hoban *'Turtle Diary'* (1975)

It was a Friday lunchtime in early May of 1996, and Alison and I were beginning to suspect that we had strayed into a particularly far-fetched and badly scripted episode of *The X Files*. [1] We were sitting in the departure lounge at Plymouth Airport, waiting to put Tony on his 'plane back to Ireland, after one of his occasional visits to Cornwall. Tony, as is his wont, was drinking Guinness, and I was sipping from a can of rather nasty, lukewarm lager, as Alison, who was driving, sat and drank her coffee in a ladylike manner. It was a pleasant interlude and I was taking advantage of a session that I could spend with Tony, when both of us were completely sober, in order to catch up on a few interviews for my book.

A few weeks earlier at the *Fortean Times* 'Unconvention 96' [2] I had been chatting to co-editor Paul Sieveking, who was kind enough to give me a present of a rare copy of *Fortean Times* # 29. [3] The back cover featured the notorious 'Doc' Shiels colour photograph of the Loch Ness Monster, and the content included a scholarly analysis of the pictures by a number of photographic and fortean experts. [4] I thought that Tony might be interested in seeing it, so I had taken it to Cornwall with us. During the general mayhem of the three days we had spent with him, (as one may have gauged from the earlier chapters in this book, time spent with the good doctor, especially when one is vainly trying to achieve certain specific objectives, is often difficult to explain, and wrapped in a surreal cloud of word play and Guinness), we hadn't actually got around, either to showing it to him, or indeed to discussing the subjects that had been on my agenda for research into this book.

I passed him the magazine, open at the article in question, but before he could do more than glance at the heading, things started to get very strange. I have always been very suspicious of conspiracy theorists. I don't know what happened at Roswell, New Mexico, in 1947, and whilst I am certain that certain people in the American Government know perfectly well what happened, I am equally certain that most, if not all the theories propounded by conspiracy theorists, UFO buffs, and paranoid schizophrenics are complete bunkum. Later that afternoon, however, I had an appointment to visit a colleague and

friend of mine, who was to give me a sheaf of papers relating to certain events that happened in Newquay in 1978.

I don't really believe that the CIA, and MI5, are tapping the 'phones and reading the mail of people engaged in UFO research (see appendix 4 where I am forced to eat my words). Anyway, I've never really been involved in UFO research - most of what I do is obscure, and slightly dull zoology - this present work is somewhat of a departure for me, so I never felt that I was in any danger from 'Big Brother'. Suddenly the airport lounge seemed to be full of security guards. There were only about half a dozen men in uniform, but there were a number of rather sinister looking men in black suits, wearing sunglasses, and looking quietly menacing. A man in plain clothes, who introduced himself to Tony as a senior police officer came over to us. I was engaged, at the time in assembling my tape recorder so I could tape an interview with Tony, but at the sound of the words:

"Mr Shiels, can I see your passport?",

which was accompanied by the practiced 'flashing' of a warrant card in a leather wallet, prompted me to put my tape recorder away very quickly. They conversed in low voices. I didn't try to overhear their conversation, but I gathered that Tony had shown the policeman all the relevant travel documents, and that all was in order.

I decided that this was the right time to go to the lavatory. Sitting in the formica-lined cubicle, I was effectively invisible, and so could overhear snatches of a conversation between one of the 'men in black' and someone else over a walkie-talkie. I only heard some of what they said, but the words 'special branch' were mentioned on several occasions. I was also shocked to hear my own name as well.

Slinking out of the 'loo' as soon as the coast was clear, I rejoined Alison and Tony. They told me, that with no notice whatsoever, Tony's plane had been cancelled. I began to feel somewhat scared. The policeman came over to talk to Tony again, and the P.A. system asked Alison, as the owner of our Transit Van to report to the information desk. She was asked to move our van on the grounds that it was causing an obstruction (it wasn't), and Tony was told that his flight would now be departing three hours late. The men in black suits were still milling around. I just sat there feeling very paranoid.

I still don't know to this day what it was all about. The harassment, such as it was continued all afternoon, but we were, by this time at least, in such a state of advanced paranoia, that even quite innocent occurrences were open to vicious misinterpretation. Was the 'target' of this activity me or Tony? Were the motives magical, ufological or, as it seems more likely, political. Were Alison and I being warned against collecting the UFO related documents which we have quoted in full later in this chapter? Or was Tony, in the words of Shane McGowan just guilty of *"being Irish in the wrong place and at the wrong time"*, [5][6] in a week when security at all airports and military bases had been stepped up because of a rumoured IRA blitz to coincide with the 80th anniversary of the Easter uprising?[7] Was Tony's flight cancelled only because he was the only passenger? Or was there a more sinister motive?

With all these questions teeming around my brain, and, I suspect, the brains of Tony and Alison, we did the only thing open to us. We went to the bar, ordered another round of drinks, some of which, by the way, we managed to get the airport authorities to pay for as some measure of compensation for the inconvenience Tony had suffered.

As we now had three hours to kill, we sat down with our drinks, and as the men in black suits looked on

with interest, I got out the 1978 copy of *Fortean Times*, and assembled by tape recorder and microphone, preparatory to finally commencing my interview.

The article, which was mostly about Loch Ness, included an excerpt from a letter that 'Doc', had written to Bob Rickard in which he mentioned the Owlman:

> *"Within the next few weeks I'm getting out of the psychic game. My witch-daughters are retiring from the monster-raising business too. As a final fling Kate and I will have a crack at Owlman and Morgawr so we can say our final farewells to them. I want to get on with other things .... Like painting and writing .... We're all fed up with the 'backlash' effect of too much psychic game playing. It's caused some misery in the last few years. We – Kate and I – would like you to announce that we're no longer playing witch and wizard after May 1st ... "*[8]

I was interested in this last 'crack' at Owlman, and asked Tony about it. He said that it had involved him doing his own inimitable thing, and Kate:

"prancing around with no knickers on", [9]

but that the Owlman had not shown himself in physical form.

At about the same time however, a series of unpleasant events took place at Newquay Zoo, on the North Coast of the county.

I don't know whether the two episodes; the Owlman of Mawnan, and what I cynically once dubbed. 'The unidentified flying wallaby slasher of Newquay', are related but I suspect they are. I am not just following quantum-fortean methodology of the interconnectedness of all things, but the more one investigates the affair, the more parallels one finds. Both episodes seem to have begun with the same symbology - that of mutilated waterfowl. It seems, as we have shown, that despite reports suggesting otherwise, the mysterious bird which had attacked the two boys at Porthowan in the 'twenties', was some unknown form of waterfowl injured mysteriously, [10] and it seems, although the accounts do not all tally exactly, from what I have been told, by one ex-employee of the zoo, [11] who has asked me to respect her anonymity, that the events of the early summer of 1978 started when, one morning staff at the zoo found a dead, mutilated muscovy duck. [12]

I first heard about the matter, sixteen years after the event in the early spring of 1992 when I was engaged in research into Alien Big Cat sightings in Devon and Cornwall. [13]

One afternoon I was engaged in an interview with a Police Sergeant from Middlemoor Police Station in Exeter. [14] I will not name him as I have not received his permission to do so, [15] and I am quite aware that certain senior officers in the Devon and Cornwall Police Force do not approve of their officers talking to paranormal or fortean researchers. It would be easy to build into this some paranoid conspiracy theory about how 'the powers that be' are trying to suppress information about fortean events, [16] but the truth is, I fear, far more prosaic. I have been told, on good authority, that the Police, especially in this region equate an interest in the paranormal with drugs and excesses of a hippy lifestyle. Indeed, they have a fair amount of justification in so doing; many so-called researchers that I have met over the years turn out to be stoned wannabe-anarchists, with wild staring eyes, dreadlocks and a thin dog on a string. Equally - just as many researchers turn out to be genuine, intelligent people with an interest in what lies beyond the next turn in the road, but in many cases the attitude of the police is understand-

185

able. [17]

I had spent something over forty minutes talking to this particular officer, when he stunned me by asking whether I had heard of the 'Wallaby Slashings in Newquay'. I hadn't, so he told me what he could. In 1976 and 1977 there was a series of inexplicable attacks on livestock at Newquay Zoo. Mystery big cats had been seen in Devon and Cornwall at that time and it was thought by many that the events were somehow connected. [18] He couldn't remember any more details but suggested that I should telephone the one man who knew more about the killings than anybody else: Mr Marshall, the head zoo-keeper at the time.

I tracked down Mr Marshall, by dint of a number of telephone calls, some bare-faced cheek and a lot of luck. I eventually found him in a small house on the outskirts of Newquay. He was long retired and in failing health, and since the death of his wife he had been living with his daughter. He was kind enough to grant me a lengthy interview, the relevant portions of which I quote in full:

> *"We had a spate of beheadings. The suggestion was, at that time, because there was no blood or gore or anything at all anywhere in the zoo, and the head had been removed, we thought that it was the same as the rustlers do in Australia. They lay sacking on the ground, and kill the sheep, and then wrap it up so there is nothing left.*
>
> *We lost, I think it was two wallabies, some black swans and some geese. All beheaded. Now this, apparently was happening all over the world at this time. It was happening in America, Japan and China as well as here, and they tried to link it up with sightings of U.F.O.'s*
>
> *There was no blood left in the animals at all, and I had the area U.F.O. compositor, or whatever he called himself come down, and the suggestion was that it was beings from Outer Space who came down and needed the blood or whatever else it was that they drew out of these animal to survive. It never developed any further than that. I believe that they got a radiation count in the wallaby paddock at that time and also the pads of the wallabies' paws, or feet – whichever you want to call them, were white".* [19]

I asked Mr Marshall whether they had ever found the culprits:

> *"No, but the same thing was happening all over the world. I can tell you that. I've got to be honest about it. As far as I am concerned, I would suggest, and I did say this at the time ... Cornwall has got Black Magic, its got witchcraft and witch covens, and if anything I think this was what or who did it. The strange thing was that there was no blood anywhere. That was a strange thing.*
>
> *There was the thing with the Geiger Counter, but I think that could have happened anywhere. You're bound to get a certain amount of radiation, and possibly it being an area of tin mines and whatever, it is an area of granite mixed with other substances. Nothing else materialised whatsoever.*
>
> *It happened on several occasions, and I've got a feeling that there was another one since I left the zoo".*

The Policeman who had originally told me of the events at Newquay had theorised that the

186

events were somehow linked with sightings of a mystery big cat in the area. I mentioned this to Mr Marshall...

> *"That did come up. It was suggested at the time. In Devon there were a lot of killings and it was suggested that they were a puma or something. If our killings had been a puma I'd have caught it.* [20] [21]
>
> *In the zoo there were a lot of areas outside the cages, and indeed inside the cages was sand. Any animal walking around at night time, a cat, a puma, or whatever, they would pad around in front of the cage, because they would want to know what was inside it, and therefore they would leave paw-marks. I would have found paw-marks somewhere, without a doubt. I did look and I found nothing.*
>
> *An animal would have left paw-prints and I found none. Just for the hell of it you check everything, and there was nothing. I'm convinced that it was something to do with a coven down here. I'm convinced that there's more than one. I don't know anything about witches and their things, but there were a lot of whispers at the time".* [22]

Mr Marshall's voice became a little strained then. He hinted that he had more to tell me, but didn't like to say too much on the 'phone. I let the matter drop, intending to bring it up again when we met face to face.

While the Owlman was active in the skies above Mawnan Woods, and Morgawr haunted Falmouth Bay and the lower reaches of the River Helford, strange 'creatures' were seen in the seas off northern Cornwall. Mr Marshall of Newquay Zoo was often contacted by the police:

> *"Any sightings of anything at all, and I would be called by the police. One night two fishermen, at night saw something and the police 'phoned me at three in the morning to say that they had sighted this huge white thing out at sea and had I any idea what it was? "I've got no bloody idea" I said, but I didn't see it. Nothing else came of that at all"* [23]

Peculiar creatures were seen in the Cornish countryside. Some, as we have seen, appear almost too strange for comprehension, others appear to be more easily explicable. One animal that almost made the fortean text books was the 'Giant Mouse of Newquay'. Mr Marshall explains:

> *"One night a wallaby escaped and a drunk going home up Treninnick Hill reported it to the Police. He saw it hop over a hedge and he thought it was a giant mouse. It soon sobered him up (laughs). The Police brought it back under a coat".* [24] [25]

By the end of the 1970's Alien Big Cats were being reported from several different locations across the West-Country. Men such as Eric Beckjord. a charming man I met at the 1990 ISC Conference in Guildford believe that these are truly 'alien animals'. [26] There is no doubt that there is a folkloric tradition of ghostly big cats in the South West, especially in Cornwall.

One particular apparition from Morwenstow in North Cornwall is said to sit on the stone pillars of a field gate. It is said to be the size of a dog with large, saucer like eyes. A local man who attacked it with a sledgehammer, (which seems both an unfriendly and a singularly pointless thing to do), was reportedly paralysed, either by fear or by some ill-defined psychic emanation when the creature reportedly de-materialised in front of him. [27]

Unfortunately for the phenomanalists amongst us, the truth behind the spate of big cat sightings in the UK. and indeed across the globe, is probably far more prosaic. It is generally agreed that they are escaped zoo and circus animals of various species and creatures released into the wild after legislation in 1976 forbade the widespread keeping of such animals as pets without first undergoing a stringent licensing procedure. [28] [29] Zoo-keepers are usually adamant in their opposition to this theory, believing that such creatures would not be able to survive undetected in the British countryside. [30] Unusually Mr Marshall agreed with me:

> *"There is every possibility that there are cats - pumas at liberty in Devon and Cornwall. The reason for this is, and I don't think that most people realise this, but as soon as the animal licensing came in in 1976 people were dumping their animals like there was no tomorrow. A chappie at Roach had lion cubs and he deliberately released them. They were caught again. He deliberately released them so they wouldn't have to go to Newquay Zoo.*
>
> *There was never any check on who had what and where. There was a chappie down at Redruth who had a bear. A Himalayan Bear".* [31]

One of the Cornish 'wild' pumas, may have been the pet of a St Ives night-club owner, known to all and sundry as 'Big Barry'. When he left the area in the mid 1970's it was widely rumoured that his pet had been released into the wild. [32]

When one starts to research the matter of exotic pet keeping during the 1970's it is surprising quite how many such animals were in private hands.

Mr Marshall again:

> *"I was landed with a puma that a chappie had as part of his act here in Newquay one summer. It was a tame puma. He went off and left it. I had it in the zoo for a while.*
>
> *It was very willy nilly at one stage. A lot of circuses, small circuses, not Bertram Mills and things, but small circuses went bust on the road, and after a while who knows. If you haven't got the money for feed then you've got to do the other, haven't you?"* [33]

Mr Marshall's final reminiscence was, perhaps the most disturbing to a fortean zoologist, who above all is an animal lover.

> *"Zoos and circuses had to be viable. If it wasn't a viable proposition to keep a certain type of animal then they were got rid of. In my day in the 70's, lions were so cheap to buy that if you bred them you couldn't sell them, but if you killed them and sold the body to a taxidermist you'd get a better price than you paid for them in the beginning. For stuffing, a taxidermist would give you £350 where you could buy one for £50. It's a weird world!"* [34]

We ended our conversation by discussing the then current set of A.B.C sightings on Dartmoor and Exmoor. Mr Marshall asked whether he could accompany me to the next set of sheep kills. I eagerly agreed, at that time I knew no professional zoologists and I was only too happy to have a 'pro' on my team.

We parted cheerfully, with Mr Marshall again hinting that he had more to tell me about the wallaby killings. Two days later he was dead.

A few weeks later I was approached by Rosemary Rhodes of Ninestones Farm on Bodmin Moor. She asked me to come and visit to investigate the spate of sheep killings and sightings of mysterious creatures on her farm, that over the next few years became known as 'The Beast of Bodmin'. [35] [36] I was only the second researcher on site, and true to my promise I wanted to take Mr Marshall along with me.

I telephoned his daughter cheerfully. She answered the 'phone in a voice thick with grief, and told me that only days after talking to me about the mysterious killings in Newquay her father had been taken suddenly ill, and died. She knew nothing more and didn't want to talk to me.

Even as I write this some four years later, a shiver goes down my spine as I remember Mr Marshall's hints that he hadn't told me the full story.

During the summer of 1994, Alison and I finally visited Newquay Zoo. We had camped in a lay-by just outside the town the night before and it was a glorious mid-summer morning. We were the first punters in through the gate. It was obvious that the zoo had seen better days. It had just been taken over by yet another change of management who were desperately trying to give it a face-lift but at the time we visited it was desperately in need of slick of paint, and looked sad and forlorn.

It was, however, surrounded by high chain-link fencing and all the paths and many of the enclosures were covered in raked sand and gravel paths. It was as Mr Marshall and other ex-employees had described. If, as it seemed was the practice, the paths had been raked each night as the zoo employees left work, then it was difficult to see how anybody, or anything could have climbed over the fence, visited the enclosures, killed sizeable creatures without a struggle and left them decapitated and exsanguinated with no footprints or traces of blood on the ground. Twenty years on it remains a disturbing and unpleasant mystery.

Much to my surprise, Tony didn't know much about the episode. He had heard about it, but hadn't taken much interest in it. I wondered whether or not to tell him of my suspicion that he had indirectly been the cause of it, by invoking the spirit of the Owlman in the spring of 1978. The coincidence in the timing, the injured geese, and, indeed the location, seemed too great and therefore I was sure that the two events were somehow, rather unpleasantly linked.

I decided against it, mainly because Tony was already under a great deal of stress over the events of the afternoon, and I didn't want to be the cause of even more. Because his plane was now going to arrive at Cork Airport three hours or more after the advertised time, he was now going to have missed his last bus back to his home in County Clare. As the song says:

"Its a long way from Clare to here".

As it was, the events of that peculiar afternoon were not yet over, as an incredibly attractive young woman, wearing, probably the sexiest air stewardess's uniform I have ever seen walked into the room and looked around her purposely. Having reached that state of what is not exactly inebriation, but is that feeling after three or four beers, when you know that what you really want from life is another three or four beers, my hormones had taken over, and I leaned across to Tony and whispered:

"I wonder what she'd look like with a sigil painted on her belly?"

and he sniggered, before turning back to me in astonishment and saying:

189

"Hold your whisht .. .she's coming over here". [38]

The air stewardess, who, it later turned was something far more senior within the airline came over to where we were sitting, and much to Tony's delight, announced that the flight was not going to be three hours late after all, and that for reasons best known to themselves the airline had decided to schedule a flight only ninety minutes after the original flight was due to leave.

He would still miss his bus, but at least he would be back in "God's own country", by soon after opening time. 'Doc' looked the happiest we had seen him all afternoon, and started to whistle a jaunty Hibernian tune beneath his breath. More ominously, however, the men in the black suits, who were still leaning nonchalantly against the walls, suddenly perked up, and started to mutter into their mobile 'phones and 'walkie talkies' as if they had suddenly been mobilised into action.

We finally saw Tony get onto his 'plane. In common with all the other passengers on the flight they had to go through the door marked 'security' rather than the door marked 'flights', so it seems that the security alert, whatever it was about, was still under way.

Three days later he telephoned us having finally, after a long series of misadventures, got home. For us, however, the episode wasn't over and we still had to get to our destination on Dartmoor to receive the next few documents in the case.

In view of my latent paranoia, following the events of that fateful afternoon, you will, I hope, forgive me, if I fail to identify where it is I was going, who I was going to meet, or how, in fact we got there. I would like to say, however, that it was a very fraught journey, made even worse by me turning around every few seconds to try and ascertain whether or not we were being followed.

It did not help our burgeoning sense of paranoia that the automatic arm on the barrier allowing us out of the car park at the airport had opened without us putting any money in the slot, and that for at least half our journey there was a large, black Mercedes with tinted windows following us three cars behind.

But that was all coincidence wasn't it?

We received a parcel of papers relating to the Newquay Zoo attacks. They consisted of the Police Report, (fairly heavily censored), the original vet's autopsy report, and a handwritten report, which appears to be from a local UFO research group, presumably the one referred to by Mr Marshall in our interview. [39]

I have decided to quote the documents in full, not only because of the historical importance of them but because they place the events within some kind of context.

The first report is that from the local police. This is, by far the most suspicious of the three documents. It has been photocopied so many times that it is almost indecipherable in parts, and large sections have been censored so the information is unreadable. I am making no claims as to whether it is genuine or not. I have several 'official' documents in my possession, which in my opinion at least are palpable fakes.

They have usually come from the UFO fraternity, they are also photocopied to a state of near illegibility, and they have large sections of them which have been censored. Unlike this document, however, they usually purport to be Ministry of Defence memoranda regarding crashed UFO's, and they usually

U.K EYES 'B'

MINISTRY OF DEFENCE

Main Building, Whitehall, London SW1A 2HB

Telephone (Direct Dialling) 01-218 ████

(Switchboard) 01-218 9000

Dear ████████,

As you know, OSI has completed a report on the landing of a craft of unknown origin crewed by several entities near RAF Bentwaters on the night of December 29/30 1980.

Interestingly, OSI reports that the entities were approximately 1½ metres tall, wore what appeared to be nylon-coated pressure suits, <u>but no helmets</u>. Conditions on the night were misty, giving the appearance that the entities were hovering above ground level.

Tape recordings were made on which the entities are heard to speak in an electronically synthesised version of English, with a strong American accent. Similar transmissions intercepted irregularly by NSA since 1975.(See attached - Flag A)

According to OSI, entities had claw-like hands with three digits and an opposable thumb.

Despite original reports (Flags B - E), OSI said the craft was not damaged but landed deliberately as part of a series of visits to SAC bases in USA and Europe. Reports that craft was repaired by US servicemen or was taken on to the base are not confirmed by OSI.

Landing is not considered a defence issue in view of the overt peaceful nature of the contact, but investigations by DIS are to be continued on ██████████ auth. ity. Precautionary plan for counter-information at a local level involving ████████ and a ████████ ███████ ███, is strongly recommended.

Sincerely

For comparison purposes (see next page) a UFO Document from the mid 1990's which is a palpable fake

Newquay .... taken over a .... bet .... and fire
.... "A" ....enclosure .... over ....
.... in ....
Western .... 2nd October 78
.... CRIMINAL DAMAGE - Newquay Zoological Gardens ....

Sir,

Over the past months a number of incidents have occurred at the Newquay Zoological Gardens at Trenance Gardens, Newquay. These incidents were, at first, thought to be unconnected and possibly due to the incursion of a marauding animal but as will be seen, this has now been discounted.

On the 3rd June 1978, a wallaby was discovered to have been beheaded in it's paddock. This was found by the staff when first opening up the premises in the early morning. The head of the animal was not found but the point of severance was unusually clean cut.

On the 17th August 1978 a black swan was found to have been beheaded also. The neck and head were missing but the body of the swan was unruffled and showed no sign of a struggle. No blood was to be found at the scene. Later the neck was discovered in undergrowth on the premises but the head was never found. The point of severance was again very clean.

Between these dates a Chinese goose, which is a fairly large species of goose, was removed from it's enclosure and it's carcass, minus head, was later discovered stuffed between a loose wooden fencing panel on the outer security fence. This was jammed tightly in a very confined space. At this spot the security fence was completely intact.

On Saturday 23rd September 1978 a young wallaby was found to have been removed from it's enclosure. It had been taken about 50 yards over several other fences to a paddock with the lower half of it's carcass remained. The upper part of the body was missing and there was no trace of blood at the scene. Marks in the grass showed signs of someone or something having flattened the grass and several particles of meat were visible. An examination of the remaining carcass in the presence of the Zoo's Consultant Veterinary Surgeon, W. Clifton Green of Edgcumbe Gardens, Newquay, and his Assistants, brought the unanimous verdict that the carcass had been dissected by a human being rather than an animal as the skin around the wound was clean cut and there were no teeth or claw marks visible on the carcass. The backbone had been deeply severed between the vertebra and some of the internal organs were missing.

The estimated value of the stock lost to date is approximately £600. Initially, the above incidents were not regarded too seriously and were thought to have been due to a marauding animal but closer examination of the facts of the incidents makes this possibility very .... The lack of wounding or marking elsewhere on the carcasses ..... ruled out this possibility and the behaviour in the most recent incident with a young wallaby, which weighed approximately 25 pounds, was taken over a fence between four and five feet in height out of the first enclosure and over several other fences of approximately four feet in height, into a paddock approximately 50 yards away, again making the involvement of any known animals most unlikely.

No pattern is discernible in the dates of the incidents, which appear to have all occurred in the later part of the night or just before first light. Moon phases have also been examined for any pattern but this is not consistent.

Shortly after the swan's death, staff found a knife in undergrowth at the Zoo but thought nothing of the article and it was then subsequently used in the food preparation room. I have examined this knife which is approximately $12\frac{1}{2}$ inches overall length with a $7\frac{1}{2}$ inch blade with a serrated edge. The blade is marked Saufax Inoxydable and the handle is of rough wood.

There are no persons known to be strongly opposed to the Zoo or any of a mental state known to the Curator of staff.

The only apparent link in these incidents is the removal of the head, and in the case of the swan and wallaby is the absence of any blood. In this respect, enquiries are being pursued into any possible link with black magic ceremonies.

There are a number of other incidents which have occurred in recent years involving the disappearance of animals and wild fowl from the Zoo but generally these were put down to foxes and other marauding animals and consequently no firm dates or information were recorded. However, if added to the recent series of incidents, these would make a very long catalogue of animals and wild fowl which have been destroyed at the premises in the last few years.

<u>Police Constable 358</u>

A pages from the supposed Newquay Zoo Police Report - a document which although not proven to be real, has the hallmarks of authenticity.

POST MORTEM REPORT ON WALLABY

The hind quarters of the wallaby were presented for examination, the anterior half of the carcass being absent. No external marks or injuries were present on the remaining skin. The carcass had been transected through the lower lumbar region at the level of an intervertebral space, through the anterior part of a lumbar vertebral centrum. The left articular process was broken but no other gross damage was present. The edges of the carcass appeared to have been cleanly transected by a sharp appliance. The wound edges were even and clean to evidence of bite wounds were present, nor was there any indication of interference with muscular tissue. The bladder and muscle skeletal system of the pelvis, but the pelvic girdle and the hind legs appeared undamaged. At the time of examination, there was no evidence of any great haemorrhage having occurred at the time of division. Nor, judging by the transection, was there any struggle.

It is thus possible that the division of the carcass occurred after death; and was not its cause. The subject inflicting the damage is uncertain, but the possibility of human involvement cannot be excluded following this post mortem examination.

Veterinary Post Mortem Report of Wallaby

have an aura about them which suggests that they were originally manufactured by a hormonally challenged teenager with an over-active imagination, sitting in his bedroom with his home computer.

This document, whilst I cannot guarantee its authenticity, has a certain stamp of professionalism about it which makes me think that it is probably genuine.

It is dated the 2nd October 1978, and the headings, titles and names of the officers making the report have all been deleted. The main body of the report, however reads as follows:

Sirs,

Over the past months a number of incidents have occurred at the Newquay Zoological Gardens at Trenance Gardens, Newquay. These incidents were, at first, considered to be unconnected and possibly due to the incursion of a marauding animal, but as will be seen this has now been discounted.

On the 3rd June 1978, a wallaby was discovered to have been beheaded in it's (sic) paddock. This was found by staff when first opening up the premises in the early morning. The head of the animal was not found but the point of severance was unusually clean cut.

On the 17th August 1978, a black swan was found to have been beheaded also. The head and neck were missing, but the body of the swan was unruffled, showing no sign of a struggle. No blood was to be found at the scene. Later the neck was discovered in undergrowth on the premises, but the head was never found. The point of severance was again very clean.

Between these dates a Chinese goose, which is a fairly large species of goose, was removed from its enclosure and it's (sic) carcass, minus head, was discovered stuffed between a loose wooden fencing panel on the outer security fence. This was jammed tightly in a very confined space. At this spot the security fence was completely intact.

On Saturday 25th September 1978 a young wallaby was found to have been removed from its enclosure. It had been taken about fifty yards over several other fences to a paddock with the lower part of it's (sic) carcass remained".. [40]

This last sentence does not seem to make more than minimal sense. One can grasp what the (unnamed) author is trying to convey, but the wording itself is meaningless.

The grammatical construction (it's instead of its) and other anomalies have been left exactly as they are in the original document. The report continues:

The upper part of the body was missing and there was no trace of blood at the scene. Marks in the grass showed signs of someone or something having flattened the grass and several particles of meat were visible.

An examination of the remaining carcass in the presence of the Zoo's Consultant Veterinary Surgeon, W.Clifton Green of Edgecumbe Gardens, Newquay, and his Assistants (sic), brought the unanimous verdict that the carcass bad been dissected by a human being rather than an animal as the skin around the wound was clean cut, and there were no teeth or claw marks visible on the carcass. The backbone had been deeply severed between the vertebra

195

and some of the internal organs were missing.

The estimated value of the stock lost to date is approximately £600. Initially, the above incidents were not regarded too seriously and were thought to have been due to a marauding animal but closer examination of the facts of the incidents made the possibility very remote. The lack of wounding or marking elsewhere on the carcasses have ruled out this possibility, and the behaviour in the most recent incident with a young wallaby, which weighed approximately 25 pounds, was taken over a fence between four and five feet in height out of the first enclosure and over several other fences of approximately four feet in height; into a paddock approximately 50 yards, again makes the involvement of any known animals most unlikely. (41)

The grammatical structure of the last section is also suspect. The structure seems rather 'americanised' and the grammar itself is of a lesser level than I would have expected from the (very British), P.C. that I interviewed in 1991, who had, apparently been the investigating officer, and was, presumably, the author of this document. The americanised name of the vet, however is perfectly genuine, and it was this surgery who had given me Mr. Marshall's telephone number in the first place.

There is, always, the possibility that this report is not genuine, and has therefore been fabricated by person or persons unknown - presumably someone with an interest in conspiracy theories, UFO's and Cattle Mutilation. Unfortunately, I have lost contact with the officer who, if this report is genuine, would have been the author of it, and therefore I cannot verify it 100%. I believe that the Police Officer concerned has now left the Devon and Cornwall Constabulary, and is therefore essentially uncontactable. (42)

Unfortunately for the continuity of the document; the next paragraph of four lines is completely censored. We are presented, therefore, with another dilemma. Assuming, for the moment that the document is genuine, and I must reiterate, that we have no reason, apart from innate paranoia, and an instinctive distrust of conspiracy theorists, to suppose that it is not genuine, what is the reason for the censorship?

It is tempting to speculate that they were added as 'icing on the cake'. Even assuming that the documents are genuine, there is no doubt that it came into my possession through the activities of conspiracy theorists and UFO buffs. Whilst I trust my personal contact implicitly I have no knowledge, for good or for ill, of the 'professional' ethics of the people from whom she obtained them, and in this business it doesn't do to ask too closely. I can imagine no reason why a document which, after all, carries no obvious security classification, should be censored at least to this extent. One has to wonder, therefore, whether the document is genuine, but the censorship isn't; whether some over eager Ufologist along the way had decided to 'censor' what was already an interesting document, by drawing thick lines through it with a felt pen, in order to produce a more 'X-Filesey' (43) effect. Unfortunately, we shall probably never find out, because in view of the events described earlier in this chapter, my paranoia suggests that it would be unwise to contact the Devon and Cornwall Constabulary direct.

The document continues, however:

"No pattern is discernable in the dates of the incidents, which appear to have all occurred in the later part of the night, or just before first light. Moon phases have also been examined for any pattern but this is not consistent". (44)

196

This paragraph also seems a little suspect. I have never yet met a police officer willing to consider lycanthropy or vampirism as motivation in an unsolved crime. If, however, as earlier parts of this report, and certain sections of my interview with Mr Marshall tended to suggest, occult practitioners of some description were serious suspects, then, hypothetically at least, the phases of the moon, might have been considered as supporting evidence by the investigating team.

Here, I would like to say, that I have uncovered no evidence at all that there was any witchcraft or black magic involved in these events. I have 'put the word about' through some contacts of mine in the area, and have not been able to uncover any evidence in favour of the 'ritual sacrifice' theory. Interestingly, however, the same scenario was resurrected about sixteen years later on Bodmin Moor in conjunction with certain events involving the Alien Big Cats, popularly known as 'The Beast(s) of Bodmin'. Since the early 1990's there had been a series of attacks on sheep on farms in the area, particularly on Nine-stones Farm at Common Moor. The farmer, Mrs Rosemary Rhodes, had invited the Centre for Fortean Zoology to investigate, and although our relationship with Mrs Rhodes was both fruitless and short lived, it awakened my interest in the phenomenon.

A few years later, after some very unconvincing video (which turned out to be of a domestic cat), and many more sheep kills, a local woman was attacked. I have spoken to two or three people who knew her, and, it seems, that despite all the speculation, (both in the media, and within the fortean world), to the contrary, that her story - that she had been walking her dog one night when something hit her on the back of the head - she later woke up to see a mysterious cat-like animal, was true. [45] She assumed that the cat-like animal was responsible for hitting her over the head. I think this is unlikely. However, I think that the speculation that she was attacked by a group of (unnamed) occultists or witches, as part of (an equally unnamed) ritual, are equally unfounded.

I have spoken to a practicing witch who lives on Bodmin Moor. (She is not, however, anything to do with Tony Shiels, and his witch colleagues). She is a friend of mine and she is also a friend of the lady concerned, and she told me that such speculation is both silly and hurtful towards those in the area who are devotees of the craft.

The Newquay police report went on to describe a weapon which may well have been used in the attacks. (It equally may well have had nothing to do with the attacks at all):

> *"Shortly after the swan's death, staff found a knife in undergrowth at the Zoo but thought nothing of the article, and it was subsequently used in the food preparation room. I have examined this knife, which is approximately 12 inches overall length with a 7 inch blade with a serrated edge. The blade is marked Saufex Inoxydable, and the handle is of rough wood".* [47]

The next paragraph, of thirteen lines, has been censored in an identical manner to the earlier paragraph. The odd word is discernable, but as it is only words like 'it' or 'the', then this is not really any use. The three final paragraphs are uncensored and read as follows:

> *"There are no persons kmown to be strongly opposed to the zoo or any of a mental state known to the Curator or staff".* [48]

(Unfortunately, I don't actually know what this last sentence means. Presumably, and here I can only speculate wildly, it means that there are no known psychotic animal killers who regularly visit the zoo, carrying knives and with a wild gleam in their eye. One would have imagined, certainly in view of my

brief acquaintanceship with Mr Marshall, who was obviously a sensible and responsible man, that this would have been self evident.)

> *"The only apparent link in these incidents is the removal of the head, and in the case of the swan and the wallaby, the absence of any blood. In this respect enquiries are being pursued into any possible link with black magic ceremonies.*
>
> *There are a number of other incidents which have occurred in recent years involving the disappearance of animals and wildfowl from the Zoo but generally these were put down to foxes and other marauding animals and consequently no firm dates or information were recorded. However, if added to the recent series of incidents, these would make a very long catalogue of animals and wild fowl which have been destroyed at the premises in the last few years".* [49]

The Report is signed only *"Police Constable 358"*.

This, I have been informed by my cousin, herself an ex-policewoman in Cornwall, was consistent with the procedure followed at the time. [30]

The second report that we were given purports to be an autopsy report on the dead wallaby. It is typed in landscape, rather than portrait, which is unusual, but would seem to suggest that it had originally been in some type of cardex system. [51] Like the previous report it was typed on a manual typewriter, (not unusual for 1978), and whilst my inate scepticism caused me to examine both documents carefully to see if they were from the same source, it seems certain that they were typed on different machines.

This document looks more genuine than the police report and there is an examining officer's name and serial number at the bottom of the report, although, tantalisingly, the photocopy is so poor that they are both illegible. The report reads:

> *"POST MORTEM REPORT ON WALLABY.*
>
> *The hind quarters of the wallaby were presented for examination, the anterior half of the carcass being absent. No external marks or injuries were present on the remaining skin. The carcass had been transected through the lower lumbar region at the level of an interverte-bral space through the anterior part of a lumbar vertebral centrum. The left articular proc-ess was broken but no other gross damage was present. The rest of the carcass appeared to have been clearly transected by a sharp appliance, the wound edges were even and clean. No evidence of bite wounds were present, nor was there any indication of interference with muscular tissue. The bladder and rectum were absent from the pelvis, but the pelvic girdle and musculo-skeletal system of the hind legs appeared undamaged. At the time of examina-tion, there was no evidence of any great haemorrage having occurred at the time of incision. Nor, judging by the transection was there any struggle.*
>
> *It is thus possible that the division of the carcass occurred after death, and was not its cause. The subject inflicting the damage is uncertain, but the possibility of human involve-ment cannot be excluded following this post mortem examination".* [52]

The descriptions of these mutilations are very exact, and are almost identical to other mutilations reported from across the world, especially in America. [53] This is, however, the only example of a wal-

laby mutilation that is in my files. One important factor, however, is the removal of the bladder and the rectum. What has been described as 'coring' of the rectum of the victim is a common part of such mutilatory attacks, and it has always been seen as being very significant by researchers, occultists, ufologists and forteans. It has also been the feature of these attacks most commonly used by those who do not believe that there is any 'un-natural' cause for these incidents, to 'debunk' them.

Many of the American cases that featured 'rectal coring' took place in relatively wild countryside. Because of a hot climate and an inaccessible terrain, the carcasses were often not discovered until several days after the attacks, and it has been suggested, quite forcefully, on a number of occasions, that invertebrate scavengers such as sexton beetles, had crawled up the rectum of the dead animal and eaten the surrounding tissue giving the appearance of 'rectal coring'. This may well have been the case in some instances, and is a convincing scenario. [54] [55] [56]

In this case, however, it can be clearly shown that it is impossible for this scenario to have taken place. The animals could only have been dead a few hours by the time they were found. The reports state clearly that the deaths took place in *"the latter part of the night or just before first light"*, [57] and it is certain that the first zoo employees would have arrived for work soon after dawn. It is impossible therefore that the 'rectal coring' could have been caused by invertebrate predation, and the temperate climate of Cornwall, compared to, say, Colorado, would seem to confirm this. If, therefore, the 'rectal coring by invertebrate predation' hypothesis has been shown to be invalid in this instance then it does, by association, cast doubt on the findings of the American Investigators, including those of the FBI who propounded the hypothesis, at about the same time in the United States.

A specialised FBI team examined several incidences of cattle mutilation which were in nearly every instance identical with the wallaby attack described above, and after much deliberation concluded that the injuries they had investigated could have been caused by natural predation from the carnivorous animals of the area. [58] This report has been scoffed at and ridiculed for years by occultists and forteans from all streams of thought, and has been used as supporting evidence for theories of government cover-ups, government conspiracies, and governmental incompetence. It seems, that in the light of this evidence, that the conspiracy theorists, for once at least, may have some substance behind their paranoia.

The third report that we received is equally interesting, although from a completely different viewpoint. Whereas the other reports are, or at least purport to be, documents issued by the official agencies involved, this third report is unsigned, and handwritten, but appears to be the work of the UFO investigators described by Mr Marshall during our interview. This document does name the two police officers involved, but for the reasons I have already given, I shall not identify them, except by their initials when quoting from the report. [59]

AUTHOR'S NOTE: The truth can now be told. I discussed the mystery with Joan Amos, for many years the doyenne of West Country ufology. She had not only heard of the case, but somehow - and I never discussed how - had managed to get hold of the official documents appertaining to the case. On our next visit to her tiny cottage she presented me with a mysterious bundle of papers containing the official police reports on the Newquay Zoo killings as well as the autopsy report from the local vet and a pile of typewritten papers from the un-named UFO investigator who had, I believe, been the only person (apart from me) to ever fully investigate the mystery. I kept her identity secret in the original book because she was terminally ill in a Tavistock hospice by the time it was published, and I felt that any publicity would have been counter productive.

"CASE REPORT: NEWQUAY ZOO.

CASE TYPE: SUSPECT ANIMAL MUTILATION.
SITE: NEWQUAY ZOO, TRENANCE GARDENS, NEWQUAY.
DATE: FEBRUARY THROUGH SEPTEMI3ER 1978.

INVESTIGATION SUMMARY.

This series of incidents came to my attention as a result of an article in the CORNISH GUARDIAN describing a case that the Newquay Police were involved in at the time.

As the published characteristics were similar to ones notified to all area co-ordinators by Derek Mansell earlier in the year, I notified Data Research immediately. Derek Mansell then wrote to the Newquay police and then received permission for me to assist in the enquiry.

I made an appointment to see the Head of CID, Chief Inspector F and the investigating office Detective Constable H". [60]

I would like to say here that 'Detective Constable H' is the police officer whom I spoke to about the matter many years later, and so, whether or not the first two documents are genuine, and although I have certain suspicions about what purports to be the police report, I have no reason to doubt the veracity of the autopsy report, the third record is, in my eyes at least, almost certainly genuine. If it is not genuine, the author, whoever he or she is, has certainly 'done their homework'.

The report continues:

"These officers briefed me on the incidents.

INCIDENT DETAILS.

9th Feb 1978: Muscovy Duck decapitated.
16th Feb 1978: Bar Head Goose decapitated.
26th Feb 1978: Muscovy Duck decapitated.
12 April 1978: Muscovy Duck decapitated.
3rd June 1978: Wallaby beheaded.
17th Aug 1978: Black Swan beheaded.
23rd Sept 1978: Wallaby beheaded." [61]

The final two incidents are bracketed together, and the report continues:

"Between the dates bracketed a CHINESE GOOSE was found jammed between the panels of the outer fence.

Two carcasses were left for analysis - the Chinese Goose and the wallaby killed in September. Of these two only the final wallaby was subjected to post mortem analysis. The body of the goose was located by me, the carcass is unsuitable for analysis as it is badly decomposed, however the enclosed bone samples were taken.." [62]

(Obviously, as the only document that I have is, what is at least a fourth generation photocopy, I have not got the goose bones in my possession, nor, unfortunately, do I know where they are).

> *"(A copy of the vet's report is enclosed)".* [63]

(This is, presumably the same report as I have quoted above as all three sets of documents in my possession came to me from the same source).

> *"The bone samples are from the upper cervical region, no traces of viscera etc remained - owing to action* of *decomposition and local animal agents.*
>
> *It would have been helpful if, at the time photographs of the other bodies had been taken in situ.*
>
> *Mr Marshall, the Zoo manager informed me that after the killings:*
>
> *'The remaining wallabies' strange swellings on the jaws and sides and the skin on the feet had turned white. This is something I have never seen before'."* [64]

(This passage has been quoted exactly as it was written in the document in my possession. Presumably the word 'had' or 'developed' or both was omitted after the third word of Mr Marshall's statement).

According to veteran zoologist and zoo-keeper Clinton Keeling, captive wallabies are prone to a necrotic disease of the jaws, (especially the lower maxillary), which is known colloquially as 'lumpy jaw'. It is not particularly surprising that the unnamed UFO investigator was not familiar with the symptoms of a condition well known only to those with intimate knowledge of the care and husbandry of the larger marsupials. [65] [66] [67]

The statement continues:

> *"This information was not notified to the vet or police which is a pity as physical causes could perhaps have been established.* [68]
>
> *As one possible cause could have been radiation exposure I borrowed a radiac survey meter measuring in MILLIROENTGEN from Derek Mansell, however this meter was found by me to be totally unusable as no operating switches are fitted and the batteries are no longer available. I therefore had to obtain the loan of a Radiac Survey Meter No. 2 measuring in Roentgens from another source. An examination with this instrument produced these results:*

> | | |
> |---|---|
> | *WALLABY COMPOUND:* | *0.2 Roentgens.* |
> | *APPROX SITE OF WALLABY CARCASS:* | *0.2 Roentgens* |
> | *ALL OTHER SITES VISITED:* | *0.0 Roentgens.* |

> *It should be stressed, however, that these readings could well be caused by other than radiation traces, for example there may be rocks which have a higher than usual background count or the meter needle may have strayed off the zero mark"..* [69]

201

Although I have quoted all the rest of all three sets of documents in full, I have omitted the next paragraph which consists of an impassioned plea to the treasurer of, whichever UFO organisation the investigator and author belonged, to purchase a radiation meter for use in cases such as this one. After this, the document continues:

> *"Other physical evidence was a paw print found by the police during their investigations. This paw print was never identified. The print was located near a hole where something had attempted to gain entrance to the lion's cage!"* [70]

This is a particularly interesting incident. I have never known any incidences where animals have tried to 'break in' to a lion's cage. On the only occasion that I have taken my own dog, Toby, to a zoo, he refused to go anywhere near the outside perimeter wire of the lion enclosure, but as soon as he came within about thirty yards, the lions, which had been dozing in the summer afternoon sun, immediately 'awoke' and started pacing up and down the wire fence nearest to us in a hungry and aggressive manner. Toby was terrified, and pulled us away, his tail between his legs. I think that it is very unlikely that any flesh and blood animal would voluntarily attempt to gain access to the cages inhabited by such impressive carnivores. [71]

Clinton Keeling has never heard of such an incident in a British Zoo, although he has a vague recollection of such behaviour being noted amongst wild foxes visiting the lion enclosure in an unnamed Dutch zoo. [72] [73]

The report continues:

> *"Another print was found in the larger pony paddock where one of the birds was found. In discussion with the keeper and the manager and police officers I found that earlier in the year reports had been made by several apparently reliable witnesses that a large 'puma' had been seen walking along the railway tracks behind the zoo.*
>
> *At this time no animals were missing from the premises. This is of interest in view of the paw-print found outside the Lion's cage - this has not yet been identified - possibly this was related to the 'puma'".* [74]

Alien Big Cats were reported from all over Cornwall in the years to come, [75] but this is one of the earlier ones on our files. This is not really either the time nor the place to discuss this particular phenomenon. There is no doubt in my mind, however, that they exist. I have seen one. There is also no doubt in my mind that many of the animals reported are bona fide, living creatures.

It is, however, equally certain that some of them are not. It is a common misconception amongst the lay-cryptozoologists, that the 'mystery cat' phenomenon is a particularly British one. This is not so. Anomalous creatures which appear to be either pumas or panthers (melanistic leopards) have been reported from across Western Europe, Australia, New Zealand, [77] parts of the United States [78] [79] where the puma is supposedly extinct [80] [81] and where black leopards have never lived, [82] and other geographical locations besides. At a conference co-hosted by the ISC and the Folklore Society [83] in 1990, when I met the notorious researcher John Eric Beckjord, who achieved the notable 'honour' of becoming effectively banned from most functions organised by the International Society for Cryptozoology, he told me that he was convinced that ABC's are not flesh and blood creatures at all, but are in fact manifestations of complex pan-dimensional entities whose nature and motivation remain obscure. [84] Whilst I do not agree with him in every instance, in some cases I suspect that be may be right.

Most, if not all of the alien big cats reported in Britain, at least those who are in fact animals, in the sense that we recognise them as such, are descendants of creatures released deliberately, or accidentally in the wake of the 1976 Dangerous Wild Animals Act. Other large cats were almost certainly introduced into the British countryside in the wake of legislation clamping down on small, badly run provincial zoos.

There are, however, a significant number of 'big cat' reports which predate this legislation. I have written elsewhere [85] of the theory suggesting that there is a recurrent gene of 'gigantism' within the British wildcat population. Animals which appear to be 'giant' wildcats are seen in Cornwall on a regular basis. One witness saw such a cat on Bodmin Moor in the late summer of 1995. She described a cat, about the same size as my Labrador cross dog; about four and a half feet in length and about two feet tall, with tabby markings, a flattened head and ears, and a very long, ringed tail. [86] Animals such as this have, in my opinion at least, been roaming the Cornish moorlands since times immemorial and are a natural part of our ecosystem. There are other reports, however, which seem to be far less corporeal in nature and, which, could have a direct relevance to the animals described in the report from the UFO investigator. [86]

To return to the report (the investigator repeats himself slightly for a line or two before continuing):

> *"The keeper informed me that a paw print had been found in the larger pony paddock where one of the birds was found, and in the corner of this paddock where a small bridge is located no horses could be persuaded to approach the bridge after the bird was found.*

> *This is interesting, in view of the commonly held belief that horses have strong extra-sensory or Psi ability and will not approach haunted spots.*

> *This area is within reasonable distance of the other affected sites and it is unusual that the horses which are accustomed to humans were 'nervous and very skittish'. The following day the paw-print was reported to the police.*

> *To rule out the possibility of a sex-seeking male cat I enquired if any of the killings occurred at a time when the female cats were in heat - there was no connection.*

> *It would seem safe to assume that whatever killed the animals did not do so as part of a feline mating ritual. However, it is difficult to reconcile a large cat with these killings as all the killings were committed with clean cuts and bore no teeth or claw marks. It would be logical to presume that if a cat had done the killings the remains would have been badly lacerated and signs of a struggle and panic would have been evident. However the situation is exactly the opposite, for example the black swan killed on August 17 1978, to quote from the Police Report:*

> *'... the neck and head were missing but the body of the swan was unruffled and showed no sign of a struggle'."* [87]

This is a direct quote from the police report quoted above. This, therefore implies that the UFO researcher had access to the same documents as I have had. It also implies that either the document is genuine, or possibly that the UFO reporter actually faked it, passing it off as a genuine police report for reasons of his own. This, I feel is unlikely, although my reservations, stated above still stand. The

investigator continued with what, by anyone's standards is a pretty meticulous piece of reporting:

> *"The method of killing would indicate that the culprit is an extremely strong 'person' or that some form of drug was used to pacify the animals. If tissue samples were available then the drug if used, could be detected.*
>
> *Certainly the killing of the wallaby on the 23rd September 1978 confirms this statement it also rules out any known local animal in the Newquay area".* [89]

Errors in syntax, like the one in the last sentence have been left as they are in the original document.

More importantly, however is the inference that a 'drug' of some kind was used. If this is so, it is not a unique occurrence. A bison mutilated at the Cheyenne Mountain Zoo in Colorado in October 1975, was found to have traces of what appeared to be an anticoagulant substance in its body. [90] The autopsy report read:

> *"It was very strange, there was an excessive amount of serosanguinous (blood tinged) fluid in the abdominal and thoracic cavities and the fluid had seeped into the body tissue and even into the eyeballs".* [91]

Hypothetically there may be a chemical substance acting both as an anti-coagulant and a tranquiliser (possibly similar to that found in the saliva of the vampire bats). [92] This is pure speculation on my part, and I feel that further speculation without hard evidence is a pointless activity.

The investigator went on to describe another aspect to the case which was strikingly similar to other cattle mutilation reports:

> *"The facet of the case which is very interesting is the lack of blood at the incident sites, at first this was thought to be due to occultists but 1 understand that the police have now discounted this after local enquiries".* [94] [95]

It should be remembered, however, that although I agree with the local police that human occultists were not involved in the affair, at least not directly, Mr Marshall was convinced, right until his death that occultists were involved. It may also not be directly relevant to this particular case, but it should be remembered that during 1978, there was a minor west-country cult based around the American mass murderer Charles Manson. [96] He was eligible for parole during that year, and although, as history relates, he did not achieve his wish, there were several TV documentaries and a feature film made about him. In the wake of the movie, *Helter Skelter*, [97] several bikers, hippies and general odd-balls in both Devon and Cornwall professed a serious interest in him and his creed. I knew some of them at the time, and to my knowledge their activities went no further than reading the book, watching the film and wearing the T-shirt.

It should perhaps be pointed out that there are some similarities between the events at Newquay Zoo over the summer of 1978, and certain rituals described by Ed Sanders in his book *The Family* [98] which described the activities of a cult called 'The Kirke Order of Dog Blood', [99] which was associated strongly with the 'Manson Family'. [100]

Cattle mutilation phenomena had been occurring for several years in the United States, and such total exsanguinations, as recorded in the Newquay Zoo case was a common feature of such attacks. A typical cattle mutilation case was described by Kenneth M Rommel, Jr, the former-FBI agent referred to previ-

ously. He described a scenario which:

> *"Involved, amongst other features, the removal by 'precision surgery' of parts of the dead animal (the sexual organs, one eye, one ear, and – with female animals – the udder), a seemingly cored rectum ('as though a large cookie cutter' had been used), and the lack of blood in the carcass".* [101]

It is difficult to reconcile such horrific injuries with the conclusions that he reached from his investigation, which read in part that these mutilations were:

> *"consistent with what one would expect to find with normal predation, scavenger activity, and normal decomposition of a dead animal".* [102]

Despite the fact that there are no other records of wallaby mutilation, at least in my files, the pattern of injuries reported at Newquay in 1978 seems pretty typical.

The investigator then went off at a tangent. We must follow him, because although the events he describes next may not have any direct relevance to the other material discussed in this book, the synchronicity is disturbing enough to be worth noting:

> *"To deviate slightly I have heard so far unsubstantiated reports of a herd of Dartmoor Ponies was found (sic), at the bottom of a gully also drained of blood".* [103]

The investigator then refers briefly to a case described in a book called *Mystery stalks the Prairie* by Robert Donovan and Keith Wolverton, [104] and complains that the book is missing from 'Data Research'.

We should presume that the episode to which he refers is that from Cherry Brook Valley in 1977. The episode has been assimilated into the canon of fortean misinformation, and should therefore, perhaps be examined in a little depth, particularly because it is an episode which I have personally investigated.

The dead ponies were found on April 11th 1977 by Alan Hicks, a shopkeeper from Tavistock who had been walking on Dartmoor with his children. They came across the fifteen carcasses in a small gully at Cherry Brook. On the 13th July that year the *Western Morning News* reported:

> *"Fears that the mystery deaths of fifteen ponies near a Dartmoor beauty spot were caused by visitors from space were being probed by a Torbay team yesterday.*
>
> *Armed with a geiger counter, metal detectors and face masks four men are investigating what leading animal authorities admit seems a 'totally abnormal happening', and are hoping their equipment will throw a new light on the three month old mystery.*
>
> *While other investigators have looked for signs of mutilation, disease or poisoning - or even gunshot wounds - the four men are seeking proof that extra-terrestrials were responsible for the deaths.*
>
> *'If a space craft has been in the vicinity there may still be detectable evidence', says the Team Leader, Mr John Wyse, founder of the Devon UFO centre.*

His team is investigating the Postbridge mystery because the ponies deaths have similarities with unsolved cases in the United States.

Many of the Dartmoor ponies - all found within a few hundred yards of each other in the Cherry Brook Valley below Lower White Tor had broken bones.

'Horses and Cattle have been found in the United States in strange circumstances with the bones smashed or the bodies drained of blood', said Mr Wyse.

'Our members have already made a preliminary investigation and we know the bodies are now decomposed but there may still be some evidence of an extra-terrestrial visit'. [105]

The same newspaper story quoted Mrs Joanna Vinson. the secretary of the Livestock Protection Society as saying that:

"I still suspect that something dramatic happened – something very strange indeed. No-one can give any logical explanation. One theory is that the ponies died of redworm – but that does not explain the broken necks and legs". [106]

A particularly bizarre aspect of the case was that according to some reports the animals had almost completely decomposed away within forty-eight hours. Even the local Chief Inspector of the RSPCA accepted that this was a mystery.

The *Western Morning News* on the following day suggested some other hypotheses. Miss Lilian Martin, a member of the Livestock Preservation Society, suggested that the ponies had been grazing in the deserted valley when a sudden rainstorm flooded the valley:

"My theory is that the ponies were in a very enclosed valley. There was a waterfall at the head of the valley, and they may have been caught in a sudden burst of water and knocked against the boulder". [107]

The same newspaper report said that the UFO research team from Torbay had:

"come across no evidence to confirm or deny any of the theories put forward". [108]

A few weeks later an unnamed representative from the Dartmoor Pony Society claimed that the ponies had died in various parts of the moor and had been dumped there by a fanner who was unwilling to bear the cost of paying for their burial. [109] Mrs Vinson replied scathingly:

"One wonders if the people who say this sort of thing can possibly have been to the valley and seen the distribution of the ponies or of the terrain". [110]

Two other theories were promulgated in the weeks that followed. A botanist from Exeter suggested that the animals had been poisoned by eating a plant called the Bog Asphodel. [111] This theory does not explain the broken bones and seems unlikely for other reasons. Ms Vonny Cornelius, a herbalist who lives in a caravan in the country outside Totnes told us that although she was familiar with the plant she had never known ponies kept in field where the plant grew, to eat them. *"They have more sense than people give them credit for"*, she said. [112]

206

Naturalist Kelvin Boot, then based at the Royal Albert Museum in Exeter was quoted by the *Western Morning News* as saying that a 1917 book called 'Plants Poisonous to Livestock', which had been written by Harold Long, [113] mentioned several cases where cows had died after eating this plant and even mentioned a case where a cat had died after drinking milk from an affected cow. [114]

None of this, however, explains the broken bones, the sheer numbers of animals involved, the extremely rapid rate of decomposition, [115] and if the investigator responsible for the 1978 Newquay Zoo report is correct, the exsanguination of the carcasses. [116]

The second theory came from Mrs Ruth Murray of the Animal Defence League. She claims that the animals were stampeded by a local fanner engaged in a feud with a neighbour, who deliberately drove the animals into the gully so they would be killed, as a deliberate act of malice. [117]

The Centre for Fortean Zoology began to investigate the affair in the summer of 1991, fourteen years after the event. We spoke to Mrs Vinson who was rather reticent [118] and referred us to Mrs Murray. We telephoned Mrs Murray, who was unwilling to speak to us at the time. She did, however tell our researcher to 'phone back a week later when she had more time. This we did, to be greeted with an extraordinary tirade from her. She shouted at our researcher, accusing her of 'pestering' her day and night and of 'not taking no for an answer'. As we had only spoken to her once and were only 'phoning back then because she had asked us to, it seemed rather peculiar. [120]

Her claim that 'we had pestered her day and night', was irresistibly reminiscent of certain events chronicled by veteran UFO researcher John Keel in his book, *The Mothman Prophecies*: [121]

> *"I kept a careful log of the crank calls I received and eventually catalogued the various tactics of the mysterious pranksters. Some of these tactics are so elaborate they could not be the work of a solitary nut harassing UFO believers in his spare time. Rather it all appears to be the work of either paranormal forces, or a large and well financed operation by a large and well financed organisation with motives that evade me"...* [122]

I can certainly confirm, that in a curious parallel to the psychic backlash reported by Tony Shiels, [123] investigators involved in some areas of forteana, including some of the matters discussed in this book, suffer from a curious 'antipathy' towards them by household machinery, especially computers, telephones and fax machines. It is almost as if there is a 'ghost in the machine', which is evoked into 'life' by one's research into certain subjects and which acts as a warning to those unwary travellers venturing into realms of investigation which should, perhaps, be left unexplored.

I can also vouch for the enormous numbers of 'crank' telephone calls which one habitually receives, and which seem to intensify remarkably, when one is engaged on research into more 'sensitive' areas of forteana.

I would not be at all surprised to find out that Ruth Murray had received a spate of these quasi-fortean annoyances soon after she had spoken to us, blamed them on us, and not surprisingly, become very angry about the whole affair.

Four years after, one of our researchers using a different name telephoned her, and this time she was reasonably happy to talk to him. She still claimed that an un-named farmer had stampeded the animals maliciously, and that she was sick and tired of 'nuts' claiming there was a paranormal element to what was, after all merely a straightforward, if rather nasty story.

We have also been informed that there was an anomaly in the dates that the animals were reported, and that the decomposition did not, therefore take place over a period of just forty-eight hours. The mystery continues, however, and has even been cited in such notorious hoaxes as the book *Alternative 3*. [126] This semi-legendary hoax started off as a TV programme which purported to be a documentary claiming that the U.S, the U.K., and the U.S.S.R had been working together for decades to establish a base on Mars. The programme claimed that the base was run by slave labour, that the earth was doomed because of massive environmental pollution, and in passing that the deaths of the Dartmoor ponies had been caused by a botched attempt to catch them prior to shipping them into outer space. [127]

Both the TV programme, and the subsequent book, were, of course hoaxes, but the controversy, and the belief that there is still a small grain of truth behind it all, persist to this day.

It should perhaps be noted that *The Mothman Prophecies* [128] is not just the only book, apart from this one, predominantly about a series of episodes involving a mysterious winged humanoid creature, but was cited by the unnamed UFO researcher in the references to his report on the Newquay Zoo mutilations. [129]

As the last word on the mystery of the Ponies of Cherry Brook, I would merely point out that Dartmoor is an ancient and strange place. This particular area of Dartmoor has been associated with strange phenomena for many years. The elemental phenomena known commonly as 'the hairy hands' have been felt, and even seen, [130] not too far away; and mysterious deaths of livestock continue.

Ian Wright, a friend of mine for twenty years or more, and a long standing associate of the Centre for Fortean Zoology saw a mutilated and disembowelled pony just below White Tor, on the edges of Cherry Brook Valley in 1992, [131] and it should also perhaps be pointed out, that in the very month that the Cherry Brook killings took place, the one time voice of a generation released a record which included the lines:

"I've got a new pony/her name was Lucifer"

and which went on to say that when he killed her it:

"hurt me more than it hurted her",

and the song was punctuated with the refrain:

"How much longer?" [132]

How much longer indeed?

The report into the Newquay Zoo killings concluded with a summary of the findings:

1. *The killings are committed in the early hours of the day, apparently without any personnel hearing anything.*

2. *Whatever is responsible kills efficiently and rapidly.*

3. *Blood and internal organs are removed by the killer, either by drinking, or by some form of suction device or container.*

4.   *The killer must be within easy reach of the zoo (if terrestrial), as no person or animal has been seen entering or leaving the zoo area.*

5.   *If a human predator is responsible, he must hide his blood soaked clothing near to the scene of his crime, as a blood soaked figure would be noticed.*

6.   *It would seem probable that if a human is responsible that he would be familiar with the movements of the zoo staff in order to make his entrances and exits unobserved and in all probability had loitered on the exterior several times planning his entry point.*

7.   *A possible disposal point for carcass parts and clothes would be the manhole mentioned in the report"...* [133]

(Unfortunately my copy of the report does not mention a manhole, neither does my copy of the police report unless of course it was contained in one of the paragraphs which have since been censored. This suggests that there are further portions of the report that I have not been able to locate).

8.   *In view of the Dartmoor case I am still trying to locate the investigating officer on that case. If I succeed details will be forwarded in a separate report.*

9.   *It would be of interest to see if any drugs for animals had been stolen shortly before".* [134]

His report ended with the following conclusions:

"Several factors remain to be investigated before a positive conclusion can be reached. These factors are:

A.   *Condition of an abandoned mine near the zoo (possible refuge).*

B.   *Exact description of the 'puma'.*

C.   *A search through past records to establish whether any similar (sic) has been reported in the past and if any similar incidents are on record for different parts of the country.*

D.   *Have any patients with a history of lycanthropy or 'vampiric' fantasies been discharged, or escaped from any mental home recently.*

E.   *Has any veterinary anaesthetic of any type been stolen.*

F.   *Any surgical equipment e.g. scalpels or post mortem kits been stolen.*

G.   *What if anything is at the bottom of the manhole in the paddock.*

H.   *Any mysterious disappearances over the relevant period.*

I.   *Any reports of unusual aircraft or incidents.*

J.   *Have the local population reported any loss of livestock.*

209

K. *Have any reports been received of any organic matter being found anywhere". [135]*

It is interesting that the investigator started to discuss vampirism. There is a long history of vampiric attacks on livestock in the west-country. Devon folklorist Theo Brown described attacks on sheep which have certain vampiric symptoms. These occurred in the 1950's but similar attacks have been reported to the present day. She believed that they were merely the work of foxes. Having studied the ecology of British foxes, and their role within the environmental infrastructure, I must beg to disagree with her.

Too many of these attacks, including some of the aspects of the Newquay Zoo killings are horribly reminiscent of the attacks on livestock described by Sean Manchester in *The Highgate Vampire*: (see footnote).

"For a number of weeks, dead animals, notably nocturnal ones, kept appearing in Waterlow Park and Highgate Cemetery itself. Further inspection revealed that what they all had in common were lacerations around the throat and they were completely drained of blood". [136]

Back in Cornwall the attacks continue. As we were putting the finishing touches to this book news came in of a horrifying attack and decapitation of a Vietnamese Pot Bellied Pig near Par. [137] There is no doubt in my mind that many of these revolting attacks are the work of sick, twisted individuals who gain perverted pleasure out of the torture and death of domestic animals.

Some of these cases, however, have an even more sinister element, and it seems incontrovertible that there is something ancient and very evil which lurks, mostly unsuspected in the darker parts of Cornwall.

FOOT NOTE: In the ten years or so that have passed since I originally wrote this book, I have learned more about the Highgate Vampire case which leads me to suggest that all information one gains about the undead in north London should be treated *cum grano salis.*

CHAPTER SEVEN: INSINUATION

*"Each incidence of anything in life is just a single dot and
my face is so close to that dot that I can't see what it's part of"*

Russell Hoban *"Turtle Diary"* (1975)

In October 1995 Tony Shiels was back in Cornwall.

I am sure that the reader of this book could well accuse me of being deliberately 'difficult' with my style of writing. I know that the narrative chops and changes between 1976, 1978 and the mid 1990's but that's the way it went. Most of the action, or at least the research for this book, took place in pubs over prolonged liquid lunches, and as Douglas Adams said:

"Time is an illusion, lunchtime doubly so" [1]

Who am I to argue with the master?

We met Tony on several occasions during the period he was in Cornwall that autumn, and it was at round about this time that our level of personal involvement suddenly expanded into what sometimes seemed like a full time occupation.

It sometimes seems like it is Tony's eternal tragedy to be famous for what he perceives as the wrong reasons. He is a painter, and a fine one at that, and he has had a loving, and quite illustrious career as such. His 'monster-raising' activities only lasted for a relatively short period of time, and it seems unfair to him that they receive so much more attention from certain quarters than do his activities as a surrealist artist.

The events of October 1995 were a case in point.

Tony was the featured artist at exhibitions in two separate art galleries, one in Penzance and the other in St. Ives. The events had attracted a reasonable amount of media attention and he had been extremely busy with photo sessions and interviews.

211

At the launch party for one of these exhibitions, he was approached by an old friend of his, Simon Parker, the night editor of the *Western Morning News*. In Tony's words:

> *"He came up to me when I was at the exhibition opening and tried to show me some letter about the Owlman or something, but I was busy drinking and talking to people..."*[3]

and Tony didn't quite forget about it, but he let the matter slide to the portion of his mind where the memories of other events of little importance rest until they are needed.

A tiny piece appeared in one of the local newspapers claiming that an un-named American student had encountered 'The Owlman' in the vicinity of Mawnan Old Church but there were few other details.

We pride ourselves on being professional even though we are dealing with a world of extremely bizarre phenomena. We keep records, we file data, and we do our best to conduct our investigations within reasonably scholarly limits. It is, therefore, somewhat embarrassing to have to admit that we have lost the original newspaper clipping. It was, I think, from the *Western Morning News*, but we have been unable to confirm this.

Although we telephoned the newspaper offices we were unable to find any further information about this sighting, until, by accident, we contacted Simon Parker.

His name and telephone number had been included in a list of names, addresses and telephone numbers sent us by Tony, as suggested avenues of enquiry. [4] We contacted him in the spring of 1996, and he was both charming and helpful. He had been more interested, he said, in the Morgawr phenomenon, and had collected a number of clippings and other pieces of information on the subject. He knew little about the Owlman, but he did have a letter that he thought we might be interested in. It was from the American student who had experienced the Owlman the previous autumn. [5]

Three days later, as promised, the parcel of photocopies that he had promised finally arrived. It had, I think, been the longest three days of our lives. We had already got one bona-fide Owlman witness, and it looked as if we were just about to get another.

The letter read:

> *"Dear Sir,*
>
> *I am a student of marine biology at the Field Museum, Chicago, on the last day of a summer vacation in England. Last Sunday evening I had a most unique and frightening experience in the wooded area near the old church at Mawnan, Cornwall. I experienced what I can only describe as 'a vision from hell'.*
>
> *The time was fifteen minutes after nine, more or less, and I was walking along a narrow track through the trees. I was halted in my tracks when, about thirty metres ahead I saw a monstrous man-bird 'thing'. It was the size of a man, with a ghastly face, a wide mouth, glowing eyes and pointed ears. It had huge clawed wings, and was covered in feathers of silver/grey color. (sic). The thing had long bird legs which terminated in large black claws. It saw me and arose, 'floating' towards me. I just screamed then turned and ran for my life.*
>
> *The whole experience was totally irrational and dreamlike (nightmare!). Friends tell me*

212

Return of the Owlman

AFTER an absence of almost 20 years a bird-like monster labelled the "owlman" has been seen in Mawan Smith. Described by a young woman as "vision from hell" it was the size of a man, with ghastly face, a wide mouth, glowing eyes and pointed ears.

"It had clawed wings and was covered in feathers of a silver-grey colour," said the woman, a marine biology student on holiday from Chicago.

She claimed the creature had long bird legs which ended in large black claws.

"It saw me and arose, floating towards me. I just screamed then turned and ran for my life," she said.

The sighting of the bird like man is not the first in in the woods around Mawnan Church.

In July 1976, the Packet reported a similar siting on a Sunday morning above the rocky beach near Mawnan Church when what appeared to be a full grown man with legs bent backwards like a bird and jumped up through the trees.

It had red slanting eyes and a very large mouth and its feathers were silvery grey. Miss Jane Greenwood of Southport reported it as having large black crab-like claws.

The week the creature was spotted was one when a booklet on Morgawr, the Monster of Falmouth Bay was

published, and there were two independent sightings of the beast in Falmouth bay.

A number of unsolicited letters were published in the Falmouth Packet without comment other than to confirm the bona fides of the correspondents.

The young student has provided her name and address but requested anonymity.

By coincidence Mrs Gertrude Stevens of Golden Bank has spotted the Falmouth sea monster Morgawr this week.

"Most of it was under water but I could observe it clearly," she said.

She described the creature as about 20 foot long with a small head on the end of a long neck and yellowish - green in colour.

Guess who's back?

LEE TREWHELA REPORTS ON THE RETURN OF MORGAWR

Above Right:
'Doc' Shiels at the Fortean Times Unconvention 2002

Left: *Falmouth Packet, 14th September 1995*

Right: *West Briton, 15th September 1985*

LEGENDARY Cornish sea monster Morgawr has been spotted again — this time heading towards Falmouth. The description matches that provided by author Sheila Bird who saw a strange creature ten years ago off Portscatho.

She is planning to write a book about Morgawr and has a bulging case file of sightings.

Fishermen and other members of the public have seen it over the years. The latest sighting was made this week by Gertrude Stevens, of Golden Bank, Falmouth.

She saw the creature 60 yards off Rosemullion Head. She says it was 20ft long with a small head on a long neck. The body was thick and bulky at the front, but narrowed down to the tail, which was broad, flat and pear-shaped.

She watched it swim slowly in the direction of Falmouth with its head and neck above the surface for a minute, then it sank down very quickly, tail first.

The last sighting was in 1992, and Sheila Bird believes it was attracted back into Cornish waters by this year's hot summer.

Carrie Ham, 86, of Helford Passage, saw the monster about ten years ago. She told *The West Briton:* "I was looking out of my window one morning at the peaceful river when I spotted what I thought was an overturned boat. Suddenly, what looked like a long arm shaking something shot out of the water — it was the head and neck.

"A lot of people don't believe these sightings, but I know what I saw."

One of the most celebrated sightings happened in 1976 when Falmouth fisherman George Vinnicombe spotted what he also thought was an upturned boat 30 miles off The Lizard before he, too, saw the head and neck.

Sheila Bird, of Grove Hill-drive, Falmouth, is adamant that it is not a legend and believes that the sightings are of, not one, but many surviving prehistoric creatures.

She told *The West Briton:* "Two independent palaeontologists have studied the descriptions and feel that these creatures are descendents of the plesiosaurus."

She saw Morgawr about 200 metres away in July, 1985, while walking on cliffs near Portscatho.

Her description of the creature — 20 feet long, slender neck, small head and enormous hump — has similarities with this week's sighting.

Sept 5, 1995.

Dear Sir,

I am a student of marine biology at the Field Museum, Chicago, on the last
day of a summer vacation in England. Last Sunday evening I had a most
unique and frightening experience in the wooded area near the old church of
Mawnan, Cornwall. I experienced what I can only describe as 'a vision from
Hell'.

The time was fifteen minutes after nine, more or less, and I was walking
along a narrow track in the trees. I was halted in my tracks when, about
thirty metres ahead, I saw a monstrous man/bird 'thing'. It was the size of
a man, with a ghastly face, a wide mouth, glowing eyes, ansd pointed ears.
It had huge clawed wings, and was covered in feathers of silver/gray color.
The thing had long bird legs which terminated in large black claws. It saw
me and arose, 'floating' towards me. I just screamed then turned and ran
for my life.

The whole experience was totally irrational and dreamlike (nightmare!).
Friends tell me there is a tradition of a phantom 'owlman' in that
district. Now I know why. I havew seen the phantom myself.

Please don't publish my real name and address. This could adversely affect
my career. Now I have to rethink my 'world view' entirely.

Yours, very sincerely scared,

"EYE-WITNESS"

This is how the 'owlman' appeared to me:

The letter from Chicago

that there is a tradition of a phantom 'owlman' in that district. Now I know why. I have seen the phantom myself. Please don't publish my real name and address. This could adversely affect my career. Now I have to rethink my 'world view' entirely. Yours, very sincerely scared,

"Eye Witness"[6]

She gave her 'real' name and address, and under the letter there is a postscript:

"This is how the owlman" appeared to me [7]

And then a picture.

We have honoured her request and kept her name and address confidential. However, it does seem as if this episode is not as straightforward as it might otherwise have seemed.
In April 1996, Tony visited our house for the first time. He was relatively restrained, and although we sat up late drinking red wine and talking about 'the case' no furniture was broken and there were no ectoplasm stains on the upholstery. We showed him the letter from the American student, and were eager to gauge his reaction. As often seems to be the case with Tony, it was not at all what we expected.

"It's a fake lads .... someone's trying to set you up"...[8]

he took an enormous swig of red wine and then qualified the statement:

"no, someone's trying to set ME up".

Tolkein once wrote that Wizards were *'subtle and quick to anger'*, [9] and in my limited experience I must say that he is right. Tony has a temper, but he is also a very subtle man, and it is this immense subtlety, which he hides, successfully behind a cloud of alcohol, profanity and Irishness, that has made him such an enigmatic target for the fortean researcher. His main objection was to the style of the drawing which accompanied the letter. He felt, with some justification, that it was the work of somebody trying to 'fake' his style.

His first thought was that it was some complicated jest on behalf of the *Western Morning News* in general, and Simon Parker in particular. At about two thirty in the morning, when we were all a little worse for wear, he telephoned Simon Parker's house. He wasn't in. Unfortunately for her, his wife was. It is a measure of the esteem in which Tony is held by all his friends, that when Mrs Parker was woken up by 'Doc' drunkenly demanding to speak to *"that gobshite of a husband of yours"*, that she was not only civil but greeted him warmly. They chatted happily for about fifteen minutes before Tony, with an affectionate roar, put the phone down, and immediately picked it up again to ring the night desk of the *Western Morning News*. Much to our surprise, we could not get an answer.

We finally managed to speak to Simon the following day, just as Tony and I were leaving the house, in order to visit my local pub. He managed to convince Tony that he had no idea of the identity of the author of the letter and that although he didn't know whether it was genuine or not he had no reason to suppose that it wasn't. Tony seemed to believe him. Simon told me that the letter, which had been posted in Cornwall, had arrived at the newspaper along with the rest of the day's mail, and had arrived on his desk, purely because he was mildly interested in such things. [10]

There was no more information that could reasonably be gathered from Simon, so we therefore had to explore other avenues of investigation.

The first and most obvious thing to do was to write to the young lady herself at the address she had given.

> *"Dear Miss....,*
>
> *Simon Parker, the Night Editor of the* Western Morning News *passed your letter of September 5th 1995, on to our organisation.*
>
> *We were very interested to hear of your experience. We are presently researching the Owlman of Mawnan, indeed I am lecturing on the subject at the FT Convention at the University of London next weekend. We are collecting material for a book on the subject and wonder whether you would like to help us further..*
>
> *We would be very interested in talking to you, or failing that having as comprehensive a written account of your experience as possible. If you could let us have a telephone number on which you can be contacted, we would be very grateful. We shall of course respect your confidentiality in the finished book and your name, address and identity will be kept secret.*
>
> *We enclose a copy of issue six of our journal which includes a trilogy of articles about the Owlman phenomenon which you may find interesting.*
>
> *I look forward to hearing from you.*
>
> *Best wishes,*
>
> *Jonathan Downes.*
> *(For the Centre for Fortean Zoology)". [11]*

We sat back to wait for her reply. The following weekend, as I told her in my letter, we drove to London for the *Fortean Times,* UNCONVENTION '96, and on the Sunday lunchtime I delivered a lecture about the Owlman phenomenon and my ongoing researches into it. [12]

After the lecture, a young man came up to me and introduced himself as Stephen Fowler. His father had been the Rector of Gerrans and Portscatho, and his ministry had, for a while included Mawnan Smith. He told me of another rumoured Owlman sighting, that involved a patient at a local group home, for either mentally handicapped or mentally ill people. He promised to find out more details for me, shook my hand and left. [13]

Many other people came up to me over the weekend to talk about the Owlman, but no-one else had any positive information for me. We were hoping, that by the time we returned to Exeter there would be a letter waiting for us from our mysterious American student - but it was not to be. Three weeks passed, and we were forced to come to terms with the fact that she wasn't going to reply to our letter. We then decided, that, although we could not force her to co-operate with us, we could ascertain, whether or not she actually existed.

Using various contacts, whose methods were, shall we say, questionable, and who shall therefore re-

main anonymous, we found out that the address that she had given us was a real one. There was no way, at least not without breaking several federal laws, that we were able to ascertain whether or not she lived at the address, or the true name of the occupant. The international Directory Enquiries service provided by British Telecom had no record of her name at that address, and whilst we found that the Field Museum in Chicago did indeed take students, including Marine Biology students, trying to identify her through the student faculty was more difficult than it might otherwise have seemed. We made repeated telephone calls to Chicago, and eventually spoke with the department heads in each department. They told us that there was no-one of the name we gave working there at the time, nor had they any recollection of a person with that name working at the museum. There was, however a catch. The museum itself is not an educational facility, and whilst students do 'work' there they do so 'on placement', or voluntarily, and so records are not as stringent as they would have been if the Field Museum had been an educational facility in its own right.

One would, however, assume that a visiting student would have left some trace of her existence behind her. Although, therefore, it is, however, not impossible that she may have indeed been a student on attachment to the Field Museum in Chicago, the evidence was beginning to pile up to the contrary. We were left, therefore with the following alternatives:

1. The young lady *does* exist. We have her name and address correctly but she is not interested in co--operating with us, and coincidentally the Field Museum of Chicago have such an inefficient record keeping department that no-one can remember who she is.

2. The young lady *does* exist. For reasons of her own she has falsified one or more of the following: her name, her address, her nationality, or her connection with the Field Museum of Chicago.

3. The young lady does *not* exist.

If the whole affair *is* a hoax, then who is behind it?

If we assume for the moment that it is a hoax, then whoever is responsible must have the following identifying criteria:

1. He/she must be conversant with American mores, and has probably either visited America, or has friends/relatives there. He/she might, of course be American after all. The address is real, and was written down in an authentically transatlantic manner.

2. Whoever posted the letter must have been in Cornwall on the fifth of September 1995. (The person who posted the letter and the person who wrote it, may, of course, not be one and the same).

3. Whoever wrote the letter either saw the Owlman or had enough knowledge of other Owlman sightings to be able to describe it. I would not, for example, think that someone who had only read the Mawnan-Peller booklet would have been able to concoct a description such as that given by the 'American student'.

4. Whoever drew the picture had fine draughtsman's skills. If 'Doc' is correct, he/she also had enough knowledge of 'Doc's' work to be able to produce a credible fake. There is something about that drawing which bothers me. I am convinced that it is based on another drawing that I have seen somewhere. It is not based on one of the published eyewitness drawings of 'The Owlman', but I feel sure that it is based on a drawing I have seen somewhere in an occult or fortean magazine.

217

5. This is pure supposition, but I also think that whoever drew that picture knew that Tony had once been to Chicago.

Tony told me the story of his Chicago trip in his own inimitable style. Apparently, he had been the special guest of honour at a Magician's Convention in Chicago. During the proceedings he managed to successfully 'raise' a lake monster in Lake Michigan, and to play piano with an all-black blues band who introduced him on stage as:

"The famous British Bluesman DOCTOR Shiels from Ponsa - where the fuck is that – nooth"...[14]

Yes. The Wizard of the Western World had definitely visited Chicago.

If we are to suppose that the 1995 letter is a fake, then the obvious suspect is Tony himself, but although he is quite happy to admit to anything that you accuse him of, I don't feel that he is guilty of this particular deception.

I have one particular reason for this deduction. I am convinced that the picture is based not only on Tony's style, but also on a drawing originally printed in one of the less reputable fortean/paranormal magazines, or possibly in a 'pulp' science fiction novel. Tony is frighteningly well read, but he has no interest in either of the above genres; indeed he has often been scathing about my interest in such things, and therefore, knowing him as I do, I think that it is unlikely that he is the perpetrator of the 1995 letter and picture.

He has, however been accused of hoaxing on a number of occasions, most recently, and perhaps importantly by Mark Chorvinsky, editor of the renowned *'Strange'* magazine. [15]

Mark spent a long time preparing a series of articles which 'exposed' Tony as the perpetrator of a series of hoaxes. The first in the series was published in *Strange* magazine #8. In tortuous detail, and drawing on source material such as some 1976 cassette tapes sent by Tony to Mike McCormick, in which he allegedly propounded the idea of an ongoing sea-monster hoax in southern Cornwall. [16]

Chorvinsky interviewed a number of people on the subject, and various people from his past, like McCormick, Roy Standish - an ex-Editor of *The Falmouth Packet*, and Alistair Boyd, the researcher who finally uncovered the truth about the infamous 'Surgeons Photo' which for well over half a century was seen as the most convincing piece of evidence of the Loch Ness Monster. [17]

They painted a convincing picture. Roy Standish said that even at the time, he had been convinced that 'Doc' was responsible for the Mary F photographs, and several people alleged that 'Doc' had sent them prints which were slight variants on the Mary F photographs several weeks before the images we have come to know appeared for the first time in *The Falmouth Packet*. [18] [19]

This was probably true. Tony even admits as much. He claims, (and knowing the way the fortean underground works I tend to believe him), that several different versions of the photographs had been circulating around the Falmouth area for some time before they were actually published. [20] [21] This makes sense, and although by implication, the story given to *The Falmouth Packet* with the photographs is probably untrue, there is no real reason to suppose that Tony is responsible for the photographs.

He has always insisted to me, except on one occasion when, I am sure, he was just being frivolous, that

he did not fake the photographs, and that he does not know who Mary F is. [22] This is a long way from saying that he believes in the veracity of the photographs, and also in the truth of the story of the lady who took the photographs having them developed by her brother and then 'selling the copyright to an American Gentleman'. [23] The fact that Tony is now the owner of the copyright (he claims to have been given it by Standish), refutes this story completely.

There are several reasons to doubt Chorvinsky's findings. The first, and probably the most important is that Tony is a very subtle man. It seems, from what I have heard from Tony and from other people, that Chorvinsky's main source of information during his research for these articles was Tony himself. [24] [25] I have interviewed many of the same people as Chorvinsky did, and have had access to much of the same source material, and have also had the advantage, that while researching this book, I have spent significant lengths of time in Cornwall itself, and, I think that it is important that Mark Chorvinsky and I have reached very different conclusions.

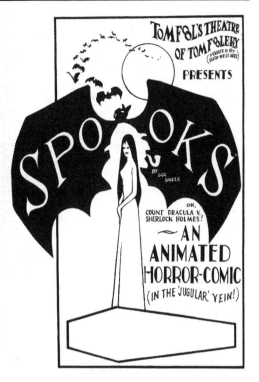

One of the contributors to the special issue of *Strange* magazine which included the work on the Mary F photographs drew a parallel between what he perceived as "Shiels versus Chorvinsky" [26] and the infamous battles between Sherlock Holmes, and his nemesis Moriarty. [27] This is an amusing parallel to draw because Tony Shiels has flirted with Holmsian imagery on a number of occasions. His book '13' includes a trick called 'The Red Handed League' [28] (a punning reference to the short story 'The Red Headed League'), [29] he invents a semi-fictional alter-ego called 'Hemlock Shiels' in 'The Cantrip Codex', [30] and one of his plays, 'Spooks' was based on a struggle between Sherlock Holmes and Dracula! [31] I think however, that all involved missed the point Tony wanted the team from *Strange* magazine to reach the conclusion that he had faked the whole thing. James Moriarty, however, never intended in be thrown over the Reichenbach Falls! [32]

Ever since I have known the man, he has been adamant that he is first and foremost a painter and that his monster-raising activities, which took place two decades ago now, were never really of more than tangential importance. He has always done his best to distance himself from forteana and fortean research, at least in the way that it has become perceived in the nineteen nineties. On several occasions he has told me that he regrets the amounts of time during his life that he has spent doing 'other things' apart from painting. [33] I think that the whole *Strange* magazine episode was Shiels' greatest hoax. It was an attempt by Tony to put that part of his life, behind him for good. It was indeed a scenario of which Sir Arthur Conan-Doyle would have been proud, but, in my opinion at least, Mark Chorvinsky was not the Great Detective, pitting his wits against the master 'criminal'. He was more like any one of dozens of minor characters in Conan-Doyle's books - the unwitting dupe of a master trickster! In saying this I intend no disrespect towards Mark Chorvinsky. He is a writer and investigator for whom I have a great deal of respect. In this particular case, however, I have a sneaking suspicion that Tony Shiels ran figurative rings around him!

There are other pieces of evidence to support my theory. Chorvinsky made an important issue out of the 1975 G.B. Gordon hoax photographs of 'Shiela' the Loch Shiel Monster, [33] which were printed originally in Tony's 1975 book *The Shiels Effect*. [34] (A punning reference to a book about another 'psychic superstar' called *The Geller Effect*). [35] These photographs, which are obviously fakes, and which according to *Strange* magazine were made with plasticene on glass, were printed together with Tony's musings on the use of Cryptozoology as an adjunct to his own form of 'Bizarre Magic'.

'Bizarre Magic' is a branch of stage magic used by magicians (note the small m) such as Tony to produce illusions based on the type that can be produced by Magicians such as Tony (note the large M). [36] It plays games with occult imagery, images from horror films, and gothic novels. Tony pointed out, very convincingly, that cryptozoology - the discipline which indeed places 'monsters' and 'beast-icons' within a modern cultural subtext, is a very useful adjunct to such surreal games.

I think that it's important to note that this book, and indeed the 'G.B.Gordon' photographs (I wonder whether this is Tony's friend John Gordon the star of at least one of his plays, [38] or whether, indeed it actually matters), appeared the year before the Mary F photographs brought the, purely local, mystery of Morgawr onto the world stage. Tony is quite happy to admit that he made those pictures and that he, together with Mike McCormick attempted to create others in the same way. [39] The results, he claims were very disappointing. He has always claimed not to have been directly responsible for the Mary F photographs. Whether or not he knows who WAS responsible is another question entirely!

The second reason for casting doubt upon Mark Chorvinsky's findings is that Tony is, and as far as I can gather, always has been a consummate artist. I have been an afficianado of his paintings for some time, and have seen a great deal of his work. For at least thirty years he has been an artist of unimpeachable quality. [40]

The main problem with viewing the Mary F photographs as a piece of art by the great surrealist painter Tony Shiels is that they are actually not terribly good, which is something that no-one could say about his other pieces of work. They are spectacularly unconvincing pictures which I have no difficulty in believing were made by using a plate of glass and some modelling clay. I just have a sneaking suspicion that if Tony had produced them, they would have been done much better.

The next piece of evidence to suggest that Mark Chorvinsky has been well and truly bamboozled, is the far superior quality of the other photographs taken by, and in conjunction with, Tony over the years 1976 to 1980. If we ignore the 'G.B.Gordon' photographs which, I am certain, were only ever intended to produce a mildly amusing illustration for a section of his 1975 book, then the other pictures: The Morgawr photographs of 1976 taken by both him and David Clarke, [41] the 1977 Nessie pictures, [42] and the Irish lake monster pictures, most notably the white animal that Tony nicknamed 'Moby Mick', [43] are far more convincing. The provenance of each photograph is plausible, and on each case there are witness(es) to the actual taking of the photograph.

It must also be remembered that Tony has never given his wholehearted support to the two more problematical monster pictures of that time; the 'Andrew the Schoolboy' photograph described earlier in this book, [45] and the picture, supposedly of an Irish animal, which was, it is claimed, taken by Patrick Kelly, a direct descendant of Edward Kelly, the notorious scryer to Elizabethan soothsayer John Dee. [46] [47]

It has been claimed that both these photographs are also the work of the Shamrock Shaman, but in view of his disavowal of them, it seems unlikely. The photographs which are unquestionably by him, how-

'The Chain Locker' on the Falmouth waterfront

ever, are of such quality that only two conclusions can be drawn:

1. They are, as Shiels claims, genuine. The photographs were taken under the circumstances that Shiels describes, and whether they show a 'real' animal, a zooform phenomenon, or a three dimensional image similar to a Kirlian photograph, [48] created by Shiel's mind and transferred psychically onto film, is a question that, for the purposes of this argument is irrelevant. 2. Shiels faked the whole thing! Mark Chorvinsky believes the latter, I believe the former. Unfortunately, Mark had devoted so much space in issue nine of *Strange* magazine to his denunciation of the Wizard of the Western World, that his loyal readers, aghast at the prospect of more of the same dominating their favourite magazine for an unspecified period, rose up in a body and voiced their disapproval of the project. [49] [50]

Mark, knowing, as any good editor must, that discretion is the better part of valour, decided to scrap the rest of the series. We contacted him a while later to suggest the possibility of us printing the rest of his findings, but he was unenthusiastic. To date therefore, he has gone little further than accusing 'Doc' of having faked the 'Mary F' photographs, and although he has mentioned tantalising fragments of the rest of his findings, they have never been made public.

'Doc' is unrepentant. I sat next to him in *The Chain Locker*, a pub on Falmouth's sea-front (which keen-eyed readers will remember was the site for the infamous press conference with Mike McCormick

twenty years before), and discussed the Chorvinsky affair with him.

> *"The trouble is with the Gobshite is that he missed the whole point"*. [51]

he said to me sadly. He explained how he had co-operated with Mark much in the way that he co--operated with me on the research for this book (except without the alcohol abuse), and how every step of the way he had fed Mark information that he knew could lead him to only one conclusion.

"And the bloody man thinks he's a surrealist", he said, shaking his head, and downing his pint of Guinness. *"Come on lad, let's go"*, he said and so we walked back into the spring sunshine.

As we shall see in the final chapters surrealism is the real key to this whole affair.

Another important thing to remember is that Tony, like all the best artists views his whole life as a work of art. Even the 'debunkers' in the *Strange* magazine piece accept that.

> *"Daily, some kind of element of myself was reflected in film that I could relate to - that I could appreciate; and understand that in a sense, the man is producing an enormous piece of art, which is his life!"* [52]

Some people seem to have an intransigent problem with reconciling Tony's activities as a stage magician with his activities as a magical magician. On his suggestion I wrote to several of his colleagues in the world of stage magick. Several of them wrote back, essentially confirming what I had already known; that Tony's magickal abilities are as real as his artistic talent. [53]

The last thing that one has to remember about Tony is that he is a consummate trickster. By his own admission he is a:

"Cheat - a fake - a thimble rigger! (....) a charlatan - a mountebank".. [54]

In the introduction to the infamous piece in *Strange* magazine Mark Chorvinsky wrote:

"To some he is a rogue - to others a genius" [55]

I have been working as a quasi-journalist and investigator, within the zoological branches of forteana, and previously within music journalism, and more specifically writing about bootlegs (which are the nearest true analogy to fortean research within rock music), for over a decade now. [56] [57] I have met a staggering amount of people and interviewed many of them. I have worked for one ex-pop star, notorious for his treatment of journalists, [58] and I have interviewed another, John-Paul Jones, late of Led Zeppelin, who were a band, infamous for their threatening behaviour towards people who asked them questions that they would rather have left unanswered. [59] Although, Tony is one of my dearest friends, and is also a man for whom I have a great deal of respect, he can, when he feels like it, be impossible to deal with on any rational level at all. We were visiting him, soon after Bealtaine 1996, when, out of the blue, one afternoon, he decided to tell us both how he had hoaxed the whole thing from start to finish.

> *"I did it. Owlman. Morgawr, the Nessie pix the whole shagging lot. It was me. I made the whole lot out of plasticene, or whatever it was that Chorvinsky claimed".* [60]

He was very drunk as he ranted on, but, all the time he was perfectly in control of the situation. He

went on to make the most extraordinary claims:

> *"I'll say whatever they want me too. I faked the surgeon's photograph, I was George Spicer!* [61] *I was Mary F! I even faked Mark Chorvinsky ... he doesn't really exist, he's really made of plasticene ..."* [62]

... and then he abruptly changed the subject, grabbed Alison by the waist and capered off to the middle of the room with her, engaging her in a most peculiar dance which, intermittently (interspersed with a lot of wine drinking) took up the rest of the evening.

I think that he was 'trying it on'. Whether or not there was any substance to any of his allegations, the way he made them negated any value that they might have had. These were direct contradictions to everything he had ever said to me, and indeed he contradicted them again the next day. This is a "case" of a wizard being playful!

He had made exactly the same claims to a reporter from one of the national newspapers only a few days before and they had refused to print the story. [63] Their refusal to print it was purely because these people, and their kind, have a vested interest in keeping mysteries such as Morgawr, Owlman and Nessie going as long as possible.

In my alternate career as a media consultant for various TV and film companies I have had no difficulty whatsoever in persuading TV companies to film interviews with even the most unconvincing 'eyewitnesses'. When, however, I have been in the position of being able to 'explode' a myth - like, for example the puma skull found at Lustleigh Cleave in 1988, [64] the TV companies have shown no interest whatsoever. When Tony claimed to have made up every piece of fortean evidence ever attributed to him (and more besides), the reporters from the national newspaper probably believed him, but refused to print the story because it 'was not what their readers wanted to read'. I, however, have printed the story, because it happened, and not because I believe those allegations that Tony made.

These were a passing fancy by a playful man who, as has always been his custom has tried to confuse matters as far as possible.

Tony can tell you a lot about national newspapers:

> *"Actually getting into the papers is not so difficult as many magicians seem to think. Over the last few years my name or my picture has been seen in most of the big British daily or weekly papers (....) All you have to do is either tell the Editor that you're about to do something newsworthy, or be in the right place at the right time .... when somebody or something else is about to interest the press boys"...* [65]

This also tells you a lot about Tony, and possibly, even a little something about me.

AUTHOR'S NOTE: Mark Chorvinsky died in 2005, and we never reconciled our differences. He went to his grave thinking of me as an ungrateful limey who thought he knew more about Cornwall than he did, and I never repented of depicting him as a "cowboy" in my cinematic retelling of the Owlman mythos., which incidentally, Tony described as 'peculiar'. Hmmmmmmm

CHAPTER EIGHT: INTERPRETATION

"They won't stop killing the whales. They make dog and
cat-food out of them – face creams, lipstick. They kill the
whales to feed the dogs so that the dogs can shit on the
pavement and people can walk in it. A kind of natural
cycle…"

Russell Hoban *"Turtle Diary" (1975)*

The story continues. This is by no means the end, but as various writers have said before, you have to end somewhere, although it is horribly frustrating to end this book with so many questions left unanswered.

'Doc' telephoned me the other day from Ireland:

"Aren't you ever going to finish the bloody thing?" he roared at me across the Irish Sea.

'It's not that bloody interesting..' [1]

I know what he means, but then, as so often within this narrative, I find myself disagreeing with him. I think that The Owlman of Mawnan is absolutely fascinating, not only because of the inherent facets of the story itself, but because of the light it sheds upon other, seemingly insoluble problems which beset fortean researchers.

I am one of the UK's very few professional cryptozoologists. This is not to say that there are only a few of us actively engaged in the search for mystery beasts - there aren't, but I am one of the only ones who manages to make any money out of it! Not much, but enough to get by.

Cryptozoology is a relatively new discipline.

The basic tenets of the science were laid down by Bernard Heuvelmans in 1954. Writing in 1988, he reiterated the aims of the science he created:

225

"Hidden animals with which cryptozoology is concerned, are by definition very incompletely known. To gain more credence, they have to be documented as carefully and exhaustively as possible by a search through the most diverse fields of knowledge. Cryptozoological research thus requires not only a thorough grasp of most of the zoological sciences, including, of course physical anthropology, but also a certain training in such extraneous branches of knowledge as mythology, linguistics, archaeology and history. It will consequently be conducted more extensively in libraries, newspaper morgues, regional archives, museums, art galleries, laboratories, and zoological parks rather than in the field!"[2]

His definition of Cryptozoology itself was exacting:

"The scientific study of hidden animals, i.e., of still unknown animal forms about which only testimonial and circumstantial evidence is available, or material evidence considered insufficient by some!" [3]

Over the last ten years there have been many suggestions that the science of Cryptozoology should be expanded to include the study of 'Out of Place Animals', feral animals, and even animal ghosts and apparitions. Heuvelmans rejects these moves with typical thoroughness, and not a little wry humour...

"Admittedly, a definition need not conform necessarily to the exact etymology of a word. But it is always preferable when it really does so which I carefully endeavoured to achieve when I coined the term 'cryptozoology'. All the same being a very tolerant person, even in the strict realm of science, I have never prevented anybody from creating new disciplines of zoology quite distinct from cryptozoology. How could I in any case?

So, let people who are interested in founding a science of 'unexpected animals', feel free to do so, and if they have a smattering of Greek and are not repelled by jaw breakers they may call it 'aprosbletozoology' or 'apronoeozoology' or even 'anelistozoology'. Let those who would rather be searching for 'bizarre animals' create a 'paradoozoology', and those who prefer to go a hunting for 'monstrous animals', or just plain 'monsters', build up a 'teratozoology' or more simply a 'pelorology'.

But for heaven's sake, let cryptozoology be what it is, and what I meant it to be when I gave it its name over thirty years ago!"[4]

Unfortunately, many of the creatures which are of most interest to cryptozoologists do not, in themselves, fall under the blanket heading of cryptozoology which is why many of us, who are interested in such phenomena as 'The Beasts of Bodmin and Exmoor' [5][6] (which logically cannot be 'unknown species' but are logically 'known species' albeit in an alien environment), and 'The Devil Dogs' of Devon and Cornwall and 'The Big Grey Man of Ben McDhui', [8] which are certainly not 'animals' or even 'animate' in the accepted sense of the word, have to look further afield for a definition of our activities.

Even if they had not been proposed by Heuvelmans with his tongue firmly placed in his cheek, I would have grave difficulty in pronouncing these alternative titles for what would undoubtedly become an extremely unwieldy bundle of pseudo sciences so in a spirit of derring do I decided to lump them all together with the unnamed study of what I have dubbed 'Zooform Phenomena', apparitions or entities

226

which appear to be animals - which take the form of animals but are neither animate, nor in most cases even corporeal.

I have called my artificial portmanteau of esoteric disciplines 'FORTEAN ZOOLOGY', taking my lead and much of my methodology from the work of the renowned American investigator and author Charles Hoy Fort (1874-1932), the self-styled 'arch enemy of science' who leant his name to a whole range of new and esoteric disciplines.

I think that it is very unlikely that anyone will have read this book without knowing who Charles Fort was. The following biography, which is included on the off chance that I am wrong is paraphrased from that given in each issue of *Fortean Times*.

Fort, who came from a Dutch family in Albany, New York spent many years researching scientific data in the New York public library and the British Museum library. (Ironically at the same time as Karl Marx [9] and Fredreich Engels [10] were also spending every day in the same London library - one wonders in lighter moments whether they ever met, and shared their epoch-making ideas with each other over a thermos of cocoa?)

He marshalled his confidence and set forth his philosophy in four books; *The Book of the Damned* (1919), *New Lands* (1923), *Lo!* (1931) and *Wild Talents* (1932). He collected research and news items on strange phenomena, portents, prodigies and curiosities. He was sceptical about scientific explanations and observed that scientists often tend to argue according to their own beliefs rather than the rules of evidence, and that inconvenient data was ignored, suppressed, discredited or explained away.

His dictum *"One Measures a circle beginning anywhere"*, (which was also used by Isaac Asimov in his 1953 book *Second Foundation*), [11] expresses his philosophy of continuity in which everything is in an intermediate state between extremes. He had notions of the 'Universe as Organism' and of the transient nature of apparent phenomena. Since his death his work has been continued by The International Fortean Association (INFO), [12] by the British magazine *Fortean Times* [13] which has gone from being a small circulation fanzine selling no more than fifty copies to being a large and glossy periodical available in every newsagent, by ASSAP, [14] the society which attempts to find a scientific explanation for anomalous phenomena, by the Fortean Picture Library [15] who have catalogued and conserved pictures, photographs and engravings of interest to the fortean researcher and in our own little way by us at the Centre for Fortean Zoology. [16]

Cryptozoology itself has always contained one inherent and fundamental dichotomy and this has been carried forward into my new discipline of Fortean Zoology. The dichotomy is that whereas some of the subjects with which we are concerned are well known. (if the study of an apparently 'unknown' creature can be described as such), such as the Loch Ness Monster, the Yeti and even the aforementioned 'Beasts of Exmoor', the greater part of what we study is by its very nature obscure and often, to the layman, insignificant. The public at large have a deep and fervent interest in phenomena which may prove to be huge, scaly lake monsters, or shambling, hairy man-beasts, but on the whole the research projects with which much of cryptozoology and its allied disciplines are concerned, such as 'The Tatzelwurm', a putative, and as yet undiscovered two foot long bipedal lizard which has been reported from much of southern France including parts of Provence and the Alps Maritimes [17] [18] and the possibility of a race of dwarf, white weasels which have been reported from the Welsh island of Anglesey [19] are of only passing interest (if that) to the public at large.

As we approach the end of the second millennium, and only sixty years or so after Fort himself died,

Forteanism is in great trouble. Mainly because it has become ForteanISM. Charles Fort would not have approved of the work he did being transformed into a cross between a religion and a marketing ploy. He refused to have anything to do with the original Fortean Society (founded by Tiffany Thayer not long before his death), [20] and he would not have liked the way that his name has been adopted by a movement which is in so many ways unlike the subjects in which he was interested. So-called 'fortean' magazines often have more in common these days with publications covering science fiction, and seem overly obsessed with television programmes like *The X Files* [21] which, though undeniably entertaining, are nothing more than well meaning fiction. The same publications are also often obsessed with fringe religious beliefs, middle class paganism, and Spiritualism, and are in great danger of losing sight of what they actually should be doing.

I 'invented' the name of Fortean Zoology, because, although I wanted to call it 'Anarchozoology', I knew that the quasi-political overtones would upset too many people and distract them from what I really wanted to achieve. I adopted the name 'Fortean' because Fort, and many of those who came after him, who have NOT been distracted by ephemeral nonsense, were some of my greatest inspirations. To my utter surprise, I eventually got to meet, and work with some of these men, and women, and together we have achieved a little of what we originally set out to do.

In the meantime, I have scandalised some of the more 'fundamentalist' cryptozoologists by adopting terms of reference, very alien to those who see the natural world purely in terms of organic, carbon-based life-forms.

I have divided the 'creatures' (the punctuation marks are intentional, as will become clear) with which we are interested into three main groupings.

- CRYPTIDS
- QUASI CRYPTIDS
- ZOOFORM PHENOMENA

The first grouping are the actual unknown animals as defined so succinctly by Heuvelmans.

The second grouping are also 'real' living and breathing animals, but are this time of 'known' species, but in an unfamiliar location. These can also be termed 'Out of Place' animals, but this term, usually used to refer to such creatures as the Alien Big Cats (or at least some of them), which are so regularly reported on the British moorlands, is open to a degree of misinterpretation.

The third, final, and in some ways the most contentious of the three groupings of apparently unknown creatures are the ones that may well not be creatures at all!

At the risk of severely angering the folk in the Yeti, and Bigfoot research 'camps' and indeed some of my friends and colleagues who have spent so much of their lives sitting on the shores of Loch Ness waiting for something to happen, this is the category into which most of the most well known members of the iconography of Cryptozoology fit in.

This is not the time nor the place to enter into a long discussion about the zoological veracity or other-wise of the most 'media friendly' cryptids, the Yeti, Bigfoot and the Loch Ness monster but even the most hardcore nessiephile or traditional cryptozoologist would admit that the volumes that have been written about these phenomena include a fair amount of evidence that suggests that some, if not all, of

their manifestations may not necessarily be of physical origin.

One of the most important books to have been written on the subject of Fortean Zoology in the forty years since Heuvelmans first published in English, is 'Alien Animals' by the well-known husband and wife team of Janet and Colin Bord. [22]

In their book they outline five types of what they call "Animals that aren't", [23] but what in a paper published by the now defunct Society for Cryptozoology and Anomalies of Nature (SCAN), I first described as 'Zooform Phenomena': [24] Apparitions which take the form of animals - usually living but which are not living things - at least in the way that we understand the term.

In my original paper I added a sixth category (mystery kangaroos), [25] to the original five propounded by the Bords and the list of Zooform Phenomena/Alien Animals/Animals that aren't, now reads:

- MYSTERY CATS
- MYSTERY DOGS
- LAKE MONSTERS AND SEA SERPENTS
- MAN BEASTS (BHM)
- WINGED THINGS
- MYSTERY KANGAROOS

The very strange thing about each of these categories is that in nearly every case zooform phenomena of a particular case live alongside actual flesh and blood cryptids of similar form and sometimes the definitions get muddied to such an extent that it is difficult to tell where one ends and the next begins.

The Owlman of Mawnan, and the similar entities described in this book are members, clearly of that fifth category. But, to categorise them is not good enough. The purpose of this chapter is to attempt to find out what they actually are!

The simple answer is that nobody knows, and until we have redefined our knowledge of the laws of Physics to a degree which I am certain the academic authorities of this century (and most probably the bulk of the next one), will find unacceptable, we are unlikely to know.

What we can do, however, is make some educated guesses. It must be stressed, however, that guesses ARE all they are.

There have been several different hypotheses suggested to explain the Owlman phenomenon. Since the original interview with 'Gavin' first appeared in *Animals & Men*, [26] several people wrote to suggest their interpretations of his experience.

Fortean researcher Janet Bord, whom we mentioned above, was the first to write:

"Dear Jonathan,

My main reason for writing is to comment on "Gavin's" account of an encounter with the Cornish Owlman. He did mention our identification of this creature as an owl, as suggested

229

in our book 'Modern Mysteries of Britain', but only in passing, and I would like to expand on it if I may. I have been interested in the Owlman ever since he was first reported in the 1970's, and I have been to the woods where he was seen in the company of Doc Shiels who was instrumental in publicising the sightings. I was uncertain what to make of the reports for some time, but tended like most people, to accept them as genuine, in view of all the other activity in the Falmouth Bay area at the time (Morgawr and UFO sightings). More recently, however, now that some doubt has been cast on certain of the Falmouth events (see Mark Chorvinsky's painstaking research as published in his 'Strange' magazine), [27] I lam much more inclined to believe that the sightings have a much more prosaic explanation. It was my own sighting in Hafren Forest (Powys), a few years ago which clarified my thinking on Owlman, as here described in 'Modern Mysteries of Britain':

"I was sitting in a car when my attention was caught by a disturbance in the trees across a stream. I saw a large bird, definitely an owl, rise up vertically, facing me with its whole face and body visible, its legs and feet hanging down. It rose straight up above the trees and flapped off in broad daylight".

This very closely resembles what the witnesses of Owlman have described - indeed the very name 'Owlman' suggests that the creature was owl-like. The creature's size is the problem - 'Gavin' says that it was "definitely a great deal bigger than any owl". But I suspect that anyone taken by surprise when an owl rises up close by them, would think the creature bigger than it really was, and with its legs and feet hanging down, and wings lifted, these would add to its apparent size and bulk. There's no doubt that owls are frightening to encounter in an eerie wood at night, and they do tend to be alarmed and fly off if people approach them. So despite "Gavin's" protestation that the creature was definitely not an owl, I have my suspicions that that's exactly what it was". [29]

Three months later John Heath-Stubbs seemed to agree with her:

"Dear Sir,

May I suggest that the creature seen by 'Gavin' in the article in 'A&M6' was almost certainly an Eagle Owl (Bubo bubo). This bird is found in continental Europe but has been found in Britain occasionally. It is about 26 inches in length, so that the five feet given by the observer is wrong. It is difficult to be accurate at night with measurements. It is characteristic of owls in general to perch with two toes pointing forward and with the outer toe reversed". [30]

By December 1995 'Gavin' had had enough. Much against his better judgement, he broke silence and wrote a reply for the letters page of *Animals & Men*:

"Dear Jon.

Forget about the whole thing? Are you kidding, for now I'll die fighting. The objections to the reality of 'owlman' recently brought up in your letters are hard to dismiss at all convincingly but at the same time, to my mind, they are ridiculous. We have some very big problems here: owlman looks like a very large owl (hey, it's not called owlman for nothing guys?), I've seen it and those who object haven't. Janet Bord wrote of her suspicions that the creature, despite my protestations was an owl. The only way to ever be sure that you have seen

230

an image as recorded in your mind is to see that image again, and, as I don't think (and hope) it likely that I will ever see the creature again, I do remain sceptical of my own conscience.

Owls tend not to grow to more than four feet in height, nor would sightings of them result in the construction of exactly the same mental image, as drawn independently by witnesses including myself. That, for me, is the biggest problem. If I see an owl I draw an owl, not the same quasi-bird humanoid that teenage girls and Doc Shiels were drawing back in the late 'seventies.

John Heath-Stubbs clearly did not read my account: if he did he considers me either a liar or a pathetic observer. 'The five feet given by the observer is wrong' ?????!!! Excuse me, but trying to say that 'owlman' cannot be five foot tall because eagle owls do not exceed two feet', is an absurd approach to the data, and a poor attempt to dismiss it. I have decided that to prove to myself if no-one else, that the animal I saw was considerably bigger than an eagle owl, I need to find the actual tree in which my sighting occurred. Photos, when obtained will be published.

John Heath-Stubbs notes it is characteristic of owls that two toes point forward while 'the outer toe' is reversed. Actually the 'inner toe' (digit 1), is reversed too. This could be the case in owlman, but the large, bulky, pincer feet (again remarked upon independently by different witnesses), don't remind me one bit of an owl's slim feet. Look at my drawings for god's sake". [31]

It is actually quite surprising how many people believe that all the owlman sightings can be explained by aberrant sightings of large owls. British Cryptozoologist, Dr. Karl P.N. Shuker, a friend and colleague of mine believes in the Eagle Owl theory. [32]

He believed that at least one of the sightings is directly attributable to that of an Eagle Owl. He points out that these huge birds are commonly kept in aviaries and bird gardens, as well as by pet-keepers and has noted that there are a large number of escapes on record. He too, cites Janet Bord's experience, (as quoted above), and whilst he has an open mind about zooform phenomena he feels that this case has a definite zoological foundation.

It is quite surprising that whereas African and Indian parakeets are well established in some British locations, [33] [34] and there are a multitude of other records of ludicrously out of place birds (my own records include an Orange Bellied Chloropsis [35] [36] in a garden in Exeter, and a Timneh African Grey Parrot from a council estate in Harlow, Essex), [37] that there are not more reports of out of place raptors.

The trade magazines are crammed with advertisements offering all shapes and sizes of predatory birds for surprisingly low prices. The small ads column of *Cage and Aviary Birds* for the week ending June 6th 1992. [38] for example, offered Golden Eagles, [39] Eagle Owls, [40] Goshawks [41] and Harris Hawks [42] as well as a multitude of smaller and less exciting raptors for comparatively small sums of money. As Gerald Summers pointed out on a number of occasions during his trilogy of books about captive birds of prey, [43] [44] [45] these birds are very adept at escaping from their quarters even after many years of seemingly contented captivity, and it would seem fairly surprising that more have not done so.

There are, in fact, well-attested records of Eagle Owls in Cornwall, as there are in other parts of Britain.

231

[46] Whether these are stragglers from the natural population in Northern Europe, or are, in fact escapees from captivity, as suggested by Karl Shuker, [47] and Devon naturalist Trevor Beer, [48] is unclear. My objections to the hypothesis which suggests that the 'Owlman' is nothing more than an aberrant large owl are the same as those voiced by 'Gavin' himself. The 'creature' he saw, which is presumably the same as the 'creatures' experienced by the other individuals listed in this book, is far too large to be an orthodox owl. It does not behave in the way that orthodox owls behave, and whereas it is certainly possible that badly frightened children like those who saw it first at Easter 1976 [49] could have misinterpreted a surprising sighting of a bird, albeit a large and unfamiliar one, into a winged, feathered humanoid, it is unlikely that some of the other witnesses could have done the same thing.

As noted elsewhere, [50] 'Gavin' was, even at the young age that he was when he experienced the zooform phenomenon of Mawnan Woods, a surprisingly experienced naturalist! He had a great deal of experience with birds of prey, especially owls, and whilst I might not necessarily accept the uncorroborated word of many twelve year olds, in this instance, and especially when one considers the depth to which I have investigated this particular incident, I feel that one should have no qualms about accepting his version of the facts.

My rejection of the 'owl' hypothesis does not only hinge on these criteria however. These incidents have taken place within a very small geographical area over a period of nineteen years. If there was a vagrant owl, of whatever species, it seems very unlikely that it would only be seen by teenaged girls in such a restricted area. There are no records, as far as I am aware, of aberrant owls being seen in other parts of southern Cornwall between 1976 and 1995, and there are, as we have discovered, no sightings that cannot be expressly linked to teenaged or very young girls.

The second most widely supported hypothesis is that Tony Shiels made the whole thing up. I have stated my reasons for disagreeing with this viewpoint throughout the book. Whilst I am certain that Tony Shiels is quite capable of having made the whole thing up, I do not believe that he did so.

His assertions in *Fortean Times* and other publications that 1976 was a particularly strange year in southern Cornwall have been borne out conclusively by my investigations into the matter. I must also say, that despite the allegations by Chorvinsky and others which were listed in the last chapter, I do not feel that he could be responsible for all of the Morgawr sightings since the mid-1970's. I am certain that he used the phenomena for his own ends. He may even have contributed to it, but I feel that the manufacture of an entire series of cryptid sightings of this magnitude is beyond even the Wizard of the Western World.

My main reason for rejecting the hypothesis that Tony Shiels faked the whole thing is the testimony of 'Gavin'. This checks out to the smallest degree of minutae that I have been able to check, and there is no possibility of there having been any collusion between him and any member of the Shiels clan.

No, I will revise that last statement. The history of fortean investigation, and indeed all branches of the natural sciences is littered with the metaphorical corpses of people who said that *"such and such was impossible"*, or that *"there is no possibility"* of something happening. I have no intention of joining this illustrious brigade of losers, and will therefore re-phrase my last statement to read:

'In my opinion it is highly unlikely that there is or has been any collusion between 'Gavin' and Tony 'Doc' Shiels, or any of his family or associates".

Another argument which could well be put forward is that 'Doc' and 'Gavin' both hoaxed their individ-

ual involvement in the phenomenon, independently of each other. As I have shown elsewhere in this book, I am completely convinced of the veracity of 'Gavin's' testimony, which in itself is corroboration of the incidents that can be directly linked to Tony Shiels and his family and friends.

We can therefore discount, with all possible margin of doubt, the hypotheses which call for all the Owlman witnesses to have been either making it up, or to have misidentified a sighting of a 'real' bird. Tony Shiels, however believes that these episodes are sightings of a surreal bird.

For the past three years Tony Shiels has been urging me to study Surrealism. Over and over again he has claimed that Surrealism is the key facet in the Owlman case, and he has always implied that if I grow to understand surrealism, I will eventually understand the Owlman phenomenon. On May 26th 1996 he wrote to me:

"You must learn about surrealism – that is an order!!!" [51]

and the word must was underlined three times. One does not disobey the orders of a wizard, especially when one is desperately trying to link up a number of disparate, and seemingly unrelated strands of thought and experience into some semblance of a cohesive whole in order to finish a book, that by the early summer of 1996 I was beginning to wish that I had never started.

Surrealism, like 'Fortean', is a severely misused word. It has been used to describe everything from 'zany' children's television programmes, to any form of art or drama into which an incongruous element has been introduced with the simple aim of attracting comment. Neither of these, nor many other usages of the noun are correct. Surrealism is something far more organic. In its true sense it has far more in common with true 'Forteanism' (if there is such a thing), than most of the current practitioners of the latter would care to admit.

In 1924 Andre Breton gave the following definition:

> *"SURREALISM, noun, masc., pure psychic automatism by which it is intended to express, either verbally or in writing, the true function of thought. Thought dictated in the absence of all control exerted by reason, and outside all aesthetic or moral preoccupations".* [52]

One could hardly ask for a better definition of some of the phenomena which so commonly preoccupy fortean researchers. Many years later, (but precisely when I am unsure because someone has ripped out the title page of my copy of the book), Patrick Waldberg wrote:

> *"Imagination, folly, dream, surrender to the dark forces of the unconscious and recourse to the marvellous are here opposed, and preferred, to all that arises from necessity, from a logical order, from the reasonable".* [53]

In the light of such a revolutionary statement as inflammatory as any call to arms by a gun toting demagogue, one ceases to regard 'surrealism' (with a small 's'), as cack-handed imitations of 'Monty Python' [54] by third rate sitcom writers, and begins to gain an insight into why The Wizard of the Western World considers surrealism as inherently germane to the issue of the Owlman (and indeed other so-called-fortean phenomena). All such phenomena are inherently surreal, and the owlman phenomenon is a particularly good example of the genre. As is becoming clear, the Owlman of Mawnan is at the centre of an immensely complicated surreal joke, which like all the best jokes is concurrently hysterically funny and terrifying. One starts to perceive the events recounted in this book as being all linked in a

What do we like......SEA HEADS!!!

fashion which is by turns both obscure and glaringly obvious.

I was brought up in the tropics, and have always thought that the practice of having a siesta during the afternoon is an eminently sensible and civilised one.

During the final work on this book, I started work at about 9.a.m and finished between twelve and fourteen hours later, but always with a break for, what my mother used to, and probably still does call, a 'zizz' in the middle of the afternoon. One afternoon, whilst I was working on the final parts of this book, and also attempting to fulfill the instructions I had been given by the Wizard of the Western World with reference to surrealism, I had a dream, or at least I think it was a dream:

From where I am sitting I perceive a schematic vision of events which feels like there is an enormous spider's web draped over the western peninsular of the British Isles. The centre of the spider's web is situated at Mawnan Old Church, and squatting in the middle, like a huge malevolent spider is the entity, described disrespectfully by Tony Shiels as "His Owliness". In the same way that the empty corpses of flies can be found in the web of any large house spider, the desiccated memories of various events both horrific, and apparently irrelevant are entrapped in various parts of the web. Several people; me, 'Gavin' and some people that I don't recognise, are walking gingerly along strands of the web towards our nemesis at the epicentre.

We are trying, both to keep our balance like strange analogues of circus tightrope walkers, and to avoid being ensnared in the webbing itself. Some grotesque bundles, some looking frighteningly ancient, dotted about the web, are proof that other people before us have made this journey, and that some, at least failed to complete it.

The final part of my vision is that the spider's web itself is made of a shiny silver substance that in parts is reflective, but only in the way that the concave or convex mirrors in a sideshow tent at a fun-fair are. Occasionally, out of the corner of my eye I see a reflection in one of these strands of webbing. It is the reflection of a large, bearded man with twinkling eyes and a tall hat. For some reason he is laughing, but whether it is at us, at the Owlman or at himself there is no way to tell...

The next day I received a telephone call from the good 'Doctor', instructing me to learn more about Max Ernst. [54]

He was one of the greatest surrealist painters, but according to 'Doc' he is possibly the central character in the whole Owlman saga.

In 1925 he wrote:

> "... he that will gaze attentively at that spot will see in it human heads, various animals, a battle, rocks, the sea, clouds, thickets and still more: it is like the tinkling of a bell which makes one hear what one imagines". [55]

Later in the same piece, eventually published in 1937, he wrote:

> "... if you consider them carefully you will discover most admirable inventions which the painter's genius will turn to good account in composing battles (both of animals and men), landscapes or monsters, demons and other fantastic things that will do credit to you. Genius awakes to new inventions in these indistinct things (...) such as the parts of animals, and as-

Mylor Marina

pects of landscape, rocks and vegetation". [56]

The same year that was published Max Ernst, originally from the Rhineland was visiting Cornwall with his lover Leonora Carrington.

Tony Shiels briefly described the events of that summer in *Monstrum*:

> *"They all descended on the Truro River house of 'Beacus' Penrose, Roland's brother, and proceeded to call forth strange animals.*
>
> *One night, Eileen Agar, Lee Miller, Nusch Eluard, and Leonora Carrington danced naked near Mylor, and probably raised the 'large snake-like creature' seen there at that very time.*
>
> *Eileen Agar had already discovered a 'bird snake' on the Dorset coast, and photographed the 'prehistoric monster', rocks, of Ploumanach, Brittany. Lee Miller pointed her camera towards 'disquieting images'. Nusch Eluard, had created some strange submarine photo-montages.*
>
> *And Leonora Carrington was obsessed with Celtic totem-beasts.*
>
> *A powerful quarternary of sorceresses. But the arch sorcerer of that particular party was Max Ernst"...* [57]

236

A recurrent image in Max Ernst's paintings and collages was 'Loplop'. This was his bird headed alter ego. Loplop is seen running past a semi naked woman in woods, in an illustration from *Une semaine de Bonte* (1933). He is pursued by two men, one of whom looks frighteningly like Tony Shiels. [58]

We have already seen how, when his essay was finally published in the year he went to Cornwall, Max Ernst predicted animal mutilation ('parts of animals') and even something called *Animals & Men*. I knew nothing about Ernst when I chose the name for the magazine. It originally came from a song on an LP called *Dirk wears white Sox* by *Adam and the Ants*. [59] [60] The spelling of 'sox' is more Edward Lear [61] than Stuart Goddard, [62] but we shall return to him later.

In the same essay he describes skyclad witches: *"Several young girls amusing themselves in beautiful poses"* and *"some very beautiful women crossing a river and crying"*.

He states his intention to *"erect a monument to the birds",* and tells how he was *"visited nearly every day by the bird superior Loplop, an extraordinary phantom of model fidelity who attached himself to my person"*. There are other clues here including a conflict with the Church in the shape of two Bishops. (Rev. Peter Mumford was only one, but he died soon after and was replaced by another), and more references to birdmen, and even mysterious big cats, but I think that we have read enough.

Did the events of the summer of 1937 act as an invocation to give some semblance of corporeal reality to Max Ernst's bird headed alter ego? If so, why was it nearly thirty years before he was seen by *"Several young girls amusing themselves"*. Perhaps the fact that 1976 was the year that Ernst died had something to do with it?

One of my favourite authors, Sir John Verney, [63] died a few years ago. I once edited a music and arts magazine called ISMO, which was named after one of his books.   For a brief time, during the last few years of his life I had the privilege of exchanging letters with him. Amongst other things, he was fascinated by Edward Lear (who, in his diaries, by the way always spelt 'rocks' 'rox' and 'socks' 'sox' hence the surrealchemic connection with *Animals & Men* - the titles of my magazines have a lot to do with this passage), and in a book called *Seven Sunflower Seeds* [65] he wrote:

"One has to learn to see beyond logic - as Lear himself did. Nothing can ever be proved beyond a shadow of doubt. How dull if it could!" [66]

Earlier in the same book, a young girl the same age as many of the Owlman witnesses is discovering Edward Lears poetry for the first time:

"I read - and soon entered the private landscape which Lear carried around with him. It was indeed a strange and beautiful country with certain pronounced features. There was usually a plain; and water near it - but a large lake rather than the sea proper, I thought. Then there were steep crags that might be 'perpendicular' or the Hills of the Chankly Bore. Often there was an old tree called variously a 'Bong', a 'Crumpetty' or a 'Twangum'. And always, but always, there was a solitary old man. He might be the Quangle Wangle, the Pobble, the Yonghy-Bonghy-Bo, The Akond of Swat, or:- My   aged Uncle Arly Sitting on a heap of Barley

and selling "Propter's Nicodemus Pills", but he was always, I felt, Lear himself".

Setting aside any considerations of *The Owl and the Pussycat* vis-a-vis Owlman and Cornish A.B.C sightings, re-read the above passage, substitute Max Ernst for Edward Lear and you have the bare bones

Illustration of 'Lop-Lop' from ' Une Semaine de Bonté' by Max Ernst (1933)

of an explanation. (Note, please that I did not say THE explanation).

As well as Loplop, Ernst created another chimera (perhaps the *'chimera in an evening dress'* he describes in the 1937 article), combining the human form with that of a nightjar. The nightjarman, with a face strikingly similar to the 1976 drawing by June Melling, was pictured in *La dame Ovale* (1939). The nightjarman is an irresistible parallel with the owlman, (especially as owls and nightjars are the only two orders of British birds to be truly nocturnal).

Tony Shiels wrote a trilogy of plays about nightjars in the early 1980's both invoking and confusing the issue further:

> *"Obeying the flexible rules of surrealchemy, the second part of the trilogy was the first to be written and staged; it had a magnificent title – Cloth Owl the Winking Curtain – and was a minor hit. The first play, which actually came second, was simply called Nightjars. Finally, the third, entitled Dr Beak Hides His Hands or Wireless Night, opened in Dublin in the early springtime of 1981.*
>
> *The Nightjar Trilogy was deeply and darkly surreal, shot through with bizarre humour. Cloth Owl and Dr Beak centred around a strange, black, horned, tent-like object, known as the 'zoobox' which housed a number of eccentric characters and a menagerie of mythical animals (unicorn, harpy, basilisk, etc) said to have been left behind when Noah hauled up the ark's anchor.*
>
> *One of the principal characters in Cloth Owl, was a stinking, hairy, cloven footed, dragon tailed, goat headed, medieval demon. The actor inside that magnificent demon costume was my eldest son Gareth, who was utterly convincing in the role and scared his audiences most gratifyingly ... especially when he performed a slow, grotesque, semi-crippled dance – to the music of a crumhorn and drum – wearing a disturbingly incongruous lurex yashmak. Gareth also played Dr Beak in the final play; his costume based on illustrations of a 14th Century 'plague doctor', with his monkish gown, broad brimmed hat, and weird beaked mask, (the wickerwork 'beak' contained – optimistically – 'protective herbs', in the days of the Black Death). Influenced by spook show blackouts, we staged Dr Beak in complete darkness; or rather, I mean that the only lighting was carried by the actors in the form of small 'pencil' flashlights and cigarette lighters. It was effectively disconcerting. Remember ... these plays were comedies, but the laughter was of a nervous kind". [69]*

We have nightjars, we have owls, we have the zoobox and we have *Une Semaine de Bonte*. A pattern is beginning to emerge, but what can we make of it?

Most cryptozoologists are baffled by this type of cryptoinvestigative methodology. As has been explained, however, the Owlman of Mawnan is not a cryptozoological problem. Most surrealists and many true forteans believe in both acausal synchronicity and in the fundamental interconnectedness of everything. Sceptical mathematicians point out that in their opinion such things are merely the result of a lamentable lack of knowledge about the laws of probability on the part of most members of the general public. I am prepared to agree with that, when one of these sceptical mathematicians is able to present me with a convincing piece of mathematics to back up his argument.

Until then, it's time for some more connections...

239

Illustration of 'The Nightjar Man' from 'La Dame Ovale' by Max Ernst (1939)

You will remember that during the chapter on 'bird men' from other parts of the world we discussed John Keel, and his book, *The Mothman Prophecies*. [70] You may also remember that in an early interview I conducted for this book Tony Shiels, made an offhand comment, suggesting that the Owlman of Mawnan might only have come into being because he (Tony) had read Keel's book. In the same letter which included his order that I learn more about surrealism Tony wrote:

'Grand Genie' sculpture by Max Ernst

Thinking about your owlman book yesterday, I remembered a character in Keel's 'Mothman Prophecies' (which I don't have to hand): Princess Moon-Owl, from the planet Ceres (which is actually an asteroid, but no matter). It just struck me that there was a curious connection with Owlman and crop circles through the names - Moon Owl and Ceres. As I remember, a Chief Corn Stalk is also mentioned in Keel's book. Another thing - David Hoy predicted the Silver Bridge disaster (this is documented in John Godwin's book on Dave) which was the climax of the Mothman saga. That doesn't really matter - but the thing that really interests me here is the Native American stuff - and the Ceres/Corn connections. Moon Owl/ Owlman - Corn/Cornwall (yes I KNOW it's a horn. I'm lexilinking). (...) Max was very interested in North American culture, and he had a large collection of Hopi/Zuni 'Kachina' dolls, some of which represented the Corn Spirit.

Leonora moved to Mexico where she fused Celtic symbolism with Native American. Now remember there is a New Mexico connection through McCormick, and he gave me my cactus core stick. He, too, is fascinated by Navaho/Hopi/Zuni culture - and made much use of owl bones in some of the 'things' he created.

I feel that there could be something important here. Obviously, Owlman is quite similar to Mothman in some ways, but I suspect that the real connection is through the Red Indian/Max Ernst stuff- and the Corn Spirit/Cornwall lexilink. If you visit Mawnan Old Church, you will discover a nicely embroidered Phoenix to remind you of Arizona and Loplop" [72]

Max Ernst moved to Arizona in 1942 (with Dorothea Tanning, and one of the first major paintings he made there was *Surrealism in Painting* [73] (also the title of a 1927 essay by Andre Breton). [74] Tony discusses the significance of this painting in some depth in *Monstrum*:

> *"Surrealism and Painting (1942) - portrays surrealism itself as a monster, a viscous, writhing creation, part bird, part serpent, part human, caught in the act of picture making".* [75]

This description is irresistibly reminiscent of the owlman, and Morgawr, two thirds of the unholy trinity of zooform phenomena which have manifested themselves in the Falmouth area (the ABC's -when the 'A' is stressed, are the third). The more one delves into the surrealchemic links suggested by Tony Shiels. the more plausible, and at the same time absurd, the whole 'case' appears.

Tony's 1996 letter concluded with:

> *"So ... I'm just suggesting a possible shamanic link (or several) between Moon Owl/Ceres/ Mothman/Corn Stalk and Ernst/Carrington/Cornwall/Owlman/Morgawr. And what of the connection between a fellow called WHEATman and my 1976 birthday? Loren Coleman*

may be able to tell you. Then there's 'Thundersqueak' (but that's almost a different story). There could be a connection, also, between the Kachina Corn Spirit and Roswell, but we'll leave that (and the 'Desert' conjectures) for now. So far as Owlman is concerned, Max Ernst is the surrealist shaman behind it. Have you seen his 1944 sculpture 'Moon Mad', made in Arizona? Oh, I'm rattling on too long. I'm sure you can make something of this anyway ...". [76]

I'm sure I can. The connections are many and multifarious both inside and outside what Tony had to say. There does, however come a time when you can have too much data, and when you have to sit down, discard the irrelevant, and attempt to reach some conclusions.

Besides this, we have travelled to some bizarre places (figuratively speaking) during the research for this book, but there are some places that I am not prepared to go.

Sir Arthur Conan-Doyle is often cited as an authority in books on fortean subjects. This is partly because of his authorship of the Sherlock Holmes stories, and partly because of his involvement with Spiritualism and psychical research, (most notably his involvement in the Cottingley Fairy photographs). His contemporary, Rudyard Kipling, is less well known in fortean circles. This is somewhat unfair, because he was a deeply spiritual man who had a profound insight into fortean matters, and his writings are well worth investigating.

Earlier in this book I quoted at length from *Puck of Pook's Hill*, [77] and briefly discussed Kipling's theory about 'The People of the Hills', having arrived on these islands as the gods and demi gods of invading armies. When the foreigners either left, or became integrated into the mainstream of British culture, the entities who once were Gods, became 'sidelined', and eventually became 'The People of the Hills'. These are what we now know as earth spirits, and some of them could well be described as zooform phenomena.

I wondered whether this model, as suggested by Kipling could also serve as a convenient explanation for the Mawnan owlman phenomena. The church itself is built in the centre of a prehistoric earthwork. This lead Janet and Colin Bord to speculate that it might be on a ley-line. I know very little about things, and will not therefore be drawn into speculation on the subject, but they found three alignments which passed through the church:

> *"1. Nare Point (SW 800251) – Mawnan Church (SW788272) – Mabe Church (SW767325) Stithians Church (SW731371). Four points in eight and a half miles.*
>
> *2. Mawnan Church (SW788272) – St Anthony Church (SW 783257) – The Three Brothers of Gugwith (SW 762198) – tumulus on Arrowan common (SW754176). Four points in six and a half miles.*
>
> *3. Mawnan Church (SW788272) – Manacccan Church (SW 764250) – earthwork, St Martin in Meneage (SW 750238) – Tumulus on Goonhilly Downs (SW 725215). Four points in five and a half miles.*
> *All alignments are on Ordinance Survey sheet 203, 1:50,000) ".* [78]

As they point out, there may well be more, but it is the ancient history of the church and the surrounding area itself, that more particularly interests me. The church was originally dedicated to St. Mawnan. (Latin: S. Maunanus). Nothing certain is known of him. One theory describes him as a Breton monk

242

who landed in Cornwall in 520 AD, and another describes him as an Irish Bishop, who with 27 disciples founded a peripetetic school. In the fifteenth century it was rededicated and given a second patron: St Stephanus. It would be tempting to theorise that this was because of unexplained paranormal phenomena in the area, but it seems almost certain that it was purely because nobody had any real idea who the original patron actually was. [79]

As far as the earthworks are concerned, there are again very few details except that it was a celtic fortress overlooking the mouth of the Helford river, and was in a good state of preservation until about 1920, when part of it was demolished during work on an extension to the graveyard. [80] There are few clues here, so we should, perhaps examine the surrounding countryside.

Although there is no direct link with the owlman, many other zooform manifestations that have been reported across the country, and especially in Cornwall, have been in conjunction with ancient standing stones. It has been theorised that some, if not many of the standing stones in Cornwall were geomantically arranged by visiting Phoenician tin traders, between two and three thousand years ago. [81] Was there, I wondered, a link between the Phoenicians, owls, or at least birds, and little girls or young women?

When I was a first or second year pupil at Grammar School in North Devon during the early 1970's I went through a traumatic experience. I was in the latin class, and for reasons best known to himself, the latin teacher used to finish off every lesson by reading excerpts from a particularly gruesome book about the Roman arenas. [82] He seemed, or so it appeared to me as an impressionable, and admittedly rather immature twelve year old, that he took a salacious and almost perverted delight in reading descriptions, of public crucifixions, burnings, disembowellings, dismemberments and ritual torture both of humans and animals to a class of about twenty small boys. I don't know what effect these stories had on the rest of the class but they completely traumatised me, to such an extent that I feel very disturbed and upset even writing about it now, a quarter of a century later.

I started to investigate Phoenician mythology and found that there were links, many of them, to the subjects discussed in this book. They worshipped a corn deity, and more significantly sacrificed both animals and small children in horrific ways. [83] I started to dig deeper into the available literature on the subject, but found myself confronted with more and more graphic descriptions of ritual tortures, burnings and dismemberments on an enormous scale. [84] My dreams, which had been relatively unfettered by visions of Owlmen, wizards and naked witches, became populated with ghastly visions of tortured children.

I decided that here was where my research should end. I had gathered enough data, and whilst there were plenty more avenues that I could explore, I had really had enough, and I wanted to get on with other things. So now was the time to try and reach some conclusions.

During the time he was in exile in France, after his release from prison, Oscar Wilde (who was residing under the alias of 'Sebastian Melmoth'), started work on a number of stories, none of which were ever finished. There are no written records of these stories, as far as I can ascertain, but they were just fragments of plot which emerged from his opium and absinthe addled brain as he chatted to his companions and attempted to re-live past glories. [85] [86]

One of these stories concerned Jesus Christ. He hypothesised that Jesus had somehow survived the Crucifixion, had indeed appeared to his followers at the first Easter, but instead of ascending to heaven on Ascension Day, had gone into hiding to escape Roman and Jewish Authorities who had become suspi-

cious and were looking for him. With the rise in popularity of Christianity, Jesus found it impossible to come out of hiding, and was forced to stay a fugitive, the only man in the world who knew that, to misquote Mark Twain; 'reports of his resurrection had been greatly exaggerated'. [87] [88]

At various times during my research on this book I wondered, whether the whole Owlman phenomenon was based on a similar scenario. What, I theorised, if Tony Shiels HAD actually invented the first sighting? There is no evidence for the existence of any of the Melling family apart from that directly attributable to him? [89] What if he had hoaxed the first sighting only to find, paradoxically and ironically, that people were actually starting to see the zooform phenomenon that he had 'invented' for fun, after reading *The Mothman Prophecies* [90] for the first time?

This is pure conjecture. I have no reason to suppose that everything Tony told me about the events of Easter Saturday 1976 were not perfectly true. I mentioned this theory to Tony one morning when I had a hangover, and he was telling me that he hadn't had one since one morning in November 1954. He just laughed, and said that

> *"As long as you don't do a Chorvinsky and say that I made the shagging thing out of plasticene, I don't care what you say".* [91]

Something definitely happened over the Easter weekend of 1976, and whatever it was it was directly responsible for the sightings which have occurred over the next twenty years.

The Easter Weekend of 1976 was a special and magickal time. I will not go into details for fear of compromising a lady, who I believe is now happily middle aged and married with several children, but that weekend was a magickal one for me as well. During all my literary and musical activities of the last twenty years, events of that weekend, across the world keep on intruding into my life. A pop star that I was to work for a decade and a half later made a momentous (and disastrous) career move that weekend. [93] Another musician, (about whom I was later to write a book), retired that weekend, [94] and on a personal level (which I do not wish to discuss in public) the quasi-synchronistic events are manifold. For whatever reason it seems that I was predestined to write this book, and have been for the last twenty years.

It was also the weekend in which the Owlman of Mawnan was given corporeal form. Whether the ghost of Max Ernst, returned to Cornwall in the form of his bird headed alter ego, whether The Wizard of the Western World carried out a practical joke that succeeded far beyond his wildest dreams, whether it was me, locked in the turmoil of an adolescent and ultimately fruitless love affair or whether it was just two little girls being frightened by the unexpected appearance of an escaped eagle owl, we will probably never know, but something happened there which has adversely effected the zeitgeist of the area ever since.

In 1985 Graham McEwan described a hypothetical mechanism which could account for a recurrent zooform phenomenon like the Owlman of Mawnan:

> *"... the theory being that events, especially if violent or tragic, can leave a 'recording' on their immediate surroundings. The energy is stored, and may be reactivated, maybe many years later, when the conditions are right. The presence of living people may be a requisite for example".* [95]

I would like to suggest that this hypothesis would be more likely to be workable, if the area itself is al-

ready 'damaged' or affected in some manner by magical ritual or some psychic trauma. Thus, an event in 1976, which may be one of the scenarios suggested above, or may well be something else entirely, 'triggered' latent psychic possibilities within the area. Whether these were caused by Tony's 1975/6 invocatory activities with skyclad witches, whether they were caused by the similar invocatory activities of the 1937 surrealists, or whether they are connected with the activities of the Phoenicians, or even if the 'damage' is a result of the reconsecration of the church in the fifteenth century or the destruction of part of the prehistoric fort in the 1920s matters little. We shall probably never know the truth.

What we have discovered, however, is that the events in the woods surrounding Mawnan Old Church are not a hoax, or a random collection of unrelated incidents.

In my more frivolous moments I wonder whether Mark Chorvinsky was sort of right after all. Maybe 'Doc' had made the whole thing up, perhaps after he had been reading John Keel's classic *The Mothman Prophecies* (about a similar apparition in West Virginia during 1967), and had decided in a spirit of genuinely surreal mischief that it was perhaps time that Cornwall had something similar to counterpoint its very own sea monster. Perhaps this very act of creation helped form a tulpa which then got out of hand. If so then I suspect that Tony was as surprised as anyone else when other people started to report sightings of the creature.

Another theory that I have adopted at various times is linked with the sex of the witnesses. With the one exception — the young man who has asked to be identified only as 'Gavin' the only people to have seen the creature have been young women. Even 'Gavin' was accompanied by a young woman at the time. Could the owlman be a sort of three dimensional, feathered poltergeist? An apparition 'invoked' by the peculiar hormonal and emotional changes which affect young women at this time?

Maybe the combination of these conditions — which as anyone who has ever shared a house with a teenage girl will know can be quite devastating, with something inate in the psychical infrastructure of the area surrounding Mawnan Old Church has a synergistic effect, producing the apparition that has become known as The Owlman of Mawnan.

My attitude towards the Owlman has changed greatly over the years. When I finished the main body of my investigations in the late spring of 1996 I was convinced, although I didn't usually say it in public, that "Doc" *had* after all made the whole thing up originally and that he was as surprised as anyone else when the animal he had created in his own image suddenly started to materialise in front of people.

Over the years I met more witnesses whose testimony had not appeared in my original book. At the Truro UFO Convention in August 1998 I met a middle aged woman who told me that she had seen the creature *'flapping around in the woods"* during the high summer of 1978. Her description of the creature was far more bird like than any of the other descriptions that I had encountered, and if it hadn't been for the fact that she described an entity with a five foot wingspan and red, glowing eyes I would have been tempted to dismiss her sighting as that of a large bird.

Various researchers, including noted west-country naturalist Trevor Beer have suggested that the sightings of the Owlman are nothing more than sightings of an escaped Eagle Owl *(Bubo bubo)* - a northern European species which supposedly became extinct in Britain about 10, 000 years ago. However both this species and other gigantic *Strigiformes* from Europe and North America are kept widely as pets and as exhibits in public aviaries and it is not uncommon for them to escape. They are also strong fliers and it is not impossible that an Eagle Owl could have been blown in a gale from either central Germany or the Pyrexes to make its home in the dense woods of southern Cornwall. However, it is highly unlikely

that if this were so then it would only ever come out to be seen by adolescent girls.

We should, I think, look elsewhere for an explanation.

Over the years as my reputation grew, and with it the fame of His Owliness, I began to receive letters and e-mails from people all over the world who claimed to have seen similar things. One, taken almost at random from my files was from a young man in Ohio:

> *Jon,*
>
> *What has been seen here in Ohio, USA, is a little different than the Owlman of Mawnan has been described. It was seen in the mid to late 60s in a desolate area of land in North Eastern Ohio called the Grand River Valley.*
>
> *There is about 150 sq. mi. of untouched land there, all which is extremely densely covered in brush.*
>
> *A road called Hoffman Norton met another called Hyde Oakfield in the south-eastern corner of the territory before its bridges collapsed and were torn down. Two men saw this 3-4 ft. creature walk across the dirt road in front of their car, pause, look in at them, and continue walking to the other side of the road. They described it most closely as having the "body of a monkey and the face of an owl, "with bright yellow-gold glowing eyes, long thin arms, a sloped beak, and hair or feathers which appeared to be pulled back from its face. The men swore it was the devil, and one will not speak of the event to this day - he only says that he fears every day that it will come back for him.*
>
> *Recently, another man has claimed that he saw the "owlman" - as my friend and I have called it, even before we learned of your book or other similar creatures. This man was 8 years old, and riding his bike in another fairly remote region across the town. He always referred to it as "the little demon" after it sat low in a ditch and watched him ride by on his bicycle.*
>
> *Several years later, in the early 70's, a series of cattle mutilations took place, whereas coyotes were blamed, until people began reporting seeing the profile of a small, thin, manlike being, escaping the pastures. The being was said to have had small pointy ears near the top of his head (like a horned owl's feathers?). The farmers were dismissed as "crazy" and the whole investigation was dropped.*
>
> *I don't know what is here (or was here), but it was real. It could still live there or have offspring. I have heard that due to its remoteness, the Grand River basin was the site of different animal testing projects. Could something have gone wrong?*
>
> *Thanks for the reply.*
>
> *Mike*

It is interesting to compare these descriptions by 'Mike' not only with the other reports in this chapter of the Cornish Owlman, but with the accounts of the Puerto Rican chupacabra of which I have written elsewhere. It is also important, I believe to note that the same explanations for the creature are also included in Mike's e-mail. He alludes to shadowy 'Black Projects' carried out by the United States Gov-

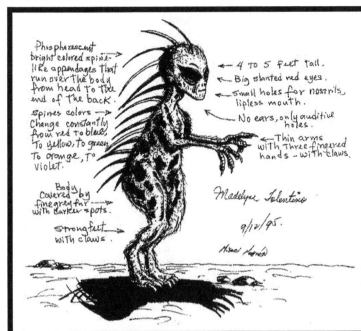

Phosphorescent bright colored spine-like appendages that run over the body from head to the end of the back.

Spines colors change constantly from red to blue, to yellow, to green to orange, to violet.

Body covered by fine grey fur with darker spots.

Strong feet with claws.

4 to 5 feet tall.
Big slanted red eyes.
Small holes for nostrils, lipless mouth.
No ears, only auditive holes
Thin arms with three-fingered hands - with claws.

Madelyne Tolentino

9/12/95.

Getting Stranger..........

The grotesque vampiric chupacabra (left) has a string of lexilinking references to the Owlman story.

The initials G. S. (for goatsucker) appear again and again, not least in the initials of the two witnesses whose testimony is most pertinent to this book).

However the goatsucker is also an archaic name for the night-jar, and as Tony Shiels has pointed out over and over again within these pages, nightjars are an integral part of THE CASE.

ernment in genetic engineering and gene manipulation. The same social paranoias have been expressed in Puerto Rico, and indeed in other parts of the world. I believe that it is a mark of the society in which we, in the western world, all live at the beginning of the 21st Century that people are so ready to believe ill of their elected Governments and to blame a frighteningly wide range of paranormal occurrences on the Government rather than on these events being just part of the natural way of things.

In my investigations across the world, although I have come across hints of Government cover-ups, they have invariably been (as recounted elsewhere in this book) at a low level in order to obfuscate mis-doings by a Government official of low rank and experience. There has never, as far as I am aware at least, been any more sinister motive. The rest is just paranoia on the part of those who are interested in such things.

Something which may also be mere paranoia, but which I am convinced is very real is the phenomenon of psychic backlash. This is a series of inexplicable and horrific outbreaks of bad luck that can overtake the hapless seeker after monstrous truth on his way to his goal. I never believed in it until, during the months that I was working on this book two of my pet cats died suddenly, two computers blew up (as did two cars) and my wife left me. I also encountered psychic backlash while investigating the links between animal mutilations and crop circles which are described elsewhere in this book.

In the spring and early summer of 1997 I was involved in an experiment to see whether corn taken from crop circles had different growth rates to corn taken from other parts of the same field. We asked listen-ers to our *Weird about the West* Radio Show to help with our experiment and grow some grain from a crop circle at home. We sent out about ten small packets of oats and sat back to await results. Two days later I got a telephone call from a worried lady who claimed that she was picking up 'terrible psychic emanations' from the corn seeds. She also claimed that she had experienced similar phenomena causing headaches and a feeling of general illness when she had visited a crop formation last summer.

The same morning I received a telephone call from a colleague who said that he had received unconfirmed reports of a formation - one of the first of the year - in a field next to the site of a serious car crash. We are not in the position of trying to make capital (financial or otherwise) out of other people's misery so the names and places have been deliberately withheld. According to another one-time colleague called Pete Glastonbury, in 1992 at Berry Pomeroy in south Devon, a formation in the shape of a dumbell with scythe attachment appeared in a field of barley. It was the first formation of the year in Devonshire. Shortly afterwards there were three simultaneous motorcycle accidents involving green Kawasakis. In each case the driver was relatively unharmed but the passenger on the pillion was killed. Pete vouched personally for one of these accidents which occurred when the bike in question crashed into his garden wall.

The weirdness didn't end there however.

During the very first journey I had made after carrying the corn samples which I had sent out, my car engine had suddenly overheated and seized. In 1992 exactly the same thing happened to a Mini Metro owned by Pete Glastonbury. To confound the situation further, last summer, I had been photographing crop circles and on my journey home the self same thing happened to my transit van. A coincidence? I hope so. To make it even stranger, the two incidents involving my vehicles took place on the same stretch of road and within five hundred yards of each other. As I jokingly said at the time I was beginning to wonder whether crop circles should carry a government health warning!

During the summer of 1998 I was revisiting the area around Mawnan Old Church on almost a weekly basis. The second edition of *The Owlman and Others* had come out and I was hitting the publicity trail in earnest. As part of the publicity machine I attended invocations to the Owlman carried out in the woods around the church at midsummer 1998, Samhain 1998 and Bealtaine 1999.

Immediately my luck started to change. Things began to go wrong and my little household found itself locked into a cycle of psychic backlash so grotesque that we had to do something to escape from it.

Although I was brought up (and confirmed) within the Church of England I have always had a leaning towards Roman Catholicism. My faith is a very private one and is not something I talk about very often. If there is such a thing I suppose that I am a pantheistic Catholic because I also believe (to a certain extent at least) in the principles of Wicca and I see no real difference (on an emotional level if not a theological one) between the twin Celtic deities of Cernunnos (the horned God) and The Mother Goddess, and the twin Christian figures of Jesus and the Blessed Virgin Mary. On New Year's Day 1998 I had my house blessed by a very wise friend of mine who is a third degree witch, and that magickal protection that she placed around me and my belongings protected us to some extent at least for the next few months. When I was in Mexico, I also began to experience psychic backlash in the form of severe physical illness and for the first time ever, and with no training I attempted to carry out a spell of protection - by myself - and without attracting the ridicule of my fellow travellers.

When I decided to carry out this ritual we were in the middle of the Puebla Desert, parked in a tiny layby next to a small roadside shrine to the Virgin Mary. It was festooned in strings of small plastic flags which fluttered gaily in the wind like the prayer flags on a Tibetan monastery. Indeed, friends of mine who are much better and more devout Catholics than I am have told me that for certain people in Central America they serve much the same function. Each time, or so they believe, the flag flutters in the wind it sends up a tiny prayer to heaven. God and his Angels can see the flags fluttering far below them on earth and they act as a reminder to the Almighty of his subjects on this planet.

My personal brand of Christianity is far less concrete than this but I found it a comforting and oddly touching belief, and whatever your school of thought on the matter, and indeed whatever your religious or spiritual beliefs, the sight of these tiny, gaily coloured flags fluttering bravely in the middle of the desolation of the Puebla Desert is a sight to warm the hardest of hearts.

A few feet away from the shrine was a concrete bunker on which a number of pieces of political graffiti concerning Subcommandante Marcos and the Zapatista Separatist Guerrillas had been painted. We have mentioned Marcos and his political movement several times in this narrative, but the time has come, I believe to examine him as a man, or at least the image which he has so carefully cultivated for the world outside. In a similar move to Gerry Adams of Sinn Fein, the guerrilla leader has become the slightly romantic poet figure, and like Adams in Ulster he has attracted a great deal of attention from people who would otherwise have little or no interest in his political beliefs.

Half way between the shrine to the Blessed Virgin and the ugly concrete bunker daubed with paeans of support to the pop-politician (who has also, or so I have been informed, recorded some of his own revolutionary songs and has a burgeoning career as a pop singer in front of him), I acquired a cactus stick of the type that the Hopi Indian medicine men once used as magic wands. It caught my eye immediately - I had to own it, and so it joined the flotsam and jetsam in the back of the car. But it wasn't just that I wanted it. I knew that one day I was going to own one like it and when I saw it for the first time, I knew that something I had been told many years before and many thousands of miles away in a pub in Cornwall had finally come to pass.

In 1976 Mike McCormick (see chapter two) gave Tony Shiels the core of one of the giant cactuses which twenty-two years later were towering all around me in the middle of the Puebla Desert. The Hopi Indian shamans had used them as magic wands, and I asked Tony what had happened to his one. He laughed and told me that one day I would have one of my own, and several years later between monuments to the two great cultural influences in the Mexican psyche, and in a deserted spot in the middle of the Mexican desert his prediction came true. It was as if I had been given a present by the desert.

As I was taking something away I had to give something in return and in what turned out to be pretty well my last act as a neophyte "Sorcerer' s Apprentice" I made a sigil out of stones in the very place where I had found the stick. The sigil that I made was Tony' s own - a sign that he has described as a Nnidnidiogram and which he claims with some justification is a powerful and potent magickal symbol which has been of great use to him in summoning up monsters.

Tony Shiels is probably the most powerful and the wisest man that I have ever met. He has the power to summon up monsters. Although I go looking for them, I would never attempt to emulate him in his invocatory activities because by the laws of magick once you cause something to happen you have to be responsible for the consequences, and whilst I can deal with the consequences of looking for something like the chupacabra and even of chronicling its activities and drawing some tentative conclusions as to its nature I cannot take the responsibility for summoning it to appear before me like a rabbit out of a hat. Indeed, I very much doubt whether I have the power to do so.

Following instructions that I had been told many thousand miles away from the little stone image in the middle of the Mexican desert I grasped my new magic wand, and cast a protective circle around me, my Nnidnidiogram and my companions. I mentally consecrated each of the four points of the compass to the four sons of Ometecuhtli and Omecihuatl and as I faced west I repeated as much as I could remember of the Aztec hymn to Quetzacoatl, the winged serpent and Aztec Dragon God, and the deity that most resembles the beneficent creator of western religions.

249

Back in the UK things slowly began to recover and did so until, at Bealtaine 1999 we were stupid enough to stir the whole affair up again. In 1978, 1980 and 1986, Tony Shiels had carried out magickal rituals either at Bealtaine or Samhain (Hallow'een) to invoke 'His Owliness' and partly as an intellectual discipline and partly out of sheer mischievous caprice we decided to emulate him on the last Walpurgis Night of the 20th Century.

Various members of the Exeter Strange Phenomena Group decided to come along for the ride, and we were also accompanied by veteran Australian cryptozoologist Tony Healy, co-author of a remarkable book called *Out of the Shadows*. [10] Tony had arrived in Exeter that afternoon. We had met him at the Unconvention, and as is our custom we had invited him to stay with us for as long as he wanted.

One of the less well publicised roles of the Centre for Fortean Zoology is that it acts as a flop house for visiting forteans from around the world and at various times one can find several well-known members of the fortean and cryptoinvestigative communities wrapped in blankets or sleeping bags on my sitting room floor.

Tony was not the only minor celebrity to accompany us on our magickal quest. One of the party was a long haired and bearded young man wearing a ragged Medieval Court Jester's outfit. Perhaps appropriately, he answered to the name of 'Jester'. Richard Freeman, in the guise of Muzzlehutch the Magician, accompanied by Jester carried out a strange and highly theatrical ritual to summon the Owlman. As I am no magician (the ritual in the Mexican desert was the only one I have ever tried to carry out) I have asked Richard to explain what he did, and what he was trying to achieve in his own words:

"The elements were called on once more. Their visual embodiments are different according to what is being summoned. Instead of the four dragons of the four quarters I called upon winged humanoids from differing cultures.

- *The north was the **Skovman**, a form of Scandinavian elf that could take the form of a giant owl.*

- *The east was the **Tengu** of Japan, grotesque bird deamons.*

- *The south was **Popobwa**, a bat winged baboon that anally rapes sleeping men in the folklore of Zanzibar.*

- *The west was **Mothman**, the red eyed, winged horror that terrorised Point Pleasant, Virginia in the 1960s.*

Into a silver brazier of hot coals I poured a mixture of certain herbs and oils. An ugly red cloud of foul smelling gas billowed up like an Arabian genie. I snorted in its noxious vapour and began to rant like a madman speaking in tongues. Jester clad in motley capered about the circle as I brayed my incantations. His presence had twin purpose: As a jester he was the embodiment of chaos, without which order is totally impotent. He also reflected the essentially absurd nature of the ritual, the phenomenon, and the universe in general.

The letters G and S, so important in the whole case were uttered in the incantation. "Great Strigiform, Girl Scarer, Goat Sucker'. I bid the beating of wings and the insidious churring to come galumphing from the inky branches. Yet even as the verbal deluge poured from my

lips like tallow from a candle, I knew the most important component of the spell was missing - there were no young women present.

However, we left Jester there for the night and when he returned to us in Exeter a few days later he told us how his dreams had been bedevilled with strange winged entities and how at one point during the long, cold night he had felt something strange and heavy clinging onto his back.

During the next few months we received more reports of sightings from the Cornish woods — they were mostly inconclusive, but three or four groups of young women reported seeing strange, grey, feathered objects fluttering around through the upper branches of the trees above them."

However, I for one should have known better. The psychic backlash that I had managed to dispel a year before returned severalfold and things at the CFZ were getting particularly bizarre. We had outbreaks of poltergeist activity as well as a horrible run of bad luck and I determined that not only was I going to have to do something to end it all, but that this time I would have no further involvement with the Owlman or any of his kin.

My attitude towards my investigations (and I hope towards my life) is that humour is an invaluable asset. As my mentor Tony "Doc" Shiels also pointed out *"humour is our greatest weapon against psychic backlash"* and I have always used humour which is one of the reasons that, perhaps, I have survived, when others who started out alongside me, and who might seemingly have been expected to achieve greater things than me had fallen (figuratively and literally) by the wayside.

We decided that the best way to dispel the malign miasma of despair into which everyone involved in the Bealtaine ritual (but especially Richard, Phil and me) had fallen, was to do something which involved the Owlman but also involved the three of us in a humorous manner.

After some soul searching we made the now notorious Owlman film. Billed as a cinematic adaptation of my book it was in fact no such thing. A homage to Tony Shiels and to another great inspiration of mine, film-maker John Walters, the movie which was eventually shown for the first time at the 2000 Unconvention at the Commonwealth Institute in Kensington High Street, London was like nothing else ever made in the annals of forteana. One of my friends from America told me, after she saw it that *"It sucked worse than any other movie I have ever seen"* and was somewhat nonplussed when I told her that this was after all the reason I had made it in the first place.

What I was not prepared for was for the film to be a success. Much to my surprise it was. One review read:

A co-production with Limited Talent Productions, it's a pseudo-documentary loosely based on the book of the same name by Jon Downes and is a blackly comic romp that sees the author and his girlfriend retrace the investigative steps in the book. Involving sea serpents, gay cowboys, wizards, mad lemonade selling tramps, transsexual nazis, inbred yokel mobs, lesbian witches, and other assorted perverts and nutters, it is a trash cinema classic in the same league as Phil Tucker's 'Robot Monster', Edward D. Wood JR's 'Bride of the Atom' and John Walter's 'Multiple Maniacs'.

Other reviews were equally enthusiastic and compared the film favourably with the horribly over-hyped *Blair Witch Project* which had no jokes and cost nearly 50 times as much to make, despite being the

cheapest budget hit film on record. Unfortunately our plan to make a silly movie that would detract from all the attention that had been given in recent years to the Owlman phenomenon failed badly. By CFZ standards at least it was a great success and gave us even more media attention which was ironically the very last thing that we had been looking for.

It was essentially just a very silly spoof art movie with little relevance to the main body of the research that the CFZ both collectively and individually has carried out into the Owlman Phenomenon. What it did do, however, almost as an afterthought, was provide my first (and only until this book) public claim that Tony Shiels had been responsible for all the original sightings and that the phenomenon proper had not started to appear until some years later after people had started to believe in the stories that had originally been produced as a joke.

Our ridiculous film has gathered a fair amount of press coverage, and as a result the Owlman is back in the public eye again. Also in May 2000 we made contact again with our old friend and mentor Tony "Doc" Shiels who told us, (quite possibly tongue in cheek or maybe not) that the feathered monster had been seen again.

Whatever has happened is still happening and will continue to happen.

Strange things are still happening in the vicinity of Mawnan Smith. In May 1996 we saw an advert in one of the local free papers. It was from a young woman in Falmouth who was working on a book about 'strange phenomena in the Mawnan Smith area'. [96] We contacted her, and offered to pool our resources. For reasons of her own she was unwilling to co-operate with us, but she told us that she had experienced several strange incidents in the area as had some of her friends. She told us of burnt out cars and even an unsolved murder, but refused to meet us. [97]

I told Tony about it in my next letter to him, and within days he replied:

> *"Of course weird things are happening there, this year. It was bound to be this way. More will happen before the summer is over. That's what the sea heads tell me. A certain amount of UFO activity will be part of it. I know that a number of Cornish witches will be doing their stuff and the results will be interesting."* [98]

The very next week I was in Cornwall again talking to a witch near Bodmin, who is involved in invocatory activities of her own. [99] I am tempted to say that there is more happening in Cornwall, even now, than even Tony Shiels knows about. But I think it would be unwise. He is The Wizard of the Western World, after all, and I have a sneaking suspicion that he knows everything. He certainly knows that you are reading this…

253

CHAPTER NINE: INSPIRATION

"Jazz acrobats is what thay are - and they seem
philosophically above such trifles as a cage..."

Russell Hoban *'Turtle Diary"* (1975)

It was a pleasant evening on the last day of August 1996, the night before the *Zoologica* Exhibition. I was sitting at a wooden bench, outside a pub at Ardingly in Sussex. With me was my long time friend, assistant and partner in 'crime' Graham Inglis. We were drinking beer and trying not to bring up the subject of my forthcoming divorce. I was beginning to have to come to terms with my new found, and enforced status as a single man, and more as a matter of form than for any other reason, I was half heartedly ogling some pretty girls who were walking along the road in skin-tight jeans.

A young man in his early twenties was sitting next to us. He is a nice bloke. I don't know him very well, but I have met him a few times, and we have exchanged many long letters. Over the last eighteen months or so readers of *'Animals & Men'* have come to know him as 'Gavin'. He was (quite appropriately) drinking a pint of Guinness.

As we watched the girls and drank, we chatted desultorily about this and that and unusually for us, never mentioned the Owlman once.

Another friend of mine was sitting at the next table, and the mobile telephone which he rather self-consciously carried in the breast pocket of his denim jacket began to ring. He hadn't had a mobile 'phone for very long, so when it rings it always takes him a few moments to realise where the noise is coming from, and to answer the call. Much to my surprise he said that the call was for me. I was very taken aback because I had not given out his number to anyone, and very few people outside the closed world of the zoological 'mafia' even knew that I was in Sussex that weekend. I swallowed a mouthful of beer and answered the call. Much to my surprise a voice with a thick Irish brogue roared at me across the satellite link:

"How are yer doin' lads? Fun and games are afoot!"

I looked at 'Gavin' and grinned, and put my hand over the receiver..

"Guess who?" I said, and we both laughed …..

255

APPENDIX ONE:

THE CASE.... FOR OWLPERSON

Tony 'Doc' Shiels

(NOTE: This piece originally appeared in issue six of Animals & Men and is reprinted with the kind permission of its author)

In 1927, at the Manoir d'Anjo. Verengeville-sur-Mer, Andre Breton hunted owls and wrote Nadja. Around this time, Max Ernst made a series of surreal 'Bird Monuments' and Salvador Dali sent a letter (to Lorca) in which he confessed that he was 'painting a very beautiful woman, smiling, tickled by multi-coloured feathers'.

A bizarre loploplot was being hatched.

Breton, (obsessed by eyes) should not have been shooting the hooting owls. Look what happened to John Fane Dingle - after he 'shot a crop-eared owl' - in the Richard Hughes poem:

>*"Corpse Eyes are eerie.*
>*Tiger eyes fierce.*
>*John Fane Dingle found*
>*Owl-eyes worse".*

Ending

*SEA HEAD and the "Admiral **G**raf **S**pee"*

"Owl-eyes, without sound
- pale of hue
John died of no complaint
with owl-eyes too".

In 1933, the Loch Ness Monster and King Kong became world famous; and Max Ernst created his superb collage novel - *Une semaine de Bonte* - full of monstrous hybrids, including birdmen and birdwomen, in a variety of dramatic/erotic situations. Also in 1933, Andre Breton met the surrealist seer, Victor Braunder, for the first time. Like Breton, Braunder was obsessed with eyes.

Loplop, *Bird Superior,* cock-a-doodled magical sigils on eggshells. Peculiar pitpatted onto Parson's Beach, Cornwall. Deep in the Helford something stirred. In 1937, Max Ernst visited Cornwall with Leonora Carrington. They conjured cryptozoological curiosities. Skyclad surrealist witches were involved. Morgawr the sea serpent was seen. H.P. Lovecraft died. Fern-Owls chirred in the Mawnan woods.

When whippoorwills call and evening is nigh....

In 1976, Max Ernst died, and a *'big feathered bird-man'* was seen hovering over Mawnan Old Church. Dover publications produced an edition of *'Une Semaine de Bonte*. I licked an ice-cream cone, performed prestidigitations with pears, and met some young girls who had seen the strange Owlman of Mawnan. Owlman has been described as being 'big as a man with a nasty owlface, big ears and big red eyes'. It had wings, grey feathers, and feet 'like big black crab claws'. Owlman could rise straight up vertically with hardly any movement of the wings. It was only ever seen by young females so far as I know. For ten years, from 1976 to 1986, in cahoots with a group of witches, I attempted to invoke the Owlman employing the techniques of Shamanic surrealchemy. From time to time the conjurations may have worked. Some very strange things certainly happened during that period. I am sure that Max

Ernst/Loplop had something to do with these happenings. My Owlman experiments ceased around Halloween 1986, when tricking and treating at Mawnan Old Church upset the ecclesiastical authorities. It was a hoot.

In 1994, something which is now known as 'The Case' captured my attention. Shortly after Paddy's day I flew from Shannon and soon found myself in London where the game was afoot and strix trix were in the city air. Somehow, it started with a crossword clue, a bag of pears, a Picasso exhibition, and the initials G.S - which could represent 'Great Strigiform'. The pears proliferated and bottles of perry soon appeared. A vaguely Fortean person asked me if Owlman was really male; was it a cock or a hen? I recalled a dream, involving Max Ernst in which I had decided that Owlman was not a cock. But then, cocks popped up everywhere, along with more pears, perry and ice cream cones. One of the young girls who saw Owlman in 1976 was called Barbara Perry. The winged thing was also encountered by the Greenwood Sisters (G.S). I thought about Hen's Teeth and Mr Punch. They were already part of The Case.

I am writing this paragraph in Ireland, on Monday morning, May 1st 1995: after an exhausting 'Eve of Bealtaine' night of conjurations and libations. Owl-eyed Dingle from the poem came to mind at some point in the proceedings. This, in turn, made me think of Dingle, Co Kerry, and the famous Giant Squid (G.S), driven ashore there in 1673. Today, one of my daughters who lives quite close to Dingle, telephoned me to announce the news that another Kerry Kraken had been netted. Something 'owl-eyed' could have invoked it.

'Doc' Shiels in his Ireland studio 2005

APPENDIX TWO:

GOING TO CORNWALL ARE WE?
....I THOUGHT YOU MIGHT

O ver the years, I have done many newspaper interviews regarding the Owlman story; most notably when the - not very good - movie of *The Mothman Prophecies* based on John Keel's famous book finally hit the big screen in 2002 starring Richard Gere.

I suppose, that having directed a completely unwatchable film loosely based on this book, I am not really entitled to criticise the big screen version of Keel's book, but - like my film (although in a less entertaining manner) - the movie had very little to do with the book on which it was based.

The following pages contain a small selection of the post 1996 press cuttings on the subject culled almost at random from our voluminous files.

Fishy goings on in the garden pond?

Blame the Owlman

By CHRISTOPHER EVANS

TO Roy Standring, the explanation for the regular disappearance of the goldfish from his garden pond was obvious.

Herons, he decided, must be to blame for the thefts. But locals in the Cornish hamlet had a more bizarre theory.

The fish, some claimed, were being preyed on by the Owlman of Mawnan — a 5ft tall half-owl half-man, a winged beast with red eyes and black talons.

According to Jonathan Downes, who studies such phenomena, the Owlman has appeared regularly to adolescent women in Mawnan churchyard.

Seventeen girls aged eight to 18 have reported sightings since 1976. The only boy to have seen the terrifying apparition was a 13-year-old — but he was with one of the girls at the time.

The Owlman never speaks or hoots. He hovers, does hiss sometimes and occasionally crackles 'like static electricity', says 38-year-old Mr Downes, who has recently published a book on the beast.

The first reports of an Owlman came when a family called Melling from the North of England were on holiday at Mawnan, which is four miles south of Falmouth.

The family's two daughters were playing in the graveyard of the 13th century church on Easter Saturday, 1976.

Suddenly, they fled screaming into the car park where their parents were unpacking a picnic lunch.

They told hysterical tales of a man covered in feathers flitting about.

The Mellings, so the story goes, reported their encounter to a local 'wizard' called Doc Shiels.

Shiels was already investigating — or, according to some, fabricating — reports of a sea serpent called Morgawr.

Other sightings of the Owlman followed, including one that July.

The most recent of which Mr Downes is aware was by an American student.

She reported: 'I experienced what I can only describe as a vision of hell.

'I was walking along a narrow track in the trees. I was

Shiels: Serpent hunter

halted in my tracks when about 30 yards ahead I saw a monstrous man-bird thing.

'It was the size of a man with a ghastly face, wide mouth, glowing eyes and pointed ears.

'I just screamed and turned and ran for my life.' Sightings and tales of the owlman precede Mr Downes's interest in the case. He has interviewed the only male witness, who is now 22. Mr Downes says: 'He's terrified even now.'

While Mr Downes remains adamant that the Owlman exists, others vary from the sceptical to the incredulous.

As the Tourist Officer for Cornwall, Roy Standring might be expected to back a myth which would not only explain the disappearance of his goldfish but might also encourage visitors to the area.

However, he rejects the existence of the Owlman.

'We've got more than enough powerful legends in Cornwall from King Arthur to the standing stones,' he insisted yesterday. 'We don't need any spurious ones.'

Part of landscape gardener Rod Good's job involves working up at the churchyard.

'I haven't seen anything supernatural,' said the 52-year-old.

But there certainly is one spot just below the churchyard where the atmosphere is very strange.'

Sergeant Alex Johnstone of Devon and Cornwall Police sighed and said: 'The Owlman is a new one on me. I look forward to seeing the proof.

'I have heard of the Hairy Hand of Dartmoor, though.

'Funnily enough, that's an excuse frequently offered by people returning from licensed premises.'

Daily Mail, 26th September 1997

MONSTERS OF THE WEST

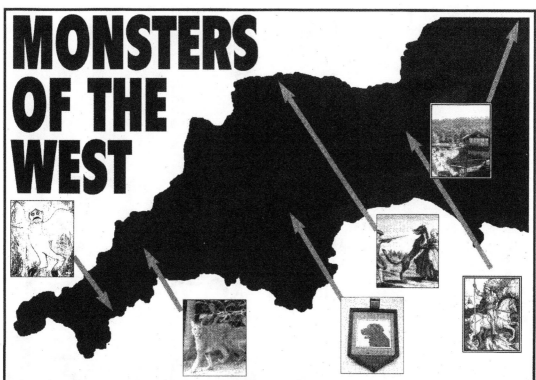

▼ SPECIAL REPORT by JONATHAN DOWNES

Author and paranormal expert

EVERYONE has heard of neighbours from hell but we could all be sharing our living space with even more sinister entities. Take a look at our monster map to see if there is a strange creature living near you.

I have spent my life studying the reality of creatures that most people believe exist solely in horror movies or comic books.

My interest in such things was sparked, when I was seven years old, by a library book called Myth or Monster which set me firmly on the path that I have followed ever since.

In recent weeks, I have been uncovering the truth behind some of the worlds most chilling mysteries in this paper.

The response to my articles has been amazing, but what most people don't seem to know is that just as many strange beasts have been reported from the West Country as from anywhere else in the world. Here, therefore, is a compendium of some of the region's most exciting and spine chilling monsters.

● Owlman of Mawnan

EVER since 1976 the woods surrounding Mawnan Old Church in southern Cornwall have been haunted by a grotesque feathered birdman.

This apparition has been seen by more than 20 people since then – mostly young girls – and seems in many ways to be very similar to the notorious Mothman of West Virginia, subject of the blockbuster movie starring Richard Gere.

● Beast of Bodmin

FOR decades people have been reporting mysterious big cat-like creatures on the wilder moorlands of the West Country.

Some people believe that these animals – like the one I saw in May 1997 – are escaped exotic pets: pumas or panthers which were liberated after the introduction of the Dangerous Wild Animals Act 1977. Other people believe that they have a more sinister nature.

● Black Dog

THE archetypal westcountry monster is the giant Black Dog.

These creatures are often believed to be the hunting pack of Satan himself. They even have a village named after them!

Each October an effigy of a giant black dog, accompanied by a parade lit by burning torches, is carried through the Devon lanes from Morchard Bishop to Black Dog village itself.

There has even been a novel based on these legends – The Hound of the Baskervilles.

● Old Boneless

PERHAPS the weirdest monster of them all – one which has no shape or form whatsoever.

This hideous entity is often encountered in the West Country, most notably on the road between Minehead and Bridgwater. One witness, about 80 years ago, said: 'It were alive – kind of woolly, like a cloud or a wet sheep – and it slid up and all over him on his bike....it was terrible cold and smelled stale.'

● Beast of Brassknocker Hill

IN 1979 there was a series of sightings of an ape-like creature in the vicinity of Brassknocker Hill just outside Bath.

It sounded as if a young chimpanzee had escaped from captivity and was lurking unsuspected in the area.

In 1999, there was another spate of sightings. We went to investigate, and although we found no solid evidence we found that many local people were convinced that something was lurking in the woods.

● The Cavemen of Lustleigh Cleave

A DEVONSHIRE Bigfoot? According to the late folklorist Theo Brown, ghostly cave men, naked and covered with hair, have been reported shambling around in the vicinity of some ancient standing stones in Lustleigh Cleave.

Similar creatures have also been reported on western Dartmoor and a quarry in Somerset. A weird monkey-like creature has been reported from Churston woods near Paignton.

● Werewolf of Lynton

THERE are many accounts of a wolfman living near Lynton on Exmoor.

One story is of a woman who was walking home alone, late one evening, when she saw on the path directly in front of her the tall grey figure of a man with a wolf's head.

Advancing stealthily forward, this creature was preparing to spring on a large rabbit that was crouching on the ground, apparently too terror stricken to move.

● The Dragon of Aller

DRAGONS are the most universal of all monsters and, even today, giant winged reptiles are reported occasionally from the more far-flung parts of the world.

One of the best West Country stories is that of the dragon of Aller who terrorised the neighbourhood and was killed by Sir John Aller with a long spear. The valiant knight was burned to death by the dragon's fiery breath.

● Devil's Footprints

IN February 1855 a trail of cloven hoofprints was found in the snow.

According to some reports, the line of prints was found to zig-zag its way from Topsham southward to Totnes, a distance of approximately 97 miles along the south Devon Coast.

Some people have claimed that these footprints were made by the Devil himself, others have claimed that they were a mixture of natural phenomena and hoaxes.

● The bird-woman of Minehead

AN old witch called Mother Leakey once lived in Minehead.

She was supposed to have the power to transform herself into a strange cormorant-like bird which would fly to the top of ship's masts and screech abuse at sailors.

This strange bird-woman was seen well into the 20th Century and even more recently was blamed, by the more superstitious, for inclement weather.

Sunday Independent, 17th March 2002

OWLMAN MYSTERY

Zoologist concludes West phenomenon could be for real

I'M A BELIEVER: West Country expert Jonathon Downes has studied the mystery for a decade

▼ Jonathon Downes is the West Country's own master of mystery, hunting down vampires and seeking out the truth about such phenomena as the Loch Ness Monster and Bigfoot. The co-founder of the Exeter Strange Phenomenon Group Centre for Fortean Zoology is undoubtedly an expert on the unexplained, but there are some things that even he cannot define. Here he tells how fact and fiction can sometimes collide in a mysterious and disturbing manner

The biggest movie of the forthcoming spring looks set to be The Mothman Prophecies, a chilling film based on the 1974 book by John Keel, starring Richard Gere and Laura Kinney.

The book and film, released on Friday, tell the story of a rise of strange and disturbing phenomena which took place in and about the West Virginia town of Point Pleasant during 1967.

These centred around sightings of The Mothman, a bizarre flying humanoid creature seen in the woods near the town.

Reports from the United States suggest that Mothman has become a booming business in West Virginia with

tourists flocking to the area.

It will now be interesting to see whether, in the wake of what is still undoubtedly a very successful film, tourists will also be travelling to their drums towards a small village near Plymouth, where a similar creature has been seen over the last quarter-century.

In April 1976, two young girls — Jane Melling, 12, and her nine-year-old sister Vicky — saw what they described as a big, feathered bird-man hovering over the church tower in the village of Mawnan Smith.

The two children, on holiday from the north of England, were so scared that the family cut their holiday short and went back three days early.

The sightings have continued over the years.

"The legs had high ankles and the feet were large and black with two huge toes on the visible side. The creature just pivots with sideways head and forwards, its wings lifted and forwards. Its wings lifted and backwards. On seeing its head jerked down and forwards. Its wings definitely closed. On seeing its head jerked down and forwards. As it did its legs folded up. We ran away."

Block

Admit

The eyes were red and glowing. At first, I thought it was someone dressed up, playing a joke, trying to scare us. I laughed at it, we both did, then it both scrapped. When it went up you could see its feet were like paws.

The sightings have continued over the years.

In 1989 a young man called Gavin described the creature he and his girlfriend saw. It was standing on a thick branch with its wings sort of held up about five feet tall (but please read on)

I am the only scientist ever to have interviewed witnesses to the Cornish Owlman, and I believe that I have the biggest collection of Owlman related documents and memorabilia in the world.

As a respectable zoologist it goes wildly against my better judgement to admit this, but after over a decade of studying the phenomenon I have reluctantly come to the conclusion that this is a very real and frightening one.

Although a creature such as the West Virginia mothman and the Owlman of Mawnan cannot exist within the framework of accepted science, I am convinced that in their own peculiar way they are as real as you or me.

The biggest mystery about the affair so far as I am concerned is, if they got Richard Gere to play John Keel in The Mothman Prophecies who will they get to play me in the sequel?

Jon Downes' book "The Owlman, and others" is available from CFZ Publications. For further information email Jon at jondownes@aol.co.uk

CHILLING: A scene from the forthcoming film The Mothman Prophecies, starring Richard Gere and Laura Kinney

Sunday Independent, 24th February 2002

In search of the MOTHMAN

The Mothman is coming. Walsall UFO writer NICK REDFERN reports from Texas on a spooky American horror – and its lesser-known British cousin

Nick Redfern: "Mothman mania is about to hit the UK."

IF SOMEONE were to come up to you and inquire whether you had ever seen a large, man-sized creature with bat-like wings and glowing red eyes, you might be inclined to smile nervously and slowly back away – and no-one would blame you.

In a few short weeks, however, your response might be different. Mothman mania is about to hit the UK.

The Mothman Prophecies is a new Hollywood movie starring Richard Gere. It tells the story of dark and sinister goings-on in an American East Coast town. It involves everything from UFOs and Men in Black-style characters to monsters and things that go bump in the night.

The film is a genuinely spooky look at a series of allegedly real events that occurred in Point Pleasant, Virginia.

From November 1966 to December 1967, the entire area was beset by a wave of weirdness. People reported seeing strange lights in the sky above their homes, mysterious men would turn up on their doorsteps and warn them not to discuss what they had seen, frightening and nightmarish visions were commonplace and a sense of doom and dread enveloped the entire area when a nearby bridge collapsed killing dozens.

And amidst all this small-town strangeness loomed the spectral presence of the Mothman.

The events in question were investigated at the time by an acclaimed author on UFOs and the paranormal, John Keel, and ultimately published in his 1975 cult classic book, The Mothman Prophecies.

The film, however, updates things to the present day and tells the story of a Washington-based political journalist, John Klein (Gere), whose wife dies in tragic circumstances following a brief battle with cancer. In the wake of this tragedy, Klein, throwing himself into his work, heads for Point Pleasant in pursuit of a story and inadvertently runs into a series of inexplicable events that would task even the best efforts of Mulder and Scully.

Thankfully, the film is not filled with scenes of a stuntman in a poorly fitting moth-suit flying shakily across the sky. Nor does it rely on shock tactic special effects to hammer home its story.

Rather, The Mothman Prophecies focuses on atmosphere, shadowy locations and subtle imagery, and accurately portrays the sense of evil and impending doom that gripped the town of Point Pleasant at the time. Gere shines, too – trying to juggle with events in his personal life as he travels along a journey further and further into unreality.

What do UFOs, collapsing bridges, Men in Black and a gargoyle-like creature that looks like it walked off the set of Jurassic Park-meets-Aliens have in common? Well, while the film supplies the answers, I wouldn't dream of giving away the ending.

Unlike most of the people who will be visiting their local cinema to see the film, however, for some, Mothman is nothing new.

JONATHAN Downes is the director of the Exeter-based Centre for Fortean Zoology (named after Charles Fort, an early chronicler of all things mysterious) and, along with his sidekick, Richard Freeman, runs the only full-time monster hunting group in the UK.

For Downes and Freeman every day is an adventure filled with sightings of Big Cats on Dartmoor, Nessie, Bigfoot and a creepy-looking winged man rumoured to haunt the wilds of Cornwall – the Owlman!

Yes, I know what you're thinking: another Batman villain. But, according to Downes, you'd be wrong.

Admittedly obsessed by the Owlman, Downes has spent years and a small fortune pursuing it and interviewing people who claim to have seen this British equivalent of Point Pleasant's flying whatsit.

So how does Downes feel about the Mothman getting the big time Hollywood treatment? Shouldn't Britain's very own version be getting the royal treatment, too?

"Indeed, he should," says Downes.

"I'm looking forward to seeing the film and hope they capture the spirit of the story. But perhaps one day Britain's Owlman will be as famous as Mothman is about to become."

And who would portray the 6ft 6ins Downes, whose resemblance to Bigfoot is startling?

"My dear boy," he tells me, "I am unique among men. I would have to play myself. Hollywood, are you listening?"

If The Mothman Prophecies lives up to all the hype, Jonathan Downes may well indeed one day see his face up on the silver screen. Now, that would be scary.

ABOVE: How the Mothman looked, according to witnesses. LEFT: Two of the film's stars, Richard Gere, who takes on the role of John Klein, and Laura Linney, who plays Connie Parker.

Express and Star, 2nd February 2002

Even the image of his Owliness has been made into collectable figures

Left: *This highly detailed figure of the Owlman was created by Heart and Co in Japan for its 'Heart of Mystery Series.'*

Right: *Another interpretation of the Owlman, created by Medicom Toy, Japan for their 'Great Mystery Museum Collection series'*

Mawnan Revisited - *For this 30th Anniversary edition members of the Centre for Fortean Zoology Mark North,, Oll Lewis and Thelma Sampson, go back on the trail of the Owlman and Morgawr in February 2006*

APPENDIX THREE:

THE OWLMAN SURFACES IN PUERTO-RICO IN 2005

Nick Redfern

In September 2005, I traveled to the island of Puerto Rico for a week, with a team from Red Star Films of Canada, to make a documentary for the nation's Space Channel on animal mutilations that was titled Fields of Fear. The focus of the filming was the vampire-like Chupacabras. Certainly, most of the many cases that we investigated did fall into the category of the island's most famous bloodsucker. One incident in particular, however, was significantly different and seemed to eerily parallel the weird events at Mawnan Church in the hot summer of 1976.

It was five days into our excursion on the island and, after a delicious lunch, we headed for a place of worship known as the Church of the Three Kings, which was a wonderful building that looked like a combination of a Medieval English castle and something you would see in a dusty Mexican town in one of those old spaghetti-westerns. But this structure was surrounded by dense, green woods on all sides rather than desert, and was topped off with a large, five-pointed star that reached out to the heavens from the church's flat roof. Our interviewee was a barrel-chested figure named Pucho who had an amazing tale to tell us.

As the crew set up the equipment, little kids, excitedly chattering, came running out of the woods to see what all of the fuss was about, and a teenager insisted on riding by at every moment on a noisy, rusty old motorbike that was definitely well past its prime. Pucho shouted something in the direction of the bike and the rider, looking hurt, vanished into the sunset, never to be seen again. Pucho then settled back, folded his arms, and proceeded to relate his story.

269

Church of the Three Kings

"Pucho elaborated, he was amazed to see a huge, feathery bird come looming out of the tree canopy"

It was long after the sun had set on a weeknight in February 2005, said Pucho, and he was walking past the Church of the Three Kings, when he heard what he described as a *"loud roar"* coming from a particularly dense section of trees adjacent to the building. And, as Pucho elaborated, he was amazed to see a huge, feathery bird come looming out of the tree canopy. Oddly, the bird did not merely fly out, but seemed to levitate vertically in the fashion of a helicopter, before it soared high into the air and headed off in the direction of a nearby farm. Stressing that he had never before or since seen such an immense beast, Pucho could only watch in stark terror and utter shock until the creature was out of sight. Notably, several days later the farm where the creature was seen flying towards suffered a number of horrifying attacks on its livestock, and of a type that Count Dracula himself would have been proud.

I was immediately struck by the similarities between Pucho's encounter and the three-decades-old events in the woods of darkest Cornwall. One of the witnesses to his Owliness, Jane Greenwood, described her sighting in the summer of 1976 to the *Falmouth Packet* newspaper, after a number of earlier reports had made the headlines:

> *"I am on holiday in Cornwall with my sister and our mother. I, too, have seen a big bird-thing. It was Sunday morning, and the place was in the trees near Mawnan Church, above the rocky beach. It was in the trees standing like a full-grown man, but the legs bent backwards like a bird's. It saw us, and quickly jumped up and rose straight up through the trees."* And as Jane had perceptively asked: *"How could it rise up like that?"*

How, indeed? It was exactly that question that Pucho wanted an answer to twenty-nine years later. Personally, I wanted to know what sort of creature it was that seemed to manifest in woods adjacent to sacred grounds on opposite sides of the world and decades apart, and where the witnesses described the appearance and movements of the animal in practically an identical fashion? It is a question I still ask myself – obsessed, as I am, with such diabolical weirdness.

Pucho was very matter-of-fact about the encounter, cared not a bit about publicity, and just wanted to know what was afoot in darkest Puerto Rico. None of us could help him, beyond confirming that the island was a truly strange place; and whatever it was that he saw, it had no place roaming around the wilder parts of the island. He laughed loud as if to say: *"You* are telling *me?"* On that note, we said our farewells. But of one thing I was certain: whatever the Owlman was, the creature was not restricting its activities to the southwest of England. The beast – be it a physical reality or some form of diabolical thought-form – was on the move.

APPENDIX FOUR:
BEYOND SUSPICION

Nick Redfern

The following was written by noted UFOlogist Nick Redfern in 2006, and is used with his permission…

"My newly published book, 'On the Trail of the Saucer Spies', reveals the way in which elements of the British intelligence community – including Special Branch, Scotland Yard, and GCHQ at Cheltenham – monitors people within the UFO research field, and, indeed, the way in which they have done so for decades.

The story I have uncovered is not one that suggests the secret surveillance was undertaken to prevent people from getting too close to the "alien truth." Rather, the official spying stemmed from the fact that Special Branch, in particular, had come to the strange conclusion that certain UFO researchers, such as me and Matthew Williams, had been "hired" by subversive groups to uncover UK defense secrets of a very down-to-earth nature, and that our UFO research was merely an ingenious "cover story" to be trotted out by us in the event that we were questioned by authorities.

Needless to say, the theory was not just outlandish: it was completely and utterly without foundation. However, I uncovered a copious amount of evidence showing that Special Branch were watching a whole range of individuals who had written about UFOs in the UK

273

in the mid to late 1990s – including the good Mr. Downes.

As one Special Branch source explained to me:

"Downes is, as you well know, the chap best known for his Yeti and Loch Ness excursions. But, as with you and your people and the UFOs, there was some concern that this was just a ruse – or partly, a ruse, at least. Downes was well acquainted at the time with a number of people in Ireland that we were interested in. The Downes thing was very low-key and didn't last long, but he was watched for a while, purely to see if he was working with certain Irish people. But there was nothing really to it: just this chap [Downes] talking with chaps in Ireland who were his friends, but who we were watching, and who were also interested in those monster pursuits."

The scenario of Special Branch monitoring the activities of full-time cryptozoologists such as Jon, purely because of the fact that they happened to have friends in Ireland sounds wholly outrageous; however, it is something that Jon himself can corroborate.

Special Branch sources also maintain that Jon was watched for two other reasons in the 1990s: one related to a Big Cat investigation he was embroiled in, the details of which had been provided to him by a British Army source. In this case, the soldier in question had deep knowledge of the secret affair between Diana, Princess of Wales and Major James Hewitt (the latter who Jon went to school with) that was not public knowledge at the time the solider had told Jon of the details.

Special Branch had come to the very odd conclusion that an unidentified subversive group was manipulating Jon to use the Big Cat story as a cover to try and uncover further details of the Hewitt-Diana affair from the solider, and then expose it as a way of rocking the monarchy. However, the investigation was hastily dropped when the official world soon learned that Jon was (and still is) an ardent royalist, and that their theories were in complete error.

The final investigation of Jon appears to focus upon a story he relates in his book The Owlman and Others about the way in which he received a batch of British Police files on animal mutilations that had occurred at Newquay Zoo in the late 1970s. In this case, Special Branch operatives mused upon the possibility that Jon had been provided the documents by subversives who were trying to recruit him into their ranks, and that the documents had been given to Jon as a kind of "dangling carrot" enticement.

I know the real story of the documents, thanks to Jon, and the Special Branch theories were completely and utterly without any foundation whatsoever. Moreover, background data on Jon and his family was incorrectly recorded in the files and the whole sorry mess was a fiasco from beginning to end. Some people might find all of the above-surveillance and such lamentable errors in the official files of Special Branch (and other agencies, too) as laughable, and a complete waste of taxpayers' money.

It is. However, there are far more serious issues to consider, too: namely the fact that, in the increasingly "Big Brother" state in which we live, Government agencies are compiling files on British citizens purely because they have Fortean interests. And the fact that those same agencies came to completely erroneous conclusions and compiled wholly erroneous data, with respect to me, Matthew and Jon regarding our Fortean interests seems not to matter to

the faceless automatons in power.

Who knows how many more files (also containing wholly erroneous data) have been opened on people in our subject by authority figures that believe our research is a cover for working with what they perceive to be subversives, remains to be seen.

It's debatable whether or not "the truth" really is out there. But there is one place where "the truth" most definitely is not: and that's in the official surveillance files of me, Jon and Matthew. Time and again, officials got it totally wrong, and practically had us walking arm in arm with subversives, when we were just doing a bit of harmless research and trying to earn a crust in the process

It really isn't paranoia if you think "they" are watching you and listening to you. They really are. But time and again, the official justification for that surveillance is so far removed from the truth as to be laughable. What next? Identity cards? Constant surveillance of the population for our "own good"? Yeah, right.

It's time that this unwarranted surveillance was highlighted for the nonsense that it certainly is and is stopped. And it's time for us, the people, to bring an end to all of this Big Brother nonsense before it gets totally out of control.

Those wanting to know how and why the British Government justified its nut-job surveillance of elements of the British cryptozoological community, can read the details in Nick Redfern's new book, *On the Trail of the Saucer Spies: UFOs and Government Surveillance*, published by Anomalist Books, New York.

<u>G</u>roovy <u>S</u>cooter

275

APPENDIX FIVE:

MORGAWR,
The Monster of Falmouth Bay

Anthony Mawnan-Peller

This pamphlet was originally produced by Morgawr productions in 1976. It is especially interesting from a historical point of view because it was as far as we know the first documentation of some very strange things that happened in Cornwall in the mid 1970's.

In this 30th Anniversary edition of *The Owlman and Others* we have included The Centre for Fortean Zoology reprint, with the original text from the pamphlet full, with additions. Including an introduction by Tony 'Doc' Shiels, the Wizard of the Western World, and an essay by Jonathan Downes describing some of the monstrous events that have happened in Cornwall since this pamphlet first saw the light of day!

MORGAWR

the
MONSTER
of Falmouth Bay

by A. Mawnan-Peller

The original front cover to the 1976 pamphlet

MORGAWR
The Monster of Falmouth Bay

A. Mawnan-Peller
with an introduction by
Tony 'Doc' Shiels

For
Martin *'Mort'* Brown
Cryptozoologist, cartoonist
and gentleman
1969-1996

Morgawr

The monster of Falmouth Bay

A Short History

by

A.Mawnan-Peller

Introduction

by Tony 'Doc' Shiels.

Two decades ago, from Parson's Beach on the Helford, I saw Morgawr, the now-famous Cornish 'sea serpent'. 1976 was a very strange year indeed in which Cornwall seemed to be a prime target area for various manifestations of para-normality.

Not only did Morgawr per-form, but there were reports of UFO sightings, 'little peo-ple', witchcraft, mysterious sounds and smells, and the grotesque Owl-man of Mawnan. As the *'Wizard of the Western World'*, I found myself at the epicentre of these happenings. As an artist and surrealist, I enjoyed the experience.

Morgawr is now, probably, the world's best-known 'sea-serpent' (the Loch Ness Monster being a fresh water first cousin), and the creature is still seen from time to time. This little booklet, which first appeared in 1976, was the first serious, though brief - documentation of the Morgawr phenomenon. Jon and Alison Downes are to be congratulated for re-publishing this important piece of cryptozoological history.

MORGAWR

In the ancient language of Cornwall, the name MORGAWR, meaning 'Sea Giant', describes an enormous marine monster which lives in the waters of Falmouth Bay. A long-necked sea-serpent, similar in appearance to the famous 'Nessie' of Loch Ness.

Cornwall is known as the 'Land of Legend' and, until fairly recently, the Great Cornish Sea-Serpent was regarded as part of that legend; a romantic rumour, a mythological beast, a figment of the Celtic imagination, along with piskies, mermaids and spriggans. However, a hundred years ago, a long necked monster was caught by fishermen in Gerrans Bay. Fifty years later, a Mr. Reece and a Mr. Gilbert, trawling three miles south of Falmouth netted an amazing creature. It was twenty feet long, with an eight foot tail, a 'beaked' head, scaly legs, and a broad back covered with 'matted brown hair'. Marine Biologists of the day were unable to identify the beast.

One sunny evening in September 1975, Morgawr was spotted off Pendennis Point. Mrs Scott, of Falmouth, and her friend Mr. Riley, saw a hideous, hump-backed creature, with 'stumpy-horns', and bristles down the back of its long neck. The huge animal dived for a few seconds, then resurfaced with a conger eel in its jaws. Mrs. Scott says that she will never forget 'the face on that thing', as long as she lives.

Shortly after the Scott/Riley sighting, Morgawr was encountered by several mackerel fishermen, and blamed for bad luck, bad weather and bad catches.

In January 1976 a strange (and, so far unidentified) carcase was discovered on Durgan Beach, Helford River, by Mrs. Payne

MORGAWR

of Falmouth. For a while it was thought that the monster was dead, until the 'Falmouth Packet' newspaper published two photographs of Morgawr, taken in february by a lady who called herself *Mary F*. They showed a long necked, hump backed creature, at least eighteen feet long, swimming in the water off Trefusis Point, near Flushing. *Mary F's*, monster was described as 'black or very dark brown', with a snake-like head and *'humps on the back which moved in a funny way'*.

After publishing those historic photographs, the 'Packet' received a flood of letters from people who claimed to have seen Morgawr. Estimates of the creature's length varied from twelve to forty five feet. At the beginning of May, two London bankers, on a fishing holiday, saw a pair of monsters in the mouth of the Helford River. Now it seems as if Falmouth Bay could contain a whole family of Sea Serpents!

MORGAWR'S MILE.

The mouth of the Helford River appears to be the area most favoured by the sea-serpents; the majority of sightings being from the stretch of coastline between Rosemullion Head and Toll Point. This is now known as *'Morgawr's Mile'*.

Duncan Viner, a dental technician from Truro, saw Morgawr, in January 1976, swimming *'a few hundred yards off Rosemullion Head'*. At first, he thought it was a whale, as only a dark hump was visible; but as he watched, it started to rise in the water and a long neck appeared. Mr. Viner estimated the length of the monster to be between thirty and forty feet.

MORGAWR

Miss Amelia Johnson, on Holiday from London, was taking a walk in the Rosemullion area when she saw a *'strange form suddenly emerge from the water in Falmouth Bay'*. She describes *'a sort of prehistoric dinosaur thing with a neck the length of a lamp-post'*.

Gerald Bennett of Seworgan, saw a creature swimming in the Helford, one afternoon. The part of it above the water was *'about twelve feet in length, with an elongated neck'*.

On Good Friday, 1976, a fifteen year old schoolboy from Helston spotted a *'weird animal with two humps and a long neck like a snake'*, moving up the river between Toll Point and the Gew. The monster was *'slimy, black and about twenty five feet long'*. He took a photograph of the animal which was later shown on BBC television in the Spotlight programme.

There have been many other sightings along *'Morgawr's Mile'*, the hottest length of coast for would be monster spotters.

THE MONSTER HUNTERS

Towards the end of March 1976, a 'professor of metaphysics', from Albuquerque, New-Mexico, USA, arrived in Falmouth with a plan to capture the monster. Professor Michael McCormick, a fire-eater and travelling showman, intended to trap Morgawr and to exhibit the beast in his 'Matchbox Circus'. But by the beginning of May, the 'professor' had left Cornwall ... without his sea-serpent.

MORGAWR

"Duncan Viner's Morgawr, 1976"

"Captain Cringle's Sea Serpent, 1893"

"The Reese/Gilbert Monster 1926"

MORGAWR

As it happens, May turned out to be a busy month for Morgawr. World-famous monster hunter, Tim Dinsdale, decided to investigate the Great Falmouth sea serpent. Mr Dinsdale is best known for his tireless efforts, over a number of years, in pursuit of the Loch Ness Monster. He has written several fascinating books on the subject of 'Nessie'.

Another writer showing an interest in Morgawr is Peter Costello, (author of '*In search of Lake Monsters*'), who regards the 'Mary F'. photographs as an '*important contribution to unraveling the mystery of the Great Sea-Serpent*'.

Folklorist, Tony Shaw, (co-author of '*The Folklore of Cornwall*'), is another keen investigator. He has collected and recorded interviews with most of the people who claim to have seen Morgawr, and is working on a book about the Cornish Sea - Dragon. Mr. Shaw, at first regarded the monster as, simply a '*modern day myth*', but is now convinced that there is a huge unidentified creature living in Falmouth Bay.

One of the strangest characters involved in the hunt for Morgawr is Tony 'Doc' Shiels, a professional wizard and well known 'psychic'. The Doc believes he can make telepathic contact with sea-serpents and invoke the creature by magical means. Doc's monster hunting exploits have been featured in newspapers and on radio and television.

Another magical personality, involved in the hunt, is Psyche, a beautiful young witch from Inverness, who, in the company of several members of her coven, swam naked in the waters of

MORGAWR

Falmouth Bay, in order to attract the monster to the surface. Since Psyche's initial dip, several nude witches have attempted to raise the sea-dragon by swimming around *'Morgawr's Mile'*.

WHAT IS IT???

There are various theories which have been put forward to explain or identify the creature known as Morgawr.

The most attractive and exciting notion is that the animal could, possibly be a plesiosaur ... a reptile which is supposed to have been extinct for over seventy million years! The 'Mary F', pictures certainly show something very large, with a long neck, small head, a large, hump-backed body, and flippers riding high in the water ... all of which fits in with most zoological descriptions of the plesiosaur. It is also true that these aquatic dinosaurs could adapt to life in both fresh and salt water. However, it is unlikely that a cold blooded reptile could survive the temperature of Falmouth Bay.

It has been suggested that Morgawr may be an invertebrate, a giant mollusc or worm. But it would be difficult for a creature without a skeleton to support such a huge body. Nevertheless, very large invertebrates, such as the Giant Squid, do exist in deep water, although they show themselves on the surface very rarely.

The most logical theory, it seems, is that the monster is a type of long-necked seal, a warm-blooded mammal. This is the

MORGAWR

'Morgawr off Trefusis Point'
One of the 1976 photographs by *'Mary F'.* © FPL

MORGAWR

explanation favoured by such experts as Peter Costello and Dr. Bernard Heuvelmans. It is possible that a so far undiscovered and very large species of seal could exist in Falmouth Bay (not to mention Loch Ness!). Seals are fairly common around the Cornish coast, and recently a black one was seen in the River Fal.

A very strange theory has been put forward by Doc Shiels. He suggests that Morgawr could be a *parapsychical entity*, a non-organic 'thing' existing in *several more than threedimensions*, capable of changing its size and shape at will, or even seeming to appear as something else entirely. Doc relates sea and lake monster phenomena to sightings of flying-saucers, dragons, and 'little green men'; all of which he describes as the *props of a cosmic joker*. Doc's theories are, to a certain extent, supported by a well-known writer on the subject of monsters, F.W.Halliday (author of *The Great Orm of Loch Ness* and *The Dragon and the Disc*.

It is unlikely that Morgawr will be properly identified until a good, clear colour photograph or a cine film is taken of the creature. Any cameraman who is lucky enough to obtain such a picture will, undoubtedly, have something of great scientific and monetary value.

'A GUIDE FOR SERPENT SNAPPERS'.

Anyone with a camera has a chance of capturing Morgawr on film.

MORGAWR

Modern, automatic, cassette-loading cameras make good photography easy; removing, as they do, all worries about exposure, shutter speed, focus and so on. However, for a really good still picture of the monster, I would recommend a single-lens reflex camera with a good telephoto lens.

Amateur movie-makers would also be well advised to try and shoot the beast. A length of cine film, showing the monster in motion, would be invaluable to zoologists. Most cine cameras, these days, use Super-8 film, and are fitted with zoom lenses. Better pictures are more likely to be obtained if the camera is tripod mounted rather than hand-held.

Colour film is to be recommended for both still and cine photography where a sea-serpent is to be the subject. A full colour picture would certainly contain far more useful information than one in black and white.

Monster-snapping is, of course, very much a matter of luck. Being in the right place at the right time is something which is not so easily planned in advance. Anyone, anywhere on the coast around Falmouth Bay and the mouth of the Helford River has a sporting chance of getting a picture of Morgawr ... so long as they don't forget to carry a camera at all times. Those who are seriously interested in photographing the creature would be best advised to station themselves in one of the less easily accessible parts of, say, 'Morgawr's Mile'. Sea Monsters are most often seen to surface during periods of warm weather and calm, unruffled waters. If and when you are lucky enough to see or to photograph Morgawr, it is advisable to make a few

MORGAWR

notes as soon after the sighting as possible, giving estimates of size, distance and so on. The more details noted, the more valuable your sighting or picture will be.

If a camera is not available when the monster is seen to surface, sketches, as detailed as possible, should be made and signed by witnesses. In this way, when all the evidence is collected and compared, an accurate picture of the creature can be built up and analysed by scientists interested in such phenomena.

MORGAWR'S RELATIVES.

Not since the year 1817 has a sea-serpent generated so much interest as Morgawr. In August of that year, a huge monster was seen in the waters of Massachusetts Bay, mainly in the area of Gloucester Harbour.

In 1846, Captain Christmas of the Danish Navy saw an enormous, long-necked beast between Iceland and the Faroes. He described the creature as having '*a neck thick as a man's waist, with a horse-like head, moving gracefully like a swan's*'.

On August 6th 1848, H.M. Corvette 'Daedalus' was homeward bound, from the East Indies. At 5 p.m. the officers were surprised to see a gigantic sea-serpent swimming past the ship. Sixty feet of the creature's body was visible above the surface of the water. It had a snake-like head and, '*something like the mane of a horse*', down its back.

MORGAWR

"The Scott/Riley Monster 1975"

MORGAWR

In 1893, the British ship 'Umulfi' encountered an eighty foot sea-serpent off the Mauretanian coast. Captain Cringle reported that the monster *was rushing through the water at great speed, and was throwing water from its breast as a vessel throws water from its bows*.

In 1919, a lawyer, Mr J. Mackintosh-Bell, was on holiday in the Orkney Islands. On the morning of August 5th, from the deck of a cod-line fishing boat, off Hoy, he saw a monster with *a long neck as thick as an elephant's front leg, all rough looking like an elephant's hide*. The head was like that of a dog, with small, black eyes.

The carcase of a sea-monster was washed up at Prah Sands, Cornwall, in 1933; the year in which 'Nessie' first became famous.

Dr. Heuvelmans lists over 550 reports of marine monsters, in his book *In the wake of the Sea-Serpents*; I have mentioned just a few of the more famous ones. Morgawr is, without a doubt, destined to become one of the best known and best documented of all. Already, Falmouth's monster has captured the attention of the international press, radio and television; as well as some of the world's best-known monster-hunters.

'CURIOUSER AND CURIOUSER'

Morgawr is not the only strange thing to have happened in the Falmouth Bay area since the Autumn of 1975. In October 1975,

MORGAWR

"The Bird-Man of Mawnan.

Based on a sketch

by

June Melling. 1976"

"Amelia Johnson's Monster 1976"

MORGAWR

a group of three UFO's was seen in the sky above Falmouth Docks. Then, in March 1976, a pair of flying saucers appeared over Perranwell.

In the spring of 1976, a group of *'real live Cornish piskies'* was photographed by one of the monster raising witches.

During the Easter weekend, the two young daughters of a holidaymaker ... Mr. Don Melling, from Preston, Lancashire ... saw a *'huge great thing with feathers, like a big man with flapping wings'*, hovering over the church tower at Mawnan (on *'Morgawr's Mile'*). The girls ... Vicky, 9, and June, 12 ... were so frightened that the family holiday was cut short by three days.

Flying saucers have, of course, been seen by many hundreds of people over the years; and Cornwall has had its fair share. There would be nothing particularly unusual (by normal saucer spotting standards) about the Falmouth sightings if they had not coincided with the other odd happenings.

'Little People' have been seen from time to time, coming out of flying saucers. Maybe that is how the piskies first arrived in the area!

Like Morgawr, it seems that the weird bird of Mawnan has ancestors in Cornwall. The *'Cornish Echo'* for June 4th 1926, carried the headline *'Boys Attacked by Strange Bird'*, and described how two young boys encountered a very peculiar, very large and very aggressive feathered thing, between Mount

MORGAWR

Hawke and Porthowan. The big bird was killed after quite a struggle, and the body examined by several people, but nobody could identify it. Coincidentally, during the early part of 1976, a thing called 'Big Bird' was busy frightening the people of Southern Texas. It was reported as being *big as an automobile, with a fifteen foot wingspan and a bat like face*.

Morgawr continues to thrive. On May 20th 1976, Falmouth coastguards received reports of several sightings in the mouth of the Helford River. At the time of writing, Cornwall's Great Sea Serpent is alive and well. Keep an eye on the water ... you may be lucky enough to see the monster yourself.

Good Hunting!

***

EDITOR'S NOTE: In the last twenty years a lot has changed. Tim Dinsdale is dead, and Tony 'Doc' Shiels now lives in Eire. The original edition included a list of recommended books about Lake and Sea Monsters. We have not included this, as they are nearly all out of print. The Centre for Fortean Zoology, (see last Page), sells a wide selection of new and second hand books on the subjects, so if you want further information do not hesitate to contact us. Will you also please contact us if YOU have an eyewitness report, photograph or video (which has since 1976) almost entirely superceded cine film), of Morgawr, the Mawnan Owlman or any other strange phenomenon.

Two Monstrous Decades in Falmouth Bay.

by

Jonathan Downes

(Director of The Centre for Fortean Zoology)

After the original publication of this booklet, the sightings continued apace. In 1980 Mr Martin and his daughter were particularly lucky (if there is such a thing as luck), to see both Morgawr AND the Owlman on the same day.

In 1985, Falmouth author Sheila Bird, and her brother, a geologist saw the animal again. This is a particularly notable sighting, because it is, as far as we are aware, the only time when Morgawr has been seen by anyone with scientific training!

They described an animal similar in shape to a plesiosaur, but as Mr. Mawnan-Peller pointed out Plesiosaurs died out over seventy million years ago .... or did they? New evidence has recently been discovered which tends to disprove Mawnan-Peller's claim that *"it is unlikely that a cold-blooded reptile could survive the temperature of Falmouth Bay"*.

It appears that some fossil reptiles, including some plesiosaurs may have been warm blooded, and more importantly it appears that the larger an aquatic reptile is, the less prone to heat loss it becomes. In a bizarre process called Gigantothermy, very large marine reptiles, like the giant Leathery Turtle or Luth, which grows in excess of nine feet in length, and is a regular visitor to our shores, exhibit the characteristics of warm blooded animals, even though they are nothing of the kind! (For more information on possible plesiosaur survival, gigantothermy and allied topics, I refer you to *'In Search of Prehistoric Survivors'* an excellent book by my friend and colleague Dr. Karl P.N.Shuker).

Although the 'long necked seal' theory is rather out of favour in some circles these days, it has always been a plausible one. It also seems quite possible that Morgawr could be either a surviving, evolved descendant of the plesiosaurs, or, just as excitingly an evolved descendant of one of the primitive whales or archaeocetes. These animals, the most primitive of which, even had flipper like legs similar to those of a sea-lion, have also been presumed extinct for millions of years, but an animal of this type has been suggested as the identity for a 38 foot long animal known as 'Migo', which was filmed in Lake Dakataua on the island of New Britain, north-east of New Guinea in 1994. Something definitely lives in that remote lake .. I've got the only copy of the video tape in the UK!

But nearer to home! Most years someone sees something mysterious in the waters of Falmouth Bay, and as recently as the autumn of 1995, a lady called Gertrude Stephens, of Golden Bank, Falmouth witnessed Morgawr swimming slowly through the primordial waters, she has haunted since times immemorial.

The Owlman sightings have also continued. The gigantic bird-man was seen again by two schoolgirls, Sally Chapman, and Barbara Perry soon after this booklet was first published, and there were further sightings in 1976, 1978, 1980, 1985, 1989 and

MORGAWR

1995. There is definitely something very strange about Falmouth Bay!

In the twenty years since this booklet originally appeared a lot has happened in the wierd world of monster hunting. Interest in the paranormal, and in strange phenomena has never been higher. It has become almost 'respectable' to admit to a taste for the bizarre, 'The X Files' is one of the most popular programmes on television, and Fortean Times - the journal of strange phenomena, which in 1976 sold only a few hundred copies of each issue now sells something like 65,000.

Cryptozoology, the study of hidden, or unknown animals was first suggested by Dr. Bernard Heuvelmans in the late 1950's and even now is treated with distrust by many 'mainstream' scientists who really should know better. The scientific establishment has insisted for decades that there are no new species of animals left to be discovered. This is palpably untrue.

Within the last few years we have discovered The Megamouth Shark, The Vu Quang Ox, the Chacoan Peccary, The Giant Muntjac and many other exciting new species. Maybe the scientific discovery of the Yeti, Bigfoot, Nessie or Morgawr, is only just around the corner!

* * *

MORGAWR

DO YOU WANT TO HELP SOLVE MYSTERIES LIKE MORGAWR, OR THE BEAST OF BODMIN MOOR?

There is something magical about Cornwall. It is a part of the country which really bears very little similarity to the rest of the United Kingdom. There are lots of strange things happening, many mysteries to solve and much research that needs to be done.

In 1991 we started The Centre for Fortean Zoology, a non-profit making organisation dedicated to researching the wierder wildlife of the world. We are presently involved in research across the world. We have representatives in thirteen or fourteen countries, and we publish a range of books and magazines about the subject, ranging from the relatively 'light-weight' to the scholarly. Books on the Owlman of Mawnan, and the Morgawr phenomenon, which will list every known sighting in a great more detail than we have done in this booklet, are also in preparation.

We are always looking for researchers, helpers, photographers, cameramen, scientists, artists, and people who simply want to subscribe to our magazine *Animals & Men*. You are obviously interested in mystery animals, and the wierder aspects of our not-so modern world, otherwise you would not be reading this booklet, so why not write to us at:

The Centre For Fortean Zoology,
15 Holne Court,
Exwick,
Exeter,
Devon EX4 2NA.

ACKNOWLEDGEMENTS

Many thanks go to the following people for their assistance in compilation of both this edition and the original of this book: My ex-wife Alison, Lisa Peach, Julia Andrews, Bob Rickard, Darren Naish, Janet and Colin Bord, Richard Freeman, the late Dave `Shento` Shenton, the late John Gordon, John Jacques, the Westcountry Studies Library, the Cornish Studies Library, The Rev. Barrington Bennetts and the management and staff of *The Seven Stars* in Falmouth, Corinna James, Graham Inglis, Oll Lewis, Mark North, Thelma Sampson, Truro Museum, Anthony 'Doc' Shiels, Nick Redfern, Jan Williams, Clinton Keeling, everyone at Newquay Zoo past and present, Simon Parker, Paul Whitrow, Vonny Cornelius, Joyce Howarth, Marco   Gianangelli, Ian Wright, Rev Lionel Fanthorpe, Craig Glenday, Uri Geller, and finally, my late mother for teaching me to love books, and my late father for teaching me to write them...

REFERENCES AND NOTES

Key of abbreviations for Chapters:

CFZ	*Centre For Fortean Zoology*
CCBR	*Cornwall County Bird Report*
FP	*Falmouth Packet. (newspaper)*
FT	*Fortean Times.*
PR	*Police Report (ref 40 etc)*
STP	*Spanish Train Publications*
TDA	*Transactions of the Devonshire Association*
WMN	*Western Morning News*
WB	*West Briton (newspaper - Truro)*
UFOR	*UFO Report (ref 59 etc)*

CHAPTER TWO

1. Cousens. S. *Tony Shiels.* Milton Keynes. Mark Space Publ. 1995
2. Adams. D. *Dirk Gently's Holistic Detective Agency.* Heinemann. London 1987
3. For non-UK readers. Captain Birdseye was a fictional sea captain with an enormous white beard, created in order to sell frozen fish fingers.
4. I would not like to compromise a lady who, unlike myself, is now happily married so I refer you to my song *Better than Dying* on my CD, The Case, 1995.
5. Shiels. Tony 'Doc'. Monstrum - a Wizard's Tale. p52. Fortean Tomes, London 1990.
6. Tony Shiels pers. comm. (video interview) April 1995. *(in the interests of readability, chapter 2 has been presented as a continuous narrative, whereas in fact I have drawn upon a number of different sources.)*
7. FT 16 p19.
8. Shiels. Tony 'Doc' op. cit. 1990.
9. Shiels. Tony 'Doc' op. cit. 1995.
10. Ibid.
11. Bord. J and C. *Alien Animals* Granada, London 1980.
12. FT 16 p19
13. Ibid.
14. Mawnan-Pellcr, A. *Mowgawr – the Monster of Falmouth Bay.* Falmouth, Mowgawr publ. 1976 (republished by STP/CFZ 1996).
15. Tony Shiels in conversation with the author.
16. Jaret Bord pers. comm. Jan 1996
17. Tony Shiitls pers. comm. Feb 1996.
18. Janet Bord pers. comm. Feb 1996
19. Tony Shiels in conversation with the author.
20. Tony Shiels cited in Rickard. R.J.M article *Birdmen of the Apocolypse.* FT 17 p17.
21. Tony Shiels pers. comm Nov 1995.
22. In Apr 1996 we visited St Ives together with Tony and asked several of his old cronies for news of Dick Gilbert, but have been unable to locate him.
23. Bord, J & C. op.cit.

24. Rickard, R.J.M. op. cit.

25. Ibid.

26. Ibid.

27. Mawnan-Peller op. cit.

28. FT 17 pl'7.

29. Darren Naish pers. comm.

30. FT 17 p17.

31. Ibid

32. Ibid.

33. Although we are perfectly aware that one of the major academic criticisms of Fortean research is that it is not thorough enough, in this case we really couldn't be bothered!

34. FPFri9 Jul 1976, p14

35. Ibid.

36. Sunday Independent Sep 1977.

37. 'Miranda'' (pseudonym) pers comm.

38. FT summer 1978.

39. Tony Shiels 1990 ob. cit.

40. The Sun 28 Apr 1978.

41. Unreferenced, because the supplier of the clipping omitted to state its source.

42. FT summer 1978.

43. We were not able to identify the *Falmouth Packet* article referred to in his letter.

44. Tony Shiels pers. comm. with the atthor, Nov 1995.

45. Tony Shiels writing to Janet Bord. 26 Jun 1978.

46. Tony Shiels 1990 op. cit.

47. Tony Shiels pers. comm. Feb 1996.

48. FP 14 Jul 1978.

49. Ibid

50. FP 21 Jul 1978.

51. FP28 Jul 1978.

52. Unreferenced clipping.

53. Tony Shiels writing to Janet Bord. Oct 1978.

54. Tony Shiels writing to Bob Rickard. 19 Jun 1978

55. Pers. comm. Jan 1996.

56. Ibid.

57. As 53.

58. Tony Shiels 1990 ob. cit.

59. Ibid.

60. Dinsdale. Tim. *Project Waterhorse.* Collins. London 1968.

61. Tony Shiels pers. comm.

62. Shiels, Tony. 1990 ob. cit.

63. The Anglicised spelling is beltane, the Celtic feast of May Eve, made famous in *Ride a White Swan* by T. Rex (1971)

64. Pers. comm. Dec 1995.

65. Tony Shiels writing to Janet Bord, 24 Apr 1979

66. Tony Shiels writing to Janet Bord. 6 May 1979.

67. Tony Shiels 1990 op. cit.

68. Karl Shuker pers. comm. Apr 1996.

69. Karl Shuker pers. comm. May 1996.

70. Ibid.

71. Petrovic.W. pers comm.

72. As 69.

73. As 65.

74. Cornwall CountyBird Report (CCBR) 1949.

75. CCBR 1958.

76. CCBR 1959.

77. CCBR 1960.

78. Ibid.

79. Ibid.

80. Petrovic,W. pers. comm.

81. McEwan,G. *The Mystery Animals of Britain and Ireland.* Robert Hayle, London 1985.

82. FT35 pp24-25.

83. Tony Shiels pers. comm. Apr 1995.

84. Tony Shiels "The Case for Owlman" *Animals & Men #6* .

85. Strange magazine #9.

86. Ibid.

87. FT48.

88. CFZ video interview with Tony Shiels, Apr 1995.

89. An extraordinarily emotive expression meaning "for the fun of it".

90. I visited Tony in Falmouth on a number of occasions, and I don't think I have met anyone else who knows so many people. A walk of just a couple of hundred yards between two different pubs can take the best part of half an hour because there were so many people wanting to stop for a chat.

91. O'Siagluil. N. *The Shiels Effect - Manual for the Psychic Superstar.* 1975 - due to be republished by CFZ 1997-98.

92. Tony Shiels pers. comm. May 1996.

93. As 88.

94. Dave Shenton pers. comm.

95. FT48.

96. Nnidnid #1. 1986.

97. As 88.

98. Julia Andrews pers. comm.

99. FP 1 Nov 1986.

100. I have visited the pub in question, the Stag Hunt at Ponsanooth, with Tony on a number of occasions. I have seen him perform magickal feats in the public bar.

101. Miranda (pseudonym) pers. comm.

102. O'Siaghail. N. 1975 op. cit. (As 91)

103. FP 8 Nov 1986.

104. FP 1 Nov 1986.

105. We contacted the office of the present Bishop of Truro and they had no record of the incident.

106. FP 8 Nov 1986.

107. Ibid.

108. *Sunday Independent* 9 Nov 1986.

109. Although the photograph of Kate which appears in the first issue of *Nnidnid* shows her completely naked, as is discussed in a later chapter, this is an image of power, rather than of erotocism.

110. As 108.

111. The most notorious of these was the one in *The Sun* headlined "The weirdest family in the Land" - see ref 40.

112. This is one of the more unpleasant aspects to the Shiels mythos. It is one which he has always denied, and with which his friends, amongst which I am proud to count myself, get particularly angry.

These accusations are whispered amongst the more salacious forteans but, as far as I know, have never made it into print.

113. To date, despite a large number of allegations, and many children having been taken into care, no successful case has ever been proven by the authorities.

114. As 108.

115. Another unreferenced cutting believed mid-1970s *Falmouth Packet.* A friend of his from the time told us how Tony's "pipe-smokers" club had prompted some of his children and their friends to start up a Silk Cut (a brand of British cigarette) smokers' club in the same pub, in a light-hearted attempt at teasing their father.

116. Unreferenced 1978 cutting, *The Daily Mail..*

117. This column was called "The Doc Shiels Cabinet of Curiosities".

118. ...so was this.

119. Truro's *Midweek Recorder.* 10 Dec 1974. about Tony's then-new book. *Entertaining with ESP.*

120. 1 will not name names - but YOU know who you are.

121. As 108.

122. Walt Disney 1959

123. Definitions of which can be found in Symons. J *The Great Beast. N.E.L. London 1975.*

124. Aleister Crowley did so; see Symons op. cit. 123.

125. Tony Shiels 1990 op. cit.5.

126a. FP 8 Nov 1986.

126k A totally unhelpful letter to me from BBC Radio Cornwall.

127. FP 15 Nov 1986.

128. Mawnan-Peller op. cit. 14.

129. FP 15 Nov 1986.

130. Ibid.

131. Bord J and C op. cit. 11

132. McEwan.G. 1986 op. cit.

133. Ibid.

134. FT48.

135. Strange magazine #9.

CHAPTER THREE

1. As is obvious from the text, the original document is unreferenced.

2. ....so is this.

3. As Elvis Costello once said, "Accidents will happen," and, as noted by Dinsdale, Shiels, Halliday, Keel, and practically everybody else involved, within cryptoinvestigative methodology, they certainly do!

4. Between Jul 1993 stat Dec 1995. Together with many parts of my "old" life, he has vanished completely with my ongoing divorce.5.   It was broadcast between Oct and Dec 1995 over a period of 10 weeks. It was produced by CST productions and has since been shownon a cable channel in the UK Midlands and satellite TV in Austria.

6. Letter to "Gavin" (pseudonym) May 1995.

7. Gavin's' memory was at fault. The book is actually Bord, Janet and Colin: *Modern Mysteries of Britain.* Grafton. London 1988.

8. Austin,OL and Singer, A: *Birds of the World – A Survey of the 27 Orders and 155 Families* pp154-155. Hamlyn. London 1962.

9. "Gavin" pers. comm. May 1995.

10. "Gavin" pers. comm. Jun 1995.

11. Filmed for reasons of cost at Dozmary Pool, Bolventor, and shown in the first episode.

12. I did another documentary on the subject in May 1996, but the definitive snall-screen discussion of "his owliness" is yet to be made.

13. Published summer 1995.

14. To date, we haven't done so.

15. Letter to "Gavin" Jul 1995.

16. Shiels, Tony 'Doc' "The Case for Owlperson" - *Animals & Men* #6.

17. Blue in Green Studios, Haytor Vale.

18. John Downes and the Amphibians from Outer Space: The Case CD and cassette, Sep 1995.

19. Tony made a guest appearance on this album as well as providing the cover art and the title.

20. Letter to "Gavin" Aug 1995.

21. "Gavin" pers. comm. Aug 1995.

22. The parallels between the summer of 1976 and the summer of 1995 are many and various and are discussed more fully in my article *"A Caseful of Cougars", Animals & Men #7,* Oct 1995.

23. A term which I believe was first used by Wolfred Mellers in his book *Twilight of the Gods* (O.U. P. 1973).

24. My fixation with such things is discussed further in my 1990 book *Road Dreams.*

25. Karl Shuker pers. comm.

26. To be discussed in a forthcoming CFZ publication.

27. As always.

28. Taylor, D: *It was Twenty years Ago Today.* Granada. London 1987.

29. Huxley, A: The Doors of Perception. 1961.

30. Taylor op. cit. 28.

31. Huxley op. cit. 29.

32. Bord. J & C: *Alien Animals.* Granada. London 1980.

33. Various telephone calls with "Gavin" in the early part of 1996.

34. Green. J: *Sasquatch – Apes Amongst Us.* Hancock House. New York 1978.

35. Encounters. Jul 1996.

36. Coleman. Loren *Mysterious America.* 1980.

37. Green, J. op. cit. 34.

38. *Encounters..* Jul 1996.

39. "Gavin" pers. comm. Apr 1996.

40. Kinsey, A.C., Pomeroy, W., and Martin, C.E *Sexual Behaviour in the Human Male.* Saunders. Philadelphia 1948.

41. Doubt has been cast on some of Kinsey's results by commentators who claim that, as some of his source material came from the testimony of convicted sex offenders, that the results extrapolated were atypical.

CHAPTER FOUR

1. Heuvelmans. B: *On the Track of Unknown Animals..* Hart-Davis. London 1958

2. Lewis. C.S.: *The Lion, The Witch and The Wardrobe.* H.C. London 1941.

3. Keel. J: Tin *Mothman Prophecies.* UK edn *Visitors from Space.* N.E.L London 1974.

4. Bord. J & C: *Alien Animals.* Granada. London 1980.

5. Rickard. R.J.M. "Birdmen of the Apocolypse" FT 17 pp14-20.

7. I have no idea when he said this originally; I got it from Monty Python.

8. See The *Unexplained.* ed. P. Brooksmith.

9. Ibid.

10. I have no more details on this book.

11. Cited in Rickard op. cit. 5.

12. Ibid.

13. There was a particularly crass reference to this type of phenomenon in an episode of *Mysterious West*.

14. Kipling, R: *Puck of Pook's Hill.* Longmans.. London 1902.

15. Ibid.

16. Shiels. Tony 'Doc': Monstrum – *A Wizard's Tale.* Fortean Tomes. London 1990.

17. White. T.H. *The Once and Future King.* Collins 1960 edn.

18. Cited in Heuvelmans. op. cit. 1.

19. *Transactions of the Devonshire Association. (TDA)* 1899.

20. *TD.A.* 1922.

21. Downes. J.T. *A Dictionary of Devonshire Dialect.* 1987.

22. Brown. T: *Devon Ghosts.* Norwich. Jarrold. 1980

23. *TD.A.* 1957

24. Theo Brown was recorder of the Devonshire Association folklore section for many years.

25. Unfortunately she died in the late 1980s.

26. Also wryly noted by Noel Stratfield in her book *Ballet Shoes,* Penguin, London 1936. ppl65-6 Puffin 1957 edn

27. *TD.A.* 1957.

28. Ibid.

29. Tongue. R. *Dartmoor Folklore.* 1965.

30. *TD.A.* unreferenced.

31. Issue 2.

32. See 26.

33. Tony Shiels pers. comm. 1995.

34. Apparently a book by novelist Leslie Thomas claims that during World War 2, GIs exploring an abandoned church in South Devon found an enormous stone phallus hidden behind the high altar. I have not been able to verify this.

35. *Goblin Universe #4.* CFZ 1997.

36. McEwan, G: *Mystery Animals of Britain and Ireland.* Robert Hale. London 1985.

37. *TD.A.* unreferenced.

38. Lewis, C.S: The *Voyage of the Dawn Treader.* 1967 Puffin edn.

39. Kipling op. cit. 14.

40. For non-UK readers, this is just a pointless pun based around a tv advertisement for a well-known brand of confectionary.

41. William Petrovic pers. comm.

42. *TD.A.* unreferenced.

43. Ibid.

44. Steve Johnson pers. comm.

45. *TD.A.* unreferenced

46. Ibid.

47. Lcegg, R. *Mysterious Dorset.* D.P.C. Sherborne 1987.

48. Ibid.

49. Legg. R., Perrott. T and Collier. M: *Ghosts of Dorset, Devon and Somerset.* 1974.

50. Perrott. Tom pers. comm.

51. *Goblin Universe #4.* CFZ 1997.

52. *TD.A.* 1933.

53. *Western Morning News* (WMN) 16 Feb 1932.

54. Steve Johnson pers. comm.

55. *TD.A.* unreferenced.

56. WMN 19 Feb 1932

57. WMN l6 Feb 1932

58. As 51.

59. William Petrovic pers. comm.

60. As 51.

61. *T.D.A.* unreferenced.

62. Cited in Legg op. cit. 47.

63. Legg op. cit. 47.

64. Ibid.

65. Ibid.

66. McEwan op. cit. 36.

67. *Fortean Studies vol 1.* ed: Steve Moore. John Brown Publ. 1994.

68. Anon. *Cornish Echo,* 14 Jun 1926.

69. Mawnan-Peller. A: *Morgawr – the Monster of Falmouth Bay.* (Morgawr Falmouth Publ. 1976, re-published CFZ 1996).

70. Bord. J & C. op. cit. 4.

71. Richard. R.J.M. op. cit. 5.

72. Ibid.

73. *CFZ Yearbook 1996*

74. *Cornish Echo* 14 Jun 1926.

75. As 51.

76. *Fortean Studies vol.1.* ed: Steve Moore. John Brown Publ. 1994.

77. *WMN* 15 Jul 1957.

78. McEwan op. cit. 36.

79. Jan Williams pers. comm..

80. See chapter 2.

81. McEwan op. cit. 36.

82. *FT35* p24.

83. Shuker. K.P.M. *In Search of Prehistoric Survivors.* Blandford 1995.

84. Loren Coleman *Mysterious America.* 1980.

85. Cited in Rickard op. cit. 5.

86. Ibid.

87. Ibid.

88. It is one of the curses of contemporary forteana that people forget that *The X Files* is fiction.

89. Shelton & Mavriedes *Idiots Abroad.* Knockabout. London 1988

90. Heylin.C: *Great White Wonders.* Omnibus. London 1994.

91. See comment at 88.

92. Coleman op.cit. 84.

93. Heuvelmans op. cit. 1.

94. Coleman op. cit. 84.

95. Ibid.

96. See my article *Mystery Kangaroos* in *Dead of Night* magazine, autumn 1995.

97. Keel op. cit. 3.98. *Animals & Men #4.* CFZ 1995.99. *Animals & Men #3.* CFZ 1994.

100. *Animals & Men #4.* CFZ 1995.101. Kurt, Cobain, et al.102. *Animals & Men #4.* CFZ 1995.

103. Ibid.

104. Rickard op. cit. 5.CHAPTER FIVE

1. Tony Shiels pers.comm. Mar 1996
2. FT 17.
3. Shiels, Tony 'Doc': *Monstrum! - A Wizard's Tale.* Fortean Tomes. London 1990.
4. This research took two days in Mar 1996.
5. Shiels 1990 op. cit. 3.
6. Tony Shiels pers. comm. Nov 1995.
7. Shiels 1990 op. cit. 3.
8. Despite the volume of information presented in this chapter, I have drawn sparingly on the source material available.
9. Tony Shiels pers. comm. Jan 1996.
10. For example. *Daemons, Darklings and Doppelgangers,, 13,* and *Something Strange.*
11. Shiels 1990 op. cit. *3.*
12. Ibid.
13. Mawman-Peller. A: *Morgawr – the Monster of Falmouth Bay.* Morgawr Falmouth Publ, repub. CFZ 1996.
14. Ibid.
15. FP 9 Jul 1976.
16. *West Britain* 15 Jul 1976.
17. Ibid.
18. Tony Shiels CFZ videotaped interview, spring 1995.
19. 1977 feature film.
20. WB 21 Oct 1976.
21. Ibid.
22. Ibid.
23. Unreferenced.
24. *West Britain (WB)* 18 Nov 1976.
25. Ibid.
26. WB 18 Nov 1976.
29. WB 9 Dec 1976.
30. Ibid.
31. Ibid.
32. WB 18 Nov 1976.
33. WB 20 Dec 1976.
34. Ibid.
35. *West Britain (WB)* 25 Nov 1976.
36. FP 9 Jul 1976.
37. FP 18 Jun1976.
38. Bernie Mace pers. comm.
39. Joan Amos writing in 1997 CFZ Yearbook.
40. FP 27 Aug 1978.
41. FT 17.
42. WB17 Jun1976.
43. Cited in FT 17.
44. WB 17 Jun 1976.
45. Ibid.
46. Ibid.
47. WB 23 Sep 1976
48. Ibid.
49. FP 16 Jul 1976

50. Reference lost.
51. FP 23 Jul 1976.
52. FP 22 Oct 1976.
53. Reference lost.
54. FP 17 Jun 1977.
55. FP 13 Aug 1976.
56. Ibid.
57. The owl family.
58. Reference lost.
59. Austin & Stringer *Birds of the World.* Hamlyn. London 1962.
60. FP 15 Oct 1976.
61. Austin & Singer op. cit. 59.
62. William Pctrovic pers. comm.
63. Steve Johnson pers. comm.
64. FP 29 Oct 1976.
65. A similar report from Hong Kong, noted by G.A. Herklots, 1953: *The Hong Kong Countryside,* S. C.M.P.
66. FP 23 Apr 1976.
67. WB 15 Jul 1976
68. Julia Andrews pers. comm.
69. William Petrovic pers. comm.
70. Reference lost.
71. FP 11 Feb 1977.
72. FP 18 Mar 1977.
73. FP 31 Dcc 1976.
74. FP 1 Oct 1976.
75. FP 24 Dec 1976.
76. William Petrovic pers. comm.
77. FP 10 Dec1976.
78. FP 31 Dec 1976.
79. Ibid.
80. FP 23 & 30 Jul 1976.
81. FP 13 Aug 1976.
82. FP l0 Sep 1976.
83. Mawnan-Peller op. cit. 13.
84. WB 18 Nov 1976.
85. William Petrovic pers. comm.
86. WB 9Aug 1976.
87. Ibid.
88. WMN 19 Aug 1976.
89. Ibid.
90. Ibid.
91. FP 30 Jul 1976.
92. WB 19 Aug 1976.
93. Reference lost.
94. FP 27 Aug 1976.
95. FP 29 Oct 1976.
96. 'Miranda the Mermaid' (pseudonym) pers. comm.
97. WB 1 Jul 1976.

98. WB 8 Jul l976.
99. Ibid.
100. WB 16 Jul 1976.
101. WB 22 Jul 1976.
102. WB 16 Sep 1976.
103. FP 24 Sep 1976.
104. WB 28 Sep 1976.
105. WB 12 Nov 1976.
106. Part of Penny Williams' poem about Beaky:

> *A sillhouette of a dolphin, black against the moon.*
> *Leaps out in a graceful curve, twisting. And is gone.*
> *Slicing through the calm in a trail of phosphorescence.*
> *Gleaming like a midnight rainbow,*
> *Defying the very stars in its brilliance ...*

107. FP 2 Feb 1977.
108. FP 18 Mar 1977.
109, 111, 113. Mawnan-Peller op.cit. 13.
110,112,114. FP 5 Mar 1976.
115. Tony Shiels 1990 op. cit. 3.
116, 117. Ibid.
118. FP 19 Mar 1976.
119. We contacted Mr Shaw but it transpired that nothing had come of his planned book and he had no information that we did not already know.
120. Mawnan-Peller op. cit. 13.
121. We wrote to Mike McCormick on a number of occasions but he never replied.
122. Tony Shiels pers. comm. Jul 1995.
123. Shiels 1990 op. cit. 3.
124. FP 26 Mar 1976.
125. Shiels 1990 op. cit. 3.
126. Ibid.
127. FP 26 Mar 1976.
128. This pub was the scene for many of the interviews carried out for this book.
129. FP 2 Apr 1976.
130. Searle, F. *Nessie: Seven Years in Search of the Monster.* N.E.L. London.
131. Witchell, N. *The Loch Ness Story.* Pan 1982 edn.
132. FP 2 Apr 1976.
133. Ibid.
134. Shiels 1990 op. cit. 3.
135. The true reasons for McCormick's departure have never been satisfactorily resolved.
136. Strange magazine #9.
137. The *Falmouth Packet* has always claimed responsibility for the name. Tony and I both contest this.
138. FP 23 Apr 1976.
139. Ibid.
140. Mawnan-Peller op. cit. 13.
141. Shiels 1990 op. cit. 3.
142. Ibid.

143. McEwan. G: *Mystery Animals of Britain and Ireland.* Robert Hale. London 1985.

144. O'Siaghail, N: *The Shiels Effect - Manual for the Psychic Superstar.* 1975: due to be republ. by CFZ 1997-8.

145. Ibid.

146. Shiels 1990 op. cit. 3.

147. Tony Shiels in conversation with the author, May 1996.

148. These allegations have been discussed in a previous chapter.

149. *The Sun* 28 Apr 1978.

150. Writing in Tony Shiels' *The Cantrip Codex* due for republ. by CFZ in 1997.

151. "Miranda" (pseudonym) pers. comm.

152. Special Agent Tina Askew pers. comm. (snigger)

153. From the 1939 movie *The Wizard of Oz.*

154. *Reveille* 7 May 1976.

155. Mawnan-Peller op. cit. 13.

156. FP 14 May 1976.

157. FP 4 Jun 1976.

158. 9 Apr 1976.

159. Ibid.

160. FP 9 Jul 1976.

161. Ibid.

162. Including *Mysterious West.*

163. FP 30 Jul 1976.

164. Mawnan-Peller op. cit. 13.

165. Shiels op. cit. 3.

166. FP 24 Sep 1976.

167. WB 2 Sep 1976.

168. FP 10 Sep and WB 16 Sep 1976.

169. *Cornish Life.* Jan 1977.

170. FP 3 Jun 1977.

171. Ibid.

CHAPTER SIX

1. "Just because they say you're paranoid, it doesn't mean you're not stored on their computers." (Crass, 1981)

2. Where, coincidently, I was lecturing on "The Owlnnn", a recording of which is available from *Fortean Times.*

3. The only issue to be A4 with a colour cover.

4. Including Colin Bord.

5. "The Birmingham Six" from the Pogues' album *If I should Fall From Grace of God* (Stiff Records 1987.

6. Shane McGowan is a friend of the Shiels family.

7. Paul Finnigan pers. comm.

8. FT 29.

9. Tony Shiels in conversation with the author. May 1996.

10. See chapter 4.

11. As with the several informants in this chapter, I will respect her wishes.

12. See police report quoted below - 40 et al.

13. For my unpublished book, *The Mystery Animals of Devon and Cornwall.*
14. The regional headquarters.
15. See 11.
16. See ref 1 and my other comments about *The X Files.*
17. Weird shit attracts weird people - and I should know.
18. Anonymous police sergeant pers. comm.
19. Interview with Mr Marshall, Apr 1992.
20. Brierley. N: *They Stalked by Night* p/p 1997.
21. Francis. Di:: *Cat Country.* Davis & Charles. Newton Abbot 1984.
22. See 19.
23. Ibid.
24. Ibid.
25. Other sightings of errant wallabies in the region have been identified as giant rabbits.
26. Eric Beckjord in conservation with the author, 1990.
27. See my article 'Zooform Phenomena" in *Scan News* # 2.
28. Dangerous Wild Animals Act 1976.
29. Shuker, K.P.N. *Mystery Cats of the World - From Blue Tigers to Exmoor Beasts.* Robert Hale. London 1989.
30. Francis op. cit. 21.
31. Marshall - see 19.
32. FT reference lost.
33. Marshall- see 19.
34. Ibid.
35. *Animals & Men.#3.*
36. *Animals & Men #7.*
37. I have no idea where this song comes from but Tony sings it a lot.
38. Gaelic dialect for "be quiet."
39. Marshall - see 19.
40. Document purporting to be a Police Report (PR).
41. Ibid.
42. I have tried, but to no avail.
43. See my other references to this TV programme.
44. PR.
45. "Trish" (pseudonym) pers. comm.
46. Ibid.
47. PR.
48. Ibid.
49. Ibid.
50. Mrs Penny Rowe pers. comm.
51. For those unfamiliar with the term, this is a metal ring binder designed to hold reference cards.
52. Document purporting to be Post Mortem Report (PMR)
53. *Reader's Digest: Into The Unknown.* 1980
54. Ibid.
55. William Petrovic pers. comm.
56. Peter Glastonbury pers. comm.
57. PR.
58. Calkins CC. (ed) *Myseries of the Unexplained.* Reader's Digest 1982.
59. Document purporting to be UFO researcher's case report (UFOR).
60-64. Ibid.

65. Clinton Keeling pers. comm.

66. Chris Moiser pers. comm.

67. This disease is apparently untreatable.

68. It is surprising that neither the vet or any of the zoo staff recognized the disease.

69. UFOR.

70. Ibid.

71. For the record, this was Dartmoor Wildlife Park in the autumn of 1990.

72. Clinton Keeling pers. comm.

73. Chris Moiser, my other "tame" zoo expert had never heard of such a thing.

74. UFOR.

75. Shuker, K.P.M. op. cit. 29.

76. Murger, M., writing in *Fortean Studies vol 1.* ed: Steve Moore.

77. Gilroy, R. *Mysterious Australia.* Nexus Books 1995.

78. Coleman, Loren: *Mysterious America.* 1980.

79. Shuker, K.P.N. op cit. 29.

80. *Animals & Men, #3.*

81. *Animals &* Men *#4.*

82. Green, R: *Wild Cat Species of the World.* Bassett. Plymouth 1992.

83. Held at the University of Surrey, Guildford.

84. Whether or not he still holds the same views, I do not know.

85. Downes. J: *Smaller Mystery Carnivores of the Westcountry.* CFZ Exeter 1996.

86. Bill Charlotte pers. comm. May 1996.

87. UFOR.

88. PR.

89. UFOR.

90. Calkins op. cit. 58.

91. UFOR.

92. William Petrovic pers. comm.

93. Ibid.

94. UFOR.

95. See the PR.

96. The notorious "hippy cult" leader responsible for the deaths of Sharon Tate, Gino and Rosemary LaBianca, and anything up to fifty others.

97. Based on the book by Vincent Bugliosi and Kurt Gentry.

98. Sanders, E. *The Family.* N.E.L 1971.

99. Whose beliefs included animal sacrifice and ritualised child abuse.

100. Properly known as "The Family of the Infinite Soul, inc."

101. Calkins op. cit. 58.

102. Ibid.

103. The true facts of this case are obscure.

104. I have not been able to locate this book.

105. WMN13 Jul 1977.

106. Ibid.

107. WMN 14 Jul 1977.

108. Ibid.

109. WMN 2Aug 1977.

110. Ibid.

111. Unreferenced press cutting.

112. Vonny Cornelius pers. comm.

113. Long, H. *Plants Poisonous to Livestock.* 1917.

114. Ibid.

115. It has been suggested that the original investigators were mistaken as to their time frame of the original incident.

116. This unfortunately is the only reference we have to exanguination in this particular case.

118. Joanna Vincen pers. comm. Jun 1991.

119. Ruth Murray pers. comm. Jun 1991.

120. Ruth Murray pers. comm. Jul 1991.

121. Keel, J. *The Mothman Prophecies* (UK: *Visitors from Space)* N.E.L. 1974.

122. Shades of *The X Files*, huh?

123. Shiels, Tony 'Doc'. *Monstrum! - A Wizard's Tale.* Fortean Tomes. London 1990.

124. Ibid.

125. Ruth Murray pers. comm. to John Jacques, May 1995.

126. Watkins, Leslie: *Alternative 3.* Warner. London 1994 edn.

127. See also Joan Amos writing in *Goblin Universe #4.* CFZ 1997.

128. Keel op. cit. 121.

129. UFOR.

130. Brown. Theo *Devon Ghosts.* Jarrold. Norfolk 1980.

131. Ian Wright pers. comm. 1992.

132. *"New Pony".* Bob Dylan, from *Street Needle* (1977).

133. UFOR.

134. Ibid.

135. Ibid.

136. Manchester, S. *The Highgate Vampire.* p/p 1985.

137. Joan Amos pers. comm. May 1996.

CHAPTER SEVEN

1. Adams, D. *The Hitch-Hiker's Guide to the Galaxy.* Heinemann. London 1978.

2. The exhibition in Penzance featured larger pictures; the one in St Ives mainly smaller ones including Sea Heads.

3. Tony Shiels pers. comm. May 1996.

4. Our files are full of people who Tony suggested we contact. We did so in about *75%* of the cases.

5. For the purposes of brevity we shall refer to this document as USA Owl.

6. USA Owl.

7. Ibid.

8. Tony Shiels in conversation with the author, Apr 1996.

9. Tolkein. J.R.R. unreferenced.

10. Simon Parker pers. comm. May 1996.

11. CFZ letter, Apr 1996.

12. An audio tape of my lecture is available from *Fortean Times.*

13. Stephen Fowler pers. comm.

14. Tony Shiels pers. comm. May 1996.

15. *Strange* magazine #9

16. Ibid.

17. See *Animals & Men #1.* CFZ. Exeter 1994.

18. William Petrovich pers. comm.

19. As 15.

20. Ibid.
21. Tony Shiels pers. comm. May 1996.
22. Tony Shiels pers. comm. Jul 1995.
23. FP 12 Mar 1976.
24. Tony Shiels pers. comm. Apr 1996.
25. *Strange* magazine #9.
26. Ibid.
27. Most notably in Conan Doyle's *The Adventure of the Final Problem,* from *The Memoirs of Sherlock Holmes,* first published 1892.
28. Shiels, Tony 'Doc': *13.* Supreme Magic Company. Bideford 1967.
29. One of *The Adventures of Sherlock Holmes,* Conan Doyle. First published 1891.
30. Shiels, Tony 'Doc': *The Cantrip Codex.* 1991 – due for republ. 1997 by CFZ.
31. Shiels, Tony 'Doc': *Monstrum! – A Wizard's Tale.* Fortean Tomes. 1990.
32. Actually, it wasn't – this is what is commonly known as, in authoring circles, a "cop-out". It was not Col. James Moriarty who Sherlock Holmes threw over the Reichenbach Falls, but his brother, Professor Moriarty.
33. Tony Shiels pers. comm. on a number of occasions.
34. O'Siaghail. N: *The Shiels Effect – Manual for the Psychic Superstar.* 1975; due for republ. by CFZ in 1997 – 8.
35. Written by A. Pucarich the previous year.
36. O'Siaghail op. cit. 34.
37. Heuvelmans, B: *On the Track of Unknown Animals.* Hart Havis. London 1958.
38. See Chapter 2.
39. *Strange* magazine #9
40. Cousins, S: Tony Shiels. Mark Space Publ. Milton Keynes 1995.
41. Shiels 1990 op. cit. 31.
42. Ibid.
43. Ibid.
44. McEwan, G: *Mystery Animals of Britain and Ireland.* Robert Hayle. London 1985.
45. See Chapter 5.
46. Shiels 1990 op.cit. 31.
47. Wilson, C. *The Occult.* Collins 1980.
48. Ibid.
49. Mark Chorvinsky pers. *comm.* 1995
50. Tony Shiels pers. comm. 1995.
51. Tony Shiels pers. comm. May 1996.
52. Mike McCormick in *Strange* magazine #9.
53. Unfortunately these letters are now lost.
54. Early publicity flyer cited in *Strange* magazine #9.
55. *Strange* magazine #9.
56. Downes, J. *Take This Brother, May it Serve You Well – An Incomplete Guide to Beatles Bootlegs.* STP 1988.
57. Also a series of thirteen articles in *Spanish Train* magazine between 1987 and 1990.
58. Steve Harley.
59. See practically any account of their career.
60. Tony Shiels pers. comm. May 1996.
61. George Spicer was one of the most famous witnesses of the Loch Ness Monster.
62. Mark Chorvinsky's main contention was that Tony had hoaxed all of the monster photographs with plasticine models.

63. Tony Shiels pers. comm. May 1996.

64. Downes, J. *Smaller Mystery Carnivores of the Westcountry.* CFZ. Exeter 1996.

65. O'Siaghail op. cit. 34.

CHAPTER EIGHT

1. Tony Shiels pers. comm. Jun 1996.

2. Heuvelmans letter to Boris Porchnev printed in *Cryptozoology,* 1988.

3. Heuvelmans *Cryptozoology.* 1980.

4. Heuvelmans 1988 op. cit. 2.

5. Shuker, K.P.M. *Mystery Cats of the World - From Blue Cats to Exmoor Beasts.* Robert Hayle. London 1989.

6. Francis, Di. *Cat Country - the Search for the British Big Cat.* David & Charles. Newton Abbot 1984.

7. Downes, J. *Smaller Mystery Carnivores of the Westcountry.* CFZ. Exeter 1996.

8. McEwan, G. *Mystery Animals of Britain and Ireland.* Robert Hayle. London 1985.

9. Usually given the misnomer "the father of communism".

10. His collaborator.

11. The third volume of the highly-acclaimed *Foundation* series.

12. Based in the USA.

13. Founded by Bob Rickard in 1972.

14. A wonderful organisation which deserves greater support.

15. Founded in the mid-1970s by Janet and Colin Bord.

16. Founded by the author in 1991.

17. Heuvelmans, B. *On the Track of Unknown Animals.* Hart-Davis. London 1958.

18. *Animals & Men* #2. CFZ. Exeter 1994.

19. Downes. J. op. cit. 7.

20. "In 1931, when Tiffany Thayer and Aaron Sussman founded the Fortean Society, Fort had to be tricked by mendacious telegrams into attending the celebratory banquet. He said he would not join the organisation himself 'Any more than I'd be an Elk'" - Damon Knight, 1974 introduction to *The Complete Books of Charles Fort,* Dover Publications.

21. If you don't know my opinions on this subject now, there's no point in my doing references...

22. Bord, J & C. *Alien Animals.* Granada. London 1980.

23. Ibid.

24. Downes, J. "Zooform Phenomena". *Scan News.* 1993.

25. Also Downes, J. "Mystery Kangaroos", *Dead of Night* magazine. 1995.

26. *Animals & Men,* CFL. Exeter 1995.

27. *Strange* magazine #9.

28. Ford, Janet and Colin: *Modern Mysteries of Britain.* Grafton. London 1988.

29. *Animals & Men* #7. CFZ Exeter 1995.

30. *Animals & Men* #8. CFZ Exeter 1996.

31. *Animals & Men* #9. CFZ Exeter 1996.

32. Karl Shuker pers. comm.

33. Ibid.

34. William Petrovic pers. comm.

34. David Bolton pers. comm.

36. Herklots. G.A.K. *Hong Kong Birds.* - S.C.M.P. Hong Kong 1968.

37. Paul Andrews pers. comm.

38. *Cage and Aviary Birds.* 6 Jun 1992.

39. Austin & Singer. *Birds of the World.* Hamlyn. London 1962.

40. Ibid.

41. Ibid.

42. Ibid. Unlike the other species which are European, the Harris Hawk is native to North America.

43. Summers. G. *The Lure of the Falcon.* Collins. London 1973.

44. Summers. G. *Where Vultures Fly.* Collins. London 1974.

45. Summers. G. *Owned by an Eagle.* Collins. London 1976.

46. William Petrovic pers. comm.

47. Karl Shuker pers. comm.

48. Trevor Beer pers. comm.

49. See Chapter 2.

50. Chapter 3.

51. Tony Shiels pers. comm. 26 May 1996.

52. Breton, Andre. *Manifested u Surrealisme,* cited in Waldburg. P: *Surrealism* Thames &Hudson. London 1965.

53. Waldburg, P: *Surrealism* Thames & Hudson. London 1965.

54. Monty Python's Flying Circus - a legendary BBC TV series first broadcast between 1969-1975.

55. Ernst, Max. "Au-dela de la peinture' in *Cahiers d'Art.* 1937.

56. Ibid.

57. Shiels. Tony 'Doc': *Monstrum! - A Wizard's Tale.* Fortean Tomes. London 1990.

58. Ernst, Max. 'Une semaine d'Onte' 1933.

59. Do It records, 1980.

60. This album, which has achieved cult status, is regarded by many as his best work.

61. 19th century traveller, artist, writer and poet.

62. The real name of the man who became known as Adam Ant.

63. The second baronet died in 1993.

64. Verney. Sir John: *ISMO.* Collins. London 1963.

65. Verney. Sir John: *Seven Sunflower Seeds* Collins. London 1968.

66. Ibid.

67. Ibid.

68. Perhaps the best-known of Edward Lear's nonsense poems.

69. Shiels. Tony 'Doc' *The Cantrip Codex.* 1991; due for republ in 1997 by CFZ Exeter.

70. Keel, J: *The Mothman Prophecies* (UK: *Visitors from Space)* N.E.L 1974

71. Tony Shiels pers. comm. May 1995.

72. Tony Shiels pers. comm. Jun 1996.

73. Shiels 1990 op. cit. 57.

74. Breton, Andre. "Le Surrealisme et la Peinture", cited in Waldberg, P. *Surrealism.* Thames & Hudson. London 1965.

75. Shiels 1990 op. cit. 57.

76. Tony Shiels pers. comm. Jun 1996.

77. Kipling. R. *Puck of Pooks Hill.* Methuen. London 1902.

78. Bord. J. & C. *Alien Animals.* Granada. London 1980.

79. Anon. *The Parish Church of Mawnan Smith.* Undated.

80. Ibid.

81. William Petrovich pers. comm.

82. Mannix. D. *For Those About To Die.* (I have no idea of the date and I would not recommendthis book to anyone.

83. William Petrovic pers. comm.

84. I sold the book in question: cannot remember the reference; and do not wish to.

85. Martin Fido. *Oscar Wilde.* Hamlyn 1973.

86. Richard Ellmann. *Oscar Wilde.* Hamish Hamilton 1987, Penguin 1988.

87. I have never been able to find out where the original Mark Twain quote came from.

88. As far as I know, the original Oscar Wilde story has never been finished.

89. I have spent the last five years trying to contact them, but to no avail. This does not mean that they do not exist.

90. Keel op. cit. 70.

91. Tony Shiels pers. comm. May 1996.

92. See *'It's Better Than Dying"* from my album *The Case,* 1996.

93. Downes, J. *Road Dreams.* CFZ (Centre for Fortean Zoology) Exeter 1993.

94. Downes, J. *Take This Brother. May it Serve You Well – An Incomplete Guide to Beatles Bootlegs.* STP. Exeter 1988.

95. McEwan. G. *Mystery Animals of Britain and Ireland.* Robert Hayle. London 1985.

96. Chris Moiser pers. comm. May 1996.

97. As she refused to co-operate with us, it is probably unethical to give her name as a reference.

98. Tony Shiels pers. comm. Jul 1996.

99. Trish (pseudonym) pers. comm.

INDEX

A

B

C

D

W

X

Y

Jonathan Downes was born in Portsmouth in 1959, and spent much of his childhood in Hong Kong where, surrounded by age-old Chinese superstitions and a dazzlingly diverse range of exotic wildlife, he soon became infected with the twin passions for exotic zoology and the paranormal which were to define his adult life. He spent some years as a nurse for the mentally handicapped but began writing professionally in the late 1980s. He has now written over twenty books. He is also a musician and songwriter who has made a number of critically acclaimed but commercially unsuccessful albums.

In 1992 he founded The Centre for Fortean Zoology, with the aim of coordinating research into mystery animals, bizarre and aberrant animal behaviour and his own particular love of zooform phenomena (paranormal entities which only appear to be animals!)

He has searched for Lake Monsters at Loch Ness, pursued sea serpents and the grotesque Cornish owlman—which inspired his most famous book *The Owlman and Others* - chased big cats across westcountry moorland, and in 1998 and 2004 went to Latin America in search of the grotesque vampiric Chupacabra. He is a popular public speaker both in the UK and the United States, where he regularly appears at conventions talking about his many expeditions and his latest research projects.

He is also an activist for Mental Health issues, having suffered with Bipolar Disorder (Manic Depression) for many years. In 2005, after having lived in Exeter for 20 years, he moved to his old family home in Woolsery, North Devon, where he intends to establish a full-time Visitor's Centre and museum for the Centre for Fortean Zoology. Following his father's death in February 2006, he inherited the old family home and announced that construction of the museum and research facility later in the year.

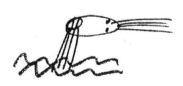

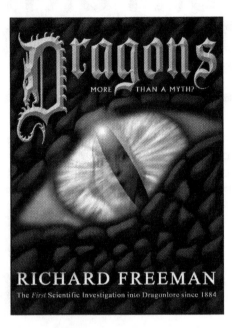

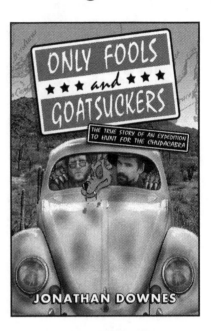

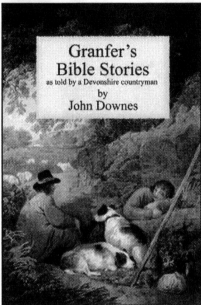

THE CASE

INVOCATION OF MY DAEMON BROTHER

MAD GASSER OF MATTOON

GOD BLESS AMERIKKA/PET SURFING

I'M ON FIRE

IRENE

LETTER TO STEPHEN

THE STRANGER

(THERE AIN'T NO SUCH THING AS A) NAKED LUNCH

BETTER THAN DYING

ENGLISH HERITAGE (PART 1 - SUMMER'S ALMOST GONE)

ENGLISH HERITAGE (PART 2 - LAND OF DOPES AND TORIES)

The legendary CD of fortean Rock Music featuring Tony "Doc" Shiels